Third Edition

It Could Happen to Anyone

D1565363

Third Edition

It Could Happen to Anyone

Why Battered Women Stay

Alyce D. LaViolette

Alternatives Counseling Association, California
Institute of Rural Management, Gujarat

Ola W. Barnett

Pepperdine University

Los Angeles | London | New Delhi
Singapore | Washington DC

Los Angeles | London | New Delhi
Singapore | Washington DC

FOR INFORMATION:

SAGE Publications, Inc.

2455 Teller Road

Thousand Oaks, California 91320

E-mail: order@sagepub.com

SAGE Publications Ltd.

1 Oliver's Yard

55 City Road

London, EC1Y 1SP

United Kingdom

SAGE Publications India Pvt. Ltd.

B 1/I 1 Mohan Cooperative Industrial Area

Mathura Road, New Delhi 110 044

India

SAGE Publications Asia-Pacific Pte. Ltd.

3 Church Street

#10-04 Samsung Hub

Singapore 049483

Acquisitions Editor: Kassie Graves

Editorial Assistant: Elizabeth Luizzi

Production Editor: Stephanie Palermini

Copy Editor: Rachel Keith

Typesetter: Hurix Systems Pvt. Ltd.

Proofreader: Talia Greenberg

Indexer: Teddy Diggs

Cover Designer: Candice Harman

Marketing Manager: Erica DeLuca

Permissions Editor: Adele Hutchinson

Printed in the United States of America

Library of Congress Cataloging-in-Publication Data

LaViolette, Alyce D.

Why battered women stay : it could happen to anyone / Alyce D. LaViolette, Ola W. Barnett. — Third edition.

pages cm

Includes bibliographical references and index.

ISBN 978-1-4522-7774-5 (pbk. : alk. paper) 1. Abused women—United States—Case studies. 2. Abused wives—United States—Case studies. I. Barnett, Ola W. II. Title.

HV6626.2.B27 2014

362.82'920973—dc23

2013000547

This book is printed on acid-free paper.

SUSTAINABLE FORESTRY INITIATIVE

Certified Chain of Custody
Promoting Sustainable Forestry
www.sfiprogram.org
SFI-01268

SFI label applies to text stock

13 14 15 16 17 10 9 8 7 6 5 4 3 2 1

Brief Contents

Detailed Contents

List of Case Studies

Foreword

A couple of years ago, when my husband was away on a business trip and my sons had a day off from school, I slipped while running from the shower to answer the phone. I had been waiting for that call all morning and, as luck would have it, the phone started ringing just as I got the shampoo into a nice lather. In what seemed like an instant, my right foot went out from under me, my body twisted, and my head hit the woodwork on the wall before slamming down on the polished slate floor. Trying hard not to pass out so that my children wouldn't find me and then bring in the neighbors to rescue their naked mother, I realized that the right side of my face was resting in a pool of blood. When I finally looked in the mirror, I saw a deep gash just above my right eye, like the kind of cut a boxer gets when an opponent connects with a left jab. The hospital is within walking distance of our house, but my sons were still too young at the time to leave home alone, so off they went with me. They were feeling guilty for not having answered the phone themselves, and they were worried about what would happen to me at the hospital. As I walked hand in hand with them and saw the fear on their faces, it suddenly dawned on me: "Damn, I look like a battered wife. This visit to the emergency room is going to take forever. They're going to ask me dozens of questions, and they won't believe me when I tell them how it really happened. Maybe they'll even question the kids separately while my face is being stitched."

Domestic violence—it could happen to anyone? Not in the eyes of the hospital staff who treated me that Friday morning. The intake clerk was more concerned about the kind of insurance I had than about my injury. The nurse asked me rather perfunctorily how I got the injury, but she never made eye contact with me as she busied herself setting out the medical supplies the doctor would be using. As the doctor examined my eye, he chuckled, and with my children sitting right beside me, he asked, "What happened? Did your husband beat you up?" That was the proverbial last straw; the ER doc got an earful. "As a matter of fact," I began, "I really expected you to seriously question me about how I got hurt. Domestic violence isn't funny. Do you know what I do for a living?" Of course, he didn't, but I filled him in. Maybe my lecture will make him think twice before he talks to an injured woman like that again, although I strongly doubt it. I am fairly certain that the experience had a more profound effect on me than on any of the hospital staff I encountered, including the ER physician.

Walking home from the hospital, I remembered my earlier thought— "I look like a battered wife"—and asking myself in the light of the ER staff's response, "What does a 'battered wife' look like? What did I need to look like for the staff at that hospital to be concerned about my safety?" In the pages that follow, Alyce LaViolette and Ola Barnett's answer to the first question is, "Any woman." In the diversity of battered women's voices that they present and in their own words, they emphasize that domestic violence can occur in wealthy households as well as poor ones; among couples of any race or ethnicity; among Native Americans and descendants of the Mayflower pilgrims, as well as recently arrived immigrants and refugees; among the young and the old, the physically abled and the disabled; among those who are straight as well as those who are lesbian, gay, bisexual, or transgendered. Nevertheless, one of the things I like most about this book is the authors' simultaneous awareness of the importance of disadvantage and marginalization in the etiology of domestic violence. Yes, it can happen to anyone, but research is increasingly showing that women who are economically and socially disadvantaged—women who are poor, nonwhite, noncitizens or refugees, very young or very old, disabled, and/or not heterosexual—are often at especially high risk of violent victimization and also are often overlooked or neglected by service providers. The irony of the dual effects of disadvantage and marginalization in terms of victimization and service provision are not lost on me in light of my own experience. When I went to the hospital that Friday morning, my statuses were pretty obvious: I am an upper-middle-class, white, U.S.-born, forty-something, physically abled, heterosexual woman—I'm not supposed to be battered because that happens to Other women. Yet, had I been one of those Other women—and this book documents this point well—abuse may have been suspected, but I would not necessarily have been asked about it, and I likely would have been treated with disdain or even hostility.

But LaViolette and Barnett do not just cite research studies or their own practice experiences to make these points; instead, they let us hear the pain, the personal conflicts, and the tremendous strength and resilience of the real experts on domestic violence—battered women. Interspersed with statistics and research findings are the stories of battered women from diverse backgrounds, stories usually told in their own words. It is these stories, I think, that do most to shatter the stereotypes of what a battered woman "looks like" and how she's supposed to think, feel, and act. Moreover, these stories document not only the diversity of battered women, but also the diversity of their experiences. They force us to rethink traditional definitions and images of battering. I have long argued that standard measures of physical and psychological abuse, with their long list of horrors, miss the point. Some batterers hit and punch to control and punish their partners, some restrict social contacts or disconnect the telephone, and some tailor the battering to the specific vulnerabilities of the victim—after all, being intimate brings with it knowledge of a partner's otherwise secret fears. Our measures of who did what to whom how many times typically do not identify these very individualized forms of abuse. Instead, we hear them in women's personal accounts, and LaViolette and Barnett must be applauded for including these women's words. As those of us in academia continue to argue over whether it is methodologically more sound to use broad or narrow definitions of abuse, this book reminds us to do what we should have been doing all along: *listen to battered women.*

Let the reader beware: This is not a "fun" or entertaining book to read. It is a powerful, often gut-wrenching book that you may have to read in small pieces, not only to deal with your emotional reactions, especially to some of the women's experiences, but also to think long and hard about the issues it raises. For me, for example, the book brought to the surface many of the conflicts I feel in working to eliminate violence against women and increase women's safety, while at the same time holding batterers accountable for their behavior. We often encourage battered women to leave abusive relationships, but leaving for some women may mean giving up eligibility for public housing, the only housing they can afford. Many of us in the battered women's movement have advocated for mandatory arrest policies only to find following the enactment of such legislation more women being caught in the police net, usually for defending themselves or retaliating against a batterer—behavior that is nonetheless violent in the eyes of the criminal justice system. Mandatory arrest laws have also had a disproportionate impact on communities of color. And do we really want to solve the problem of domestic violence by locking more men away in prisons and jails that have abandoned the goal of rehabilitation?

In *Why Battered Women Stay,* Alyce LaViolette and Ola Barnett challenge us to think critically about how we *imagine* battered women and batterers, and about how we *respond* to battered women and batterers. As we embark on a new century, I think that unfortunately *inclusivity* remains an elusive goal of the battered women's movement. LaViolette and Barnett and, most important, the battered women whose voices we hear in these pages remind us that if we exclude any group from our work, we will not succeed in ending violence. This goal of inclusivity remains elusive to some extent because of the current political climate dominated by a "lock 'em up and throw away the key" mentality. However, not all women and men are equally likely to be locked up; it is the disadvantaged and marginalized who, as always, bear the brunt of this burden. As we begin the 21st century, then, we must reevaluate our current policy goals for meeting the needs of battered women and addressing men's violence. And that reevaluation must include a critical analysis of how each policy may impact—for better or for worse—women and men from *all* social groups in our society.

When I sat down to read this book, I certainly didn't think I had all the answers, but I was pretty confident I had a good bit of the puzzle sorted out. This book substantially shook my confidence, and I'm grateful to Alyce LaViolette and Ola Barnett for the wake-up call.

—Claire M. Renzetti

St. Joseph's University
Philadelphia, Pennsylvania

Acknowledgments

The authors wish to thank Sage's award-winning acquisitions editor, Kassie Graves, for her support and commitment to the third edition of this book. We also wish to express our appreciation to Claire M. Renzetti for her dramatic and heartfelt foreword. We wish to give special thanks to Carol V. Harnish, who critiqued and edited all the editions of this book and also provided some contextual content. We also wish to thank Lesley Blake and Devin Blake for their editing and technical preparations of the manuscript. A big thanks to Don Barnett for being a "man of the hour" whenever needed.

Alyce LaViolette wishes to thank her mother, whose life was an inspiration, whose advocacy touched many lives, and whose death has left an incredible void. Alyce wishes to thank her father, who is a role model of courage and dedication to family, friends, and community; a man who is a constant source of strength to his children and grandchildren; and a man who is what a Hallmark Father's Day card is all about. Alyce also wants to thank her partner, Gail, for her ongoing encouragement and editing. She wishes to acknowledge her children, Jay and Corinne, for their spirit and audacity. Alyce also wishes to acknowledge the best coauthor anyone could wish for. Ola's integrity is exceptional and her friendship invaluable.

Ola Barnett wishes to thank her many professors and colleagues who have motivated her throughout a lifetime of academic pursuits. Because of their efforts, she has this unique opportunity to contribute to society's efforts to eliminate family violence. She treasures her supportive husband, daughters, and grandchildren. Ola wishes to thank Alyce for her lifetime of dedication and advocacy on behalf of battered women. She too values her friendship with Alyce, extending over 30 years. Ola also wants to call attention to Alyce's success in making battered women's case histories come alive in this book.

Introduction

Vignette

On May 2, 1982, Michael Connell visited his estranged wife, Karen, and their son, Ward. Karen and Michael had been separated for over a year but were seeing each other again. A friend of Ward's was also visiting and the four of them were going to go on a picnic. They never made it.

Around noon, Karen staggered from the house, bleeding profusely from the neck. She collapsed into a neighbor's arms, gasping that her husband had stabbed her and was still in the house with their five-year-old son and his friend.

The South Pasadena Police arrived on the scene to investigate. After several attempts to make contact with Michael or the children failed, they contacted the LA Sheriff's SWAT team. The SWAT team, using a bullhorn, requested that anyone inside the house come out.

Two boys walked out of the house with their hands up, pleading, "Don't shoot; we're the good guys." The SWAT team forced entry into the house at about 3:00. They found a man lying on the bathroom floor. He had massive slash wounds to his neck area and a stab wound to his chest. The wounds were self-inflicted. Michael Ward Connell was dead.

At the same time, Karen was undergoing an operation at Huntington Memorial Hospital. She had lost seven pints of blood and her vocal cords had been severed. Her young son, Ward, had saved her life by jumping on his father's back and hitting him, screaming, "Don't hurt my mom!"

The coroner's report stated, "Decedent apparently had marital problems with his wife for quite some time." Karen and Ward had been residents of Haven House, a refuge for battered women and their children. At the time of the attack, Karen had been a member of their outreach counseling group.

Karen's story mirrors some of the most horrifying events that surround domestic violence. While grassroots advocates have recognized the potential danger, many social agencies have ignored the looming violence. In the final analysis, one wonders to what extent society will assume responsibility for controlling male violence toward women and to what extent society really values women's lives.

The following pages are an attempt to provide understanding and empathy regarding this complex issue and to present an integrated learning theory explanation of the conditioning that culminates in wife abuse, in the resulting state of the survivor, and in the decision to stay with an abuser. We have asked battered women why they stayed in their abusive relationships, or why they left. We have asked about their survival both in and out of the relationship. This book represents, in part, their answers to these and other questions. Information has been gathered from the scientific and clinical sectors to formulate a comprehensive explanation that is also congruent with grassroots experience. Our work is anchored in empirical data, especially data collected from the battered women themselves.

Actual case histories furnish graphic illustrations of the topics covered. Our case studies represent a range of battering situations. We have heard from a number of battered women who were unable to relate to the severity of abuse in many case studies. They may have been in a state of denial, but battering relationships do vary in degree of injury, types of abuse involved, severity, and frequency. Some may seem lacking in drama if you have seen *The Burning Bed*, but not to the women and children involved. Fear, both emotional and physical, is present in every case.

When we talk about battering in this book, we are *not* talking about an isolated instance of aggression. According to Geffner and Rosenbaum, "Aggression is an action, abuse is a dynamic. Women may hit their male partners, but infrequently batter them, because battering or abuse includes a pattern of coercion, intimidation, and control, which is less frequently present in female-to-male aggression" (2001, p. 1). We are talking about an atmosphere that is created by many forms of abuse—a repetitive cycle that rarely occurs as a single incident and sometimes increases over time in frequency and intensity (Hirschel & Buzawa, 2002; U.S. Department of Justice, Office for Victims of Crime, 2002). One form of abuse does not occur by itself apart from all others, and physical abuse does not have to occur frequently to create a climate of fear. D. C. Adams (1988) defines the battering control pattern as involving intimidation and pressure, withholding of financial or emotional support, issuance of ultimatums and accusations, and employment of children as confederates against the woman.

We are using a definition of battering that includes six areas: (a) *physical* (slapping, pushing, kicking, restraining, using a weapon), (b) *sexual* (raping, beating genitalia, sodomizing, forcing unusual sex acts), (c) *psychological* (making threats, name-calling, ridiculing), (d) *stalking* (harassment, unwanted attention, use of technology to spy on or intimidate the victim), (e) *destruction of pets and property* (breaking furniture, destroying valued possessions, misusing pets), and (f) *dominance/control/isolation* (controlling assets, controlling clothing choices, controlling the victim's selection of friends, preventing the victim from seeing friends or family) (see Hall, Walters, & Basile, 2012; Stark, 2007).

Men who batter often find it difficult to recognize their own verbal and psychological abuse as abuse. They do not relate to the fear it can create and find it very difficult to change these kinds of behaviors. Much of the work that must be done in effective batterers' programs revolves around recognition of these forms of intimidation and halting nonphysical as well as physical abuse in the relationship (Chamberland, Fortin, Turgeon, & Laporte, 2007).

We will attempt to address some of the myths surrounding domestic violence. There is an old saying that goes, "If there are two stories, the truth is usually somewhere in the middle." Lenore Walker (personal communication, 1985) has created the new, improved version as it relates to partner abuse: "If there are two stories, the truth is usually worse than either one of them." We have also found that the truth is closer to her story than to his. Riggs, Murphy, and O'Leary (1989) found that perpetrators of abuse purposefully conceal undesirable interpartner aggression (see also Babinski, Hartsough, & Lambert, 2001).

That revision of reality makes sense. Emotional survival depends on our ability to look at ourselves and to conclude, "I am a decent person." If our deeds are incongruous with that statement, it may be necessary to modify our perceptions and recollections of the deeds. For instance, it is more satisfying to our egos to say, "My partner and I mutually decided we were not compatible" than it is to say, "I got dumped."

When a man hits, belittles, or bullies someone he loves, he needs to create a framework that makes that behavior seem reasonable. His emotional well-being depends on it. Provocation is a great equalizer in this perceptual battle. Minimizing or forgetting details or the degree of injury is a tool that can be used to construct this framework (Henning & Holdford, 2006). A British inquiry provided an example of this type of behavior. Male partner violence suspects being interrogated by police frequently talked about two types of men. These men constructed an "other" category of "men who hit ladies." They categorized themselves, however, as "men who do not hit ladies" (Stokoe, 2010).

Case Study: A Couple's Report to a Therapist

He says: I wouldn't have hit her, but she attacked me with the phone.

She says: I wouldn't have thrown the phone at you, but you were very angry and came across the room, ranting and waving your arms. You were on the attack and I was defending myself.

He says: Oh yes, that's right.

This classic case of "he said, she said" illustrates how difficult it is to judge the veracity of each person's recollections. The participants, the therapist, and any researchers who may study the different accounts all have their own biases that greatly influence their interpretations.

History of the Battered Women's Movement

Fortunately for battered women, batterers, and their families, the issue of domestic violence has come out of the closet. In the early 1970s, the women's movement spawned the shelter movement along with advocacy for women's rights. When media attention focused on issues affecting women, such as jobs, pay equity, and child care, the violence directed at women in their own homes came to public attention. The *New York Times* indicated an increase in articles on wife abuse from zero in 1970 to 44 in 1977. By 1978, battered wives had become a separate topic, distinct from records on assaults and murders (see R. E. Dobash & Dobash, 1979).

Tierney (1982) sums up the issue of public awareness as follows:

> Wife beating has become the object of media attention and government policy, not because of an increase in its frequency, or because the public has become more concerned, but because a social movement developed in the 1970's to help battered women. The growth of the battered women's movement illustrates both successful resource mobilization and the creation of a social problem. (p. 207)

Although the women's movement of the 1970s gave necessary impetus and attention to battered women through media focus and education, the first shelter for battered women and their children was started in 1964. Haven House, in Pasadena, California, was established through the efforts of Alanon members who saw the need to provide safety and shelter for the families of physically abusive alcoholics. These Alanon members held bake sales and small fundraisers to pay rent on a house in Pasadena. From 1964 to 1972, there was no more than one paid staff person. All other staff were volunteers, and the only program (until 1974) was Alanon. Chiswick Women's Aid, established in London, England, in 1971, was the first widely publicized shelter for battered women. In 1972, Women's Advocates, Inc., established a crisis hotline in St. Paul, Minnesota. Rainbow Retreat opened in 1973 in Phoenix, Arizona. In 1975, the National Organization of Women (NOW) formed a national Task Force on Battered Women/Household Violence. Activists lobbied successfully for passage of broader protection laws for battered women in 1976 (see Barner & Carney, 2011).

Domestic Violence: The Facts

The drama and tragedy of abused women will touch most of us, at some time in our lives, in a very personal way. Battering could happen directly as a result of our own intimate relationships with lovers, or indirectly through the experience of other family members, friends, or both. Whether or not we have been raised in an abusive family environment, we are almost certainly going to have close contact with, and be affected by, someone who has. And that someone, unless he gets help, will carry the legacy of violence with him into his intimate relationships. Understanding battering becomes a significantly relevant issue when applied to our own personal experience:

> Violent crimes, particularly rape and violence against intimates, are vitally important to understand and to prevent. The debilitating effects of these crimes, most of which are against women, are dramatic and long-lasting for the victims and for society. Yet the very nature of these crimes and the consequences of them mean that victims are often unwilling or even unable to report them to the police or to a National Crime Survey (NCS) interviewer. (Harlow, 1991, p iii)

Under the leadership of Senator Joseph Biden of Delaware, the U.S. Congress passed the Violence Against Women Act (VAWA) in 1994 and reauthorized it in 2000 and 2005 (U.S. Department of Justice, Office on Violence Against Women, n.d.). VAWA includes sweeping changes affecting nearly every aspect of criminal justice responses to battered women. It calls for the expenditure of $1.62 billion in five different areas, or titles, related to gender-based violence (C. F. Klein, 1995):

Title I: Safe Streets for Women increases efforts to prosecute repeat offenders who commit crimes against women.

Title II: Safe Homes for Women centers attention on domestic violence crimes.

Title III: Civil Rights for Women creates civil rights remedies to combat gender-based discrimination.

Title IV: Safe Campuses provides monetary grants for violence encountered by women at college.

Title V: Equal Justice for Women in the Courts offers judicial training to counteract gender bias in courtrooms.

Although some court challenges have occurred, as well as problems in implementation, no other set of laws has ever tackled domestic violence so directly and aggressively. (See Appendix D.1 for additional details about VAWA.)

Another event occurred on June 12, 1994. Nicole Brown Simpson, ex-wife of American football hero O. J. Simpson, and her friend Ron Goldman were found murdered with their throats slashed. A shocked nation had trouble reconciling their picture of O. J., the Heisman Trophy winner, with a man who had previously beaten two ex-wives and now was charged with double murder with special circumstances (Turque et al., 1994). The excessive media coverage painfully turned a national spotlight on the tragedy of domestic violence.

The story did not end with the juries' verdicts, not guilty in O. J.'s criminal trial and liable in his subsequent civil trial. The Simpson case continued to reverberate in family court, where California judge Wieben Stock granted custody of O. J.'s minor children to him rather than allowing the children's grandparents to retain guardianship (McGuire, 1999). Later, an appeals court overturned the judge's decision, stating that domestic violence and homicide (even alleged) of a parent are critical elements in determining whether the surviving parent should be awarded custody of his or her children (Fields-Meyer, Benet, Berestein, & Dodd, 1998). As an aside, a jury found Simpson guilty of armed robbery in a Las Vegas hotel in December 2008, and a judge sentenced him to a minimum of nine years in prison (Powers & Ryan, 2008).

Statistics on Violence Against Women

Statistics on domestic violence clearly challenge the notion that women are safest in their own homes. By the mid-1980s, domestic violence had reached such epidemic proportions that the U.S. Centers for Disease Control and Prevention (CDC) in Atlanta began to treat partner abuse like any other epidemic by gathering statistics to include in its measurement section on the epidemiology of homicide and suicide ("Epidemiology of Domestic Violence," 1984). Because of the serious and long-lasting health consequences, the CDC has continued to characterize interpersonal violence as a national public health problem (Chrisler & Ferguson, 2006).

The magnitude of male-to-female violence is staggering. The U.S. Department of Justice ascertained that of 3.5 million violent crimes committed against family members between 1998 and 2002, 49% were crimes against spouses (Durose et al., 2005). The National Crime Victimization Survey (NCVS) indicated that male-to-female intimate partner violence constitutes about 85% of intimate partner violence (IPV) cases (Rand, 2009). Separated women are victimized about 3 times more often than divorced women and about 25 times more often than married women

(Bachman & Saltzman, 1995; see also Sharps, Campbell, Campbell, Gary, & Webster, 2003). It is important to note that victims had reported only about half of the violent incidents to the police (see Greenfeld et al., 1998). (See Appendix A.1 for a variety of estimates on nonlethal intimate partner violence.)

The NCVS found that about half of female victims of partner aggression claim some sort of injury, and about 20% seek medical assistance (Greenfeld et al., 1998). In the 1994 National Electronic Injury Surveillance System (NEISS) assessment of 1,417,600 hospital emergency room patients, 84% of persons treated for injuries inflicted by intimates were women. Several investigators have shown that female victims of spouse abuse suffer unusually high rates of head injuries (Deering, Templer, Keller, & Canfield, 2001). (See Appendix A.2 for estimates of injuries of and by intimate partners. See also Appendix D.2 for additional information about injuries to women caused by IPV.)

Homicide is the least likely outcome of a domestic assault, but it is the most feared and the primary basis for formulating criminal justice policy. Women in America are killed in overwhelming numbers by the men who profess to love them. The U.S. Bureau of Justice Statistics reported the following statistics compiled from 2008 data: (a) there were 696 known spousal murders, and (b) of those murders, 82.10% were husband-to-wife killings and 17.10% were wife-to-husband killings (U.S. Department of Justice, Bureau of Justice Statistics, 2011). The rage displayed by the men who kill their loved ones amazes analysts. Over half of the women in one inquiry had been stabbed, strangled, beaten, kicked, burned, punched, hit, or thrown from windows (Wilt, Illman, & Field, 1997).

Because the relationship between the perpetrator and victim is known in slightly less than two-thirds of the deaths, most statistical summaries rely on data that actually undercount the number of domestic homicides. In 1997, the New York City Department of Health released a review of coroner records. Of crucial social significance was the fact that in 67% of the cases, at least one child was physically present during the murder; in 26% of the incidents, at least one other person was killed; and in 44% of these murders, the other person was a child (see also Sharps et al., 2001). (See Appendix A.3 for estimates of intimate partner homicides [IPH]. See Appendix B.1 for additional estimates of IPHs.)

Statistics of Intimate Partner Abuse Among Racial and Ethnic Groups in the United States

While experts seem willing to accept stereotypes of racial differences in frequency of violence, they usually ignore any important differences that, if recognized, might contribute to a lessening of domestic violence in these communities (C. M. Graham, Tsuge, & Soucar, 1998; E. Klein, Campbell, Soler, & Ghez, 1997).

NCVS data provided the following estimates of nonlethal violence per 1,000 women: 0.8% for whites; 0.9% for Hispanics; 1.2% for blacks; and 0.6% for other groups, such as Native Hawaiians and Asians (Greenfeld et al., 1998). When other researchers have adjusted for socioeconomic status, financial stress, social desirability, and alcohol use, distinctions between various ethnic groups have been found to be greatly diminished (Neff, Holamon, & Schluter, 1995). Experts believe that rates of intimate abuse are as high or higher for immigrants than for other groups (e.g., Tjaden & Thoennes, 2000). (See Appendix A.4 for estimates of differences in intimate partner violence among ethnic groups.)

Statistics of Intimate Partner Abuse Within Cross-Cultural and Global Communities

In most countries, wife beating is an acceptable form of control, whether legal or not (Schuler, Hashemi, Riley, & Akhter, 1996; Waltermaurer, 2012). Many countries have been slow to identify wife assault as a social problem. On the broadest scale, only more recent research has begun to capture the overlap among wife assault, community violence, and violence within and between countries (see Walker, 1999, for a review).

Throughout the world, injury-causing assaults routinely reflect a pattern of male-to-female violence, whether in Austria, Nigeria, Hong Kong, or Japan (see Bernard & Schlaffer, 1992; Chan et al., 2009; Ezechi et al., 2004; Garcia-Moreno, Jansen, Ellsberg, Heise, & Watts, 2006). Marital assault rates in Canada, Australia, and New Zealand are analogous to those found in U.S. national family violence surveys, but slightly higher (Heise, Ellsberg, & Gottemoeller, 1999; Moffitt & Caspi, 1999). In countries such as Korea, Nicaragua, and Bangladesh, rates are much higher (Heise et al., 1999). Russia seems to have one of the highest wife murder rates in the world, with approximately 14,000 to 16,000 female homicides per year (Horne, 1999; Veltishchev, 2004). According to estimates made by the United Nations, between 17% and 38% of the world's women are victims of intimate partner violence. In developing countries, the rates are as high as 60% (Levesque, 2001; Yoshihama, 2002).

Intimate Partner Violence Within Special Populations

Populations other than married women also experience varying amounts of intimate partner violence: dating couples, same-sex couples, rural women, disabled women, and elderly women.

Dating couples. Being young and in love does not protect men and women from interpersonal violence. Self-report evidence suggests that dating couples may be even more violent than married couples and that dating violence is more reciprocal than adult intimate violence (Whitaker, Haileyesusm, Swahn, & Saltzman, 2007; see also Hettrich & O'Leary, 2007). Most dating violence studies base their assessments on the Conflict Tactics Scale (CTS), which measures isolated acts of aggression rather than patterns of abuse (e.g., Sabina, & Straus, 2008). (See the pros and cons of the CTS measurement scale outlined in Barnett, Miller-Perrin, & Perrin, 2011, pp. 68–70.)

NCVS data have established that among boyfriends and girlfriends, 14.1% of victims are male and 85.9% are female (Rand, 2009). Statistical data from both the U.S. Department of Justice and the FBI support findings of gender differences among dating couples (Durose et al., 2005; U.S. Department of Justice, FBI, 2000). Durose and colleagues (2005) also showed that 75% of dating partner murderers are male. (See Appendix A.5 for estimates of dating violence. See Appendix B.2 for additional information on dating violence.)

Same-sex couples. Same-sex couples also experience intimate partner violence. Historically, gay men and lesbians have been adversely affected by homophobic prejudice. Many people believe that women will not really hurt each other and that they are not aggressive or violent. These and other factors influenced early researchers to exclude gay and lesbian couples from their studies of intimate partner violence. Research reported in 2005 (Craft & Serovich, 2005) determined prevalence rates to be as low as 11% to as high as 73%. Official reports for same-sex intimate partner violence are lacking in part because police agencies and the FBI do not have appropriate categories and often list victims and offenders as friends or acquaintances instead of partners. Renzetti (1992) stated that more than half of the victims of lesbian battering in her study had experienced more than 10 abusive incidents during their relationship. (See Appendix A.6 for estimates of intimate partner violence among lesbians.)

Rural women. Rural women live in virtual closed societies (enclaves) of patriarchy, where they are isolated and have little access to services, making them especially vulnerable to intimate partner violence (DeKeseredy & Schwartz, 2008). Well-known correlates of wife abuse, such as youth, poverty, unemployment, and low educational achievement, are all more prevalent in rural communities than in urban areas (Websdale, 1995b). A sample of 378 rural women with protective orders reported several types of abuse, including lifetime physical abuse (97.6%) and lifetime sexual abuse (30.2%) (Shannon, Logan, Cole, & Medley, 2006; see also M. Johnson & Elliott, 1997).

Disabled women. The amount of intimate violence perpetrated against disabled women is slowly coming to light. The number of people of both sexes with disabilities (either physical or mental) in the United States is approximately 19% to 20% of the population (Rand & Harrell, 2009). The NCVS found that the rate of male-to-disabled-female intimate abuse is 16.1%. Of women with multiple disabilities, the rate rises to 56%. This rate is 1.5 times higher than the rate for nondisabled people. The CDC has analyzed data that distinguish disabled victims of abuse from those who are not disabled. Disabled women are less likely to be in a relationship than nondisabled women. Disabled women are abused by various caretakers as well as intimate partners. According to this comparison, women with disabilities are more often abused than either nondisabled women or disabled men. These women also suffer abuse for a longer duration (Rand & Harrell, 2009).

Elderly women. Measurement of elder abuse has increased over the last decade. The U.S. Census Bureau (U.S. Department of Commerce, Bureau of the Census, 2008b) estimates that there are over 36 million elders (65 years and older) in the United States. Studies of elder abuse have been more limited than those of younger individuals. It is still the case that researchers use unique definitions and nonstandard measurements, and they usually lack control groups. It is also true that individuals who gather data on elder abuse (e.g., the police, adult protective services [APS]) are sampling vastly different populations. Adding to such problems is the fact that elders are frequently loathe to report abuse. What data are available are undoubtedly underestimates. Elder abuse is typically perpetrated by family members and romantic intimates of the victims (Acierno, Hernandez-Tejada, Muzzy, & Steve, 2009; Laumann, Leitsch, & Waite, 2008). (See Appendix A.7 for estimates of elder abuse and the identity of abusers. See also Appendix B.3 for a comparison of two prevalence estimates of elder abuse using different data.)

The Truths of Domestic Violence

Patterns of Violence

Lenore Walker's (1979) pioneering research and work with battered women led her to develop a theory of why women stay in abusive relationships. The Cycle of Violence theory describes interpersonal aggression in three phases:

1. *Tension building*: The phase in which minor incidents of violence may occur along with a buildup of anger. This phase may include verbal put-downs, jealousy, threats, or breaking things, and may last for an indefinite period of time. Eventually, this phase will escalate to the second phase.

2. *Acute or battering*: The phase in which violent outbursts occur. This violence can be seen as the major earthquake and the episodes during tension building as the foreshocks. Following the second phase, the couple (or family if there are children) will enter the third phase.

3. *The "honeymoon" or loving respite*: The phase in which the batterer is remorseful and afraid of losing his partner. He goes on a charm campaign. He may promise anything, beg forgiveness, buy gifts, be effusively communicative with a passion fueled by guilt, and basically be the man she fell in love with. Rhodes and McKenzie (1998) speculate that this type of behavior greatly sways a battered woman's decision to return. Over time, there is a change in this phase as the batterer externalizes the blame (blames others, primarily his wife) and she internalizes it (blames herself, not him) (see D. K. Anderson, Saunders, Yoshihama, Bybee, & Sullivan, 2003, and Towns & Adams, 2000).

Eventually, Walker (1979) herself and other researchers (e.g., Carlisle-Frank, 1991) modified this conceptual framework. Information from both women and men indicated that in many cases, the alleged "honeymoon" was simply a cessation of violence and that for the abuser, repentance was short-lived. In addition, data from other studies did not uniformly find cyclical patterns of abuse or, in fact, any uniform patterns (Aldarondo, 1996; Cavanaugh & Gelles, 2005). Instead, some studies emphasized the unpredictable nature of batterers' violence (e.g., Langford, 1996), and one study uncovered a pattern in which one type of abuse persisted while a different type stopped (Jacobson, Gottman, Gortner, Berns, & Shortt, 1996).

The Reality of Domestic Violence

Some of the realities of domestic violence are reflected in domestic violence statistics. Most of these realities, however, are revealed in the emotional, economic, familial, cultural, and legal burdens placed on battered women as they attempt to make decisions that will greatly affect their lives and the lives of their children.

Battered women face a number of difficult decisions as a result of living in a violent household. The most fundamental of these is the decision to stay or leave. If a woman remains with her abuser, she is criticized and quite often blamed for her own victimization. If she leaves, she is judged as demonstrating a lack of commitment and concern for the welfare of her children and her spouse.

It is not uncommon for theories in behavioral science to portray victims as provocateurs, people who incite the hapless culprit to violence, robbery, rape, or mayhem. We have held persons responsible for being burglarized because they did not have better locks or alarm systems. We wondered whether the victim of a drive-by shooting was actually an innocent victim or a gang member. It seems as if the mere act of victimization casts aspersions upon the character of the victim. This is a dilemma that few women can resolve.

As crimes become more "personal" or "intimate," we more closely question the culpability of the victim. We hold the rape victim accountable for her whereabouts after dark, question her dating practices, and wonder if her turtleneck sweater was cut too low! Defense attorneys have asked rape survivors, "What did you do to indicate you did *not* wish to be raped?" By contrast, how frequently did we ask the victim of a burglary, "What did you do to indicate that you did not want to have your house burglarized?"

Similarly, there is a feeling on the part of some that battered women have "asked for it." Overall, there is little understanding of the reasons why battered women stay and little empathy for their plight. These problems are compounded by the ability of nuclear families to insulate and isolate themselves from neighbors, family members, and societal repercussions, and also by the reluctance of the "system" to interfere in the private sphere of a sacrosanct institution. Nonetheless, spouse abuse parallels the existence of humankind. It has been an unwelcome, yet unchallenged, stepchild residing in our families for generations.

Understanding Battered Women

Most of us say that we don't understand people who put up with abuse from a spouse or lover. Most of us say we would leave if that happened. To understand the battering relationship, it is necessary to understand that most relationships don't start out with one partner seriously injuring the other. Unless you are with someone who has battered several partners, the onset of battering is usually gradual and subtle. Our own theory is that you could live with Jack the Ripper or Ma Barker for at least a year, and if you were in love, you wouldn't figure it out. That would happen because most of us aren't looking, we're just feeling, and because Jack and Ma would be on their best behavior.

Let's make this a personal issue. We would ask the reader to think about a time when you were in an important relationship (with a lover, friend, boss) and left that situation only to look back on it and wonder why you stayed so long. Or did you find yourself asking how you had gotten there in the first place? You might also ask yourself how you feel about your own anger and the ways you express it. What feelings do you usually have after you've gotten angry?

Put yourself in the beginning of your love relationship. Think about the intensity of your feelings and beliefs regarding your partner and the relationship itself. Most of us enter a marriage or important relationship feeling we will be nurtured, loved, and protected. Let's call our hypothetical couple Sam and Diane (for those of us who have watched *Cheers*).

Case Study: The Story of a Typical Battered Woman—Diane

Sam and Diane have dated for over a year and decide to get married. They know each other's friends and family. They have spent birthdays and holidays together and share many common interests, including religious beliefs. Diane's family and friends like Sam and vice versa, and everyone's excited about their marriage.

They are married and move into an apartment with their cat and two goldfish. They set up their home with many of the gifts they've received. Sam and Diane have had a few arguments while they've been together, but nothing serious. After they've been married about six months, Sam comes home from work late again. He's been putting in lots of overtime. Diane's upset because dinner is cold, he hasn't called, and they haven't had time together. Sam is tired and grouchy, and they begin to argue. Sam yells louder than he ever has before, calls her a bitch, and throws his glass of water down, breaking a glass that was a wedding gift. How many of you think you would leave the relationship or call the police? Think about it.

Diane and Sam don't. Sam apologizes. They really talk to each other for the first time in a few weeks. He says he's tired and didn't mean to break anything. Diane feels his pain and remorse. He takes her out to dinner, and they feel close again. She understands, and when they get home, they make love. Diane may feel upset, but she puts it aside as she empathizes with Sam. After all, she thinks, people aren't perfect. It's important to be tolerant.

They go on a camping vacation that year to celebrate their first anniversary and share time with both families. Sam likes Diane's brother, and they enjoy going to ball games together. Sam and Diane get rid of some hand-me-down furniture and buy a new couch and chair. They even own a laptop computer and Seal-a-Meal. At the end of their second year of marriage, Diane announces she's pregnant, and shortly after that they have a major argument. They yell at each other, call each other names; then Sam hits the wall and slaps Diane once. How many of you would leave now? Why or why not?

After the birth of their first child, the families celebrate the baby's baptism at Sam and Diane's new home. There is reminiscing about the last three years and enthusiastic anticipation of the next holiday with the first grandchild. There have been several serious arguments during the first pregnancy, but only the one

(Continued)

(Continued)

episode of hitting. Diane does find herself feeling apprehensive when Sam gets angry, but she reassures herself that it's only the financial pressure that set him off.

Sam begins to fear his anger and tries not to get mad, but finds the harder he pushes anger away, the angrier he gets. He remembers his father's outbursts, the terror on his mother's face, and his own fear. He knows he can control himself—except sometimes, Diane just really pushes his buttons.

When the baby is one year old, Diane discovers she's pregnant again. Everyone's excited. Two days after her announcement, she and Sam argue over finances and her desire to return to work. Sam slaps her twice and pushes her. Then he leaves the house. Diane cries; she is almost hysterical. She is also afraid that Sam is gone. He calls several hours later, crying and begging for forgiveness. She is not ready to forgive, but she tells him to come home anyway. He returns, they reconcile, and neither of them tell anyone what happened.

Both Diane and Sam feel embarrassed about the aggression, and they don't want their friends or family to know about it. It has been three and a half years, one broken glass, two holes in the wall, two episodes of slapping, one push, 18 months of increasing fear, one house, many joyous holidays, one and a half children, shared memories, love, religious connections, economic security, and family bonds. How many of you would leave now?

As Diane and Sam develop their own pattern of abuse, they begin to close off emotionally from their friends and families. The process is subtle. It begins with the first little lie. It continues when Diane and Sam don't go to friends for dinner because "Diane tripped and hurt herself," or because "she got the flu"—when really she's upset because she's been slapped.

The lies chip away at the couple's integrity and separate them from others. The lies also cement a bond between the two people (or more if there are children) involved. Isolation develops slowly. Can you imagine telling your close friends that you have been slapped and pushed by your husband (whom they like, and whom you still like)? Most of us want shared friends, want others to like our partners, and want others to think we have good taste.

Most of us establish "bottom lines" about relationships before we become involved. Bottom lines are the lower limits of our basic expectations of a relationship. "If she ever had an affair," "If he ever hit me," and "If she doesn't have children" are all examples of bottom lines. These basic expectations remain until they are confronted. Then, for most of us, it is easier to lower or alter them than it is to change our lives (see Lovik, 2011a; see also Fleury, Sullivan, & Bybee, 2000).

Why Does She Stay?

The most commonly asked question regarding abused women remains, Why does she stay? This question is based on the naive assumption that it's easy to leave. Contrary to frequently held beliefs, most people would not stop liking or loving an intimate partner who hit them. Most of us would say that we don't want to be hit by someone who loves us, but there are conflicting values that occur after the first incident. Most of us make promises and commitments that define who we are as people and in relationship to others. We promise to stick with our partners—to be compassionate, to be forgiving, to keep our families together. Which values weigh more when we are confronted with a push, slap, or more from our intimate partners?

In addition, a web of oppression, fear, and confusion occurs over time based on the violent and nonviolent strategies employed by the intimate perpetrator. It is important for helping professionals to understand the intricacies of this web, the individual differences between victims, and the ambiguities of gender that create this entanglement. Intervention strategies should be tailored accordingly.

It is our purpose to demonstrate that battered women have learned to endure abuse and remain in their unhealthy relationships. Their learning occurs not only through common and "normal" socialization processes, but also through exposure to the abuse itself. We hope to point out convincing analogies between learning in the laboratory, using animal subjects, and learning in the lives of battered women. That is, the principles of learning that control behavior discovered by such scientists as Pavlov, Skinner, and Seligman will ultimately be linked to the same principles of learning affecting the behavior of battered women.

Our theory of battering is eclectic. It includes the effects of male-female socialization, sex-role stereotyping, family history, and gender-related power differences. It also rests upon research conducted from neurobiological, behaviorist, and cognitive learning perspectives, as well as on social learning research and theory. In general, we assume that family violence has multidimensional causes: intrapsychic dynamics (individual), intrafamilial dynamics (family), and environmental dynamics (social and cultural). The decision to leave an abusive relationship may be determined by a convergence of factors (Frisch & MacKenzie, 1991).

Experiences that cause stress-induced symptoms in other populations (e.g., war veterans) can be likened to the experiences of a battered woman. She is a human being responding to a crisis brought on by abuse, and her response is like the response of other human beings who experience similar intense trauma, prolonged trauma, or both.

A woman cannot know with complete certainty that the man she loves and plans to marry will not eventually abuse her. A battered woman could be any woman or *every woman*. It is truly a case of "There but for the grace of God go I."

1

Weaving the Fabric of Abuse

Learned Helplessness and Learned Hopelessness

Men are taught to apologize for their weaknesses, women for their strengths.

—Lois Wyse

The enigma of battering relationships and why women remain in them begins with the long journey of learning to be female in this culture and others. To cover the topic of sex-role socialization, both in the family and in the world, is to explore the Wonderful World of Women. The fundamental principle underlying female sex-role socialization is that female identity rests upon a woman's attachment and affiliation with an intimate partner, chiefly through marriage. The mores of the culture provide a psychosocial foundation for understanding the complexity of abusive relationships.

Case Study: Lisa—For Better or for Worse

"I believe that you stay with your partner for better or for worse. I didn't know what 'worse' was when I made that promise, but I promised. I believe my husband loves me, and I'm starting to believe he could kill me. I'm not sure how long I should stay and how 'bad' is 'too bad.' I know I don't believe I should be hit, but I do believe if my relationship is a mess, I should stay to help make it better."

Socialization

P. J. Berger and Berger (1979, p. 9) define *socialization* as the "process through which an individual learns to become a member of society." Learning applies not only to observable behaviors, but also to cognitions (thoughts) and attitudes. Learning is strengthened through reward and punishment, as well as through observation of others' rewards and punishments (i.e., modeling [Bandura, 1971]). Ideally, an individual learns to discard nonproductive behavior and to retain healthy behaviors and beliefs through reinforcement. (Turn to Appendix E.3 and E.4 for descriptions and explanations of technical learning terms such as *reinforcement*.)

Society exposes men and women, boys and girls, to differential expectations as part of learning their gender identities. Sex roles tend to magnify biological disparities. Carol Tavris (1992) believes that male and female behavior is not governed so much by genetic sex (chromosomal variation) as by the social context (see Lorber & Farrell, 1991). In other words, if customs were reversed, men, who had sole responsibility for the care of their children, would learn to be child focused and nurturing, while women, whose experiences centered on climbing the corporate ladder, would learn to be aggressively business oriented (see Birns, Cascardi, & Meyer, 1994; Mihalic & Elliott, 1997). Opportunity to develop these aspects of personality plays an important role in their acquisition. "Practice makes perfect," and gender limits practice (see Blau, & Kahn, 2007; Silverstein, 1996).

The culture permits and encourages male aggression but monitors its form (J. Klein, 2006; Maccoby & Jacklin, 1974). Peers exert considerable pressure on males to be masculine, to devalue women, and even to be abusive (DeKeseredy, 1990; Parrott & Zeichner, 2003). Female aggression, on the other hand, is tolerated primarily in defense of a loved one, particularly children (J. B. Miller, 1976). Marlo Thomas highlights this point with a bit of sarcasm: "A man has to be Joe McCarthy to be called ruthless. All a woman has to do is put you on hold."

In adulthood, traditional success is governed by gender (Josephs, Markus, & Tafarodi, 1992). Masculinity is characterized by independence and competence, while femininity is typified by interdependence. In men, but not women, self-esteem is highly dependent on traditional tasks or occupational success (Overholser, 1993). While boys are afraid of failing at tasks, girls may actually be afraid of succeeding; furthermore, girls may become anxious about task success because they anticipate or expect negative consequences (Horner, 1972). They are in a double bind (Pipher, 1994). To avoid the conflict between achievement (male defined) and affiliation (marriage and motherhood), most girls learn to equate achievement with affiliation (see Mickelson, 1989).

Society still values male traits more than female traits. One can go so far as to say that women are actively devalued (see Murphy & Meyer, 1991; D. A. Myers, 1995). Television continues to depict masculine characters as much more appealing than feminine characters. This discrepancy reinforces teenage girls' recognition of their subordinate status. One of the most powerful needs expressed by today's teenage girls is their desire to be seen as equal to young men (see Labi, 1998; McDowell & Park, 1998). A large survey of 57 societies revealed that sexist attitudes within a culture not only create gender inequality, but also increase its severity (Brandt, 2011).

Affiliation and Socialization

Ferguson (1980, pp. 159–160) says that "women's identity is forthrightly and consistently defined in terms of the contexts of social relationships. . . . For most women, connection with others is a primary given of their lives, not a secondary option to be contracted at will" (see Woods, 1999). "A woman's very sense of herself becomes organized around being able to make and then maintain affiliations and relationships" (J. B. Miller, 1976, p. 83). To a certain extent, her sense of well-being depends on her marital relationship with her adult partner (Mookherjee, 1997).

In Landenburger's (1989) judgment, a woman's conception of herself acts like a filter through which she interprets the world. Girls learn to value themselves as they are esteemed by others. Girls first become defined as daughters or by their relationships with their parents. Daughterhood is a common bond for all women and a beginning step toward knowing and learning what it means to be feminine, to be a wife, and to be a mother. The only change in adulthood is that the most important source of esteem is no longer the woman's parents but her romantic partner (Gilbert & Webster, 1982).

The need to develop and retain heterosexual relationships forces girls to abandon some of their selfhood, to actually stifle their own ambitions and their own personalities (Woods, 1999). The socialization process used to accomplish this goal is called the *silencing of the self*. While preteen girls are still able to be honest and authentic about themselves, most teenage girls are no longer able to do so. Teens have come to realize that revealing who they really are is not socially desirable. Too much authenticity may lead to affiliation losses (Pipher, 1994).

One thing women learn is that to obtain the prized possession of a harmonious relationship, it is important to be nice. Oprah Winfrey (Harpo Productions, 1992) calls this inclination the "disease to please." A glance at the titles of some current magazine articles gives an indication of the enormous societal pressure placed upon women to find and maintain a relationship with a man.

"Beating the Man Shortage—Cosmo Finds the Best Places to Meet Them"

"Supporting a Husband Isn't the Worst Idea"

"Three Ways to Learn to Live With Your Husband's Infidelity"

"Sexy Ways to Calm Your Savage Beast"

"Five 'Come-and-Get-Me' Tricks"

"Making Every Minute You Spend Together Spectacular"

Case Study: Cindy

Cindy was abandoned by her parents at an early age and raised by strict, moralistic relatives. She and her sister were taught to be nice girls with traditional values. Disagreement was not tolerated; nor was unladylike behavior. Verbal abuse in the form of put-downs or threats was part of normal life. Slapping and pushing were common forms of discipline for unacceptable behavior.

Cindy decided early in life that the price of breaking family rules was too high. She had very few friends, did not stay out late, got good grades, and did not date often. She married young and quickly learned that her husband's rules were much like her aunt and uncle's. Cindy believed that she had no power to change the situation. Mild abuse was chronic, a familiar pain, endurable. She believed that maintaining her marital relationship was the most important achievement in her life.

Affiliation pressures on battered women are even more intense than those placed on women in general. A battered woman may think that her partner's violence represents a failure in her relationship, rather than an impulsive act by her abuser (Gilligan, 1982). The threat of a rupture in her adult relationship, fear of isolation from her partner, or rejection by her partner may cause her even more apprehension than sporadic physical aggression (see Vandello, Cohen, Grandon, & Franiuk, 2009). As research has progressed, it has become clearer why battered women, and indeed most people, fear rejection. MRI studies of the brain have now shown that the pain of rejection is quite similar to the pain of a physical injury (Kross, Berman, Mischel, Smith, & Wager, 2011). As one assessment revealed, showing rejected partners photographs of their previous partner caused the pain regions in the brain to "light up." That is, rejection and physical pain activated the same neural pathways in the brain (for a review, see Weir, 2012).

As part of fulfilling attachment mandates, women have learned how to support men emotionally. A description of today's woman includes adjectives that have described virtuous women over the centuries: patient, self-sacrificing, and long-suffering. Self-sacrifice for women has a long and noble history (Sansone, Wiederman, & Sansone, 1997). As Anna Quindlen (1992, p. 10), a columnist for the *New York Times*, wrote in an editorial:

> The fact is that there's still a tacit agreement in American society, despite decades of change that women support. Like a French word that always takes "la," self-sacrifice remains a feminine noun. It is a deal that works beautifully for men, which is why you hear so much about how natural it is, even that it was God's idea; that there is a theological basis for women's inevitable compromises.

Women who are supportive and self-sacrificing, but are not physically battered, are considered good women; those who are battered are not. Women who are abused are significantly more self-sacrificing than nonabused women (Woods, 1999). Ascribing traits such as martyrdom or masochism to battered women not only fails to take female socialization into account, but also fails to acknowledge research evidence refuting this myth (Caplan, 1984; Symonds, 1979).

Sexism

> *As a Catholic and the daughter of a cop in Washington, I grew up in a triple play of patriarchal culture. The Church was run by men. The nation's capital was run by men. The law was run by men. Besides that, I had three older Irish brothers who liked to be waited on.*
>
> —Maureen Dowd (2005)

Sexism is a system of combined male controls: physical control, psychological control, derogatory beliefs about women, and institutional policies and regulations that discriminate against women (D. C. Adams, 1984; see also Gay, 1997; Messner, 1997, for other viewpoints). Sexist thinking and political principles were part of the founding of America (Kann, 1998). In a newspaper article, Tucker (1999) describes a stunning reversal of fortune for Zimbabwe women. The nation's supreme court overruled or challenged nearly every law relating to women's rights. In a 5–0 decision, the court declared that "women are not equal to men, especially in family relations" (p. 14).

Assaultive men generate higher need-for-power themes than nonassaultive men (Arriaga & Capezza, 2005; see also Gondolf, 1995). From a behavioral learning perspective, a batterer's ability to gain control, to feel powerful, and to be sexually aroused through intimidation is reinforcing (as in D. Dutton, Fehr, & McEwen, 1982), and therefore the aggression will increase (see also Wood, Gove, Wilson, & Cochran, 1997). Perhaps it is fair to say that part of the job description for being male is the ability to control women, or as West and Zimmerman (1987, p. 130) have put it, "in doing gender, men are also doing dominance and women are doing deference."

Sexism occurs in the family, in the media, in psychiatry, in medicine, in language, in organized religion, in government, and in the legal system. Acceptance of sexist stereotypes has been used to justify unequal treatment of women. In fact, many observers present evidence for the feminization of poverty (Brenner, 1991). "If you are a female, that's one strike against you; if you are either a poor female or a nonwhite female, that's two strikes against you; if you are a poor, nonwhite female, you have struck out" (Julian & Kornblum, 1983, p. 337).

Sexism and Power

In 1947, Webster (cited in Murphy & Meyer, 1991, p. 152) defined power as the "probability that one actor within a social relationship will be in a position to carry out his own will despite resistance." Interestingly, the definition fails to incorporate personal power and the ability to accomplish goals in a participatory fashion. Other related concepts are decision making and dominance. Gilbert and Webster (1982) contend that power is the reward for doing masculinity well; powerlessness is the reward for doing femininity well. A girl who becomes the woman she is meant to be receives love, but never power.

Coleman and Straus (1986) examined the relationships among marital power, marital power consensus, conflict, and violence in 2,143 representative American couples. Contrary to the view that the customary model of male head-of-household best preserves the family unit, the research found that an egalitarian, shared-power, marital relationship exhibits the lowest level of conflict and aggression. This finding was true even when both partners agreed that the husband's role should be dominant. In fact, consensus about marital power reduces the level of marital strife. When discord does arise, it is associated with much higher levels of violence in nonegalitarian marriages (see also Anson & Sagy, 1995).

Almost uniformly, professionals in the field have proposed some variation of a control theme to explain male-to-female aggression (e.g., Arriaga & Capezza, 2005; Gondolf, 1995; Tinsley, Critelli, & Ee, 1992). Studies of power, control, and dominance suggest that batterers' violence may stem from men's need to control, or relatedly, not to feel powerless (see Hamby, 1996, for a review).

Violence is a deliberate, chosen behavior that batterers believe is warranted, given the situation (Kernsmith, 2005a; Ptacek, 1988). From the perspective of learning theory, battering is a goal-oriented mechanism that maintains an imbalance of power between the batterer and battered woman (see Barnett, Lee, & Thelen, 1997; Felson, 1992; Hamberger, Lohr, Bonge, & Tolin, 1997). Others conceptualize power needs more within the realm of interpersonal needs (Coan, Gottman, Babcock, & Jacobson, 1997).

From a sociological perspective, battering can be viewed as the extreme end of a continuum of controls meant to reinforce male dominance over women (DeKeseredy, 1990). Murphy and Meyer (1991, p. 97) state that "there are striking parallels between the use of violence as a means of control in marriage and in the larger culture outside of the family." Overall, a battering relationship is both the cause and effect of stereotyped roles and the unequal power relationship between men and women (S. Smith, 1984).

Cultural Support for Male-to-Female Violence

> *The attitudes of the public, the court, and even many helping professionals condone a certain level of abuse in the home, and support the patriarchal structure of the family which perpetuates the abuse from generation to generation.*
>
> —Maertz (1990, pp. 48–49)

Many experts believe that a focus on individual psychology, such as the psychopathology of some male batterers, cannot end wife abuse. Their belief partially rests on the fact that at least half of tested batterers fall within the normal range on assessments of psychopathology (Chambers & Wilson,

2007). They hold that only by changing the social and cultural institutions that permit wife abuse will a permanent solution be realized (Goodman, Koss, Fitzgerald, Russo, & Puryear-Keita, 1993). Sadly, women in patriarchal societies in which wife abuse is a cultural norm also uphold such precepts by accepting male-to-female partner abuse (e.g., Agoff, Herrera, & Castro, 2007).

One example of changing a cultural institution to reduce violence against women occurred in Pakistan. A bank credit program was implemented to assist women in obtaining a financial foothold toward independence by channeling to them economic resources that would expand their employment and income-generating opportunities. As one woman told a researcher,

> In the past my father-in-law would never stop my husband from beating me. But after I joined the Grameen Bank he said to my husband, "You had better stop beating and scolding your wife. Now she has contact with many people in society. She brings you loans from Grameen Bank. If you want to you can start a business with the money she brings." (Schuler, Hashemi, Riley, & Akhter, 1996, p. 1738)

A review of the literature suggests a number of behaviors reflecting male peer support for abusing women: (a) offering information and advice to a male abuser (e.g., "get an attorney so she can't ruin your career"); (b) keeping silent when told about the abuse (seeming agreement with abuse by failing to support the victim's position); (c) pressuring women for sex as a badge of male prowess, even at a woman's expense; and (d) providing admiration for male dominance and "keeping the upper hand" (DeKeseredy, 1990).

Additional empirical evidence shows that patriarchal norms contribute to wife beating. These beliefs include the following: (a) the man has the right to determine if his wife may work; (b) the man has the right to decide if his wife may leave home at night; (c) it is important for the man to show his wife that he is the head of the household; and (d) the man is entitled to have sex with his wife even if she does not want to do so (the woman-as-chattel theme) (M. D. Smith, 1990; see also D. A. Myers, 1995; O'Toole & Schiffman, 1997).

The following quotation from *Newsweek* magazine sums up the need to counteract the negative aspects of misogynous male socialization:

> Men's aggressive, powerful, domineering approach, their negative social attitudes toward women, and their belief in rape myths seem to have implicated men as perpetrators, while exonerating women. Perhaps the time has finally come for a new agenda. Women, after all, are not a big problem. Our society does not suffer from burdensome amounts of empathy and altruism, or a plague of nurturance. The problem is men . . . or more accurately, maleness. ("Guns and Dolls," 1990, p. 62; see also Levant, 1995)

Asher (1990, p. 7) says, "With the recent findings linking testosterone with aggressive behavior, the thought of dumping estrogen in the water supply certainly did come to mind."

Case Study: Trisha

Trisha called the hotline for information. She wanted to find out whether her marriage was typical in terms of highs and lows. She said that she didn't get black eyes; she was just pushed and shoved. Verbal outbursts and threats were just a fact of life. She said, "The kids and I just don't make Daddy mad." Her husband's male psychiatrist had told her that she needed to "take the good with the bad." Her male minister had told her to "turn the other cheek and be more loving."

Trisha's husband, the psychiatrist, and the minister are symbols of power. Male authority figures in the community tell women that they must keep their families intact at all costs. The culture encourages women to become chameleons, to adapt to their environments, to camouflage themselves and their feelings.

Battering happens partially because, somehow, society has given its consent. Married men approve of slapping women for some of the following reasons: (a) she insults him privately, (b) she insults him publicly, (c) she comes home drunk, (d) she hits him first, (e) she has an affair, and (f) she does not do what he tells her to do (see O'Toole & Schiffman, 1997, for a review).

Although society pays lip service to the belief that male-to-female violence is unacceptable or at least less acceptable than the reverse, reality provides a conflicting norm. There may be a dichotomy between what people say and what they actually believe, and culturally, there may be a state of cognitive dissonance residing in our collective psyche (Harris, 1991). Marvin Kahn (1980), a professor from the University of Arizona who studied aboriginal islanders, offers a final word on this topic. He commented about the custom of wife beating: "Severe injury or damage . . . cannot be condoned, but to totally condemn the practice [of wife beating] may be to negate an important aspect of island culture" (p. 731). (By the way, we were unable to reach these women for comment!)

A Change of Attitude

In 1992 and 1995, researchers conducted two different types of public opinion polls, including questions about attitudes toward domestic violence (E. Klein, Campbell, Soler, & Ghez, 1997). The 1992 poll found that Americans ranked domestic violence as fifth on a list of public concerns, with only 34% of the total agreeing with the notion that it is an extremely important topic. By 1995, 79% thought domestic violence was an extremely important social issue. At this time, Americans also thought that public intervention was necessary (82%), especially if an injury occurred (96%). The principal reason that people thought that public intervention was necessary, however, was to protect children, not women.

Sadly, it took the murders of Ronald Goldman and Nicole Brown Simpson in June 1994 to bring domestic abuse to the forefront of the nation's attention. Of respondents replying to questions about information learned from the O. J. Simpson trial, 93% ranked domestic violence as a very serious problem (E. Klein et al., 1997).

In the 1992 poll, arresting batterers was unpopular. Most respondents chose counseling as the best alternative for intervening in wife abuse. At a minimum, a man would have to hit a woman hard (53%) to deserve arrest, but if he punched her, 94% agreed arrest was appropriate. One disturbing and persistent belief among 38% of the participants was that "some women provoked men into abusing them" (E. Klein et al., 1997). Even judges have shocked courtrooms by sympathizing with a batterer's justification for assaulting or murdering his wife (Schornstein, 1997). On the positive side, research-based educational strategies designed to impact beliefs in schools, clinics, the media, and the courtroom (e.g., speakers, posters, classes, and films) are beginning to diminish acceptance of wife beating (Chalk & King, 1998; Goelman & Valente, 1997; O'Neal & Dorn, 1998).

One aspect of male-to-female violence that should impact public attitudes is the tremendous economic toll for victims and taxpayers. To estimate this financial burden, Max, Rice, Finkelstein, Bardwell, and Leadbetter (2004) used approximations of the total number of women affected by intimate partner violence from the National Violence Against Women Survey (NVAWS) (Tjaden & Thoennes, 1998a). In categorizing these expenses, they provided the total costs of rapes, physical assaults, stalking, and murders. They further categorized medical costs from injuries into "hospital care," "physician care," "ambulance/paramedics," "dental care," and "physical therapy." (See Appendix B.4 for a table of these costs.) A different team of researchers estimated the total costs of treating injuries, providing mental health care, homelessness and welfare, and criminal justice system processing at $8.3 billion in 2003 dollars (Ulrich et al., 2003).

Sexism and Therapy

Sexism seems to flourish even among mental health professionals (see Eisikovits & Buchbinder, 1996). In a revealing early study, Swenson (1984) investigated the judgments of experienced psychotherapists concerning the relationship between sex roles and mental health. Results indicated that the psychotherapists rated a healthy person (sex unspecified) as having masculine traits. They did not rate as healthy individuals who possessed both favorable masculine and feminine characteristics. These findings coincide with those of early researchers showing that subjects valued masculinity more highly than femininity (Broverman, Vogel, Broverman, Clarkson, & Rosenkrantz, 1972).

Gender bias can also affect a therapist's ability to recognize intimate violence. During a counseling session, a therapist reacts to what he or she believes about the power dynamics in relationships (Petretic-Jackson & Jackson, 1996). Hansen, Harway, and Cervantes (1991) used two hypothetical cases to study the ability of family therapists to recognize marital violence and recommend appropriate protection strategies. In one of the two test stories, Carol told her therapist privately that she had sought an order of protection because James had "grabbed her and threw her on the floor in a violent manner and then struck her." In the other vignette, Beth claimed that Tony had "punched her in the back and stomach and caused her to miscarry." Tony asserted that Beth tried to hit him and punched herself in the back.

Of the 362 therapists, 22% correctly identified the problem as violence or battering and 17% as an abusive relationship. Others classified the problem as conflict (8%), anger (5%), a power struggle (4%), lack of control (1%), or other (4%). The remaining therapists did not categorize the problem as any type of conflict. Only 45% of the therapists advised crisis intervention; 48% called for further assessment, 60% suggested work on a nonviolent marital problem, and 28% recommended couples counseling. Only 10% addressed the need for protection. Even when psychologists are appropriately involved, they often fail to take domestic violence into account (Ackerman & Ackerman, 1996).

Gender bias may be diminishing in some quarters. Ten years after the Ackerman and Ackerman (1996) investigation, researchers used intimate partner violence (IPV) themes other than violence (such as partner control) to test therapists. The outcome demonstrated considerable improvement. Of the participants, 57% recognized the behaviors (e.g., control) as indicative of IPV, and 45.9% actually responded to the possibility of violence. Knowledge about IPV became more widespread in the 10-year period following the first investigation (Dersch, Harris, & Rappleyea, 2006). Similarly, a contemporary appraisal revealed that students in law enforcement programs, non-law-enforcement criminal justice programs, and social work programs correctly identified domestic violence in scenarios containing IPV. Students in law enforcement programs, however, were less sensitive to domestic violence than students in either social work programs or non-law-enforcement criminal justice programs (McMullan, Carlan, & Nored, 2010).

Health care professionals also need to improve their recognition and understanding of domestic violence. "Developing successful practices both in identifying survivors of domestic violence and in preventing further victimization requires a broad understanding of the effects of domestic violence and the challenges for health care professionals in dealing with it" (Husso et al., 2012, p. 347). Over the last few years, researchers have developed quite a few screening questionnaires that help identify specific categories of battered individuals, such as battered women and battered elders. Specialists within fields such as medicine and psychotherapy often use screens developed for the special needs of personnel working in those fields (L. K. Brown, Puster, Vazquez, Hunter, & Lescano, 2007; Reis, 2000; Steigel, 2001; U.S. Preventative Services Task Force, 2004; Yut-Lin & Othman, 2008).

Practice and Policy With Immigrants

The most common call for change is for service providers to become *culturally competent*. Not only should practitioners demonstrate cultural competence, but so too should policy makers and those organizing prevention programs. Although most professionals agree with this idea, there is still disagreement about how to turn the concept of cultural competence into specific guidelines (American Psychological Association, 2006; see also Rodriguez, Valentine, Son, & Muhammad, 2009). Since there are different barriers for different ethnicities, treatment should be tailored accordingly. Research suggests the need for more education about partner violence targeted at the Latina community (S. L. Williams & Mickelson, 2004; see also Kugel et al., 2009). Another idea is to improve outreach and advocacy for immigrants (Gabbidon & Greene, 2005).

Fifty percent of the Haitians living in the United States are undocumented. Specific recommendations for service providers assisting Haitian victims include having medical, legal, and housing services staffed by people who can speak the language. Practitioners should discuss immigration status, because it affects everything the woman is doing (Latta & Goodman, 2005).

Mainstream treatment for partner abuse may not be meeting the needs of African American women. In the past, findings about white women have been misapplied to black women. Investigators assumed that the findings for one ethnicity applied to all other groups. Also, many members of the African American community are suspicious of the criminal justice system because of their experience with racial bias. As a result, women may not want to add to the high number of black males in jails by reporting their abuse, and/ or they may be shunned by their community if they do report it (Hampton, LaTaillade, Dacey, & Marghi, 2008; see also Gillum, 2009).

Gillum's study (2009) found that staff awareness of these ethnic differences enabled them to restructure shelter services in several ways. First, staff provided transportation to and from the group. Second, staff provided victims accompaniment to court, and a "big, burly man" to accompany a woman to her home to collect her belongings after she left. Staff were able to adopt a holistic approach that included assistance with finding a place to live and getting a job. Other immigrant group service agencies should adopt these practices (see Hampton et al., 2008; Houry, Kaslow, & Thompson, 2005).

Very high rates of alcoholism, unemployment, and HIV infections plague Indian tribes. Consequently, this population needs programs dealing with alcohol and drug addiction, jobs, and medical care and education for HIV. Behaviors such as respecting privacy and autonomy are important. Within Native American communities, which are different from other ethnic groups, making informal connections rather than holding formal group sessions is basic to successful helping. Service providers need to know the laws and to understand how the "jurisdictional maze" hampers law enforcement among Native American communities (Farberman, 2007; National Sexual Violence Resource Center, 2000).

An increase of funding from the Violence Against Women Act (VAWA) has greatly assisted tribes in strengthening their response to intimate partner violence. One step forward has been the availability of protective orders in 93% of tribal court jurisdictions. In addition, there have been innovative approaches to tribal prosecution. Shelters and safe houses are now located on reservations (see Luna-Firebaugh, 2006).

Asian immigrants are especially unlikely to disclose abuse by intimates because family privacy is so highly valued (Leung & Cheung, 2008). A survey of organizations serving female survivors of intimate partner violence uncovered the types of assistance needed by South Asian women (Merchant, 2000). The organizations present literacy classes, women's social groups, and training for police departments. Successful programs deal with differences in religions and castes and provide culturally matched service providers.

Immigrant populations can be overwhelmed by cultural differences when they arrive in new countries. Shelter advocates can help by providing information explaining the role of police, social services, and the court regarding intimate partner violence. For the empowerment of *all* victims of IPV, practical assistance, such as transportation to and from support groups, child care, court accompaniment, housing assistance, and job training, makes a substantial difference (Gillum, 2009; Latta & Goodman, 2005). Shelter staff make greater inroads with their clients when they demonstrate sensitivity to the feelings abused women have for their partners that make leaving difficult (Gillum, 2009).

Is It Safe to Use Couples or Family Therapy With Abusive Couples?

Many studies rating the effectiveness of couples counseling have been inconclusive for abusive couples (Chalk & King, 1998). Many traditional couples and family therapists have not been sensitive to the impact of gender on family relationships and have inadvertently imposed a patriarchal view as the standard of normal family functioning (Pence & Paymar, 1986; see also Goodman & Epstein, 2008). At the core of these allegations is the lack of certainty about the causes of male-to-female violence (see Mankowski, Haaken, & Silvergleid, 2002). Some therapists are disposed to blame battered victims for the violence (Whatley & Riggio, 1992), and a number of theorists blame battered women for not leaving. One such theorist expressed his feelings in a very victim-blaming way (D. M. Allen, 1988):

> In my experience, well-coached (metacommunication) patients will not incite a target (abusive spouse) to violence if they attempt to metacommunicate empathetically, no matter how clumsy the initial attempt. This is true even in families where violence is a routinely occurring pattern. The reason is that family violence against adults is invariably cued by the person to whom it is directed. A battered wife, for instance, helps the abuser play the role of abuser. If a victim did not wish to do that, she would leave the relationship as soon as the spouse caused her significant injury, no matter how much financial hardship she had to bear. (p. 318)

Counselors, psychotherapists, psychologists, and psychiatrists must give special consideration to the dangers inherent in providing family or couples counseling to violent families. The primary issue is safety. A battered woman may be afraid to speak out in front of her abuser about what has happened; or she may feel safe in the therapist's office, speak out, and pay for it later. A second concern is that an individual issue (e.g., control and violence) may become confused with a family issue (e.g., communication and parenting). It is critical to recognize that a battering problem belongs to the person who batters (Gondolf, 1998a; Hansen et al., 1991). Recognition is especially critical because abusive partners attempt to explain their violent behaviors by overemphasizing what they perceive as provocative behavior on the part of the victim.

Case Study: Bernice—A Tall Woman

"We are both therapists. Trying to find someone to counsel us without feeling completely exposed was difficult, and I was desperately seeking help. I was afraid and feeling trapped at this point. We finally found a marriage counselor who was well known; he had written books and articles on relationships.

During the second session, I mentioned the battering. I began to get angry and agitated when the marriage counselor did not address the violence directed at me. Instead, he talked about MY height and MY anger. He said I was very tall for a woman, something I was always self-conscious about. He asked my partner if my size, my anger, and my verbal ability (otherwise known as nagging) were intimidating to HIM."

Family therapists can reject the tendency to legitimize a power imbalance in the family. When exploring interpersonal power and control issues, therapists can too readily misperceive a battered woman's attempts at adaptation as a contest over power. From this position, it is a short step to succumb to the familiar victim-blaming routine. Failure to address gender issues minimizes the support battered women need and deserve (LaViolette, 1991). The rationale for using systemic approaches may be to make violence seem more manageable than it is (Bograd, 1992; Yllö, 2005). Newer studies imply that a one-size-fits-all approach may cast too large a net. While conjoint (couples) therapy remains extremely controversial, it may be appropriate and effective for some couples whose relationships are marred by infrequent, mild, and non-fear-provoking violence. Safety concerns are so compelling, however, that therapists undertaking this type of counseling must carefully prescreen couples for suitability (e.g., Hanks, 1992; O'Leary, 1996). The U.S. Preventative Services Task Force (2004) has developed a screening device that, taken together with other information, should alert psychotherapists to the potential for relationship abuse. Detection of this risk factor could contribute to the overall therapeutic treatment plan.

Families

> One is never finished with the family. It's like the smallpox—it catches you in childhood and marks you for life.
>
> — Jean-Paul Sartre

In families, mothers and fathers struggle with the obligations and restrictions of their sex roles. Although both parents may share the breadwinner role to some degree, they do not equally share the nurturing and domestic duties (Brines, 1994). Conflict arises not only from daily hassles and workloads, but also from power struggles and the challenge of changing sex-role expectations (Levant, 1995). Although times have changed, old stereotypes have remained intact, such as cooking, yard work, and child care (Snodgrass, 1990). Marital harmony is difficult when one lives in a democratic country and in an autocratic home.

It is important to recognize that the family is a powerful cultural transmitter of behavior, both positive and negative (Langley, 1991). Family members may learn unhealthy ways of coping, such as suppressing anger and other emotions, or using drugs, alcohol, and aggression (Belmore & Quinsey, 1994). Children tend to accept the family standards, whatever they are, as normal, and they often go on to practice them, regardless of their later uselessness. These skills become internalized responses, and their expression is almost reflexive. When an adult feels pushed against the wall, the old behavior patterns (survival skills) rear up to meet the challenge. People do what they have learned to do, and they do it with the rapidity of a knee-jerk reaction (Kovan, Chung, & Sroufe, 2009).

Overlap of Intimate Partner Abuse and Child Abuse

There is a large volume of available literature that addresses the overlap between the abuse of intimate partners and the abuse of children. Evidence overwhelmingly shows that in households where women are beaten, children are also abused (Graham-Bermann & Howell, 2010; O'Brien, John, Margolin, & Erel, 1994; Peled, 1993). In an article reviewing 35 studies, Edleson (1999) found that in 30% to 60% of families, both types of abuses were taking place at the same time (see also UNICEF, 2006; Valencia & Van Hoorn, 1999). The most recent surveys have determined that child abuse is present in 18% to 67% of families where intimate partner abuse is occurring (Jouriles, McDonald, Slep, Heyman, & Garrido, 2008).

Children living in maritally violent homes experience many risk factors simultaneously: direct physical and sexual abuse, neglect, parental alcoholism, low income, stress, and maternal impairment (see Chapple, 2003; Gibson & Gutierrez, 1991; Suh & Abel, 1990). Empirical data support the notion that exposure to marital violence, coupled with other forms of abuse, increases the severity of adverse consequences experienced by children who live in these families (J. J. Chang, Theodore, Martin, & Runyan, 2008; Holden, Geffner, & Jouriles, 1998b). The most severe forms of abuse, of course, lead to the death of a child. Child fatalities are especially likely to occur in families where males abuse their female partners (e.g., Pecora, Whitaker, Maluccio, Barth, & Plotnick, 1992; U.S. Department of Health and Human Services, Office of the Inspector General, 2008).

Most families involved in a child's death are two-parent households, and a majority of the perpetrators are either the child's father or the mother's boyfriend (see Felix & McCarthy, 1994; Klevens & Leeb, 2010). In a review of 99 partner homicides, authorities established that 56 children under the age of 18 had seen their mother being killed, their father committing suicide, or both; had found their parents' bodies; or had been killed themselves (Morton, Runyan, Moracco, & Butts, 1998; see also Sharps et al., 2001). Other people connected with a battered woman are vulnerable to violence (Riger, Raja, & Camacho, 2002). For the deaths of other family members (and friends) that occur with spousal homicide-suicides, the terminology *collateral deaths* has come into use (Washington State Coalition Against Domestic Violence, 2000).

Children exposed to parental violence often present a complex and heterogeneous diagnostic picture that blends elements of trauma symptomatology with features of more traditional disorders, such as hyperactivity (Holden, 2003; McCloskey & Lichter, 2003). A number of elements of parental violence affect the children exposed: (a) the nature and amount of the abuse witnessed; (b) the target of the abuse; (c) the severity and frequency of the interparental abuse; (d) the degree of assumed responsibility for the abuse and its outcome; (e) the age and gender of the children; (f) mediating factors such as familial, interpersonal, and community resources; and (g) the suitability and presence of interventions (P. G. Jaffe, Hastings, & Reitzel, 1992; Turner, Finkelhor, & Ormrod, 2010).

The effects of living in a domestic war zone are myriad and fall into several categories. Marital conflict and violence have the potential to make children feel insecure by interfering with parent-child bonding. Insecure attachment, in turn, places children at risk for behavior problems (Erickson & Egeland, 2010). On the more extreme end of the continuum, their experiences may fall into Hart and Brassard's (1990) category of "terrorized," manifesting symptoms of posttraumatic stress disorder (PTSD), including dissociation and hypervigilance (see also M. A. Dutton, 2009).

On the less extreme end, exposed children, compared with nonexposed children, tend to exhibit significantly higher levels of adverse effects: (a) behavioral problems (e.g., aggression, delinquency, hyperactivity, substance abuse, promiscuity), (b) mental health problems (e.g., anxiety, depression, anger, shyness), (c) health problems (headaches, rashes, stomach aches), (d) learning problems (school failure, absenteeism), and (e) social problems (poor social skills, difficulties in forming relationships) (Finkelhor, Turner, Ormrod, Hamby, & Kracke, 2009; Gleason, 1995).

According to an address by Lynn Loar (1997), a children's advocate,

> Children from violent families sound old, flat, and parentified (i.e., having to assume the responsibility of parenting their parents by acting like parents) [Van Parys & Rober, 2011]. These kids are hypervigilant, walking psychotherapists to their parents who can't tie their own shoes. They know about safety, but don't know how to share a toy. They know what they need to know and are accelerated in certain areas, especially survival. When a child gets a message in a state of arousal and fear, the message tends to stick.

Later research has connected violent prenatal familial interactions to in vivo development of fetal brain organization and function. After all, it is not the hand, knife, gun, or penis that ultimately creates the act of violence; it is the brain, the self-talk, the emotional reflex. Experiences that can be tolerated by an older child can destroy an infant. In the developing central nervous system, there are critical periods during which the brain is the most sensitive to environmental cues and organizing experiences. The ability to feel remorse, empathy, and sympathy are all experience-based capabilities. The effects of emotional neglect in childhood predispose individuals to violence by decreasing the strength of inhibition and decreasing the capacity to empathize and sympathize (Crittenden, Kozlowska, & Landini, 2010; Kotch et al., 2008; Perry, 1994, 1996). Factors that increase the reactivity of the lower brain stem (e.g., chronic abuse) and factors that decrease the moderating capacity of the midbrain and cortex (e.g., neglect) will increase an individual's propensity for aggression and impulsivity (Halperin et al., 1995). If during development, events require the stress response apparatus to be persistently active, the central nervous system will develop special stress-response neural systems. A child growing up in a violent, chaotic environment becomes hypersensitive to external stimuli and ready to respond to what he or she perceives as a threat (see also National Scientific Council on the Developing Child, 2006; Rossman, 1998).

Children Exposed to Marital Violence

There is no longer any doubt that children exposed to marital violence are learning harmful lessons about interpersonal relationships. Until the 1980s, intergenerational transmission of violence was not a focus; nor was the link made between random acts of violence and its incubation in a violent family (Holden et al., 1998b; see also Barnett, Miller-Perrin, & Perrin, 2011, for a review).

A number of factors greatly affect research on children who are exposed to adult intimate partner violence. These factors include the kinds of samples obtained, where and how they are obtained, how abuse between adults is defined, and how the child's exposure to abuse is defined. For instance, child witnesses may observe a violent act, overhear an abusive exchange, or see the results of an assault (e.g., bruises, broken household objects). Most advocates and many authorities consider exposure to marital violence a form of psychological maltreatment or trauma (Kilpatrick, Litt, & Williams, 1997; Sedlak et al., 2010; Somer & Braunstein, 1999). In fact, experts who investigate acute stress reactions classify exposure to a broad spectrum of situations (e.g., war, killings, seeing dead bodies, listening to horrifying stories) as traumatic (Gore-Felton, Gill, Koopman, & Spiegel, 1999; Hurlburt, Zhang, Barth, Leslie, & Burns, 2010; Zinzow, Grubaugh, Frueh, & Magruder, 2008).

Children of battered women are frequently exposed to recurrent male-to-female violence (P. G. Jaffe, Wolfe, & Wilson, 1990). M. A. Straus (1991b) estimates that the number of children in the United States exposed to marital violence every year is nearly 10 million. Estimates vary according to the sample of respondents queried (e.g., mothers, fathers, children), but parents seem to underestimate what their children have seen or heard (O'Brien et al., 1994; Tomkins et al., 1994). One Memphis medical team accompanying local police on domestic violence calls discovered that most children in these homes had directly witnessed the assaults. A few had not only witnessed their mother's assault, but also had been assaulted themselves when they tried to intervene (Brookoff, 1997; see also Hilton, 1992).

The most accurate estimate of children's exposure to domestic violence stems from the Adverse Childhood Experiences (ACE) comparison conducted by the Centers for Disease Control and Prevention (CDC) in conjunction with Kaiser Permanente (U.S. Department of Health and Human Services, CDC, 2006). In a sample of more than 17,000 adults, 13.7% of women and 11.5% of men reported childhood exposure to male-perpetrated intimate partner violence (see also Finkelhor, Turner, Ormrod, & Hamby, 2010).

Children exposed to IPV may also experience neglect. In a recent study using a small sample (10 children ages 8 to 12 years), several themes emerged through the qualitative interviews: (a) children did not describe their fathers as engaged or as responsible caregivers; (b) children described their fathers' parenting as "good enough" if they were simply not violent; and (c) mothers were seen (by the children) as the providers of the children's needs (Cater & Forssell, 2012).

Learning to Be Violent

The majority of children traumatized by family violence do not become remorselessly violent, but they have learned to believe that violence and aggression are viable options or solutions to problems. Their first emotional language is a reflection of the environment in which they live.

> Belief systems, in the final analysis, are the major contributors to violence. Racism, sexism, misogyny, children as property, idealization of violent heroes, cultural tolerance of child maltreatment, tribalism, jingoism, nationalism— all unleash, facilitate, encourage and nurture violent individuals. Without these facilitating belief systems and modeling, neglected and abused children would carry their pain forward in less violent ways. (Perry, 1995, p. 8)

A large body of evidence has shown that the effects of childhood exposure to parental abuse frequently extend into adulthood (e.g., Bedi & Goddard, 2007; Downs & Miller, 1998; Graham-Bermann & Howell, 2010; Kracke & Hahn, 2008). Even if a child seems to be functioning adequately when examined, sleeper effects (latent effects) such as anxiety, depression, substance abuse, aggression, promiscuity, and low self-esteem often show up later (e.g., E. M. Cummings, 1998; Graham-Bermann, 1998; D. Russell, Springer, & Greenfield, 2010).

Social Learning

Social learning theory provides an explanation for the interaction between socialization and family violence. At the core of this theory is a process Bandura (1971) called "modeling." In other words, people learn by observing and imitating others. Initially, and most important, children learn by observing and imitating their parents or primary caregivers. There is abundant empirical evidence based on laboratory research with humans that aggression can be learned through modeling (Bandura, 1971). Children exposed to violence in their families are more likely to model this behavior in their own adult relationships (Afifi, Brownridge, Cox, & Sareen, 2006; Carr & VanDeusen, 2002; Gershoff, 2008; A. H. Green, 1998).

Neuroscientists have introduced a third line of evidence from *mirror cell* (neuron) research that applies to observational learning (E. Jaffe, 2007). Mirror cells in the brain respond to actions (behaviors) in the same way whether an individual has personally *executed* the action himself or simply *observed* the action. Extrapolating from this research, the mirror cells in a child observing his father assault his mother would react as if the child were carrying out the assault himself. One can reasonably argue that observed violence may function to teach such behaviors. The stability of the findings reaffirms intergenerational accounts of family violence (Stith et al., 2000; see also Ehrensaft et al., 2003).

Social learning theory proposes that children model specific violent behaviors and attitudes, conflict resolution styles, and alcohol misuse. Although the social learning theory explanation for family violence has many proponents, some skeptics find this explanation to be either over-stated or too narrow, and others believe that the research thus far has had methodological shortcomings (Newcomb & Locke, 2001). Also counting against this theory as totally causal is the fact that many, if not most, indi-viduals exposed to violent family models do not go on to emulate abusive behaviors later in life (e.g., Mihalic & Elliott, 1997). Even when behavior is learned, there seem to be other factors, such as whether child abuse or com-munity violence were present, that contribute to its imitation (Valentino, Nuttall, Comas, Borkowski, & Akai, 2012).

Childhood Socialization

A relatively large volume of literature indicates that exposure to inter-parental violence or direct physical or sexual abuse during childhood is associated with later aggression toward others (e.g., Kracke & Hahn, 2008; Trull, 2001; Widom & Maxfield, 2001; see also Stith et al., 2000). A Finnish national survey found that 41% of men who saw their fathers perpetrating violence against their mothers went on to perpetrate violence in their own intimate relationships (Heiskanen & Pilspa, 1998). According to Hotaling and Sugarman (1986), observing abuse may be a more power-ful predictor of future partner violence than experiencing abuse directly, and paternal violence may be a better predictor than maternal violence (see also Blumenthal, Neeman, & Murphy, 1998).

Harsh treatment in childhood may also lead to the development of an antisocial orientation, which in turn is associated with chronic male-to-female violence (Simons, Wu, Johnson, & Conger, 1995; see also Ehrensaft et al., 2003). Later studies have indicated that childhood abuse also increases the risk of antisocial personality disorders in adults (Ehrensaft, Cohen, & Johnson, 2006; see also Farrington, 2000).

Conrad and Morrow (2000) proposed that children who suffer trauma such as sexual and physical abuse may learn to cope by dissociating (see also Simoneti, Scott, & Murphy, 2000). By adulthood, this coping mecha-nism can lead to the formation of borderline personality organization or disorder (Dutton, 1998). When this type of individual is threatened with abandonment, rage is the byproduct. This rage may be expressed symboli-cally (threats) or by direct violence toward his intimate partner (see also Ehrensaft et al., 2006). Rage is an emotional response to the pain and fear that he feels. It is easier to express anger than to experience pain, which can be unbearable. According to one of the participants in Alternatives to Violence therapy programs (LaViolette), "I would rather beat up 10 men than to tell a woman how I feel. Those feelings scare me."

Contrary to myths about battered women's backgrounds, certainly not all come from dysfunctional or abusive families. Coming from a healthy family is no guarantee that a woman will find a healthy partner (Kessler et al., 1994; Kessler, Molnar, Feurer, & Appelbaum, 2001). In fact, many battered women come from loving families. The family history of battered women is much less uniform than the histories of men who batter (Hotaling & Sugarman, 1990). The common denominator for women is that they were all raised in a culture where females are one-down in terms of actual power, and where the incentive to hope, to believe in change, and to "stand by your man" is paramount (see Moss, Pitula, Campbell, & Halstead, 1997).

Lenore Walker (1985b) cites several modern myths about battering relationships. One myth is that it is impossible to love someone who hits you. Love and physical force often occur together. The commonly heard phrase, "If he ever lays a hand on me, I'll leave," does not mirror reality. As Lloyd (1988) noted, physical aggression does not herald the demise of a marriage. By and large, battered women do not leave their relationships the first time their partners push, slap, or hit them (Follingstad et al., 1992; Raghavan, Swan, Snow, & Mazur, 2005). Actually, most adults have grown up in homes where loving parents spanked them as a form of physical discipline, for the child's own good (Flynn, 1996; Watts-English, Fortson, Gibler, Hooper, & De Bellis, 2006). Adults have come to believe that in families, a certain amount of physical force is not a denial of love, but can even be tangible proof of it (Gershoff, 2008). (See Appendix F.1 for a review of Ayllon and Azrin's 1966 study.)

Case Study: Bianca and Damien

Bianca had lost her husband after an 11-year marriage. She had two children and a supportive family, but she was depressed and vulnerable. After 18 months, she met a man at work who was understanding, seemed to love children, and was divorced. He had two children of his own. She began to date him.

After Bianca and Damien moved in together, the emotional and verbal abuse began. He became angry when she spent too much time with her family, calling her "Mama's girl." He was jealous of her friends and wondered why he wasn't enough for her. He got upset when their plans changed because her children were ill. His kids were older and out of the house most of the time. He wanted quiet, romantic dinners alone, sans children, on a routine basis. She gave up what was important to her a little at a time.

Bianca came from a family that was close and enjoyed time together. She had no context for understanding abusive behavior. When she confronted Damien, he told her that she was too sensitive. By the time Damien began to hit her, she was confused about her own perceptions.

Human beings tend to adapt to their situations regardless of the quality of their environment, a sort of chameleon effect. In the isolation of a battering relationship, the batterer's reality becomes the family's reality. In the words of Claudia Black (personal communication, April 1981), who works with adult children of alcoholics, "When you invite a healthy person into a sick family, you give him or her opportunity to become sick."

The Role of Learning and the Pattern of Violence

A scientific analysis of such processes as socialization and emotional dependency leads inevitably to an inquiry about the common, underlying mechanism—learning. That is, women learn to be feminine, to rely on a husband, and to follow prescribed religious concepts. The following illustration demonstrates the basic role that learning plays in behavior. (See Appendix E.2 for a brief review of operant conditioning, a type of learning based on the consequences of actions.)

Case Study: Heather and Ron

Heather had learned to iron her husband Ron's shirts just the way he wanted them. She had mastered nearly all of his favorite recipes, and she had worked very hard to teach the children to be quiet and pleasant when Ron was home. She graduated in the top 10% of her Fascinating Womanhood course (Andelin, 1963).

If Heather performed well (e.g., ironed, cooked, and got the children to bed quietly [operants]), she and Ron often had an enjoyable evening watching TV and just hanging out together (reinforcement). At such times, they shared happy, intimate moments and often ended the evening by making love. She had learned that having a pleasant evening with Ron depended upon her ability to please him. (Heather had been operantly conditioned.)

Walker's Cycle of Violence Theory

As summarized previously, Walker's Cycle of Violence theory describes a recurrent sequence of behaviors typical in battering relationships:

1. *Tension building*: A phase in which minor incidents of violence may occur along with a buildup of anger.

2. *Acute or battering*: A phase in which the major violent outburst occurs.

3. *"Honeymoon" (respite) phase*: A phase in which the batterer woos his wife.

Walker's (1979) theory provides a valuable illustration of operant conditioning. The cessation of violence in the third phase can be seen as a reinforcer. At this time, a battered woman receives discernible validation of her identity as the good wife and of her importance to her partner. Here, she recovers from her battle scars. Here, she remembers that abuse is not the only significant aspect of her relationship. She recognizes that she loves him too, that she cares about how he feels, his health, his survival if she leaves, his reputation, and about his life in general. She seems concerned about his relationship with the children and with friends and family. In fact, if she has already left him, she may return because of love (Goldner, Penn, Sheinberg, & Walker, 1990; Simpson, Atkins, Gattis, & Christensen, 2008).

It is not much of a conceptual leap to consider an abusive male partner's loving behavior as a form of intermittent reinforcement. The fact that intermittent reinforcement has powerful effects on behavior has been known for many years. Laboratory research on many species of animals and on many human populations has repeatedly documented that intermittently reinforced behaviors are difficult to alter (D. Dutton & Painter, 1993a). (See Appendix E.3 for information on intermittent reinforcement and other variables controlling reinforcement.)

Learned Hopefulness

For many women, the honeymoon stage provides reason to hope. Muldary (1983) called this outcome *learned hopefulness*. Learned hopefulness is a battered woman's ongoing belief that her partner will change his abusive behavior or that he will change his personality (see also Moss et al., 1997).

A survey of shelter residents identified the following list of reasons for staying or returning to a battering relationship: "I wanted to save the relationship," "I thought we could solve our problems," and "I loved my partner" (Muldary, 1983; see also Allison, Bartholomew, Mayseless, & Dutton, 2008). Barnett and Lopez-Real (1985) found "hoped partner would change" to be the number one reason women said they remained with their abusive partners ("feared revenge" was number two). Some women in their study made the following comments:

"That he would change was still a thought in the back of my head."

"I was always hoping, since he had gone to AA."

"I kept making excuses for him."

"After living together for so long without the abuse, I was hoping he would go back to his old self. I don't understand the change in him."

Relationship hope is an especially powerful influence on female intimate partner abuse survivors. In fact, research has revealed that just feeling optimistic appears to be beneficial. Optimism is linked with greater persistence toward goals, better coping, and improved health (Sweeny, Carroll, & Shepperd, 2006). Both men and women generally want their marriages to succeed. Procci (1990) observed that the failure of a marriage to meet one's expectations causes bitter disappointment.

Pagelow (1981a) found that 73% of the victims in one shelter sample returned to their homes because the batterers repented and the women believed the men would change. Both Okun (1986) and Thompson (1989) discovered that the hopes of battered women were rekindled by their male partners' attendance at even one counseling session, even before the men had made any real changes in their behavior. Similarly, 95% of the victims whose husbands were in court-ordered counseling believed their husbands would complete the program, although only half typically do (Gondolf, 1998c). D. K. Anderson, Saunders, Yoshihama, Bybee, and Sullivan (2003), in a study of 485 women, reported that the two most frequently cited impediments to leaving an abusive relationship were the woman's partner's promises to change (70.5%) and his apologies (60.0%).

Hope also springs from the fact that an abusive male's behavior is intermittently rewarding rather than continuously abusive. As Alexander Pope says in his "Essay on Man," "Hope springs eternal in the human breast." Male-to-female violence perpetrators can be kind, romantic, and intimate as well as intimidating and assaultive (Hastings & Hamberger, 1988). Periods of kindness interspersed with violence not only create hope, but also allow the victim to deny the side of the abuser that terrifies her (D. L. R. Graham, Rawlings, & Rimini, 1988). Exposure to negative events, however, *can* foster a downward shift in optimism that can also be beneficial. A downward shift allows an individual to prevent overwhelming disappointment by better preparing herself for a negative outcome (Sweeny et al., 2006).

Case Study: Sylvia and Dan

Even after Sylvia left Dan, she was torn by mixed feelings. Dan would call and offer support. He sometimes picked up the children and would spend a little time with them. He sounded interested in her and what she was doing for the first time in years. After they talked, he would ask her to consider reconciliation. Between the bouts of reason, he would call her, screaming and condemning her as a wife and mother. He harassed her at work. He had his mother call Sylvia to implore her to "think of the children." As the holidays approached, they talked less, and Sylvia felt relief. Dan began to pay the back child support he owed her and saw the children more regularly.

(Continued)

(Continued)

Then, one day Sylvia met Dan in the park. He came to pick up the kids. Instead, he attacked her. He choked and hit her. The children were terrified and began crying. A passerby pulled Dan away so that Sylvia and the children could escape. Dan threw himself in front of her car, screaming to his daughters, "Mommy is trying to kill me!" He has called her since the incident, alternately asking for forgiveness and blaming her for his rage. He threatens to kill her.

This pattern of hope and caring followed by brutality and fear kept Sylvia confused and immobilized for years. Dan's vacillation continues to keep her off balance, even eight months after their separation.

Relationship hope seems to be an internalized and reinforced notion characteristic of women in general. Families, friends, song lyrics, literature, religion, and the media all encourage women to hope and believe that they can change their male partners, and that they should persevere to see the results of their labor of love—the reward will be great. Isn't it true that behind every good man is a woman (who changed him)?

Relationship Commitment

Commitment to a relationship is usually seen as a positive attribute. Society urges couples to stay together through thick and thin, "for better or for worse, in sickness and in health." There are numerous illustrations of well-known women who have demonstrated marital commitment under very painful and humiliating revelations of their partner's infidelity: Hillary Clinton, Kathie Lee Gifford, Elizabeth Edwards, and Mary Alice Cisneros. So strong is public sentiment about the virtue of marital sacrifices that Hillary Clinton's approval ratings skyrocketed when she remained with Bill (P. Rogers, Krammer, Podesta, & Sellinger, 1998; Roloff, Soule, & Carey, 2001; Schindehette, 1998).

Commitment is an important issue, because keeping a relationship together no matter what significantly differentiates women who leave an abusive relationship from those who do not (Frisch & MacKenzie, 1991; see also Bauserman & Arias, 1992). It seems that for battered women, keeping a marriage covenant is a sign of pathology. Observers tend to judge their commitment as a sign of mental illness. To define seemingly healthy traits (such as keeping marital vows) as sick because of their context, however, pathologizes behavior learned through the ordinary socialization process.

According to Rusbult (1980), the degree of commitment to an intimate relationship rests on the fulfillment of certain needs: (a) relationship satisfaction (perceived rewards versus costs); (b) the quality of one's alternative (another partner, job, education, place to stay); and (c) the magnitude of investment in the relationship (time, effort, children, finances). The abused partner's commitment is a mediating factor in the decision to stay or leave. Rusbult calls commitment based on these factors the investment model. The findings of one comparison by Rhatigan, Moore, and Stuart (2005) support this model. Rhatigan and colleagues (p. 313) reported that "lesser relationship satisfaction, greater alternative, and fewer investments contributed to lower levels of commitment and greater intentions to leave those relationships" (see also Bauserman & Arias, 1992; Givertz, & Segrin, 2005).

Gager and Sanchez (2003) noted that the failure of a marriage to meet one's expectations causes bitter disappointment. Both abusive and nonabusive couples devise plausible reasons for hanging on to unhappy relationships (Vaughn, 1987): (a) belief in commitment, (b) legal bonds, (c) desire not to hurt the partner, (d) fear of not finding a better partner, (e) belief in one's ability to make the relationship better, (f) avoidance of being a quitter, (g) the need to protect children and parents, and (h) religious convictions. In general, couples hide their troubled relationships from others. They develop rationalizations, such as "All relationships have trouble," or "After a while, all couples lose interest in sex." (Regarding rationalizations: A friend of one of the authors [A. L.] asked her whether she would rather give up sex or rationalizations. As she was thinking about her answer, her friend inquired, "Have you ever gone a week without a good rationalization?")

Marital Satisfaction

One inquiry compared battered women still involved in abusive relationships with those who were not (Ellard, Herbert, & Thompson, 1991). Similarities existed in regard to psychosocial attributes such as mutual trust, love and respect, satisfaction with sex, and sharing of household chores. The key difference was that entrapped women assumed that other women had comparable problems (see Anson & Sagy, 1995).

Nonetheless, battered women are aware of the discrepancy between their actual marital relationships and their ideal relationships. On one clinical scale, a large group of battered women rated their actual relationship as extreme—rigidly disengaged with excessive emotional separation. In these marriages, one individual is highly controlling, roles are strictly defined and constrained, both partners are likely to be manipulative, and each individual is likely to do his or her own thing. Another group of battered women rated their actual relationship as chaotic (characterized by impulsive decision making and unclear, ever-changing role expectations).

The type of relationship the battered women desired and idealized was balanced (healthy, with normal give and take) (Shir, 1999).

Surprisingly, research has *not* uniformly shown that all couples involved in maritally violent relationships inevitably report marital dissatisfaction. Research has provided some ideas about the configuration of factors that make it possible for intimate partner abuse victims to stay with their abusers. In a national sample of 185 survivors who had endured abuse for an average of 10 years, Horton and Johnson (1993) found that only 27 had been able to retain their relationships with the men who abused them. Of these, only 16 rated themselves as feeling "satisfied" or "very satisfied" with the relationships. Compared with dissatisfied survivors in this sample, satisfied survivors tended to be younger, had been more severely abused, had pursued more methods for ending the abuse, had abusive partners who had become involved in the change process, had sought drug and alcohol treatment more readily, were more committed to their partners, and felt more hopeful about their relationships. By comparison, dissatisfied survivors had fewer job opportunities, a strong fear of failure, more children, and male partners who were more likely to have sexually abused them and physically abused their children. In fact, dissatisfied survivors were more than three times as likely as satisfied survivors to have been forced to have sex.

Evaluations have continued to show that not all violent couples report relationship dissatisfaction (S. L. Williams & Frieze, 2005; see also Cavanagh, 2003). The importance of *marital satisfaction* separate from or in spite of intimate partner violence has emerged in other investigations as a variable in leave/stay decisions (Jacobson, Gottman, Gortner, Berns, & Shortt, 1996). Lawrence, Yoon, Langer, and Ro found that women exposed to more emotional abuse were more likely to leave than those exposed to lesser levels. Relationship dissatisfaction played a role in these women's decision to leave.

Finally, Bodenmann, Pihet, and Kayser's (2006) analyses of intimate coping styles (i.e., styles of coping with one's partner) in a community sample found that *men's negative coping styles* (hostile, ambivalent, superficial dyadic coping) were strongly related to women's marital satisfaction, but not the reverse. These findings may suggest that women's perception of their partner's lack of investment in the relationship has a connection with women's perceived marital quality.

There are a number of other variables linked with battered women's level of marital satisfaction. Research has shown that alcoholism among husbands, for example, is related to lower marital satisfaction among female partners (Dethier, Counerotte, & Blairy, 2011). Another variable is avoidance of attachment. This type of avoidance describes an individual who avoids intimate connection (Mondor, McDuff, Lussier, & Wright, 2011; see also M. A. Dutton, 2009).

Failure to Recognize Abuse

Women who were raised in nonviolent families may not recognize abusive behavior in its early stages because they have no frame of reference. According to McLeer (cited in "The Battered Woman," 1989, p. 108),

> Early on, she may be trying to figure out how to decrease the violence but keep her relationship intact. It can take a long time for her to recognize that she can't do anything about his violence—he's a violent man—all she can do is get out.

In a 2003 study, Kate Cavanagh qualitatively detailed the stages that occurred for 136 Scottish battered women in their process of leaving their violent relationships. Women's "strategies of resistance," their attempts to keep themselves and their children safe, occur *interactively* along with men's various efforts to control them. In general, women are highly invested in their intimate relationships, and they want to save them while ending the violence. Women usually have to experience several episodes of male-to-female partner violence before they recognize and define their male partner's behavior as violence.

> First, the women treated the initial incident as an aberration (Cavanagh, 2003). Both men and women minimized or outright denied the man's violence. Complicating women's reactions were that the men nearly always apologized, and then the women accepted the apology. Many even felt sorry for their partner. As the men blamed the women for causing the violence by their failure to follow the men's "rules," many women made efforts to comply with their demands. Concomitantly, most of the men felt justified in establishing rules.
>
> Eventually, however, the women noted that compliance did not eliminate the violence; they recognized that they could not control it. Even though they acknowledged the abuse to themselves, most women did not wish to disclose it to others. Many felt too ashamed, and most continued to hope they could change it.
>
> Second, many women hoped that talking with their partners would change the abusive behavior or give them incentive to change it. They believed awareness would help, but it did not.
>
> Third, some women adopted various strategies that they thought might end the violence. As illustrations, a woman might start agreeing with everything her partner says, or she might repeatedly tell him how much she loves him.

Instead, none of these strategies works to create real change, and the woman's fear can increase while her self-esteem decreases.

Fourth, a number of women tired of these tactics and challenged the men's use of aggression. As women began to consider the violence as life threatening, they became more confrontational. As their anger got bigger than their fear, some of the women verbally or physically confronted their partner, left the relationship (at least temporarily), and told others about their partner's abuse. Occasionally, remorse about hitting their partners seemed to induce some men to stop their violence at least for a time, but it antagonized other men further.

Fifth, many women decided to "go public" about their partner's male-to-female intimate partner violence. For example, a woman might leave her house, letting others see her black eyes. These women hoped that letting others see what was going on would shame their partners. If the women were criticized and blamed, rather than understood and helped, they often did not seek assistance again.

Lastly, some women left their homes or called the police to have their partner forcefully removed. However, many women returned.

Approach-Avoidance Conflict and Entrapment

Early psychologists, attempting to understand human conflict through studies using rats, demonstrated all of the following kinds of conflicts (translated below into human examples): approach-approach, avoidance-avoidance, and approach-avoidance (e.g., N. E. Miller, 1959). (See Appendix F.2 for a description of this study.)

When an individual has a choice between two desirable options (e.g., going on a vacation to Hawaii or going to Alaska), an approach-approach conflict arises. That is, the person would like to go to both Hawaii and Alaska but must make a choice. At other times, a choice occurs between two undesirable alternatives (e.g., cleaning the oven or cleaning the garage: caught between a rock and a hard place). This circumstance also gives rise to ambivalence (avoidance-avoidance conflict). When a single choice includes both desirable and undesirable features (the house you want to buy is affordable, but it's 60 miles from your job), one may enter an approach-avoidance conflict. People caught in such conflicts vacillate, first going toward one goal and then retreating and next going toward the other goal and then retreating, and so forth.

Approach-avoidance behavior is relevant to comprehending the reasons why battered women remain. The combination of benefits (a strong attachment to one's partner, economic support) and costs (fear, humiliation) inherent in many battering relationships leads to ambivalence, conflict, and frustration. A battered woman may become trapped in an approach-avoidance conflict as follows: On the one hand, her relationship meets many of her emotional and economic needs, but it is degrading and danger-ous (Fleury, Sullivan, & Bybee, 2000; Hydén, 1999, 2005). She wants to approach the love that is hopeful and run from the abuse that is frightening. She wants to retain her relationship but move toward safety. For a while, the conflict is reflected by her ambivalence about staying or leaving.

Summary

This chapter has attempted to explain the role cultural mores and sex-role socialization play in a woman's decision to remain with her abuser. A woman learns gender identity in her family. She learns that affiliation with a man gives her status and worth. Battered women form attachments and become emotionally dependent upon their male partner in the same way that other women do, following the same path as their nonbattered sisters.

Society's acceptance of male dominance and aggression, along with its stated disavowal of male-to-female violence, creates a societal dissonance. Battered women also experience this conflict as they recognize the abuse in their own relationships. They may erroneously assume that their relation-ship struggles correspond to those faced by other women in their marriages.

A woman also learns about hope and commitment in her family, qualities continually nourished by cultural messages. A primary reason for remaining in or returning to a battering relationship is her hope and need to believe that her abuser will stop the violence, a need called learned hopeful-ness. Some of the traits most valued in women, such as commitment and tolerance, may be used to pathologize her behavior and to blame her for staying. Cultural mores, coupled with the likelihood of meeting a dysfunc-tional mate, support the contention that becoming a battered woman could happen to anyone.

2

Institutional Battering

The Power of the Patriarchy

The thing women have got to learn is that nobody gives you power. You just take it.

—Roseanne Barr

In ancient times, virgins were sacrificed to appease vengeful gods. A virgin was not a high price to pay for rain or a bounteous crop. It was an honor for the parents and the hapless virgin herself to be offered up in this way. As civilization has advanced, the powers that were, and are, no longer sacrifice maidens. They ask only that the maiden agree to sacrifice herself (Roiphe, 1986).

This chapter explores some of the practical issues faced by battered women trying to leave their abusive partners. Among these issues are economic dependency; patriarchal, social, and religious practices; and the inadequacies of the medical and criminal justice systems' responses. Battered women find little institutional support for leaving an abusive relationship.

Below the Poverty Line and Below the Belt

Women often put up with men's violence because they see no acceptable alternative and their lack of alternatives is often part of the larger cultural logic that sanctions the violence.

—Sidney Ruth Schuler, Syed M. Hashemi,
Ann P. Riley, and Shireen Akhter (1996, p. 1729)

Over the course of their lives, women are at much greater risk than men for an economic loss. Women represent 57.8% of economically poor adults (U.S. Department of Commerce, Bureau of the Census, 2008a). The Bureau of Labor Statistics (U.S. Department of Labor, 1999) shows that women make approximately 77 cents for every $1 a man makes. The median income of women who work full time is $35,745 a year; for men, it is $46,367 (U.S. Department of the Census, Bureau of the Census, 2008a). "Though business leaders say they are aware of and deplore sex discrimination, corporate America has yet to make an honest effort toward eradicating it" (Faludi, 1991, p. xiii). Despite the rumor that women have made it to the executive washroom and through the "glass ceiling" in large numbers, economic realities paint a not-so-vibrant picture.

According to Eleanor Smeal, the gender gap was alive and well in the 2010 midterm elections. Women office holders lost ground in Congress for the first time since 1979. In the 112th Congress, 10% of the Republican seats in the house and 25% of the Democratic seats were held by women. Only 17 women (12 Democrats and 5 Republicans) held seats in the Senate. This statistic places the United States at a disgraceful 72nd in women's representation among 188 countries with national parliaments (Smeal, 2011).

Women as a group have much to fear from poverty, and poverty is increasing. Nearly half of all Americans are either poor or in a low-income bracket in the United States (U.S. Department of Commerce, Bureau of the Census, 2008a). Poor women are disproportionately exposed to crime and violence (Byrne, Resnick, Kilpatrick, Best, & Saunders, 1999; Kury & Ferdinand, 1997), to illness and death of children (Belle, 1990), and to inadequate housing ("Federal Sex Discrimination Lawsuit," 2001). Male violence affects 21% to 64% of female clients in homeless shelters (Bassuk et al., 1996). Women who break away from battering relationships often become vulnerable to poverty and homelessness. One evaluation of 2,863 women extending over three years, for example, revealed that victimization by interpersonal violence increased women's risk for unemployment (Byrne et al., 1999; see also Kimmerling et al., 2009). Women usually have fewer financial resources and little social support to help them surmount the host of institutional and social obstacles that impede their progress toward self-sufficiency (see Browne & Bassuk, 1997; Kocot & Goodman, 2003).

While unemployment and lack of education are the primary causes of homelessness in general, family violence and other forms of victimization are the major causes of female homelessness (e.g., Virginia Coalition for the Homeless, 1995; Waxman & Trupin, 1997). One reason why domestic violence is such a potent contributor to homelessness is that some abusers sabotage or prevent their female partners from working. The U.S. Government Accounting Office (1998) indicated that 16% to 60% of male batterers discouraged their female partners from working, while 33% to 46% actually prevented their partners from taking jobs (see also Tsesis, 1996; J. Zorza, 1991). Many women also suffer from inadequate incomes related to lack of job training. A new federal program aimed at diminishing this problem assists low-income women in obtaining training at community colleges for higher-paying jobs (Institute for Women's Policy Research, 2012).

Finding a safe place for a woman alone or a woman with children is a critical early step in ending a battering relationship. Many battered women are unaware of the existence of emergency shelters. Even those who know about them encounter difficulty finding one with space available (Frisch & MacKenzie, 1991). A 1994 survey in Los Angeles ascertained that shelters turned down requests by 8,800 families (Burke, 1995). Older women, lesbians, immigrants, and disabled women may find it nearly impossible to obtain refuge (Irvine, 1990). Most shelters also do not accept women with teenage boys over age 13, those with felony drug convictions, and those who admit to female-to-male abuse (Melbin, Sullivan, & Cain, 2003).

In an article examining low-income women from four different cities, data consistently revealed that high percentages of women on Aid to Families With Dependent Children (AFDC) were currently abused by their partners. The percentage of these abused women reporting interference from their intimate partners with education, training, or work ranged from 15% to almost 50% (Raphael & Tolman, 1997; see also Riger & Kreglstein, 2000). It is interesting to note the broad range of ethnicities of the recipients: (a) Caucasian, 5% to 45%; (b) Hispanic, 22% to 49%; (c) African American, 10% to 55%; and (d) ethnicity not specified, 1% to 4% (Raphael & Tolman, 1997). Depending upon the assessment used and the sample tested, domestic violence (psychological, physical, sexual, stalking) appears to affect 33% to 67% of women on welfare (see Raphael, 1999, and Tolman, 1999, for reviews).

Even when battered women are employed, their abusers negatively impact their performance (S. N. Goodwin, Chandler, & Meisel, 2003).

In a survey of working women, battering resulted in absenteeism from work in over half of the women, lateness or leaving early in nearly two-thirds, job loss in about a fourth, and job harassment in over half. According to the women's reports, abusers also prohibited (33%) or discouraged (59%) them from working, prohibited (24%) or discouraged (50%) them from attending school, and successfully prevented 21% of them from actually obtaining a job (Swanberg, Logan, & Macke, 2005). Ending abuse, however, can enable many women to change their employment situation or school status (Browne & Bassuk, 1997; Moe & Bell, 2004). Despite the general findings of employment sabotage by batterers and improvement in working when abuse is not present, one federal court concluded that the law offered no protection against dismissal from employment because of spousal violence ("Federal Court Finds," 1996).

Ferraro (1981) highlighted the hurdles that battered women living in a shelter face in their attempts to achieve economic independence. Most of them are young mothers of one or more small children. They are high school graduates with relatively few job skills. They also lack a number of essentials: (a) cars, public transportation, or both; (b) timely access to subsidized housing units; and (c) affordable child care (Koepsell, Kernic, & Holt, 2006). For a moment, stop and imagine yourself in this situation. How would you cope?

Case Study: Liz

Liz arrived at the shelter following a two-week stay in the hospital for a fractured ankle that required surgery. Over the course of her eight-year marriage, she had developed a first-name relationship with several nurses. Staff had stopped believing that she was accident prone, and on this occasion, medical staff persuaded Liz to call the local shelter.

Liz was an at-home mother with two young sons, three-year-old Ben and six-year-old Patrick. She was taking medication to control the occasional seizures she suffered because of head injuries inflicted by her husband. Over the course of the relationship, she had received numerous injuries such as broken bones, concussions, facial lacerations, and torn ligaments, not to mention a myriad of cuts and bruises.

Her case was a complicated one. She was virtually unemployable because of her injuries, and she had an inconsistent job history prior to her stay in the shelter. She was financially dependent on her husband, and although he made a decent living and they owned a home, she had no independent funds. After she entered the shelter, her husband took all of the money from their joint savings account, leaving Liz with absolutely no money.

Within a week of their entry into the shelter, her sons, Ben and Patrick, tried to stab another child with a dinner knife. Liz had a difficult time keeping up with the boys, as she was on crutches and discipline was not her strong suit.

Filing for divorce was the only avenue she saw to have access to any money so that she could leave the shelter. She appeared at the initial hearing to obtain a restraining order, which included a kick-out order (her husband would have to leave the home), temporary custody, and child support. Although the judge ordered her husband to pay temporary child support, the judge determined that she should be restrained from staying in the house, as her husband would know where to find her and she wouldn't be safe.

Liz's husband remained in the house, but selectively forgot to pay child support. He filed a counter-petition demanding visitation with his children. That order was granted by the court. Liz had been in the shelter for five weeks, still had no money, was dependent on emergency food, and was unable to return to her home. She was also now in contempt of court for failure to allow visitation while living in the shelter. (As a safety precaution, staff may not allow visitation during a shelter stay.) Her husband's refusal to pay child support left her and the children penniless and unable to leave the shelter.

Liz felt discouraged as she watched other women and their children come and go. At the end of eight weeks, Liz received her first disability payment, which she needed to save for rent on her own apartment. She had just begun to look for a job, but with her injuries and few marketable skills, she was financially better off with disability. Another month passed before she received her second disability payment and her first child support check. Liz and her husband finally put their house up for sale. Liz looked for an apartment and was able to find an affordable one-bedroom in a poor section of town. With the assistance of the shelter staff, she and the boys moved in. The boys had calmed down, as they had some consistency and nonviolence in the shelter. All together, it took almost four months before Liz was able to leave the shelter, and another year before she was able to find a job. Ten years after her stay in the shelter, Liz called to serve as a volunteer.

Much like Liz's husband, other men have penalized their wives and children economically. A 1990 U.S. Census Bureau survey (cited in Waldman, 1992) showed that only half of 5 million women received full court-ordered payments; one-quarter received partial payments; and the last one-quarter received nothing. According to the 2008 U.S. Census Bureau Population Survey, women not living with their children's father most often bear the economic costs of raising the children. In fact, 8 in 10 custodial parents are women, and custodial mothers are twice as likely to be classified as poor as custodial fathers. One account of women seeking protection orders revealed that the court awarded child support payments to only 13% (Rowe & Lown, 1990).

The Personal Responsibility and Work Opportunity Reconciliation Act (PRWORA) of 1996 transformed welfare from an entitlement program that provided ongoing cash assistance to needy families to a program that grants only temporary assistance (Tolman, 1999). Advocates for battered women expressed concern that certain provisions of the act could place battered women and their children in harm's way. Requiring paternity identification in order to compel child support payments, for example, could be very dangerous. A batterer, enraged over payments, could gain access to public court documents containing information about survivors' whereabouts. Because of these safety issues, federal guidelines demanded that survivors of domestic violence be given exemptions, as needed, from participating in activities that place survivors and their children at risk.

Such exemptions for the sake of keeping women and children safe fell under the rubric of the Family Violence Option (FVO). Welfare staff charged with qualifying welfare applicants, however, frequently and illegitimately denied exemptions (see Lindhorst, Meyers, & Casey, 2008; see also Brandwein, 2003, for a review).

Economic Dependence and Remaining With an Abuser

Many researchers have observed that economic dependency is one reason many women fail to leave the relationship (e.g., Grigsby & Hartman, 1997; Morrow, Hankivsky, & Varcoe, 2004). In two surveys of shelter residents, the probability of staying in the violent relationship was highest for women whose husbands were the sole breadwinners (Aguirre, 1985; I. M. Johnson, 1992). In a study of 141 shelter residents, researchers found that most of the women interviewed were in need of material goods and services (84%), social support (79%), education (71%), health care (70%), finances (64%), legal assistance (62%), employment (62%), transportation (58%), and child care (57%). A significant number were also in need of housing (39%). The racial distribution of this group of women was as follows: 45% Caucasian, 43% African American, 8% Hispanic, and 1% Asian American. Sixty-eight percent of the women had at least one child (Sullivan, Basta, Tan, & Davidson, 1992).

Marital discord, by itself, increases the likelihood that married women will seek employment (S. J. Rogers, 1999) and the likelihood of divorce (Byrne et al., 1999). One investigation determined that women who did not escape, compared to those who did, were significantly more likely to feel unable to make it in the work world because of poor job skills (Frisch & MacKenzie, 1991). It is probable that survivors who decide to return to their abusive relationships perceive their alternatives within the marriage as more rewarding and less costly than their alternatives outside the marriage (Horton & Johnson, 1993; I. M. Johnson, 1988).

Barnett and Lopez-Real (1985) reported a constellation of reasons for staying given by the battered women that could be labeled resource and economic dependence. These were some of the comments:

> "I still feel scared of supporting the kids and bringing home enough money because I can't depend on him."

> "I'm facing eviction now. I'm scared."

> "I've never worked and have no high school education."

> "I am disabled because of his battering."

> "I feel one of the keys to this whole thing is for women to be economically independent, so as soon as they find themselves in a destructive relationship, they have the means to get out."

> "I only left once, but I came back because I didn't have any money, but money isn't everything."

> "I know I'll eventually get out of this situation, that is, finding a place to live, getting a job, and supporting my children."

Corporate America has begun to look at the effects of intimate partner abuse on their employees and on their businesses. Victims of intimate violence have higher levels of absenteeism, tardiness, job errors, and apathy, which cost employers millions of dollars annually. A 2004 estimate places the cost of intimate partner violence for businesses at nearly $6 billion annually (Max, Rice, Finkelstein, Bardwell, & Leadbetter, 2004). Of the 20,000 workplace crimes actually reported to the police between 1992 and 1996, intimates perpetrated 60.7% (Warchol, 1998). The leading cause of female occupational death is homicide (Jenkins, 1996; J. Lee & Trauth, 2009).

A survey of 11 Employee Assistance Programs (EAPs) in 1992 (Magee & Hampton, 1993) indicated that none of the EAPs had written policies covering issues relevant to domestic violence victims. While 9 of the 11 EAPs referred self-identified victims to shelters and women's services, less than half provided victim protection.

A few corporations, such as Liz Claiborne, Marshall's Department Stores, and Polaroid Corporation, have spearheaded efforts to assist survivors and to educate their own employees. State Farm Insurance Company, motivated by the efforts of K. C. Eynatten, formed the Corporate Alliance to End Partner Violence (CAEPV). Some of its members include Archer Daniels Midland, American Express, Avon, Prudential Financial, and the Colorado Bar Association (see "Fighting Discrimination Against," 1996).

Shelters are also experiencing institutional battering as a result of the economic downturn that has occurred over the last decade. The Mary Kay Foundation (2012), in its Truth About Abuse Survey spanning four years, found several significant facts: (a) 78% of domestic violence shelters nationwide were reporting an increase in women seeking assistance from abuse; (b) 74% of survivors were staying with an abusive partner longer because of financial issues; and (c) 92% of shelters had had to end or scale back specific programs and services.

Fortunately, corporate awareness and responses to workplace violence related to intimate partner violence (IPV) are mushrooming. Kim Wells, the director of CAEPV, generates a newsletter with up-to-date information on legislation, corporate programs, research, and innovations in both teen and adult IPV response (www.caepv.org). Safework has a program that teaches managers to "recognize, respond, and refer" survivors of partner violence (www.safework@safehorizon.org). Work Safe is a Canadian program targeting domestic violence in the workplace (www.worksafebc .com/domesticviolence).

In 2010, the Allstate Foundation created the Allstate Against Abuse Team. Agents and financial representatives, along with the foundation, have a goal of empowering 500,000 survivors of domestic violence by 2015 by educating them on financial basics. These basics include budgeting, debt reduction, and credit repair (K. Wells, 2012b).

The Avon Foundation awarded more than $1.5 million to fund staff for 32 shelters across the country in 2010. This project is called the Domestic Violence Survivor Empowerment Coordinator Program. In 2011, the foundation selected 15 of these programs as model programs and awarded additional funds. In 2012, the Avon Foundation brought these programs together in New Orleans for a day-long meeting. The coordinators are based in family justice centers across the country (K. Wells, 2012a).

Maslow's Hierarchy of Needs

A well-known psychological theory describing human behavior and growth seems to apply to a battered woman's decision making. Maslow's Hierarchy of Needs describes the path to self-actualization, or becoming a whole human being (Maslow, 1970). The scale ascends from basic needs, such as air to breathe, food and water, shelter, and safety, on to affiliation, esteem, cognitive or intellectual needs, aesthetic needs, and needs for self-fulfillment. The basic tenet of this theory is that movement up the ladder is contingent upon meeting lower-level needs. It is obvious that a battered woman whose needs for food, shelter, and safety are not met will have little physical or emotional energy to invest in fulfilling higher-level needs. Social expectations imposed on battered women to move up the ladder usually fail to address survival needs. For many battered women, it may feel like "two steps forward, one step back."

Case Study: Glenda

Glenda attended a women's group run by the YWCA in her hometown in the Midwest. The group's theme was "Women and Self-Esteem." She had been in the group for several months before she hinted at "not having her needs met" in her marriage. A few weeks later she came to the group with bruises on her face and an Ace bandage on her wrist. After she told the group that her husband had hurt her, the other women comforted her and wanted to help.

The group leader had heard about a shelter for abused women somewhere in California. None of the other women knew of any safe place where Glenda could go. After a two-day search, the group facilitator obtained the information about the shelter. With the help of other group members and the counselor, Glenda packed up her children and her household belongings and boarded a bus to California to become one of the first women to enter one of the first shelters in California.

Religion

It's hard to fight an enemy who has outposts in your head.

—Sally Kempton

The Judeo-Christian ethic has greatly affected American culture. God and religion are mentioned in the Declaration of Independence, the United States Constitution, the Gettysburg Address, and the Pledge of Allegiance. The Judeo-Christian heritage exerts an influence on anyone who lives in this country, whether he or she denies it, condemns it, actively participates in prescribed religious practices, or somewhere in between.

Marie Fortune (1987), an ordained Christian minister and author of *Keeping the Faith*, made the following claim:

The majority of women in the United States were raised in Christian homes or as adults have affiliated themselves with a Christian Church. This is a sociological reality. Therefore, when a woman is battered by a member of her family, she will likely bring to her experience her background and values as a Christian woman. Also likely, is that her experience of violence in her family will not only be a physical and emotional crisis, but also a spiritual crisis. (p. 2)

This crisis of faith is not limited to Christian women. Most women of faith struggle with their spiritual principles when confronted with personal violence inflicted by the person whom they have loved and trusted. It is essential to acknowledge the dilemma of those who feel bound to their relationships by the very tenets of their religious beliefs. A woman with deep convictions may look to her minister, rabbi, priest, or imam to interpret God's word and to ensure her eternal consequences. She turns to her spiritual adviser and to other members of her religious community for support. For a battered woman in particular, the quality of the assistance she receives can have life-or-death consequences. At the very least, the advice she is given can alter her life, and her children's lives, and perhaps have a significant effect on the life of her batterer.

As R. L. Clarke (1986) states, in her book *Pastoral Care of Battered Women*,

> Theological beliefs become an integral part of one's being and these beliefs are very powerful for a religious woman in a battering relationship. If a battered woman's religious convictions lead her to believe that a wife is subordinate to the husband, that marriage is an unalterable lifetime commitment, or that suffering is the lot of the faithful, then those convictions have the sanction of God. (p. 61)

Case Study: Claudette—A Christian Woman

"Hitting had gone on for a few years before we went for help. We were members of a strict Protestant denomination. They had a counseling center and we wanted Christian counseling. We talked to the counselor about our marriage, our children, about everything, except the violence. Finally, I told him I was afraid of my husband. The counselor told me in front of my husband to be a better wife and mother, to pray harder, to be more submissive. He told my husband he shouldn't hit me. When we got home, my husband only remembered the part about how I should be more submissive."

[As long as] God is male, then the male is God.

—Mary Daly

Nineteenth-century suffragist Mathilda Gage (Stanton, Anthony, & Gage, 1881/1889, p. 763) asserted that "The church, which should have been the great conservator of morals, dragged women to the lowest depths." Gage went on to explain that "the most grievous wound ever inflicted upon women has been in the teaching that she was not created equal with man, and the consequent denial of her rightful place and position in Church and State" (p. 754).

Many of the writers who assert that a sexist society is the fertile soil that allows for woman abuse also contend that traditional theologies have contributed to the victimization of wives by supplying biblical evidence that God ordains patriarchy (R. E. Dobash & Dobash, 1979; Walker, 1979). Stacey and Shupe (1983, p. 97) conclude that "the overwhelming role played by religion in the lives of the violent couples . . . was a regressive, and unwholesome one." "The major religions legitimize the power of men over women as a God-given right, and there are strong historical traditions indicating approval of men beating their wives—within certain limits—as a way of controlling their behavior" (Archer, 2006, p. 149).

One example of the strong role religious beliefs can exert on the treatment of women has come to light in the Taliban sect. Since the Taliban militia seized control of Afghanistan, it has instituted severe restrictions upon women. The Taliban, a fundamentalist Islamic sect, forces women to wear robes and shawls that totally cover the body. Taliban men forbid women to work outside the home or to pursue college educations. An egregious regulation prohibits medical doctors from touching female patients (Fields-Meyer & Benet, 1998). Religious police beat wo men who they feel are insufficiently covered (Norman & Finan, 2001). As of July 2009, men could legally deny food to their wives for failure to meet their sexual needs (Starkey, 2009; see also Amowitz, Kim, Reis, Asher, & Iacopino, 2004; King, 2009).

The sex abuse scandal that has rocked the Catholic Church for over a decade shines a glaring spotlight on the status of women and children in the all-male hierarchy of Catholic leadership. Former FBI official Kathleen McChesney, who was enlisted to intervene in the American version of the scandal in 2002, said, "It's just men listening to themselves. To my knowledge, there's no woman in the Vatican who's involved in sex-abuse issues" (L. Miller, 2010). Kerry Robinson, executive director of the National Leadership Roundtable, sees the sex abuse scandal as "sins and crimes committed by men, covered up by men and sustained by men. To overcome that, the church has to absolutely include more women" (L. Miller, 2010, p. 39).

Pamela Cooper-White (1996), who has served as a priest-associate in an Episcopal church, concluded that among several possible precipitants, sexual inequality is the overarching cause of violence against women. McDonald (1990) claimed that in systems such as patriarchy, the dominant group uses ideology to force conformity on the subordinate group.

Beliefs in sexual inequality have arisen from religious dogma and have spread beyond the confines of specific denominational groups to permeate the entire legal system (Ruether, 1983). "As long as religions continue to create and maintain a patriarchal system paralleled in the secular society which writes the laws, women will be able to advance only as far as the male creators of this system permit" (McDonald, 1990, p. 253).

Clergy's Responses to Intimate Partner Violence

Alsdurf (1985) believes that his research data show that clergy's beliefs mirror society's acceptance of patriarchal practices. He mailed a two-page questionnaire to 5,700 ministers from Protestant churches in the United States and Canada. Responses indicated that 26% of the surveyed pastors agreed that a wife should submit to her husband and trust that God would honor her action by either stopping the abuse or giving her the strength to endure it. About 50% of the pastors expressed concern that the husband's aggression not be overemphasized and used as a justification to break up the marriage. About one-third of the ministers felt that abuse would have to be severe to justify a Christian wife's leaving her husband. According to 21% of these clergy, no amount of abuse would justify a separation. Only 17% believed that seldom-expressed physical violence was compelling enough to allow a woman to separate from her husband.

A newer survey of 22 religious leaders of several faiths (Catholicism, Judaism, Islam) uncovered their responses to several questions about male-to-female intimate partner violence:

1. *Who is responsible for male-to-female violence?*
   (a) 20 of 22 said that perpetrators must assume responsibility, but victims bear some of the blame
   (b) 9 of 20 thought staying with the abuser made victims blameworthy

2. *What are the causes of male-to-female intimate partner violence?*
   (a) 15 of 22 thought some causes were lack of control and respect
   (b) 15 of 22 thought that social learning was the cause

Additional comments: Conflict is the culprit, and couples (especially women) must halt the escalation of an argument before abuse starts. Battered women's low self-esteem and their wish to be victims play a role in male partner violence.

3. *What is the best approach for dealing with male-to-female intimate partner violence?*

21 of 22 supported a proactive approach that fostered healthy marriages before violence occurred

4. *Is divorce acceptable?*
   (a) 20 of 22 declared that divorce should be a last resort
   (b) 4 of 20 said that women's power to divorce is limited by sacred documents
   (c) 6 of 22 claimed that the only acceptable rationale for divorce is infidelity or desertion, and the severity of abuse cannot be considered.

Additional comment: Scientific evidence about the harm done to child observers of male assaults is a lesser issue than divorce.

Source: Levitt & Ware, 2006.

The emphasis on maintaining marriages regardless of the cost to individual family members appears to be a tenet of many conservative religious and political groups espousing their version of family values. President George W. Bush and the Heritage Foundation considered marriage to be a safe haven for poor women and those needing protection from violence (Bush, 2002; Family Violence Prevention Fund, 2002). DeKeseredy and Schwartz (2006) referred to this family values approach as "misguided wedfare" programs.

One unusual legislative approach developed in Louisiana has been to make some marriages (covenant) harder to dissolve than standard marriages. While most experts agree that stable families have many benefits and provide the best climate for raising children, they reject the notion that making divorce harder to obtain is productive. Turning attention away from individual predilections and toward devising practical social policy changes should help attain more stable marriages (Marano, 1997).

Case Study: June

June was married for 22 years to a mental health professional who battered her and terrified the children. They were both faithful church members and she prayed daily. Her faith was the fundamental factor in her decision making. She was a devout and very intelligent woman, yet she felt confused and guilty in regard to her own angry feelings that had recently surfaced.

(Continued)

(Continued)

June's husband broke things around the house, screamed, threatened, and beat her and the children. When he attacked their older son, she tried to stop it, but he hit her and threw her out of the way. Chaos was a way of life in their family. The mood of the family changed when her husband came home from work. June and the kids ate dinner silently. They responded to any quick movement from the head of the household and were ready to duck or run to defend themselves.

When she spoke of her fear and some of the problems at home to her friends in the church women's group, she was advised to submit to her husband and not to even think of leaving him, as leaving would damn her children's souls. Her husband was, after all, a deacon and very well respected. After that first attempt to gain support, June didn't risk approaching anyone at her church for a while. Her next attempt was with an assistant minister, who advised her to pray and to endure; her husband would eventually change.

Several years later, after a particularly violent argument, June went to the minister in charge. This time she had evidence. She pulled up her sleeves to show the bruises on her arms and pulled down her turtleneck collar, revealing the finger marks on her throat. She explained calmly about hearing her children's screams as she lost consciousness. At that point, the minister decided the situation was very serious and wanted a conference with June and her husband. After the conference, June's pastor advised her to take the kids and run. And so she did.

Although battered women may seek help from clergy because they do not wish to tell outsiders about being battered, in Horton, Wilkins, and Wright's study (1988) only 14% of women who typified themselves as religious and 3% of nonreligious women rated clergy as helpful. Actual responses of clergy to victims were limited. They furnished information about treatment programs, provided extended counseling, or suggested that the survivor obtain professional therapy. Much less frequently, they advised the woman to call the police, obtain a civil protection order, or separate from the abuser. They rarely assisted women in leaving, although over half relayed information about shelters (S. E. Martin, 1989). Responses by clergy rated as helpful included validating and supporting women's reports and emphasizing safety issues even if divorce might result. Unhelpful responses included recommending that battered women remain with the abuser or change their behaviors to be more pleasing to their husbands (Horton et al., 1988). It seems important to point out that congregants within various religious communities may be unsupportive of battered women by simply remaining silent about abusive male behavior (Pyles, 2007).

Some clergy alleged that they did not help because they were seldom asked. Other considerations were clergy's lack of information about treatment programs or state laws, lack of time to meet the congregation's needs, and lack of training in counseling. Although J. M. Johnson and Bondurant (1992) documented an increase in ministerial training (from 30% to over 50%) about domestic violence from 1982 to 1988, they found that clerics remained ambivalent. Theirs has been an institutional nonresponse.

In July 1997, the California Hospital Medical Center received a grant to provide domestic violence prevention education to community groups. The grant staff selected the faith community as one group that might profit from training. For the first workshop, held in October, they invited 21 ministers; 8 attended. Over the next 15 months, volunteers mailed out personalized invitations to 300 clergy, alerting them to the workshop schedule. In response, an average of 5 or 6 ministers attended each of the five training programs. During 1998, the staff sent out additional question-naires to over 325 clergy. Of this group, 7 expressed interest in domestic violence education (Reyes, 1999).

There has been some good news on the clerical front. According to a community-based study of 476 women, 80% of the women who responded rated clergy as helpful. The women who felt helped experienced higher self-esteem, less distress associated with low social support, more self-efficacy, and greater life satisfaction (Neergaard, Lee, Anderson, & Wong Gengler, 2007).

Morality: A Reason for Staying

Guilt is the gift that keeps on giving.

—Erma Bombeck

Barnett and Lopez-Real (1985) reported that battered women also identi-fied other reasons of principle or morality for staying with their abusive spouses: (a) "children need both a mother and father" (the most significant of these ethical reasons); (b) the woman thought it would be distressing to leave her children; and (c) the woman considered divorce or separation a social disgrace. These comments reflect this conflict of convictions:

"Divorce is a personal failure."

"I believed you married forever."

"I wanted to make it because of family pressure."

"I have two boys; I'm afraid of them becoming feminine."

"I would never leave my children under any circumstances."

Battered women expressed concern about the negative status of being divorced and about the social stigma associated with being a divorcee. Many religious precepts, in fact, hold that divorce is a sin. Most spiritual groups extol the virtues of the family unit: a father, mother, and children. Religious groups center most of their activities around family events (not a single parent and her children).

Case Study: Amanda and Ray

Amanda had three children under the age of five. She was the devout Christian wife of a devout Christian batterer. She asked for church counseling after Ray broke her nose. Her husband went with her. He explained that he had been angry, and that she had been "nagging" him. She said she had been pushing him to do some chores around the house. He explained that he had no intention of hurting her and how sorry he was. She said she believed him. The pastor prayed with them. He reminded Ray and Amanda of the importance of maintaining a Christian home for the children.

By the time Amanda contacted the shelter hotline on the advice of a friend, she had received pastoral counseling on two additional occasions and had appeared before a board of elders. She was also spending three nights a week in her car with her children to avoid an incident. She was very concerned about receiving censure from the church and losing that very significant support group in her life. The church was not only a spiritual and emotional support, but also a possible source of financial assistance for her and the children. Amanda did not believe she could maintain her resolve to leave the relationship if her wish for peace and safety conflicted with her moral obligations.

Shelter staff agreed to intervene, and they scheduled a meeting with two shelter workers, the board of elders, and Amanda. With reassurance from her advocates, Amanda was able to tell her story in more complete detail. Church members were appalled and agreed that Amanda and her children needed to be at the shelter. Censure was applied to Ray, not to Amanda, and Amanda was able to leave because she had clergy support.

The Failure of Military Responses to Intimate Partner Violence

A military institution, ensconced in violence that is not only allowed but encouraged, provides an environment conducive to IPV, especially stress-related abuse (Taft, Street, Marshall, Dowdall, & Riggs, 2007). One frequent question that arises is whether spouses in the military are more violent than nonmilitary spouses. Surveys trying to assess this issue have arrived at diverse results, probably because of differences in the measuring scales used. One fairly early survey found that severe violence rates were 3.5% for the military and 0.7% for civilians (Heyman & Neidig, 1999). Although one survey (J. E. McCarroll et al., 2008) found no significant differences between the groups, several other surveys have reported elevated rates of IPV among military personnel (A. D. Marshall, Panuzio, & Taft, 2005). Assessments have also found high rates of child abuse in the military (S. L. Martin et al., 2007).

The armed forces spend $150 million a year on family advocacy to support service members, their spouses, and their families. For the most part, base commanders do not lend their support to these advocacy programs. Authorities seem routinely to disregard threats and evidence of abuse. Soldiers are able to avoid court-ordered counseling by claiming work-related assignments. On one base, the officer in charge of the family advocacy program held this position until he admitted to beating his own wife. In reaction to these dangerous oversights, domestic violence survivors have filed a class action suit against the military for negligence (Radutsky, 1999; see also Chawla & Solinas-Saunders, 2011).

According to one young serviceman (personal communication, 2008), "Before I went to Iraq, I thought before I acted. When I got back, I acted before I thought." In a separate interview, his girlfriend, whom he had recently hit, said the same thing. For some servicemen and servicewomen, this "combat readiness" is situation-specific and a new behavior. For adults abused as children, this combat readiness is more chronic, just another series of traumatic events. In a sample of more than 10,000 substantiated spouse and child abuse cases, male soldiers perpetrated the violence in 89% of the cases and female soldiers were the perpetrators in 11% of the cases (E. K. Martin, Taft, & Resnick, 2007).

Sexual Assault in Battering Relationships

Two institutions have combined forces to maintain the status quo in regard to marital rape: the institution of marriage and the institution of government. Marital rape has a long history of social acceptability and a continuing history of neglect by service providers, and even battered women's groups (Bergen, 1995; R. Campbell, 2008; Finkelhor & Yllö, 1982; D. E. H. Russell, 1983). Historically, English law of the 1700s confined legal rape to unmarried individuals because marriage was a legal contract affording husbands irrevocable sexual access to their wives (Hale, 1736/1874). Laws in the United States exempting husbands from wife rape, however, began to change after the first successful prosecution in 1979 (see Barshis, 1983). Thereafter, the evolution in laws was relatively rapid. By 1990, only three states still retained marital exemption laws (Small & Tetreault, 1990), and by 1993, all states criminalized marital rape in at least some situations (see E. K. Martin et al., 2007).

While the laws prohibiting marital rape have changed considerably over the decades, public opinion has lagged behind. Convictions about the sanctity of marriage, the need for privacy, and adherence to traditional sex-role beliefs have served to maintain greater social acceptance of wife rape than of stranger rape (Monson, Byrd, & Langhinrichsen-Rohling, 1996). So widespread are such beliefs that married women themselves may not recognize that their experiences qualify as rape (Bergen, 1995). Nonetheless, marital rape is common.

The National Crime Victimization Survey (Rand, 2009) found that of 255,630 reported rapes, intimates perpetrated 60.9%. A study of male batterers in treatment indicated that 53% of the men admitted to having sexually assaulted their female partner at least once (Bergen & Bukovec, 2006). Other findings from the research indicated that 40% of the men had emotionally coerced their female partner into having sex against her will; 8% had threatened to withhold money unless she complied with their demand for sex; 17% had raped their partner while she was asleep; 13% had threatened physical harm if she did not comply; and 15% had forced her to have sex after a fight. (See Appendix A.8 for an estimate of sexual assaults of intimates. See Appendix B.5 and B.6 for additional estimates of sexual assaults and rapes of intimates.)

Justice and the System

Historically, laws regarding the handling of intimate partner violence have mirrored American society's "hands-off" approach. Until the late 1970s, police in all 50 states could arrest a violent partner only if they had reason to suspect he had committed a felony or if he actually committed a misdemeanor in the presence of an officer. Police responded to intimate partner violence with policies that protected the privacy rights of families. Police departments traditionally trivialized family violence as noncriminal, noninjurious, inconsequential, and primarily verbal "spats" (Berk, Fenstermaker, & Newton, 1988). It is ironic that the police have tended to dismiss domestic disturbances as family spats that women can handle on their own, while feeling gravely endangered themselves when called upon to intervene. Similarly, male police may resent female cops because women are physically weaker than men, but still decide that battered women are strong enough to handle assaultive partners.

Studies have varied in their findings and interpretations of the degree of danger faced by police in responding to domestic disturbance calls. FBI statistics for the 10-year period from 1973 to 1982 revealed that responding to disturbance calls was the category of work most frequently associated with felonious assaults on officers (U.S. Department of Justice, Federal Bureau of Investigation, 1984). A later reclassification of the 1973–1982 data indicated that next to traffic calls, disturbance calls were the least dangerous (see Garner & Clemmer, 1986). In a three-year study conducted in Charlotte, North Carolina, between 1987 and 1989, police received 1,078,571 calls for service. Domestic disturbance calls accounted for 7.8% of the calls (Hirschel, Dean, & Lumb, 1994). These calls ranked fifth (of 10 categories) in terms of assaults on police officers and sixth in regard to injuries.

Case Study: Rachel and Abe

Rachel had two children, a temporary restraining order, and an abusive husband who violated it regularly. The order had not been difficult to get, but enforcement was a joke. The first few times Abe violated the order, the police did not arrive until he was long gone. The next few times, the police demanded that he leave the premises. They finally arrested him, but he was out of jail within 24 hours. It was only after four more arrests and court appearances for violating the restraining order that a judge sentenced him to eight months in jail. The judge was finally persuaded by Abe's continued threats on Rachel's life ("I'll kill the bitch") despite his demands that Abe "stop threatening her or I will have to incarcerate you."

Police Policies Concerning Intimate Partner Violence

The practices of police around the world can play a pivotal role in helping IPV victims escape by informing them of available community services. On the other hand, the police can choose to put up serious barriers that make it much harder or even dangerous for victims to leave (Grigsby & Hartman, 1997). In the United States, the literature on police responses to calls for IPV-related services reveals notable inconsistencies. Inadequate police responses add to society's tendency to normalize violence. This tendency empowers the abuser by signifying his actions are admissible under law (Belknap & Melton, 2005). Furthermore, arresting violent intimates is costly. According to the New York State Committee on Investigations, Taxations, and Governmental Operations, police made 12,724 domestic violence arrests at an average cost of $3,241 per arrest. All told, New York City paid at least $41 million for police costs and court and detention costs (see J. Zorza, 1994).

The British criminal justice system has taken three paths in dealing with the problem of IPV: (a) victim choice, (b) proarrest policy, and (c) victim empowerment. The victim choice position assumes that the victim has sufficient information (options) to make a reasoned choice about whether arrest of her abuser will improve the situation. The proarrest policy implies that subsequent prosecution will be undertaken in such a way as to prevent retaliation against the victim by the perpetrator. The victim empowerment view attempts to understand the individual victim; to educate her about available services; and to find out what might work best for her, including no arrest (Hoyle & Sanders, 2000).

One important factor in assessing police policies is whether IPV victims even call the police for services. Several studies have consistently indicated that victims do not uniformly seek help (Brownridge & Halli, 2001; Kaukinen, 2002; Rennison & Welchans, 2000). In an analysis of more than 9,000 IPV cases, Felson, Messner, Hoskin, and Deane (2002) found that factors making it less likely that victims will call police include the following: privacy concerns, fear of economic or physical reprisal, threats by the perpetrator to report a partner for child abuse, and the victim's desire to protect the offender (Wolf, Ly, Hobart, & Kernic, 2003). Circumstances that make it more likely that victims will call the police are self-protection needs (current and future), perception of IPV assaults as serious, victim injury, perpetrator history of abuse, and offender intoxication (see Bent-Goodley, 2001; Felson et al., 2002; Hutchison, 1999).

Research on Police Policies

A popular topic among researchers who examine the criminal justice system's response to IPV has been the determination of police rationales for involvement or lack of involvement in addressing the violence. Research findings suggest that some of the following attitudes influence police decision making: (a) IPV may be the victim's fault, or "justified" (Ford, 1999); (b) if he beats her and she stays, there is no real victim (see Waaland & Keeley, 1985); (c) battered women are manipulative or unbelievable (Rigakos, 1995); (d) police involvement is not the best way to stop IPV (Feder, 1998); and (e) responding to IPV calls is not "real" police work, which is catching "real" criminals (see Mastrofski, Parks, Reiss, & Worden, 1998). Illustrative of negative police attitudes is the statement of one police officer, who said during a training session that arresting batterers was hard to accept because a perpetrator might have married a "Nazi Bitch from Hell, like I did" (quoted in Ford, 1999, p. 14).

A particularly troublesome complaint about police responses to intimate partner violence centers on a perceived double standard in determining probable cause for making an arrest: one for IPV and the other for stranger assaults. Police may fail to arrest some of the most violent IPV perpetrators, including those who have used guns, knives, or clubs, or who have thrown female partners down flights of stairs (Buzawa & Buzawa, 2003; Fyfe, Klinger, & Flavin, 1997). For whatever reasons, police have often treated domestic violence perpetrators differently than they have treated other assaultive men (see Avakame & Fyfe, 2001; Bourg & Stock, 1994).

In a review of 25 studies, Erez and Belknap (1998) substantiated the hypothesis that police show leniency to intimate partner violence perpetrators—that is, police typically avoid arresting batterers compared with other violent perpetrators. Looking at these data brings up the question of male batterer accountability. According to one report, however, both police and courts appear to be even more lenient with female IPV perpetrators than with their male counterparts. Police in one study were significantly more likely to issue citations to female perpetrators than to arrest them (Tollefson, 2002). Attempting to reduce gender bias by arresting both men and women backfired against battered women. Dual-arrest policies led to an unwarranted increase in female arrests. That is, researchers determined that the arrested women were most likely victims and not perpetrators (S. L. Miller & Meloy, 2006).

Opinions also clash over police sensitivity to female victims during on-scene handling of IPV calls. One survey ascertained that IPV victims were significantly more dissatisfied with police responses than were victims of other crimes (Byrne et al., 1999). Two more-contemporary studies, on the other hand, have indicated that battered women's perceptions of police responses may be improving. One assessment of 95 female victims indicated that 75% gave the highest rating possible for police intervention, and only 9% gave the lowest rating (Apsler, Cummins, & Carl, 2003).

Another qualitative investigation of 25 female survivors revealed that about 70% described police behavior in positive terms. An encouraging finding among immigrant survivors was that 84% to 94% "felt police were responsive to their concerns" (e.g., R. C. Davis & Erez, 1998, p. 5). Similarly, some studies, but not all, have found that police treat intimate partner violence cases involving members of minority groups about the same as cases involving nonminorities (e.g., Hutchison, Hirschel, & Pesackis, 1994). A study of Canadian survivors also indicated that the vast majority were satisfied with police behavior (Brownridge & Halli, 2001).

The Need for Rational Consequences for IPV Offenders

A synthesis of several different analyses revealed that about one-fourth of batterers are arrested, about a third of those arrested are prosecuted, and 1% of those receive jail time beyond the time served at arrest (often just a few hours) (see Bourg & Stock, 1994; Yegidis & Renzy, 1994).

Concerns About Police Discretion

The attitudes of police officers definitely affect their response to partner abuse: Should they arrest the perpetrator or not? Frequently, police officers simply decide that no crime has been committed and therefore no arrest is necessary (Hirschel, Hutchison, Dean, & Mills, 1992). Other police officers persist in doing exactly what they please in response to partner abuse, despite changes in the law and training (Buzawa, Austin, & Buzawa, 1995).

Police discretionary arrest policies often rest on the relationship between the victim and the perpetrator. The more intimate the relationship, the more blame that seems to be assigned to the victim and the lower the arrest rate of male perpetrators (Buzawa et al., 1995; Fyfe et al., 1997). Police often require higher standards of probable cause for arrest in domestic violence cases compared with acquaintance and stranger arrests (Mordini, 2004; U.S. Department of Justice, Bureau of Justice Statistics, 1994).

A recent study of 378 Spanish police officers demonstrated attitudinal differences based on the victim's willingness to press charges. One group held a *conditional* preference to enforce the law dependent upon the victim's willingness to testify against the batterer. The other group held an *unconditional* preference to enforce the law. These officers felt inclined to enforce the law even if the victim did not plan to press charges. Compared with the conditional group, the unconditional group held attitudes more favorable toward domestic violence victims. This group of police felt more victim empathy, were less sexist, thought intimate partner violence was serious, and believed they had a personal responsibility to enforce the law (Gracia, Garcia, & Lila, 2011; see also DeJong, Burgess-Proctor, & Elis, 2008).

Case Study: Joe and Shauna

Joe sat in his first group for men who abused their partners, angry and disbelieving. It wasn't the first time he had pushed his wife around or screamed at her. It was the first time he had choked Shauna, but nobody knew about that. When he finally talked, it was to tell the group about his wife, who was immature and used drugs. He had stopped using a few months before. He was bewildered by his experience with the police and the courts. He had been arrested, had had to go to a group, and had had to spend 200 hours picking up trash on the freeway. "I've hit her before. I've pulled her hair. I know she didn't like it, but this is the first time anybody ever told me I couldn't do it—that I couldn't get away with it."

Dunford, Huizinga, and Elliott (1990) found that the effects of three different police dispositions (mediation, separation, or arrest) did not produce different rates of recidivism (reoffending) six months later. In fact, Sherman and his colleagues (1991) maintained that the superiority of arrest was only temporary and lasted 30 days. On the basis of a Dade County analysis, Sherman (1992) concluded that the deterrent effect of arrest was limited to employed offenders. Taken together with previous research, these findings suggest that arrest might even escalate violence in unemployed men.

One research team compared three types of police response to domestic violence calls: (a) advising and possibly separating the couple, (b) issuing a citation to the offender, and (c) arresting the offender. Results showed conclusively that arrest was not superior to the other treatments in terms of recidivism or in terms of the victim's evaluations. The researchers concluded,

> The dynamics of domestic violence in general, and the abuse of female spouses in particular, are so complex and intertwined with historical, traditional, psychological, political, and social forces that it may be unreasonable to expect any short-term action by the criminal justice system to have a significant deterrent effect. (Hirschel, Hutchison, & Dean, 1992, p. 31)

In newer research, there were three factors related to police decisions to arrest: (a) belief in the usefulness of police involvement, (b) less traditional attitudes about women's roles, and (c) knowledge of the department's proarrest policy (Feder, 1998; see also Feder, 1997). The results showed relatively low rates of arrest in domestic assaults, but even lower rates in nondomestic assaults.

Mandatory Arrest

Mandatory arrest laws require police to arrest violent intimates if probable cause exists. Such laws stemmed from findings that police discretionary responses were inadequate. Primarily, when police exhibited leniency, it often led to lack of safety for partner abuse victims. Advocates for battered women assumed that forcing police to arrest the violent partner would better protect victims.

Experts have held contrasting assumptions about the purpose of mandatory arrest. Positions on when police should arrest are as follows: It should be done (a) when necessary to protect the victim; (b) only after screening indicates that the specific offender is dangerous (e.g., under the influence of drugs); (c) upon request of the victim, to gain her satisfaction with the police; (d) on every call, to control police behavior and to avoid civil suits; (e) with great discretion to avoid racial bias; (f) to indicate that society condemns battering as a crime, in contrast to nonintervention, which suggests battering is acceptable; (g) only in extreme cases so that the family unit can be preserved; (h) when needed to compel the offender to obtain treatment; (i) only with great caution to avoid an escalation of violence directed at the victim; (j) to remove victims from isolation and to empower them; (k) to motivate women to call again, especially when they feel gravely endangered; and (l) because battering violates women's civil rights (Stark, 1993; see also L. G. Mills, 1998).

In an attempt to determine the efficacy of mandatory arrest laws, several researchers commenced investigation of mandatory arrest outcomes. Unexpectedly, mandatory arrest laws had led to a large number of arrests of women. In one study in Connecticut, police had even charged a greater portion of women with assault than men: 34% and 23%, respectively (M. E. Martin, 1997; see also Erez & Belknap, 1998).

According to Hamberger and Arnold (1991), police in a midsized community of 85,000 evidenced a twelvefold increase in arrests of women and a twofold increase in arrests of men over the previous year when following mandatory arrest policies. Upon further investigation, most of the women arrested (67%) had indeed acted violently, but in self-defense. A later investigation affirmed these findings—women are usually violent in self-defense (Durfee, 2012). Hamberger concluded that the new laws created a new criminal: the battering wife. He does not believe, however, that the women arrested are true batterers (Hamberger & Arnold, 1991; see also Kateiva & Bowker, 2010; Zeoli, Norris, & Brenner, 2011).

Larry Sherman, the most influential criminologist on the topic of mandatory arrest, operated under the premise that the value of mandatory arrest should be considered in terms of its effects on violent behavior. If mandatory arrest reduced future violence (deterrence), it should be continued; if not, it should be abandoned (Sherman et al., 1991). R. L. Davis (1998), however, rejected this logic because it would lead to a policy of arresting no one. Why? Convincing evidence supporting the deterrent effect of mandatory arrest on *any* criminal behavior (e.g., child abuse, burglary) is nonexistent (Sigler & Lamb, 1995). Consequently, mandatory arrest of batterers might not decrease battering any more than arrest deters other crimes (R. L. Davis, 1998).

Batterers' attitudes about being held accountable for their domestic violence affect their behavior. Carmody and Williams (1987) surveyed 1,626 men, 174 of whom were physically assaultive, concerning their views about the certainty and severity of the sanctions for battering. Sanctions reported by the batterers as possible outcomes included retaliatory force by the wife, arrest, wife-instigated separation or divorce, and social condemnation by friends and associates. Over half of the men, both assaultive and nonassaultive, perceived no possibility of arrest. Similarly, K. R. Williams and Hawkins (1989) reported that 494 men, including 146 spouse abusers, generally perceived loss of their partner as not very likely. Rather, they saw their marital relationship as quite resilient.

In an Iowa study, individuals convicted of domestic assault did receive greater penalties, but other problems arose. Because fewer wife abusers were willing to plead guilty and because victim cooperation was more problematic, conviction rates actually declined (C. Carlson & Nidey, 1995). Other findings suggested that while battered women might call police to terminate a current violent episode, they might balk at taking further action. They often feared giving evidence against their partners or did not want their partners to go to jail (Sirles, Lipchik, & Kowalski, 1993; Wolf et al., 2003).

Several researchers and women's advocates have noted serious problems flowing from mandatory arrest policies. Primarily, one size does *not* fit all. Some of the complications include failure to identify the primary perpetrator, failure to recognize women's self-defensive violence, and further hardships for women, such as loss of economic resources (Hamberger & Arnold, 1991; M. E. Martin, 1997). Overall, mandatory penalties do not uniformly have the desired effects.

Dual Arrest

Dual arrest is the arrest of both individuals involved in the violent incident. This policy calls for police action even if the police cannot identify the primary aggressor. Some police departments adopted a policy of dual arrest if police called to a scene believed any IPV had occurred (see Asher, 1990). Despite the specific nature of the laws, dual arrest rates varied widely by both the size of the department and the size of the city. Investigations showed that women were arrested 17.0% to 30.8% of the time. Some researchers showed no gender bias in regard to dual arrests (Hirschel, Buzawa, Pattavina, & Faggiani, 2007), and other researchers showed that dual-arrest policies led to the inappropriate arrest of women who hit in self-defense (abused women). These women were then sent to batterers' intervention programs designed for male perpetrators (Kernsmith, 2005b; Osthoff, 2002; see also Bair-Merritt et al., 2008).

In light of the controversy, a number of domestic violence experts collaborated on devising an integrated approach to batterer interventions and criminal justice strategies. This group recommended that law enforcement officers should comply with four major guidelines: (a) they should identify the primary aggressor, (b) they should execute a proarrest or mandatory arrest policy, (c) they should gather evidence at the scene for use in prosecutions, and (d) they should arrange for a temporary restraining or no-contact order (Healey, Smith, & O'Sullivan, 1998).

Domestic Abuse Response Teams (DARTs)

Government officials have sought new methods for making police intervention in IPV cases more effective. In 1996, the U.S. Department of Justice awarded a $385,000 grant to the City of Los Angeles to implement a program aimed at reducing domestic violence. The grant money enabled the Los Angeles Police Department (LAPD) to train officers to identify and arrest suspects in domestic abuse cases and to respond more appropriately to victims ("City Receives Grant," 1996). The consequence was the establishment of DART teams (available in the northeastern section of Los Angeles and other locales across the nation). DART teams usually include two specially trained uniformed police officers accompanied by a victim advocate. When called to a possible IPV scene, the police handle arrest decisions and emergency protective orders as needed, while the advocate provides crisis intervention and furnishes information about shelters and other resources. Team managers have also posted two emergency hotlines for seeking help that are available 24 hours a day, seven days a week (www .peaceoverviolence.org/emergency/domestic_abuse/dart).

Community IPV Response Teams

A federally funded Judicial Oversight Demonstration (JOD) project investigated the effects of collaborations between community agencies and the criminal justice system in three locales: Dorchester, Massachusetts; Milwaukee County, Wisconsin; and Washtenaw County, Michigan. This study recruited 1,034 IPV victims and 454 IPV offenders who had been arrested and charged with IPV. Approximately 95% of the offenders were male. The investigators tested whether strong judicial oversight of offenders combined with extensive graduated sanctions for perpetrators and comprehensive victim services would have favorable outcomes. Half of each group received the JOD intervention while the other half served as comparison research participants.

Overall, the project resulted in a significant reduction of repeat offending. These effects occurred most strongly in certain situations: (a) when both victim and offender were young, (b) when the victim received medium to high social support, (c) when offenders of these victims had had a higher number of arrests, (d) when the victim and offender had no children in common, and (e) when the victim and offender had had a relatively short relationship—about three years.

Police as Batterers

A modification to the Gun Control Act of 1968, known as the Lautenberg amendment (after Senator Frank Lautenberg), took effect in January 1997. It bans individuals convicted of domestic assault from carrying weapons. Unlike many previous laws, it does not exempt law enforcement officers or any government employees ("Domestic Violence Conviction," 1997).

Throughout 1997, the Lautenberg amendment sparked investigations of law enforcement officers across the nation. In December 1996, even before the law went into effect, Sheriff Block of Los Angeles County announced that he intended to comply with the law and that he would reassign convicted officers to desk jobs ("Sheriff Won't Contest," 1996). Within the Los Angeles area, police chiefs in Glendale and Burbank asserted that none of their men had been convicted. In the 9,300-member LAPD, approximately 150 officers may have had arrest records ("Three Deputies," 1997).

Various inquiries suggested that the LAPD's handling of officers convicted of domestic violence was insufficient (Braidbill, 1997; McGreevy, 1997). Under public pressure to comply with the law, the Los Angeles City Council hired additional investigators to check the conviction records of all LAPD personnel. Investigator General Katherine Mader reached several conclusions: (a) the LAPD had made arrests in only 6% of cases within its jurisdiction involving LAPD officers, while outside agencies had made arrests in 16% of incidents in other jurisdictions; (b) almost 90% of the allegations were against male employees; (c) the Internal Affairs Department (IAD), charged with evaluating these accusations, had judged only 38% of the male employees to be guilty but had found 58% of the women guilty; (d) reports turned into the IAD were often flawed by inappropriate language describing and blaming victims; and (e) the IAD often took almost a year to investigate domestic violence charges.

A review of 84 Internal Affairs Department incident reports disclosed that the LAPD had not made a single arrest of an officer between 1991 and 1993, even though 48 of the victims had multiple, visible injuries. Reports often described female victims as suffering from fatal attraction or as being overly possessive, while describing the accused male officers as productive and hardworking. One report concluded that "there is no fury like a woman scorned" (Braidbill, 1997).

In the final analysis, investigators identified seven convicted domestic violence abusers from the list of 150 officers, relieved them of their weapons, and assigned them to other duties (Orlov, 1997). Police union officers point out that some convictions are over 10 years old and no longer relevant. A loophole in the laws has allowed some convicted police to expunge their records, and it is expected that other officers will attempt to do so as quickly as possible ("Domestic Violence Conviction," 1997).

The Court's Management of IPV Cases

Judges

Some judges continue to rule unjustly in favor of male perpetrators and against battered victims (Stone & Fialk, 1999). The fact that a father who fails to protect his children from a child-abusing mother is rarely held responsible appears to reflect yet another gender bias in the judicial system (Bemiller, 2008; Dragiewicz, 2010; National Council of Juvenile and Family Court Judges, 1994).

Protection Orders

When battered wives ask the court for protection, the criminal justice process often victimizes them further ("California Panel Urges," 1990). The following is an excerpted quotation from the Maryland Special

Joint Committee on Gender Bias in the Courts ("Violence and Women Offenders," 1989):

> The thing that has never left my mind from that point to now is what the judge said to me. He took a few minutes and he looked at me and he said, "I don't believe anything that you're saying."

> "The reason I don't believe it is because I don't believe that anything like this could happen to me. If I were you and someone had threatened me with a gun, there is no way that I would continue to stay with them. There is no way that I could take that kind of abuse from them. Therefore, since I would not let that happen to me, I can't believe that it happened to you."

> I have just never forgotten those words . . . When I left the courtroom that day, I felt very defeated, and very powerless and very hopeless, because not only had I gone through an experience which I found to be very overwhelming, very trying and almost cost me my life, but to sit up in court and make myself open up and recount all my feelings and fear and then have it thrown back in my face as being totally untrue just because this big man would not allow anyone to do this to him, placed me in a state of shock which probably hasn't left me yet. (p. 3)

Under Title II of the Violence Against Women Act (VAWA), crossing a state line to violate a protection order is now a federal crime. A valid protection order based on due process issued in one state must be treated and enforced as if it were an order originating in the new state. Some previous state laws and practices concerning protection orders, however, conflict with the new federal law and require modification. For example, an individual who obtains a valid protection order against a same-sex partner in one state is entitled to have the order enforced in a different state that does not recognize same-sex relationships (see also "Model Police," 1999).

In some cases, judges have issued restraining orders against both partners, giving the false impression that the female victim has been violent as well. Brygger (quoted in Youngstrom, 1992) says that restraining orders are effective "only if the batterer has had no contact with the criminal justice system and 'fears the consequences' of violating the order" (p. 45). A contemporary Swedish study revealed that the effectiveness of restraining orders was linked with an assessment of the man's risk for intimate partner violence. In this sample of 214 male partner abusers, restraining orders were effective for only a subset—those at low to medium risk for IPV (those less likely to reoffend) (S. Strand, 2012).

Another favorable change in protection order laws appended to the VAWA addresses the issuance of mutual protection orders and their mandatory enforcement by other states. Congress acknowledged the problems with mutual orders and put a limit on their uses. Generally, they negatively impact battered women in other court proceedings, such as divorce and child custody determinations.

Case Study: Omar

Omar's wife obtained a restraining order. What she did not know, however, was that Omar was violating it on a regular basis "after hours," usually between midnight and 2:00 a.m. He would "just check up on her" by driving around the house or by stopping and looking through her windows. One night at about midnight, as Omar was peeking through her bedroom window, the police pulled up and arrested him. He spent the night in jail, where his shoelaces were stolen at night. Omar had a "religious" experience; he did not violate the order again.

A research project conducted by the National Center for State Courts assessed battered women's views on the effectiveness of civil protection orders. Interview data from 285 women indicated that 72% thought their lives had improved one month after receiving a protection order. At a six-month follow-up of 177 women, 85% reported improved lives, 90% felt better about themselves, and 80% felt safer. While 72% experienced no continuing problems at one month, the percentage dropped even further to 65% at follow-up. Among the batterers, 65% had an arrest history. Results suggested that judges should use abusers' criminal records to craft even more effective protection orders (Keilitz, Davis, Eikeman, Flango, & Hannaford, 1998). These findings fit with evidence that the probability of reabuse significantly declines following issuance of protective orders (M. J. Carlson, Harris, & Holden, 1999). Researchers also concluded that protection orders are only one element of many services needed by battered women (Riger, Raja, & Camacho, 2002).

Specialized Domestic Violence Courts

One attempt to improve services for battered women is the establishment of specialized domestic violence courts. One such court is the Solution Oriented Domestic Violence Prevention Court in Michigan. The mandate of this court is "to fill the gaps left by the current personal protection order system by using a solution-oriented approach to the issue of domestic violence in family division cases" (Halloran, 2011, p. 40). Its ultimate goal is to enhance safety for survivors, increase offender accountability, and provide better overall abuse prevention. No outcome data are currently available. However, anecdotal data from both shelter advocates and batterers' intervention program group facilitators are overwhelmingly positive.

Custody Issues

An antiwoman bias in family court has included finding mothers less fit as the custodial parent if they work, especially if the father has remarried and has a stay-at-home wife (Winner, 1996). Such findings occur in the absence of any research on children's relationships with their violent father (Holden, Geffner, & Jouriles, 1998a). According to a report by Taylor in 1992 (cited in P. G. Jaffe & Geffner, 1998), some judges believe that a child's estrangement from the father is more traumatic than the child's exposure to the father's battering (see also Bancroft & Silverman, 2002; Lamb, 2012).

The activities of child protective service (CPS) workers appear to have compounded the problems that battered women face in court (S. P. Johnson & Sullivan, 2008). The primary directive for CPS workers is to safeguard children. From their perspective, it is obligatory to take action (i.e., remove the child from the home) if a mother is unwilling or unable to protect her children from her violent male partner (Berliner, 1998). Members of the general public appear to hold similar opinions. In one study, two-thirds of a sample of community members judged battered women neglectful if they did not immediately find a way to stop the violence against their children (Weisz & Wiersma, 2011). One social scientist has termed this type of plight "powerless responsibility" (Rich, 1976). The law may simultaneously classify a battered woman as an assault victim and hold her criminally responsible for her male partner's child abuse (see Hulbert, 2008; Sierra, 1997)!

In trying to ascertain what is "in the best interests of the child," judges often rely on child guardians to conduct an investigation. Guardians, however, may have little or no training, behave unprofessionally, and demonstrate gender bias to such an extent that mothers feel unfairly treated (R. Berger & Rosenberg, 2008). An approach that has been problematic in the past, yet continues in some areas of the country, is to remove a child from a mother only to place the child in an abusive foster home (McKay, 1994).

The assumption that a woman can protect her children from abuse by simply leaving her batterer is not borne out by the facts and tends to ignore the deleterious effects that victimization has had on her (McMurray, 1997). In fact, a battered woman's attempt to leave her abusive partner may place her at greater risk for further abuse and even homicide (DeKeseredy, Schwartz, Fagen, & Hall, 2006; Harper & Voigt, 2007).

In one sample of battered women, 75% of women who were killed by their male partners and 85% of those who were severely beaten had left or had tried to leave during the previous year (Sharps, Campbell, Campbell, Gary, & Webster, 2003).

Some lawyers have succeeded in attributing two syndromes to mothers that have undermined their attempts to gain custody (see P. G. Jaffe & Geffner, 1998, for a review). Malicious mother syndrome (Turkat, 1995), updated to divorce-related malicious parent syndrome (Turkat, 1999), ascribes behaviors such as unjustified attempts to punish a parent and deny him or her access to the couple's children. By the author's own admission, the syndrome has no supportive empirical evidence. Parental alienation syndrome (Gardner, 1987) covers false allegations of child sexual abuse (Garber, 2011). This syndrome has no empirical validation and is alleged with some regularity against women who make accusations charging their estranged or former male partners with partner abuse or child abuse (Emery, Otto, & O'Donohue, 2007). Several empirical investigations have shown that women rarely make false allegations of sexual abuse in domestic violence cases (Bruch, 2001; Dallam & Silberg, 2006; Drozd & Oleson, 2004).

Bancroft (2011) pointed out that abused parents (usually protective mothers) need lawyers who understand the complexity that an abusive partner adds to custody proceedings. First, protective mothers need a lawyer who will have as his or her priority the safety of the mother and the children. Second, family law attorneys need to be able to properly emphasize the issue of mother and child safety to the court. Third, lawyers must properly implement the expertise and testimony of professionals, such as expert witnesses, evaluators, and mediators, during the hearings. Last, lawyers should adjust their clients' expectations about the length of the legal process and prepare them for the expensive, often grueling nature of drawn-out legal proceedings (see also Humphreys & Absler, 2011).

The Bar's response and gender bias in the court. In 1997, the American Bar Association's (ABA's) Commission on Domestic Violence convened to assess the Bar's response to survivors of domestic violence (Goelman, Lehrman, & Valente, 1996). So generally flawed was the legal profession's representation of survivors that the commission issued a series of recommendations concerning legal education. Interestingly, the commission also reemphasized the necessity for disciplinary committees to include professional consequences for lawyers who abuse their own partners and children (see Goelman & Valente, 1997, for a review).

Under the leadership of Los Angeles Superior Court judge David M. Rothman, the gender-bias committee forwarded a number of recommendations to the court that revolved around the handling of domestic violence cases. Courts handling these cases should have metal detectors, secure waiting areas, and parking lot escort programs to protect survivors. The panel further pointed out the need for two types of curative legislation: (a) legislation that would better maintain court protection of domestic violence survivors when emergency protective orders expire, and (b) legislation that would exempt domestic violence cases from mandatory mediation in child custody and visitation disputes. In addition, legislation could mandate domestic violence training for judges and attorneys.

Gender bias in the criminal justice system continues to reflect male privilege and lend credence to the argument that wife abuse is an outgrowth of patriarchy. Karen Winner, a policy analyst for New York City, documented widespread overcharging, misrepresentation, and failure to litigate diligently for female clients. Many of these deceptive practices are exacerbated by judges. For instance, judges rarely punish husbands who hide their assets during the discovery phase of the trial. When perpetrators take advantage of the criminal justice system, it creates yet another reason for survivors to feel trapped by their partners' coercion, making it all the more difficult to leave the relationship (Lovik, 2011b).

To reduce gender bias in the court, a 2011 special issue of the *Michigan Bar Journal* (Lovik & Shiemke, 2011) published several articles that help explain domestic violence and what attorneys can do to help survivors. One article provides a list of online domestic violence resources for legal professionals. Other articles cover such topics as batterers' exploitation of the justice system, custody and visitation issues, economic justice, legal remedies in other states, domestic violence court, foster care, and parenting.

Prosecution of domestic violence offenders. A 1997 analysis of prosecutions established that district attorneys prosecuted women (11%) in dual arrests more often than men (6%) (M. E. Martin, 1997). Although current research has shown improvement in prosecutorial procedures, gender bias is still problematic (Lesher, 2009).

M. A. Dutton, Goodman, and Bennett (1999) found a number of factors within the court system itself that contributed to survivors' reluctance to prosecute: (a) confusion about the court system (e.g., lack of knowledge about differences between the civil and criminal courts); (b) frustration with the criminal justice system (e.g., concern about the system's slowness, fear triggered by lack of action, lack of contact with the court); (c) conflict over incarceration (e.g., lack of child support or help in taking care of children, lack of a father in the home, views of the criminal justice system as racist and oppressive); (d) fear of not being believed; and (e) fear that the abuser would be found not guilty (see Belknap, 2000; Tomz & McGillis, 1997).

Despite the increasing number of jurisdictions with vigorous prosecution policies, court resources are so minimal that court personnel are unable to guide battered women through the court system in a way that meets their needs. There is little follow-up. Survivors concerned about their abusers' incarceration, for example, may have no information about alternatives such as mandatory counseling or community service for convicted batterers (Healey & Smith, 1998). With better court services, there is reason to believe that many more battered women would choose to cooperate with a decision to prosecute than currently do (Belknap, 2000). Current research has uncovered the importance of survivor participation in court proceedings. When survivor assistance (advocacy) was provided, both survivor cooperation and successful prosecution increased (Bechtel, Alarid, Holsinger, & Holsinger, 2012).

Syers and Edleson (1992) pinpointed two crucial variables affecting recidivism: number of previous arrests and duration of court-ordered counseling. In this inquiry, men arrested the first time the police visited the residence and who were mandated into counseling programs for a relatively longer period of time were significantly less likely to violently revictimize their female partners than their counterparts. Syers and Edleson also called attention to cases of lowered recidivism rates brought about by community intervention projects that coordinated components within the criminal justice system.

Survivor Compensation

Availability of survivor compensation, especially for survivors of domestic violence, has been problematic ("Victim Agencies," 1992). Regulators have used statutes intended to exclude participants in a fight (e.g., a barroom brawl) as a rationale to exempt battered women survivors whose behavior was provocative. The laws also require that survivors cooperate with law enforcement agencies (i.e., make an official complaint). A battered woman, however, may choose not to prosecute for a variety of reasons, such as fear. If the battered survivor does get financial compensation and the money might somehow assist her batterer, regulators could deny her application based on the principle of unjust enrichment of a perpetrator. The Office for Victims of Crime has made some headway by publishing newer guidelines that more clearly identify populations in need of such services and by specifying the combination of services most needed by victims (Tomz & McGillis, 1997). A review of assistance over the years 1986 to 2000 indicated vast improvements in services for battered women (Tiefenthaler, Farmer, & Sambria, 2005).

New intimate partner abuse laws have been written and older laws modified. In this country, every state has at least one statute pertaining to battered women (J. E. B. Myers, Tikosh, & Paxson, 1992). The Urban Institute in Washington, DC, issued a March 1997 report on implementation of VAWA (Burt, Newmark, Olson, Aron, & Harrell, 1997). Reauthorization of the bill in 2000 and 2005 mandated legislation aimed at rectifying remaining problems with VAWA 1994 and apportioning funding. Within the states, interested individuals formed committees to monitor implementation of VAWA. In particular, the National Network to End Domestic Violence (NNEDV) has accrued records across states and posts them on the Internet (www.nnedv.org/projects/otherprojects/vawa.html; see also Castro, 2010). Some good news about prosecutions: The Court Statistics Project gathered caseload information from over 16,000 trial courts in the United States on topics such as torts and contracts, domestic relations, and drugs. The criminal justice system focused more effectively on domestic violence, and, as a result, filings increased over 200% from 1985 to 1995 and then leveled off during 1996 (Ostrom & Kauder, 1997). Shelter workers have provided anecdotal evidence that victims are just not reporting as often because of their experiences with the system.

Summary

A number of institutional forces have routinely erected barriers that prevent battered women from obtaining sufficient help. Patriarchal practices within society, religious institutions, and the criminal justice system have created a gender imbalance and removed power from the hands of women. Even child protective services have held women accountable for the father's child abuse. Ordinarily, women do not have a level playing field to compete in the marketplace. They cannot usually find equal employment opportunities, even with equivalent educational backgrounds, and as a rule they do not receive comparable pay. Although there has been change, much more must be done to create a safe environment for those who have not traditionally had institutional power.

Following a divorce, the legal system does not uniformly enforce existing laws or compel men to assume financial responsibility for their children. Despite newer legislation, some judges still fail to take a partner's violence into account when issuing custody orders. The financial and caretaker burden placed on women creates havoc in their lives and in the lives of their children. When battered women turn to welfare agencies for temporary help, welfare workers are prone to ignore laws designed to safeguard battered women. On the whole, society allows men to vent their anger and frustration upon wives, ex-wives, other intimates, and their own children without fear of reprisal. If a battered woman tries to escape, there may be no place for her to go. She may even become homeless. Policies such as mandatory arrest and dual arrest have been ineffective and have often resulted in unfair arrest of women acting in self-defense. Despite newer mandates to police departments to protect battered women, they cannot count on being safe. What would you do if you had several young children and no job? Call your cleric? Call the police? Call your congressperson? Stay tuned.

3

Victimization

Why Does It Happen to Her?

Experiencing violence transforms people into victims and changes their lives forever. Once victimized, one can never again feel quite as invulnerable.

—Mary Koss (1990, p. 374)

It is important to address the question of whether victims are different from other people. Researchers who study female victims (battered women survivors, adult survivors of incest, survivors of rape) have often attempted to describe them in terms of their presumed deviance—that is, the characteristics that distinguish them from other people. The underlying assumption seemed to be that victims are to blame for their own victimization and that they are inherently provocative by nature or behavior. The concept of victim provocation formed a framework for understanding all victims. Observation of victimization phenomena brought on by captivity and extreme trauma, however, began to challenge earlier beliefs. This chapter explores victims, the myths surrounding them, and some of the forms and consequences of victimization.

Case Study: Zari and Ahmed

Zari sat in the office shaking and confused. She had nothing left. She had given up her friends and family, a Fifth Avenue apartment, and a lucrative job as a media consultant to help Ahmed start his business. She had been in other relationships and had maintained friendships with those other men. Ahmed was different. At first, he did everything she liked to do. They jogged and worked out together, went to plays, and socialized with her friends. He said that he wanted children, and that was very attractive to her.

"Mr. Hyde" did not appear for some time. The negative behavior started with criticism of her appearance and her friends. Over time, he began to follow her and read her diary. For a long time, she didn't notice that cash was missing from her drawer. When she saw Ahmed searching through her dresser, she told him to leave. Ahmed, however, hung on, trying to get her to take him back. He called her friends and family, and had his therapist call her to plead his case. She took him back.

Criticisms and put-downs began again after they had gotten back together and moved across the country. He began to break her things. She didn't realize the extent of her dependence, isolation, and humiliation until most of her furniture had been destroyed. She realized that in helping him start his business, she had lost her independent source of income and her support group. Although he didn't pay her a salary, he did pay her expenses. She felt like a child dependent on her parents for her allowance. She felt imprisoned.

He started pushing her around, and he accused her of being crazy and breaking his things. It was only after he choked her and threw her into his glass coffee table, which shattered and cut her leg, that Zari escaped.

The police took pictures of her injuries and wanted her to press charges. She found out that Ahmed had previous charges against him for stalking and terrorizing a business associate. Although he was gone, her freedom did not restore her self-confidence and security. She had escaped from her captor, but she hadn't stopped feeling controlled and intimidated. She wondered if she would look in her rearview mirror one day and see Ahmed's eyes staring at her. She wondered if he would ever stop following her.

Are Battered Women Different?

People still want to know if battered women like Zari are somehow different from other people. The real underlying question appears to be whether battered women come from poor, nonwhite families with no education or have some psychological maladjustment that predisposes them to provoke their mates, behave in sick ways, or choose men who will eventually batter them (e.g., Follingstad, Runge, Ace, Buzan, & Helff, 2001; Harrison & Esqueda, 1999). Potter and Thomas (2012) point out a newly identified type of blame: blaming white women who marry men of color who become violent. Even modern-day college students are prone to blaming battered women (Capezza, & Arriaga, 2008; Haj-Yahia & Uysal, 2011).

Finding something wrong with battered women makes it possible for the rest of us to distance ourselves from them: "If I am different from battered women, I will not be battered." "If she is different from other women, I do not have to do anything to help her."

Victim Differences

Many researchers have gathered racial and ethnic data to search for possible differences between women abused by their male intimates and those who are not (e.g., Harrison & Esqueda, 1999). Early researchers, for the most part, did not find substantial racial disparities (Sorenson & Telles, 1991), although more current surveys have found racial differences (e.g., Grossman & Lundy, 2008; E. L. Smith & Farole, 2009). Actually, rates are highly dependent on a number of reporting biases. African American women are troubled by the prospect of contributing to negative racial stereotyping of black men as criminals by reporting them (see Donovan & Williams, 2002; S. A. Hill, 2006; Moss, Pitula, Campbell, & Halstead, 1997).

Comparisons of Male-to-Female Intimate Partner Violence by Ethnic Groups Based on the Federal Government's Previous Classification Systems

- American Indians/Alaska Natives reported the most male partner violence (30.7%), and Asians/Pacific Islanders reported the least (12.8%) (Tjaden & Thoennes, 2000).
- Black female survivors have a rate 35% higher than that for white females and 2.5 times higher than that for other races (Rennison & Welchans, 2000).
- Relative to African American women, about four times as many Hispanic women and three times as many white women reported sexual abuse (Grossman & Lundy, 2008).
- Partner victimization rates of South Asian men and women were 16.4% (P. Leung & Cheung, 2008).
- Sexual coercion among 292 Latinas, including migrant workers, was 20.9% (Hazen & Soriano, 2007).

Source: Barnett, O. W., Miller-Perrin, C. L., & Perrin, R. D. (2011). *Family violence across the lifespan* (3rd ed., p. 497). Thousand Oaks, CA: Sage. Adapted with permission.

According to estimates made by the United Nations, between 17% and 38% of the world's women are survivors of intimate partner violence (IPV). In developing countries, the rates are as high as 60% (Levesque, 2001; Yoshihama, 2002). In addition to their racial and ethnic differences, persons involved in IPV vary along socioeconomic lines. Although IPV occurs at every socioeconomic level, it is more prevalent in blue-collar and lower-class families than in others (O'Donnell, Smith, & Madison, 2002). In fact, poverty is the variable most highly correlated with all types of child abuse and intimate partner violence (Kohl & Macy, 2008; Rennison & Welchans, 2000). Nonetheless, prevalence rates detailing socioeconomic status are flawed to some extent. Statistics based on police arrest records, for example, seem to overrepresent minorities and the poor because of differential arrest policies (Bachman & Coker, 1995). In other words, fewer people from Beverly Hills and Scarsdale may be included in arrest and prosecution data (see also Bowker, 1984; Schuller & Vidmar, 1992). Furthermore, poor women struggle with their survival at a very practical level (see also Byrne, Resnick, Kilpatrick, Best, & Saunders, 1999; Cucio, 1997).

Special Populations

Teenage and College Women

Levy (1990) suggests that several factors exacerbate teen dating violence: (a) pressures, insecurities, and romanticism of adolescence; (b) misperceptions about jealousy and control as loving behaviors rather than unhealthy behaviors; (c) conformity to traditional gender roles; and (d) lack of experience. Generally, teenagers do not recognize dating violence as a problem (Levy, 1993; Parrot & Bechhofer, 1991). The same is true of other segments of the population. Law enforcement, health professionals, legislatures, and society as a whole have tended to ignore teenage dating violence (Betz, 2007).

In a review of published articles, Jackson (1998) suggests that violence rates range from 10% to 50% of dating couples. Two studies of teen dating violence in North Carolina ascertained that dating violence victimization was almost gender equivalent. Male victimization was 44.7% in 2005 and 51.1% in 2007. Female victimization was 55.3% in 2005 and 48.9% in 2007 (Kim-Goodwin, Clements, McCuiston, & Fox, 2009; see also M. Allen, 2011). Official surveys, however, have arrived at very different effects for each gender. The Office of Juvenile Justice and Delinquency Prevention (OJJDP), for instance, reported that while 3% of juvenile assaults occur between intimate partners, 73% of the survivors are girls (Snyder & McCurly, 2008). The majority of sexual assaults are male-on-female (Saewyc, Pettingell, & Magee, 2003).

For teen victims seeking relief, the major stumbling blocks are the legal requirements for both adult and marital status (Brustin, 1995; Kuehl, 1991; Suarez, 1994). The 2000 Violence Against Women Act (VAWA) included some legal provisions for teens. The American Bar Association (ABA) has become more active in finding ways to safeguard teens (see Lowenberg & Fulcher, 2008). Currently, a bill is pending in Congress (H.R. 789) that would help prevent teen dating violence (see U.S. Department of Health and Human Services, Centers for Disease Control and Prevention, 2010, for a brief review of the warning signs of dating violence, excuses for dating violence, and why teens find it hard to leave violent relationships).

Several college-based studies have characterized courtship violence as largely reciprocal (e.g., Archer, 2000; Sabina, & Straus, 2008; Worth, Matthews, & Coleman, 1990). One aspect of the reciprocal nature of dating violence was the finding that "inflicting dating violence" by either sex was the greatest predictor of becoming its recipient (O'Keefe & Treister, 1998). Nevertheless, experts criticize these findings because of numerous measurement concerns, such as overreliance on the Conflict Tactics Scales (CTS). Other methodological concerns include the failure to adequately evaluate the seriousness of the assaults (see Cunradi, Bersamin, & Ames, 2009; Graham-Kevan & Archer, 2005; Hays & Emelianchik, 2009). Even presumed mutual abuse, however, is clearly not mutual. In one study, 54% of the primary aggressors were male (Weston, Temple, & Marshall, 2005).

Older Women

Prior to 1985, researchers paid little attention to older women who experienced domestic violence, and even now, most research on elder abuse focuses on elders living in nursing homes. The causes of abuse of older women are unclear in many cases, as are the reasons why some women leave and some do not. Women abused throughout a marriage may leave in old age as they recognize that their inability to withstand abuse places them at even greater risk of injury and stress-related conditions, such as heart attacks. Others believe older women remain because of real or assumed financial dependence (Pillemer & Finkelhor, 1989).

Domestically abused elders are most often mistreated by people with whom they live. At least some domestic elder abuse is actually "spouse abuse grown old" (Acierno, Hernandez-Tejada, Muzzy, & Steve, 2009). Most elder abuse, however, occurs at the hands of other family members, such as adult children and grandchildren (Laumann, Leitsch, & Waite, 2008; A. Klein, Tobin, Salomon, & Dubois, 2008). Nonfamily caregivers perpetrate a considerable amount of elder abuse as well (Teaster et al., 2006). Financial abuse by both family and nonfamily members is especially common (Stiegel, 2001). Service providers tend not to view older women as victims of spousal violence but as victims of elder abuse. Their typical response consists of in-home services to reduce dependency on the abuser and reduce caregiver stress (Vinton, 1991).

Experts have observed several problems that make helping older abused women challenging. First, elderly women are extremely likely to refuse services of any type (A. Klein et al., 2008). Second, many service providers, such as medical practitioners, fail to detect elder abuse (Thompson-McCormick, Jones, & Livingston, 2009). Finally, elder abuse investigators may be poorly trained (Ramey-Klawsnik, 2004). Innovative pilot programs to detect and prevent elder abuse, such as community outreach groups, are being studied (Brandl, Hebert, Rozwadowski, & Spangler, 2003).

Currently, many older abused women are falling through the cracks (D. D. Sorensen). Experts have begun to call for broader recognition of abuse across all fields. Domestic violence workers, for example, need to know more about the domain of adult protective services, and vice versa (see Bulman, 2010; Nerenberg, 2008). Recently, at the University of Kentucky, experts attempted to remedy this problem by developing a comprehensive elder abuse network. Participants included university scholars from different disciplines, social service providers, legal professionals, and health educators. Although the effectiveness of the program has not been evaluated, the team cooperation and effort is impressive (Blowers et al., 2012).

Rural Women

Information about battered women who live in rural areas or who have special needs is just now coming to light. Women living in nonurban areas often lack access to transportation and service providers, but guns are abundant. Women are often isolated in the most literal way, and their tight communities and local law enforcement can exacerbate rather than expose the secret. They live in a virtual patriarchal enclave (DeKeseredy & Schwartz, 2008; Krishnan, Hilbert, McNeil, & Newman, 2004; Websdale, 1995a, 1995b).

Case Study: Daleen

Daleen Berry's family moved from California to Appalachia when she was five years old. According to Daleen, domestic violence and child abuse are so prevalent there that people have all but stopped noticing when it happens. The rural nature of the terrain; the lack of resources, such as money and transportation; and the culture itself can cut off the residents of rural communities from outsiders and the help that may be needed.

Daleen married the man who had begun sexually abusing her when she was age 13. She was attending West Preston High in West Virginia, which was featured on national television for having the highest rate of teen pregnancy in the country. By the time Daleen was 21, she had four children by her violent husband. "The violence in my home was so bad that I sat down on the bathroom floor and planned to kill all of us," Daleen said.

Her husband lost his job in the coal mines, and the abuse got worse. In 1998, Daleen took a risk. She walked into the office of the *Preston County Journal* and asked for a job—a job that would allow her to leave her abusive partner and support her children. They hired her because she was persistent, despite the fact that she lacked a college degree and experience.

"Journalism gave me a mentor [Linda Miller Benson] who impacted my life in a profound way because she believed in me and saw something in me that I couldn't yet see myself," Daleen said. Today, Daleen is an award-winning author. Her book *Sister of Silence* took first place at the West Virginia Writers' Conference in the "Appalachian Theme" category. She is also the recent (and first) winner of the Pearl Buck Writing for Social Change Award.

Source: Used with permission of Daleen Berry.

Professional Women

Financial reasons have always been at the top of the list in explaining why battered women do not leave their partners (Strube & Barbour, 1984), but what about women who do have financial resources and the support of family and friends? Since 1984, one of the authors (A. L.) has been working with a base of battered women: women with jobs, careers, and the money to leave. In the setting of a private practice and in a training environment, she has met with hundreds of women who judge themselves very harshly for staying with abusive men (and women, in lesbian relationships) because they see themselves as fully able to leave. It has been a challenge to work with these women over time and to develop with them explanations— theories, if you will—that assist them in the process of problem solving, self-forgiveness, healing, and for many, leaving or staying away from their batterers.

Of course, "there ain't nothing new under the sun," so the ideas anchoring this fresh rationale are a reframing of the work done by earlier pioneers in the field and early feminists such as Del Martin, Lenore Walker, and Barrie Levy. One restructured theoretical rationale for explaining why professional women do not leave their batterers appears in the theme of self-blame for emotional responding that may be termed *spiraling reactivity:* "I am smart enough to have figured this out." "Why didn't I or why can't I leave?" Several studies have demonstrated that battered women blame themselves (e.g., Barnett, Haney-Martindale, Modzelewski, & Sheltra, 1991; Fry & Barker, 2001).

A better question might be, "How does a woman think clearly when she is operating at the level of emotional reflex?" When a woman lives with abuse, the batterer becomes the linchpin of her existence. It is necessary for peace and survival to respond promptly and accurately to perceptions of a batterer's needs and wants. Over time, these reactions metamorphize into a response pattern that is emotionally based, not cognitively based. These battered women are too busy reflexively reacting at a gut level to enter the world of objective and clear thinking (see Lazarus & Folkman, 1984; MacNair & Elliott, 1992).

Most often, the problem solving that is done has a relatively nonproductive focus. These battered women are trying to stop the violence or change the batterer (Evans, Gonnella, Marcynszyn, Gentile, & Salpekar, 2005; Halligan, Michael, Clark, & Ehlers, 2003). They are not focused directly on their own escape. They become caught in a pattern of reactions that over time spirals out of control. For many battered women, "out of control" is the description they have for their own lives and feelings. When the focus begins to shift to what they can control, the cycle of reaction changes.

From the perspective of battering relationships, women are in an economic no-win position. Hornung, McCullough, and Sugimoto (1981) provided evidence linking educational and occupational differences in couples with an increased risk of psychological abuse, physical aggression, and life-threatening violence (see also K. L. Anderson, 1997; McCloskey, 1996). Other investigators have judged a woman's higher economic status relative to a man's to be a risk factor for male-perpetrated homicide in the United States (Gauthier & Bankston, 1997) and Russia (Gondolf & Shestakov, 1997). C. Smith (1988) summed up this status conflict for women as follows:

> In the case of lower status husbands, resource theory explains how traditional values of male dominance can lead to violence against higher status wives. Conversely in the case of higher status husbands, the distributive justice hypothesis explains how more contemporary values of status advancement may lead to violence against lower status wives. (p. 15)

Lesbians

Battered lesbians have a history of being both underserved and marginalized by researchers, advocates, and the criminal justice system

(Levy, 1997). Service providers are less likely to evaluate a lesbian seeking help as a true victim (Basow & Thompson, 2012). "The violence in a lesbian relationship takes place between two social outlaws, both of whom may experience discrimination in employment, housing and at the hands of social agencies" (Margolies & Leeder, 1995, p. 141).

Attitudes of the public toward same-sex partner abuse. One word academics use to describe the rejecting attitude of society, police, juries, medical professionals, and others toward persons with a same-sex orientation is *homonegativity*. According to some experts, the public seems to accept many false beliefs (myths) about gay men and lesbians and their sexual activities because of heterosexist socialization and victim blaming. See Table 3.1 for a list of false beliefs about lesbians.

Many people assume that it is easier for gay men and lesbians than for heterosexuals to leave their violent relationships. After all, there are no legal contracts and often no social contracts, and gay and lesbian relationships do not last. The latter assumption is not true. Lesbian couples are as committed and involved in each other's lives as straight couples are. In fact, lesbians may have a particularly difficult time leaving their partners because they have so little social support and may be alienated from family. Isolation appears to be the major reason lesbians stay in battering relationships (Renzetti, 1989). Growing up gay, lesbian, or bisexual predisposes an individual to isolation, harassment, and violence from family and peers (Jerome et al., 1998; Lytle, Foley, & Aster, 2012).

Significant numbers of lesbian, gay, and bisexual youths report that they have been verbally, physically, or sexually assaulted by family members and peers (Craft & Serovich, 2005; Rotheram-Bokes, Rosario, & Koopman, 1991). Anti-gay and anti-lesbian attitudes also permeate communities, causing gay men and lesbians involved in battering relationships to face

Table 3.1   False Beliefs About Individuals With Same-Sex Orientation

Offender must be *butch;* victims must be *femme*	Gays deserve AIDs
Lesbian relationships are egalitarian	Homosexuals have low morals
Same-sex abuse is actually mutual abuse	Homosexuals deserve abuse
Rape of a homosexual is not a serious crime	Gay IPV is less violent than heterosexual IPV

Source: Barnett, O. W., Miller-Perrin, C. L., & Perrin, R. D. (2011). *Family violence across the lifespan* (3rd ed., p. 517). Thousand Oaks, CA: Sage. Adapted with permission.

special hostilities. Lesbians experience layers of oppression; they live in a culture that is not only sexist and racist but homophobic as well. Fewer resources are available to gay and lesbian survivors and perpetrators (Todahl, Linville, Bustin, Wheeler, & Gau, 2009). Of the 138 batterers' programs approved by the Los Angeles County Department of Probation, only 8 are listed as sensitive to gay and lesbian issues (Los Angeles County Department of Probation, 2010). Accessing these services is synonymous with coming out. Coming out, for many gays and lesbians, is synonymous with isolation and rejection. This sense of isolation can be compounded by feelings of shame and guilt. Seeking help is frightening for the lesbian survivor, particularly if she is closeted (Levy, 1997).

Case Study: Sandy and Linda

Sandy and Linda had been best friends for three years before they became lovers. No friends, classmates, or coworkers knew about their relationship, and they certainly kept it hidden from family members who were deeply religious. When the violence started, it was verbal and precipitated by Sandy's jealousy. The couple pulled closer together.

Their love for each other grew, as did their dependency, isolation, and fear—fear not only of physical violence and abandonment, but also fear of exposure. Sandy often threatened to tell Linda's family about their relationship.

They risked calling a battered women's hotline after Sandy broke Linda's eardrum. Linda made the calls and eventually found a counselor who would see them. They were eager for help. Neither of them talked about Sandy's threats to kill herself if Linda tried to stand up for herself or talked about leaving. To everyone in their lives (except the therapist), they continued to "play" at being straight friends.

The physical violence virtually disappeared, but the threats and verbal abuse continued. Sandy's fear of losing Linda, who was quite literally "everything" to her, became even greater as she began to look at what she was doing to her partner. Their hope of being able to live together had been rekindled, and their need to look good for the therapist, who was the only intrusion into their isolation, also increased.

One night after a particularly violent verbal phone argument, Sandy made good on her threat; she took her own life. Linda was the only person privy to Sandy's plan. She had carried it out in every detail. Linda found the music Sandy had in her tape deck that she had always said would accompany her suicide. She found a note and a scrawled will. She saw the writing drift off and the ink form a wavering line to the bottom of the page. She saw her lover's blood on the bed. But she wasn't able to share her grief with anyone except the therapist. In fact, one of her friends from church said to her, "I hope you're not going to tell me that you and Sandy had anything more than a friendship. I would never be able to speak to you again."

The system has become more responsive to domestic violence in the gay and lesbian community. In an interesting twist, gay men and lesbians cannot legally marry in most states, but they can be treated as spouses in a court of law when they are involved in domestic disputes. As of 1995, 35 states had domestic violence laws covering same-sex relationships (National Center on Women and Family Law, 1995). In 1997, the Ohio Court of Appeals held that the definition of cohabitation in the context of domestic violence covered same-sex couples (J. Zorza, 1997).

Immigrant Women

It seems obvious that language barriers, racism, employment stress, cultural beliefs, isolation, and immigration status compound a woman's vulnerability (Abraham, 2000; Huisman, 1996). An immigrant woman may be completely dependent on her husband to maintain her status. Her ability to remain in the United States may rest on an application filed by her husband in which she is included as a derivative applicant. If her spouse becomes abusive, she may be afraid to leave him or to seek protection for fear that he will withdraw a pending petition or remove her name from a pending asylum application. Until recently, immigrant women had little success in pursuing such claims when they needed protection against gender-based violence.

Several important developments have provided hope for women seeking lawful and independent immigration status. The first is the Violence Against Women Act, which contains provisions that allow battered immigrant women to assert their rights more independently. An early memorandum by the Immigration and Naturalization Service called for consideration of political asylum claims for women seeking protection against gender-specific persecution (Orloff & Kelly, 1995). When VAWA was reauthorized in 2005, it addressed the problems of immigrants more carefully. Citizenship and Immigration Services, for example, became responsible to oversee changes, such as providing interpretation and greater access to legal services (Erez, Adelman, & Gregory, 2009).

Cross-Cultural Issues

*The men say: So he beat her up? Yes he did. Well, let that be a
lesson to her. The women say: Why was she so arrogant? A woman
should learn to be cautious and calm. Men like a quiet woman.*

—Rosemary Ofeibea Ofei-Aboagye (Ghana, 1994)

An analysis of cultural practices across the globe makes clear why the plight
of women is still a human rights issue (e.g., Levesque, 2001). In too many
nations, females are third-class, dispensable citizens who can be beaten,
raped, burned, mutilated, enslaved, sold, tortured, and murdered with
impunity. Some societies still follow traditions that target women, such as
selective malnourishment, selective abortion, infanticide, forced prostitu-
tion, genital mutilation, dowry deaths, honor killings, denial of education,
and rigid codes of dress and conduct (e.g., Counts, Brown, & Campbell,
1992; d'Olivera & Schraiber, 2005; Norman & Finan, 2001; Starkey,
2009). Illustrations such as these, where women are so routinely the targets
of male aggression, have helped foster patriarchal explanations of wife
abuse (Hunnicutt, 2009).

Marital violence seems to occur in nearly every nation. Most societies
accept wife abuse as part of the culture and do not define it as criminal
(e.g., Chester, Robin, Koss, Lopez, & Goldman, 1994; Walker, 1999). One
survey in New Guinea reported that 18% of married women had gone to
a hospital for injuries sustained during a beating. In Bombay, one of four
deaths in women between the ages of 15 and 24 is caused by accidental
burning, also known as dowry death (a means of murdering a wife in order
to get another dowry through another marriage). Most victims had been
married less than five years (Prasad, 1994; Rastogi & Therly, 2006; see also
Barnett, Miller-Perrin, & Perrin, 2011).

Surveys of practices in other cultures indicate that wife assault is more
likely to be permitted in societies where men control family economic
resources, where conflicts are solved by means of physical force, and where
women do not have an equal option to divorce (J. K. Brown, 1992; Chavez
et al., 2005). Examples of ongoing, current abuses of women are not
difficult to find. Potentially deadly customs, such as female circumcision
and infanticide, illustrate the powerlessness of women in many cultures.

When Afghanistan's Taliban sect came to power in the mid-1990s, leaders
forbade the education of girls past the age of eight and prohibited all women
from working outside the home except in medical professions (Norman &
Finan, 2001). Honor killings in countries like Jordan are a special form of

regulating women's sexual behavior. With self-righteous persistence, male family members slaughter female family members guilty of disobedience or infidelity to save the family from unbearable disgrace (Kulwicki, 2002). These killings represent a cultural belief that a man's honor lies between the legs of a woman (Chesler, 2009; Vandello & Cohen, 2003). Kosovo women raped by Serbian soldiers during ethnic cleansing find it necessary to hide or deny the assaults, or never to return home. Even under the circumstances of brutal war crimes, Kosovar men reject rape survivors and find them guilty of bringing shame on the family (C. J. Williams, 1999).

Responses of Arab Palestinian husbands in one survey revealed that 41% thought that "it would do some wives good to be beaten by their husbands." Another study showed that even a substantial percentage of women (66%) still considered wife beating justified under certain circumstances, such as when a wife is sexually unfaithful or when she challenges her husband's manhood (see Haj-Yahia, 1999).

Female activists in the Middle East and Africa have been involved in the Arab Spring. In most of these countries, women are subject to oppressive legislation such as "guardianship laws," which relegate them to the status of minors. Even minor males may have more freedom. The Jasmine Revolt in Tunisia, a relatively progressive and secular country, kicked off the Arab Spring and had a strong female presence. Women flock to rallies in miniskirts, jeans, and veils. All ages are represented. Raja bin Salama, a critic of fundamentalist subjugation, called for Tunisia's new society to have laws based on the Universal Declaration of Human Rights. Feminists in Tunisia call for a separation of mosque and state (Pharaon, 2004).

Women in Egypt created a Facebook page. They collected and assembled a photo gallery of women's roles in the protest. The fear for many Arab women is that they will be left behind by their revolutionary brothers post-revolution. According to Nawla Darwish of the New Women Foundation, "We are living in a patriarchal society. Revolution may not be enough to change that" (Morgan, 2011).

In 17th-century Russia, it was lawful for men to murder their wives. A manual, the *Domostroi,* instructed peasant men how to whip their wives according to legal guidelines (e.g., with their blouses removed). Upper-class men, in contrast, were to banish their recalcitrant wives to *terems* (segregated rooms), allowing them to leave only rarely. In today's Russia, police have the statutory right to refuse service to women who claim that their husbands have beaten them (Stickley, Kislitsyna, Timofeeva, & Vågerö, 2008a). In fact, in a number of countries, such as Egypt, women find it useless—if not dangerous—to report victimization by an intimate to police (Ammar, 2006). In Peru or Pakistan, for instance, an assaulted woman's visit to a police station puts her at risk for being raped by the police (Human Rights Watch, 1992)! An analysis of 770 calls made to a hotline in Belgrade revealed that 83% of the perpetrators of assaults against women were husbands, former husbands, or partners. When fathers and sons were included, the percentage of family perpetrators rose to 94% (Mrsevic & Hughes, 1997).

In the United States, feminism has been denounced as antifamily, anticapitalist, and philosophically socialist or communist. In socialist or communist countries, feminism has been labeled procapitalist, Western, and an enemy of the state (Mladjenovic & Libriein, 1993; Mrsevic & Hughes, 1997). It appears that when women get together for anything other than a Tupperware party, insurgency is in the air.

In a survey of 1,700 Thai households, approximately 20% of the men admitted to having hit, slapped, or kicked their wives at least once in their marriage (Hoffman, Demo, & Edwards, 1994; see Edwards, Fuller, Vorakitphokatom, & Sermsi, 1994). Among female partners in Matlab, Bangladesh, 42% reported having been physically assaulted by their male partner over their lifetime and 50% reported having been sexually assaulted (Garcia-Moreno, Jansen, Ellsberg, Heise, & Watts, 2006).

Childhood Abuse

It is logical, from an intergenerational perspective, to expect that women who have experienced or witnessed abuse during childhood will have a tendency to accept violence in their own adult relationships as normative (Kalmuss, 1984). Over the last decade, evidence has emerged showing that battered women are more likely than nonbattered women to have been abused during childhood, and childhood abuse is linked with staying in an abusive relationship (Finkelhor, Ormrod, & Turner, 2007; Raghavan, Swan, Snow, & Mazur, 2005). Battered women are also more likely than nonbattered women to have been sexually abused during childhood (e.g., Polusny & Follette, 2008). The incidence of childhood sexual abuse in battered women, however, does not consistently differentiate them from women in the general population (Holtzworth-Munroe, Smutzler, & Sandin, 1997). In addition, women who have been battered and have suffered sexual abuse often find little understanding from their medical doctors. Battered women may report chronic pain, and their doctors may find no physical reason for the pain even after extensive medical tests. Consequently, medical professionals can feel frustrated. Increased training could help resolve these dilemmas (Nelson, Baldwin, & Taylor, 2011).

Repeat Victimization

A newer line of research has focused on the effects of repeat victimization (for a technical definition, see DeValve, 2004; Farrell & Sousa, 2001; see also Lauritsen, Owens, Planty, Rand, & Truman, 2012). One study found that individuals victimized earlier in life develop higher levels of fear than those who were victimized later (see Kury & Ferdinand, 1997), and research has increasingly suggested that the effects of trauma are cumulative (Polusny & Follette, 2008). Congruent with this thesis, childhood sexual abuse does place adult women at greater risk for a variety of revictimization experiences by partners and other males. Several reviews have found that, over a lifetime, sexually abused girls later suffer comparatively more sexual assaults, rapes, and physical violence than girls who are not sexually abused (e.g., Nurius, Furrey, & Berliner, 1992; B. Sanders & Moore, 1999).

Actually, data have accumulated showing both strong revictimization and polyvictimization (i.e., different types of victimization) effects for both men and women, although gender effects exist. In regard to polyvictimization, Finkelhor, Turner, Ormrod, Hamby, and Kracke (2009, p. 7) stated, "A child who was physically assaulted in the past year would be five times as likely to have also been sexually victimized." Research shows that child abuse victims experiencing any type of victimization (psychological, physical, sexual) are more likely to be involved in dating violence during adolescence, college, and adulthood (Finkelhor et al., 2007; Polusny & Follette, 2008). (See Appendix B.7 for estimates of repeat victimization.)

Even when relationships are found between battered women's childhood abuse and their current IPV, however, one must question the logic of blaming and typifying battered women as deviant because they grew up in such homes. In the experience of one of the authors (A. L.), chronic victimization seems to affect a woman's ability to pick healthy partners and increases the likelihood that she could have multiple abusive relationships. However, an idyllic childhood does not keep a woman from becoming abused in her intimate relationships. Women from healthy families are often unprepared for the manipulations of an abusive partner.

Personality Traits

While some researchers focused on race, socioeconomics, and child abuse as precursors to adult battering, other social scientists explored individual differences in personality traits. Some searched for personality problems that would indicate battered women were abnormal. Battered women do not fit a particular personality profile or fall within a singular diagnostic category (Walker & Browne, 1985).

The Minnesota Multiphasic Personality Inventory (MMPI) (S. R. Hathaway & McKinley, 1967) provides a comprehensive assessment of abnormal personality. Using MMPI scale scores, M. A. Douglas and Colantuono (1987) detected no typical personality profiles of battered women. Rhodes's (1992) study using a comparison group of nonbattered women from a clinical population, however, found that battered women scored substantially higher on the Psychopathic Deviate score of the MMPI. Using the MMPI-2 (R. L. Green, 1991), Khan, Welch, and Zillmer (1993) found elevations in scales associated with depression, anxiety, and subjective distress. Taken together with findings from other victimization studies (e.g., Taft et al., 2006), elevations such as these most probably represent the effects of victimization. In fact, a synthesis (meta-analysis) of relevant studies showed that battering was a risk factor (associated factor) for mental disorders, especially depression and posttraumatic stress disorder (PTSD) (Golding, 1999; Sabina & Straus, 2008).

One historically held contention is that low self-esteem is a precursor to being abused (see T. Mills, 1985). Early investigations found few differences between battered and nonbattered groups of women (M. N. Russell, Lipov, Phillips, & White, 1989). The majority of later studies, however, do suggest that battered women have lower self-esteem than nonbattered women (Haj-Yahia, 2000; Rhatigan & Nathanson, 2010; Woods, 1999).

In a sample of severely battered women, Cascardi and O'Leary (1992) ascertained that as the frequency, form, and consequences of physical aggression increased, the level of self-esteem decreased. Abuse can lower self-esteem by creating a sense of personal defectiveness. All in all, the general consensus today is that battered women's low self-esteem, when exhibited, is the result of the battering, certainly not the cause of it (Anitha, 2011; Matud, 2005; see Holtzworth-Munroe et al., 1997, for a review).

There can be little doubt that battered women are depressed (Al-Modallal et al., 2012; Basile & Smith, 2011; J. C. Campbell, Kub, Belknap, & Templin, 1997; Haj-Yahia, 2000; Shortt, Capaldi, Kim, & Owen, 2006). Depression is often the primary emotional response to abuse (McCauley et al., 1995; Saunders, Hamberger, & Hovey, 1993). There is a significant relationship between polyvictimization and depression (Sabina & Straus, 2008). Women who have been severely abused suffer four times the rate of depression and suicide attempts that nonbattered women experience (Seedat, Stein, & Forde, 2005; see D. K. Anderson, Saunders, Yoshihama, Bybee, & Sullivan, 2003; Kaslow et al., 1998). In fact, physical victimization by an intimate partner is positively related to levels of depression in both men and women (Samp & Abbott, 2011; Zlotnick, Kohn, Peterson, & Pearlstein, 1998) and in both lesbian and heterosexual victims (Tuel & Russell, 1998).

As shown by newer studies, such symptoms are often more situational than characteristic of a personality type. Battering is a cause, not just a correlate, of depression (Von Eye & Bogat, 2006).

Previous studies have also established an association between a battered woman's self-esteem and depression. The daily impact of living in a context of fear, as well as the abuse itself, is directly related to depression (B. E. Carlson, McNutt, Choi, & Rose, 2002; Cascardi & O'Leary, 1992). One longitudinal study found that psychological attitudes, such as depression, had less to do with remaining with a violent partner than relationship and economic factors (e.g., marital satisfaction, dependent children) (Beach et al., 2004). Another longitudinal study revealed that when battering stopped, depression decreased (Kernic, Holt, Stoner, Wolf, & Rivara, 2003).

Victim Blaming

Most early writers who described battered women failed to ascribe the violence to the perpetrator. They frequently said or implied that the battered woman was to blame; it was something about her that caused him to be violent. Quite often, members of society blame the victim without regard to the context. They blame people who are robbed for leaving their doors unlocked, and they blame battered women for nagging. They even blame rape victims for having their turtlenecks cut too low. Golda Meir, former prime minister of Israel, highlighted this lopsided point of view. When her male cabinet members concluded that they should impose a 10:00 p.m. curfew on women to reduce the incidence of rape, she opposed them. Since men did the raping, why not subject them to the curfew? She was overruled.

Ewing and Aubrey (1987) demonstrated that public opinion about battered women rests upon widely held and false assumptions. A random selection of 216 community members completed a questionnaire after reading a scenario about a violent couple. Over 60% of the respondents agreed that if a battered woman were really afraid, she would simply leave. (It is interesting to note that people seldom ask "abused" men why they don't leave [Henning & Connor-Smith, 2011].) More than 40% decided that she must have been at least partly to blame for her husband's assaults, even though the story provided no rationale for such a belief. There was some tendency for respondents to believe that the woman must have been masochistic or emotionally disturbed if she stayed, that the couple had serious marital problems, and that the woman could avoid the beatings if she entered counseling. By and large, people seemed reluctant to place the blame on the perpetrator.

More current research has replicated the finding that people are reluctant to blame batterers. One survey of college students showed a differential type of blaming. They were more likely to blame battered women who stayed with abusers for internal reasons, such as loneliness, than for external reasons, such as being threatened with death. They also rated battered women who were more traditional as less to blame than women with more contemporary values (Follingstad, Runge, Ace, Buzan, & Helff, 2001).

Beliefs defining the survivors of intimate partner violence in stereotypical detail create a battered woman that society loves to blame. Excerpts from Hotaling and Sugarman's (1986) review of research on battered women emphasize the misplaced focus on women as the provocateurs of marital violence: "Very little heuristic [future research; explanatory] value can be gained by focusing primarily on the victim in the assessment of risk to wife assault" (p. 12). "What is surprising is the enormous effort to explain male behavior by examining the characteristics of women" (p. 120). There does not seem to be a psychological profile that predicts a woman's likelihood of developing a relationship with an abuser (see Rhodes, 1992, for a review; see also A. R. Moore, 2008). Overall, research lends credence to a "just like anybody else" viewpoint (Harway, 1993).

Attributions in Violent Relationships

Survivors of aggression usually search for explanations to the question, "Why me?" A common attribution (an idea or thought generated to explain behavior) made by battered women is that they somehow provoke the violence. Therefore, they can or should be able to prevent or eliminate it by changing their own behavior (Prange, 1985). Painter and Dutton (1985) speculated that this belief, along with the contradictory belief that one is powerless, leads to enmeshment in the relationship: "As long as she continues to believe that she causes the violence, and that changes in her behavior might prevent the violent behavior from occurring, she is locked into the battering relationship" (p. 373).

When battered women no longer believe they "provoked it," they often begin to blame themselves for staying. Alfred Adler (1927), in a discussion about causalistic thinking, asserted that one of the major outcomes of victim blaming is that it excuses the perpetrator from responsibility. For instance, when people blame social conditions for criminal behavior, offenders lose accountability for their actions (and victims seem to acquire it).

Battered women need to explain the very existence and cause of the violence, not just its occurrence. Some common rationalizations given by battered women are that his aggression happened when he was "not himself" and was "temporarily out of control"; that he was a "victim of child abuse," "an alcoholic," or "unemployed" (see Ragg, Sultana, & Miller, 1999). When a battered woman says, "It's my fault," she is not only accepting blame but also absolving or partially absolving her assailant. Battered women in one study blamed themselves for initiating partner abuse when other evidence (narrative data) indicated they had not. Instead, the women misinterpreted their anger as the precipitant and made a subjective judgment (Olson & Lloyd, 2005). Similarly, another study indicated that college women exposed to hypothetical male aggression held the men less responsible if the female partner had been confrontational or negative (Rhatigan & Nathanson, 2010).

Survivors of negative events often exaggerate or misconstrue the extent to which they are responsible for their own victimization (Towns & Adams, 2000). Gilbert and Webster (1982) detected a common theme emerging from interviews with women who had experienced assaults at the hands of men (rape, incest, battering): They (a) blamed themselves; (b) denied the magnitude of the events; (c) denied their anger and wish to retaliate; (d) felt unable to set limits or fight back; and (e) found it difficult to indict the men who injured them, wanting instead to protect them. The inability of women to condemn the aggression directed at them by a loved partner seems directly proportional to their level of involvement in the relationship. Prange (1985) found that women who returned to their abusers made internal attributions about their physical abuse: that something was wrong with them. Attributions made by battered women about being assaulted are important determinants of the degree of blame they personally accept (see also Moss et al., 1997; Nichols & Feltey, 2003).

Case Study: Laura

Laura didn't want to argue with her husband anymore. They fought about everything, from religion to his job. He said that he was tired of her nagging, and that he wouldn't have to hit her if she'd just shut up. Laura began to see her behavior as provocative and tried to change it. She even began to believe that it must be her responsibility to change her husband's behavior. At that point, her husband told her that she was a sick woman and making him crazy. She was convinced.

In one comparison of 31 battered women and two groups of 62 nonabused women, battered women had significantly higher levels of self-blame (Barnett et al., 1991). In the Barnett and Lopez-Real (1985) investigation, battered women reported that they were "to blame" more than any other option listed (e.g., anxious, angry, powerful). They blamed themselves for behaviors such as "not being strong enough" or "not helping effectively." The women also reported an increase in blame correlated with the belief that their "efforts to escape were unsuccessful."

Although most family violence experts have speculated that battered women feel to blame (i.e., responsible) for being victimized (e.g., Fry & Barker, 2001; Towns & Adams, 2000), some disagree. Holtzworth-Munroe (1988), for example, states that "abused women generally do not blame themselves for their husband's violence" (p. 331), and J. C. Campbell (1990) found that only 20% of the battered women reported feeling to blame. Also, a number of investigators found that battered women blamed their husbands more than themselves for the violence (e.g., Cantos, Neidig, & O'Leary, 1994).

Landenburger (1989) proposed that battered women may either blame themselves for causing the abuse or blame themselves for tolerating it. In either case, blame is the end result, and blame tends to produce guilt. As Erica Jong so cleverly phrased it, "Show me a woman who doesn't feel guilty and I'll show you a man."

Some theories of depression contend that self-blame both causes and maintains depression (Peterson & Seligman, 1984). Andrews and Brewin (1990) studied depression in 286 British victims of violence. Of the women who had suffered partner assault, 53% currently involved with the perpetrator experienced self-blame for causing the violence, compared to 35% of those who were no longer in the relationship. Within the self-blaming group, 68% blamed their behavior while 32% blamed their character.

> *In passing, also, I would like to say that the first time Adam had a chance he laid the blame on women.*
>
> —Nancy Astor, British politician

According to Finkelhor (1983), the literature on domestic violence consistently portrays abuse as occurring in the context of psychological exploitation. Batterers use their power to manipulate victims' perceptions of reality. Battering coupled with self-blame diminishes a battered woman's belief in herself, erodes her self-esteem, and reduces her integrity. She feels demeaned as she responds to the demands of her batterer. She may jeopardize her relationships with her children, other family members, friends, and community contacts. The more extensive her compromises, the greater the erosion of her self-respect.

Social Support

Social support theory assumes that exposure to environmental duress leads to personal stress, and that social support may act as a buffer after the event occurs (Thoits, 1982). In one comparison, social support was extremely important to recovery, but gender differences occurred in kinds and levels of support offered survivors. Whereas the male survivors generally found their bosses sympathetic and their colleagues jokingly accepting, battered women experienced pay suspensions and bosses who were characteristically unsympathetic and victim-blaming (Shepherd, 1990). Lack of support, both personal and social, creates a dilemma for battered women that ensnares them in their relationships (Ellsberg, Caldera, Herrera, Winkvist, & Kullgren, 1999; Kocot & Goodman, 2003; Krugman et al., 2004; Stenius & Veysey, 2005).

One large national survey of both men and women disclosed that survivors of partner abuse received as much actual social support as nonvictimized individuals (Zlotnick et al., 1998). In a comparison of battered women's perceptions contrasted with those of two nonbattered groups, battered women reported receiving less social support than the other groups (Barnett, Martinez, & Keyson, 1996). Apparently, judgments about receiving social support rely somewhat on subjective perceptions rather than objective reality. Furthermore, social support may occur unevenly within different areas of a person's life (M. H. Davis & Morris, 1998; Postmus, Severson, Berry, & Yoo, 2009). Some dissimilarities between the findings, of course, undoubtedly reflect differences between community and clinic samples and the differences inherent in including males in one survey.

Sometimes, so-called social support from friends and family is harmful rather than helpful. It is not helpful, for instance, to suggest to a battered woman that she stay with her abuser. Some other unhelpful responses are to insinuate that the survivor is stupid, to refuse to talk about the abuse, or to stop seeing the survivor (Kocot & Goodman, 2003). Helpful support can be practical, such as offering a woman a place to stay or urging her to call the police, get an attorney, or seek counseling (Goodkind, Gillum, Bybee, & Sullivan, 2003).

On the other hand, victims of family crimes may not be very open to support when it is offered. Gondolf (1998b) found that very few battered women involved in court cases were willing to accept support services from a shelter outreach program. Of the 1,012 reached by phone from a group of 1,895, 644 refused all services for themselves (e.g., 12-session support group, individual counseling, weekly phone counseling). None of this group had ever been in touch with a shelter before. Almost half of those who refused help did so because they "did not need it." Some women were already in counseling; some had scheduling problems; some had left their abuser; a few had no transportation. Some expressed worry about triggering a child protective services (CPS) referral if they accepted help. Given the tendency of CPS personnel to blame and threaten battered women instead of abusive fathers, battered women are justified in their apprehensions (H. Douglas & Walsh, 2010).

It is interesting to note that in another analysis, the level of social support did not predict whether battered women whose batterers had been arrested and charged with misdemeanor assault would cooperate with prosecution efforts. The lack of tangible support (e.g., babysitting, transportation), however, was a predictor of noncooperation (Goodman, Bennett, & Dutton, 1999). Newer research has uncovered an appalling lack of social support from various service providers. Poorly trained service personnel may be unpleasant, unhelpful, and judgmental, thus magnifying survivors' problems (Krugman et al., 2004; Lindhorst, Meyers, & Casey, 2008; see also L. V. Davis & Srinivasan, 1995).

It is probable that even in a troubled marriage, people tend to isolate themselves from friends and family and focus on repairing the relationship. Although support is often offered, individuals may be so humiliated or stressed that they ignore or pull away from such aid. One report determined that some battered women would not seek help from relatives because they feared harm would come to them at the hands of their batterer (Riger, Raja, & Camacho, 2002; see also Thapar-Björkert & Morgan, 2010). In fact, a qualitative study of homeless battered women revealed a phase in their abusive relationships that the researchers labeled "isolation/shame and harassment/humiliation" (P. N. Clarke, Pendry, & Kim, 1997).

Blaming Alcohol

Most people seem to be looking for someone or something to blame in their attempts to explain wife beating. Violent couples and observers alike are prone to allege that alcohol is the major factor precipitating a violent episode (e.g., Flanzer, 1993). Battered women in particular have clung to the "demon rum" hypothesis (Sapiente, 1988). One explanation for such beliefs is that some abusive men commit more severe and frequent violence when they are intoxicated than when they are sober (Fals-Stewart, 2003). The amount of alcohol consumed during abusive incidents, however, is often minimal. Furthermore, most men who batter when they are drinking also batter when they are not (Bennett, Tolman, Rogalski, & Srinivasaraghavan, 1994). Some evidence suggests that batterers and their victims are more likely to drink after a violent episode than before (Barnett & Fagan, 1993).

In one analysis of arrested spouse abusers in Memphis, 92% had used alcohol or drugs the day of the arrest (Brookoff, 1997). Hirschel and Hutchison (2011) gathered data on 3,078 cases in 25 selected jurisdictions in which police made a service call because of partner violence. Neither the offender nor the victim had been drinking in 59% of the cases. Of the 41%

of the cases where there had been drinking , only the offender was drinking in 23.8% of the cases, both offender and victim were drinking in 12.3%, and only the victim was drinking in 4.9%. Further data analyses revealed that police were more likely to make an arrest when alcohol was present.

Processes of denial and minimization constitute a basis for both batterers and battered women to blame some agent other than the abuser for the aggression (Katz, Arias, Beach, & Roman, 1995). For an alcoholic, getting drunk is the goal. For a spouse abuser, getting drunk is the mechanism; hitting is the goal. Research does not support the notion that batterers are out of control when they assault their partners or that drug-induced disinhibition prompts battering (Bennett et al., 1994). Nonetheless, alcohol and drug use are highly correlated with intimate partner violence, and the role of alcohol in family violence is complex (Greenfeld et al., 1998; Schumacher, Homish, Leonard, Quigley, & Kearns-Bodkin, 2008; Stalans & Ritchie, 2008).

A study of 8,629 adult health maintenance organization members revealed significant problems for children growing up in homes where either or both parents abused alcohol. The data indicated significant correlations among parental alcohol abuse, childhood abuse, child neglect, and household dysfunction. Men who had grown up in homes where both parents abused alcohol had had much greater exposure to male-initiated partner violence (Dube et al., 2001).

Because of the numerous negative alcohol-violence connections, experts often attempt to require offenders to undergo treatment for both violence and alcohol abuse. One group of counselors working with incarcerated males devised a program to treat both conditions simultaneously. The intervention successfully reduced prisoners' scores on anger-related aggression and feelings of effectiveness in controlling drinking (Bowes, McMurran, Williams, David, & Zammit, 2012).

Effects of Captivity

Investigators have pointed to parallels between women in abusive relationships and hostages. Battered women exhibit hostage-like behaviors, such as praising their abuser, denying the battering, and blaming themselves (Mega, Mega, Mega, & Harris, 2000). These behaviors may in actuality represent a struggle for survival ("Abusive Relationships," 1991).

Many victims of violent crimes or impending violence identify with the person or persons who seem to have control over their well-being. As perceived power differences intensify, the person with less authority generally forms a more negative self-appraisal and feels less capable of taking care of himself. Thus, the person with less power becomes more dependent on the person with greater power (Freud, 1942). This phenomenon is called *identification with the aggressor* and becomes manifest in brainwashing and the Stockholm and prisoner of war (POW) syndromes.

The term *brainwashing* came into being during the Korean War when imprisoned American soldiers denounced the United States or supplied information to the enemy. Patty Hearst, a wealthy socialite-turned-bank-robber, provides another alleged example of this phenomenon. People condemned the Korean prisoners of war as traitors, and the courts sent Hearst to prison. It seems that those who sat in judgment went on with their lives believing that the brainwashed were innately weak and completely culpable.

Stockholm Syndrome

One of the most dramatic examples of identification with the aggressor occurred in 1974 in Stockholm, Sweden, during a bank robbery. Three tellers were held hostage for a period of 10 days. For the first few days, the robbers intermittently threatened them, held them at gunpoint, and pushed them around. At first, the robbers also denied food and bathroom privileges to the tellers. After the initial intimidation, a period of normalcy ensued. The robbers-turned-kidnappers were kind to the hostages, letting them go to the bathroom and walk around. Captors and hostages had conversations with each other and began the process of getting acquainted. Think about what you might do to survive in this situation. Forming a bond, becoming a real person to your captors, could save your life.

After 10 days, the ordeal ended with the release of the hostages and the incarceration of the hostage-takers. During the trial, two of the three tellers testified in defense of their assailants. Indeed, one of the tellers married her former captor after he was released from prison. In other rare cases, hostages have been known to post bail or to have emotional relationships with their captors (Strentz, 1979). These seemingly strange occurrences have become known as the Stockholm syndrome (Lang, 1974), and have come to represent a specific combination of emotional responses and behaviors that can occur when someone is held hostage (Kuleshnyk, 1984).

D. L. R. Graham, Rawlings, and Rimini (1988) have successfully applied the Stockholm syndrome to the psychological victimization processes undergone by battered women. There are five hypothesized precursors to the development of the syndrome: (a) perceived threat to one's physical or psychological survival, (b) belief that the captor (abuser) could carry out the threat, (c) perceived kindness of the captor toward the victim, (d) perceived inability to escape, and (e) captor-controlled perceptions (monopolization of the victim's perceptions, resulting from isolation) (D. L. R. Graham, Rawlings, & Rigsby, 1994; Rawlings, Allen, Graham, & Peters, 1994). Threats to survival and isolation are the most powerful antecedents for predicting development of the Stockholm syndrome (Ott, Graham, & Rawlings, 1990; see also Nielsen, Endo, & Ellington, 1992).

D. L. R. Graham and colleagues (1994) have observed that these astonishing types of Stockholm syndrome characteristics are typically found in battered women. The following are a condensation of these aspects: (a) a bond between victim and abuser; (b) intense gratitude for kindnesses shown by the abuser; (c) denial or rationalization of violence and anger toward the abuser; (d) hypervigilance to the abuser's needs; (e) adoption of the abuser's perspective of the world; (f) a view of authorities as "bad guys" and the abuser as a "good guy"; (g) difficulty in leaving the abuser after release from the hostage situation; (h) fear of the abuser's revenge, even if the abuser is dead or in prison; and (i) experiences of PTSD (see also D. L. R. Graham et al., 1995).

The Stockholm syndrome explains the paradoxical behavior of hostages who profess to love their captors. The theory appears to overlap attachment theory in terms of explaining reactions to abuse but differs in terms of the groups of individuals involved. While attachment theory developed from observations of relationships within families (e.g., mother-child, husband-wife, boyfriend-girlfriend), hostage theory developed from observations of captor-hostage relationships (Borochowitz & Eisikovits, 2002).

Traumatic Bonding

Some features of imbalanced relationships resemble the experiences of captivity. In all cases, the maltreated person is dominated by the other person and abuse is intermittent. D. Dutton and Painter (1981) termed the process of forming strong emotional ties in a relationship where one person intermittently abuses, harasses, threatens, beats, or intimidates the other *traumatic bonding*. Researchers have increasingly expanded and applied attachment theory to help explain the behavior of individuals involved in abusive relationships. One important aspect of attachment formulations is that they help clarify the finding that love and violence do not seem to be opposite forces as one might expect, but may coexist (e.g., D. Dutton & Painter, 1993b; Kesner, Julian, & McKenry, 1997).

Case Study: Jane and Lewis

Jane and her husband, Lewis, have been married for nine years. Both are professionals working in the same field. They share many of the same interests, own a home together, are involved with their families, participate in the same organizations, and share an abusive relationship.

Lewis is a soft-spoken and shy man. Rage doesn't appear to fit him well; it is confusing. His temper tantrums are usually verbal. He rants, he raves, he threatens and demeans. Sporadically, there is an accompanying physical outburst.

Over time, Lewis's verbal outbursts have diminished Jane's sense of self-worth. Some of the attacks were subtle: questioning her decision making at work, wondering if this or that person really liked her, commenting on the quality of her performance, and then jumping to her defense if her family insulted her or her boss didn't appreciate her. Lewis was concurrently Jane's best friend and her worst critic.

Jane became focused on obtaining Lewis's approval and emotional support. She poured her emotional energy into analyzing their relationship, leaving her with little energy to maintain other emotional attachments. Her job performance nosedived and she questioned her abilities—even her ability to contribute to her profession. As her self-confidence waned, her conduct as a friend, family member, coworker, and wife suffered. The feedback she received began to support her diminished self-approval, but Lewis remained steadfast, her loyal friend and her avowed enemy.

Currently, Jane's emotional dependence on the relationship has increased. She supports her own negative self-view with quotes from her husband. She fears that without Lewis, she is nothing. She has been brainwashed.

Treblinka

In Steiner's (1966) book *Treblinka*, he describes the victimization of inmates existing in the extermination camp. He asks and tries to answer a number of questions: (a) How do inmates in a death camp stay alive at all? (b) What did living under such conditions do to their souls and to their sense of themselves as humans? (c) Why did they go on when it was easier to die?

At Treblinka, the commanding officers of the SS (an armed unit of the Nazi party in Germany) morally disarmed the camp inhabitants by creating an environment replete with panic and uncertainty. Moral disarmament forces a victim to make minor concessions that lead to others, and eventually leads to humiliation, self-hatred, and submission. The strategy was to make victims accomplices in their own victimization.

The SS removed vestiges of humanity by dividing families and removing social life. The notion of time and space were lost. The commandant of Treblinka committed random acts of violence, including verbal threats, beatings, and executions. This intermittent punishment caused fear and helplessness. The unpredictability of his attacks made his authority seem mystical. Prisoners felt the exaggerated presence of a permanent menace. With a gun and a few guards, the SS controlled 600 captives and created a psychosis of fear.

Case Study: Melinda and Jason

As the headlights made a path into the driveway, the three children and their mother in the house stopped laughing. By the time the key turned and the door was pushed open, the children were quietly doing their homework and Melinda was ladling soup into bowls. As Jason came in the front door and went upstairs, he didn't say anything except "Hi." No one could read his mood. The atmosphere screamed with tension, but the house was silent.

The older boy was afraid that Dad had had a bad day; he worried about what would happen when Dad found out that his report card wasn't good. The younger boy sat in a corner and tried to make himself invisible. The little girl was afraid that Dad could read her mind and would know that she hated him. She knew that he would hurt her when he figured out what she was thinking.

Melinda didn't do much outside of the home. It was almost as if HE knew when she saw family or friends during the day. She wondered if he had friends around who told on her, because his anger seemed to intensify in direct proportion to her happiness. Two weeks before, he had chased the boys around the house, screaming about the need for discipline, and had finally beaten them with a belt. She had used to intervene, but it never worked; she could not even protect herself, much less the children. She felt confused, paralyzed, and disoriented.

Jason came down to dinner. His mood seemed calm. He began to talk. Everyone listened. After a while, the whole group was talking and more relaxed. They eased into laughter, but they wondered when everything would change. Mom never quite joined in. Her eyes were a little dull. You never saw much excitement or change of emotion from Mom. In time, the four prisoners finished their meals and went to bed.

Until someone is physically abused, they could never know: the humiliation—the damage that is done to your self-respect. To become diminished—to feel less than a human being. To be debased—to be lowered in character, dignity, and value. Emotional scars that never heal.

—Hearing transcript (cited in Nerney, 1987, p. 9)

As a battering relationship continues, there is an exaggerated belief on the part of a battered woman that her batterer is omnipresent. She becomes less able to see the connection between her behavior and the nature or rationale behind her batterer's aggression. Although his violence may occur randomly, the odds are better than 600 to 1 that she will be the target of his abuse (see also Kandel-Englander, 1992).

Forced Institutionalization

Examination of data gathered from battered women living in an Israeli shelter convinced Avni (1991) to apply the concept of institutionalization to circumstances in a battering relationship. Her deduction rested on several comparisons:

1. In an institution, staff make all the rules and punish noncompliance. In the home, the batterer makes all the rules and punishes noncompliance.

2. In an institution, inmates suffer from constant exposure to the staff. In the violent home, the battered woman suffers from constant exposure to her husband's surveillance.

3. In an institution, mortification of the self occurs by such procedures as strip searches and shaving the head. In the violent home, mortification occurs as a result of the husband's suspicion and humiliating attacks.

Battered women in Avni's study said they felt like prisoners. Indeed, a number of the women reported having been locked in their homes. In one case, a spouse plastered the door shut before he left for work. In another, a batterer locked his wife inside the house, even though she was nine months pregnant. The isolation experienced by these women led to greater dependence on their abusers. The suspicious climate in their homes led to hypervigilance and, for at least one woman who was repeatedly interrogated about alleged infidelity, total self-doubt about her sanity: "Maybe I really did it without being aware of it. I was going crazy" (p. 145).

Case Study: Sandy and Jim

Jim: My wife, Sandy, is a teacher and I'm self-employed. I don't fit in with her friends at work and I don't like to go to her parties. One night, I let her go with a friend and I'll never do that again. Two guys took their clothes off and jumped into a hot tub. They were drunk and acting crazy. When my wife told me what happened, I went off. I threw her against the wall and grilled her about what she did. Then I beat her up like she was a man. I don't tolerate infidelity. I've only had sex with prostitutes, never an affair.

Sandy: Jim never trusts me. He thinks I'm flirting with everyone and that I dress up for other men. I was surprised when he said I could go to the party and relieved at his attitude. Sometimes he literally questions me for hours. It feels like a police interrogation. Sometimes I wonder if he's right. Am I trying to attract other men? When he beat me up after the party, I wondered what I had done to encourage these guys to strip and jump into the hot tub.

Conformity and Obedience

Syndromes do not describe the behavior of all individuals subjected to terror or captivity, but they do portray what happens for most. Even under circumstances less catastrophic than life at Treblinka or institutionalization, individuals exhibit a propensity to conform to authority. In one of the most influential studies ever conducted by a psychologist, Stanley Milgram (1963) explored the extent to which people will obey an authority figure. Before conducting his research, Milgram asked psychiatrists to predict the percentage of individuals who would shock another person simply at the request of an authority figure. Psychiatrists estimated an obedience rate under 1%.

In this experiment, the investigator requested the teacher-subjects to shock learner-subjects whenever they made a mistake in a verbal learning experiment, and to increase the shock level with every successive error. (Unknown to the teacher-subjects, the shocks were not real; they did not occur.) The experiment was designed so that the learner, who was sitting behind a screen out of sight, appeared to cry out in pain and to beg the teacher to stop. Most teachers stopped at the request of the learner and informed the experimenter that they did not wish to continue. Amazingly, however, the experimenter had only to issue a directive phrase, such as "You have no other choice" or "The experiment must go on," to encourage them to continue. Every teacher conformed to some degree. The unexpected result was that 65% of the participants were willing to administer shocks at a level marked "dangerous" to obviously suffering human subjects.

The outcome of this research was so startling that other scientists tended to doubt its authenticity. Replications, however, demonstrated its validity. For example, Hofling, Brotzman, Dalrymple, Graves, and Pierce (1966) devised a real-life experiment in which a doctor unfamiliar to a nurse ordered her to give an extremely large dose of an unusual medicine to a hospitalized patient without the required written prescription. Even though the doctor ordered administration of an amount of medicine that was twice the maximum dosage printed on the label, 95% of the nurses tried to obey the order before being interrupted by a confederate of the experimenter (see also L. Sanders, 2011).

Summary

Women entering relationships that eventually become abusive do not appear to differ from their nonbattered counterparts in terms of demographic variables and most other psychological attributes. Evidence has accumulated over the years, however, that battered women, as a group, have been exposed to more childhood abuse than have nonbattered women. Battered women also suffer from victimization-linked PTSD and low self-esteem. Society is nonetheless inclined to place the blame on them rather than on the perpetrators, where it belongs. These proclivities, along with a batterer's tendency to manipulate his partner's feelings, add to the probability that a battered woman will blame herself for being beaten or for her failure to escape.

Victimization is a profoundly negative experience with long-lasting effects. Phenomena like the Stockholm syndrome and the events at Treblinka demonstrate how individuals who are seemingly normal can become psychologically entrapped. An extrapolation of these processes to battering relationships helps clarify a battered woman's emotional quandary. Compliance with the demands of individuals in positions of authority is well understood by anyone with a parent or boss, or who has suffered past consequences. Although conformity is an everyday occurrence, the effects of conformity, as evidenced by Milgram's research, are no less significant than the behaviors resulting from captivity. Conformity experiments reflect these dramatic effects on people in general and on battered women in particular. Given the nature of victim-blame and the victimization process, becoming trapped in a battering relationship "could happen to anyone."

4

Living With Fear

The Force That Holds, Molds, and Controls

Case Study: 911

Woman: I'm Robin Prunty calling on Donald Prunty. I'm at work at Smitty's and he's stalking the parking lot at Smitty's. He's supposed to be wanted in Chandler, and they haven't picked him up yet, and he's breaking the order. I have an order of protection.

Dispatcher: You said your name is Donna?

Woman: My name is Robin Prunty, P-R-U-N-T-Y.

Dispatcher: Has he already been served?

Woman: Yes he has. It's been a good month now.

[Pause: 16 seconds of confusion, muffled sound]

Dispatcher: Is he there shooting?

Woman: I'm supposed to be safe . . . Oh my God.

Man's voice: Get over here, get up, get up right now. C'mere. C'mon out here.

[Loud bang]

Dispatcher: I think there's a shooting going on . . .

—"I'm Supposed to be Safe," *Tribune Newspapers of Arizona*, 1992, p. A6

Robin's call was the prelude to a shooting spree. Her estranged husband burst into the coffee shop where she worked. Before he shot himself, he killed Robin's pregnant friend, who had given her refuge, and a stranger who was having his morning coffee. Robin was seriously wounded but survived.

Fear, both emotional and physical, is a significant feature in battering families. Its functions include control and entrapment. A discussion of male-to-female injury and homicide clarifies the tangible nature of men's threats of aggression. Laboratory research, clinical impressions, and case studies substantiate the development of fear as a learned response. Denial and minimization are consequences of escalating fear that allow a woman to remain in her violent home and make it difficult to see the forest for the trees. Gender dissimilarities in the motivations for aggression as well as the experience of fear provide a context for understanding why she stays. The pervasive nature of fear affects not only the family who experiences it, but also those involved peripherally.

Recognizing Marital Violence

To a certain extent, violence is in the eye of the beholder. For example, Sedlak's (1988) study demonstrated that perceptions of intimate abuse depended on the nature of the observer's own personal history with aggression. Both male and female subjects who had experienced violence in their own relationships did not recognize battering in the test cases. Perpetrators are prone to describe their own violent behavior as comprehensible and as isolated events, while victims portray the perpetrator's behavior as arbitrary, incomprehensible, and as the last in a series of provocations (Baumeister, Stillwell, & Wotman, 1990). Males may be more likely than females to perceive aggression as mutual (Laner & Thompson, 1982). Laner (1990) noted that students seem to believe that becoming jealous, upset, and subsequently violent is not unusual in dating relationships (see also the website of the National Center for Victims of Crime, www.ncvc.org). Similarly, society has generally regarded hitting a spouse as acceptable and a private matter, even though the same actions perpetrated by strangers would be termed violent if not criminal (Levesque, 2001). "If you are afraid, then whether it is a tickle or a smack, it's abusive. If you are afraid that you are going to be hurt, that's abuse" (battered woman cited in E. Klein, Campbell, Soler, & Ghez, 1997, p. 55).

The Subjective and Objective Nature of Fear

Fear is a powerful element in producing behaviors that are characteristic of victims in general and battered women survivors in particular. Fear is also the most common response to dating violence in women, with emotional hurt ranked second (O'Keefe & Treister, 1998). Safety issues are a primary concern for both battered women and the individuals who work with them. In a 1998 study of calls to the National Domestic Violence Hotline, telephone operators and advocates tallied comments and requests. Over half of the callers cited "apprehension about retaliation" as their principal reason for remaining with an abusive partner (Danis, Lewis, Trapp, Reid, & Fisher, 1998; see also Alsaker, Kristoffersen, Moen, & Baste, 2011; Jacobson, Gottman, Gortner, Berns, & Shortt, 1996).

The survey findings of 43 battered women by Barnett and Lopez-Real (1985) were congruent with those from the hotline calls. Fear, specifically "fear of revenge," was the second most frequently given reason by women for remaining in their violent relationships. ("Hoped partner would change" was the first.) Women in this study listed some of the following concerns:

"He kept seeking me out and finding me."

"I felt other people would die if I left."

"He was suicidal; I feared he would come after me."

"I have left and still have trouble getting out from under abuse and fears and threats. My ex-partner is continuing abuse any way he can. I now see why it truly is hard to get out and why it took me so long."

"I remember feeling many times afraid to go and afraid to stay. That very real fear of revenge is so powerful a deterrent to doing anything constructive."

"I think that police protection should be questioned a lot."

Painter and Dutton (1985) believe that a combination of hope and fear entraps battered women. Attachment to an abusive mate, reinforced by socialization, produces a very powerful connection described as traumatic bonding (D. Dutton & Painter, 1993b). There is a significant link between an abused woman's style of attachment to her batterer and her ability to leave (D. Dutton & Haring, 1999; Henderson, Bartholomew, & Dutton, 1997). For instance, if a woman believes that she is not a good person but her partner is wonderful (preoccupied attachment), she is inclined to separate from and return to the relationship very frequently. Furthermore, she maintains her emotional involvement with her abuser even after leaving (see also Vazquez, 1996). Conversely, a batterer's attachment style to his adult partner can make it impossible for him to let her leave (D. Dutton, Saunders, Starzomski, & Bartholomew, 1994).

Case Study: Betty and Henry

Betty and Henry were married and had a 14-month-old daughter, Melissa. Henry was self-employed but unmotivated. He was also possessive, controlling, and insecure. When Betty's independence got the better of him, he became abusive. Betty had gone to work on numerous occasions with bruises on her face and arms. For the most part, nobody talked about what was happening. (It is often easiest for friends and family to deny abuse, to minimize the severity of discord, and to ignore evidence.)

Betty's friends and financial security were a threat to Henry. He became more controlling, and he threatened to kill her if she tried to leave. His obsession culminated in Betty's two-week confinement. He stayed at home to watch her. Eventually, he needed money and took her to the bank to make a withdrawal from her savings account. While they were at the bank, personnel helped Betty to escape and find refuge at a local battered women's shelter.

Henry threatened to sue Betty for custody of the baby unless he was allowed to visit her. A third-party visitation was set up by the shelter through her attorney. No one at the shelter felt good about this arrangement, but everyone felt compelled to go ahead with the plan because of the legal ramifications of noncompliance. Betty and the baby were to go to her attorney's office accompanied by a male friend of Betty's (the father of one of her friends). While they were in the parking lot, Henry grabbed the baby and told Betty to get into his car or she would never see Melissa again.

Betty's body was not discovered for several months. Henry was charged with murder. He had taken Betty to an isolated spot in the desert, where he beat and shot her. Melissa was in the car while her mother was fighting for her life. Her body had to be identified through dental records.

At Henry's trial, one of his previous wives admitted to the abuse she had experienced at his hands. She was still afraid of him. Henry was eventually convicted of second-degree murder. Betty's last words to one of the authors (A. L.) as she left to meet Henry were, "If I don't come back, it is because he killed me."

Battered women in the Barnett and Lopez-Real (1985) study reported that in addition to being physically assaulted, they had been threatened. Of the 43 women in the study, 41 reported that their husbands had threatened to kill or injure them. The men had also threatened to harm other family members and coworkers, take the children, destroy property, or take all the money (see also Pearson, Thoennes, & Griswold, 1999).

In a subsequent study, Barnett (1990) analyzed the responses of 87 men who confessed to intimidating their wives. Relative to comparison groups of nonviolent men who were either happily or unhappily married, the abusive men more often threatened their wives with various actions: (a) to destroy property, (b) to hurt a child, (c) to lock their wives in or out of the house or room, (d) to take all the money in the house, (e) to leave their wives, (f) to hurt or kill their wives, and (g) to kill themselves (see also Barnett, Lee, & Thelen, 1997).

It is commonplace to hear battering men talk about their behavior as occurring in the past. Over the course of the relationship, most men expect their partners to ignore the threats and not to take them seriously. Abusive men also expect their wives to believe that they will never really hurt them, that they will know when to stop. For the victims, in contrast, threats can engender terror and have a long-term effect (Lindgren & Renck, 2008). Not only do battered women feel fearful, but extended family members and acquaintances of battered women also express fear. So strong is their fear that they may refuse to interact with the battered woman (Riger, Raja, & Camacho, 2002).

Strong differences in perceptions of fear emerged in a review of experiences related to sexual aggression. While women reported significantly higher levels of intimidation, men were unaware of or unconvinced by these reactions. They either ignored or discounted women's fear (Tinsley, Critelli, & Ee, 1992). Research has left no doubt that female partner abuse victims experience more fear than males do (Cercone-Keeney, Beach, & Arias, 2005; Melton & Belknap, 2003; see also Lovik, 2011b).

Case Study: Jack

Jack was mandated to an abuser's program because he had made terrorist threats to his ex-wife. Jack was a former officer in the special forces. He had been trained to use force, even lethal force when the situation called for it. When he called his ex-wife and told her that unless he saw his son, he'd take her on a one-way trip to Mexico in the trunk of his car, she believed him.

Jack, on the other hand, did not believe her. He thought his ex-wife was exaggerating her fright. He hadn't ever hit her. He thought the therapist was overreacting when she said she understood his ex-wife's terror. He minimized and denied the intent and the outcome of his threat.

After the session, two of the biggest and most volatile men in the group came to the therapist and expressed their apprehension regarding Jack's future behavior: "We think that guy will come back to group next week and shoot all of us. He's one of those quiet, dangerous guys." The therapist encouraged the two men to confront Jack the following week, and they did. It was the first time that he believed his ex-wife could really be afraid.

In battering relationships, it seems as if nothing is really left in the past. The past keeps happening over and over again. Despite the promises of change, change rarely happens, and if it does, it does not seem to last. Moreover, leaving and safety are not synonymous. Many abusive men will continue to harass and intimidate their partners even after they leave. They stalk their ex-partners (Basile, Swahn, Chen, & Saltzman, 2006). Research has also focused on the serious nature of stalking, including its consequences, such as forcing a victim to change her residence (e.g., Baum, Catalano, Rand, & Rose, 2009; Spitzberg, 2002) or actual killing of the victim (McFarlane, Campbell, & Watson, 2002). Batterers now use electronic technology to stalk their victims and may even convince their friends to help them (e.g., Barak, 2005; Southworth, Finn, Dawson, Fraser, & Tucker, 2007; see also Heyman & Slep, 2006)!

Many women experience violence as they attempt to separate or divorce (Block, 2003; Toews, McHenry, & Catless, 2003; see also Rand, 2009). In 1992, the victimization rate of women separated from their husbands was about 3 times higher than that of divorced women and about 25 times higher than that of married women (Bachman & Saltzman, 1995; see also Bossarte, Simon, & Barker, 2006; L. P. Sheridan, Gillett, Blaauw, Davies, & Patel, 2003). One study revealed that 55% of wives who had been raped were no longer living with their husbands (Hanneke, Shields, & McCall, 1986). Family, friends, and associates almost uniformly advise battered women to just leave, as if leaving will afford them safety. Such well-meaning advice, however, can be fatal (DeKeseredy, Schwartz, Fagan, & Hall, 2006).

An in-depth analysis of 57 women killed by their male partners indicated that 43 (75%) of the women were separated or trying to terminate their relationships at the time the murder occurred (cited in New York Commission, 1998). An examination of 119 women killed in North Carolina between 1988 and 1992 determined that current or former male partners had killed 99 of them and then killed themselves. In 29% of the murder-suicides, there was documentation of prior domestic violence. The impetus for 41% of these murders was victim separation from the perpetrator (Morton, Runyan, Moracco, & Butts, 1998). For some abusers, "till death do us part" is taken quite literally.

It is common to hear threats made by men who either do not follow through with them or follow through at a lesser level. No one really knows, however, whether a violent partner will make good on his threats (Langford, 1996). Efforts to predict dangerousness, while improving in their validity, are never 100% accurate (J. C. Campbell, 2005; Foran & O'Leary, 2008; Hilton, Harris, Rice, Houghton, & Eke, 2008). Battered women's ability to predict their male partners' violence is often more accurate than researchers'

Case Study: Rosa and Poncho

Leaving Poncho became the most dangerous action Rosa could take. Her husband had threatened to hunt her down if she ever left. He told her repeatedly that no other man could ever have her and that if she ever left he would kill her or "mess up her face so that no man would ever look at her again." He also threatened to kidnap the children if she did not stay.

Rosa knew that he was not making idle threats. The judge awarded him visitation, and he was always able to find her. Rosa reasoned that if she stayed, she would at least know what he was doing and have some control over what would happen. Her paranoia was really an accurate perception of reality.

statistical predictions (Heckert & Gondolf, 2004; Langford, 1996). On the other hand, a survey revealed that one in five women murdered or severely injured by intimate partners had no previous warning (Block, 2003).

Learning to Fear

Fear is a powerful emotion capable of creating behavioral and psychological change. To clarify how emotions such as fear are learned, Watson and Raynor (1920) applied Pavlov's conditioning procedure to an infant named Baby Albert. (The mental health of Albert's parents remains questionable at best, since they consented to this research.) Watson showed Albert a white rat (that Albert had previously liked and did not fear) and then made a loud sound behind the baby's head. After Watson repeated the process a number of times, Baby Albert began to cry and act startled whenever he saw the white rat, whether or not the sound occurred. It did not take long for Albert to demonstrate a fear response. Albert had learned to anticipate a noxious event when he caught sight of the rat, and the anticipation created fear. Classical conditioning can scientifically explain learning to fear (Mineka & Zinbard, 2006; see also Lindgren & Renck, 2008). (See Appendix E.2 for an explanation of classical conditioning.)

Advances in the neurological sciences and brain imaging processes (e.g., positron emission tomography [PET] scans) have revealed a wealth of new information about emotional learning. One section of the brain (the amygdala) is highly involved during fear conditioning (Poulos et al., 2009). Changes in this area of the brain are enduring and offer an explanation for repeated responses to specific stimuli and recurrence of trauma symptoms (Killcross, Robbins, & Everitt, 1997; Rausch, van der Kolk, Fisler, & Alpert, 1996). Nearly all studies indicate that men and women experience fear as a response to interpersonal violence very differently (Barnett et al., 1997; Cercone-Keeney et al., 2005).

Hamberger and Guse (2002) studied men and women who were arrested for domestic violence. The men in their sample were more likely than the women to be amused by their partner's aggression. In contrast, the women were more likely to call the police and to feel angry, insulted, and afraid. Such gender differences in fear reactions are concrete and consistent across a number of investigations (e.g., Kleim, Wilhelm, Glucksman, & Ehlers, 2010; Phelan et al., 2005). Men and women not only experience fear somewhat differently, but they also tend to be afraid of different things (Rabasca, 1999). For instance, a man walking alone down an empty street at night might not experience fear at the sight of three unarmed women walking toward him (unless they are Mary Kay Commandos). The reverse is most likely not true.

Previous research has found that, in general, women do not inspire fear in men as men do in women (Hamberger, 2005; Langhinrichsen-Rohling, Neidig, & Thorn, 1995). Swan and Snow (2002) studied 108 primarily African American, low-income, inner-city women who had used violence against a male partner. Women in this sample used equivalent levels of emotional abuse and more moderate levels of physical abuse. They were also, however, victims of more serious types of violence (sexual, injurious, coercively controlling abuse) than their male partners. According to Swan and Snow, women can be jealous and controlling but do not often have the ability to maintain significant control of a man's behavior. This type of control is maintained by and is a direct byproduct of fear.

Society readily acknowledges the reality of women's greater vulnerability to victimization and socializes girls to take self-protective measures (Stanko, 1988). Most women experience a chronic low-level apprehension about being victimized (see Kury & Ferdinand, 1997; May, Rader, & Goodrum, 2010). An analysis of 37 professional women recognized that women routinely take a number of precautions to protect themselves. Respondents reported walking to their cars with someone else whenever possible, keeping their keys between their fingers, and carefully checking the back seat of their cars before they get in. Half of the women had taken self-defense classes, and over three-quarters had mentally planned rape prevention strategies.

Theoretical explanations of avoidance behavior have brought further attention to the role that environmental cues play in maintaining fear. Rats learned to fear the tones that were followed by shock. Later, when these rats were able to eliminate these tones by escaping (running away), they learned to escape much faster than rats that had not learned to fear the tones. (See Appendix F.2 and F.14 for reviews of approach-avoidance behavior.) In fact, getting rid of the fear cues was very rewarding to the animals (J. S. Brown & Jacobs, 1949). A critical problem faced by battered women is that they often cannot leave the scene with its fear cues after a traumatic incident. As long as the batterer is nearby, his presence can produce fear. Over time, fear reactions can become chronic (Clemmons, Walsh, DiLillo, & Messman-Moore, 2007; Follette, Polusny, Bechtle, & Naugle, 1996).

Abused women are even more afraid than other women (M. N. Russell, Lipov, Phillips, & White, 1989). Battered women learn that their spouses may be quiescent for a time (like the Kilauea volcano), but sooner or later there will be an eruption. For women caught in a battering cycle, there is a nonviolent time, but not necessarily a time of feeling safe. Battered women learn to anticipate abuse (i.e., punishment), much as the subject of experimental conditioning learns to anticipate shock. The implied construct in both situations is fear (Healey, 1995; Wirtz & Harrell, 1987).

Several important factors become apparent given the content, quality, and quantity of violence-elicited fear in most battering relationships. First and foremost, there is the apprehension about another beating. Aversive cues such as yelling, breaking things, and particular facial expressions can precede a fight. Even though a physical assault is less common, the possibility is always present (Langford, 1996). Although a batterer may believe that his mate should feel safe because he says he "won't really hurt her," she does not.

Emotional/Psychological Abuse

Psychological abuse can stand alone as a stimulus that induces fear. Newer research is beginning to show that psychological abuse generates fear even more definitively than physical abuse (Arias & Pape, 1999). Despite several commentaries on the extreme harm caused by psychological abuse (e.g., Follingstad, Rutledge, Berg, Hause, & Polek, 1990; L. L. Marshall, 1992b), society tends to denigrate its significance in comparison with physical abuse. Instead, society has legally channeled (probably reasonably) its efforts in responding toward coping with physical abuse (O'Leary, 1999).

Definitions of psychological abuse are emerging in recognition of its significance in creating an environment characterized by fear; for example, "acts of recurring criticism and/or verbal aggression toward a partner, and/or acts of isolation and domination of a partner" (O'Leary, 1999, p. 19). Psychological and emotional abuse are extremely common, and they exact a higher toll on women than men (Vivian & Langhinrichsen-Rohling, 1994). A review of empirical evidence ascertained that psychological abuse increases depression, lowers self-esteem, and nearly always precedes physical aggression (see O'Leary, 1999). Newer evidence from brain studies shows that emotional pain can stimulate the same circuits in the brain as physical pain (Eisenberger, 2012).

Case Study: Becky and Arnie

Becky: He used to smile at me in this funny kind of way when he was really angry, and then all hell would break loose. I still get scared when I see that smile, and I stop whatever I am doing.

Arnie: I'd go home and he'd be quiet. It was a very loud quiet. I'd always say, "Are you okay? Is anything wrong?" He'd always say everything was okay, but I knew I was in trouble. Sometimes the quiet would last a while—two, three days, a week. And sometimes it would end quickly with an ugly remark or yelling or worse. But that quiet was like the "quiet before the storm," a signal telling me I had been bad and would be punished.

Cues associated with an assault become conditioned (discriminative) stimuli that bring about terror when encountered again. Learned fear has a way of mushrooming and spreading into new areas (generalization). Since stimulus generalization occurs, events that are similar to the punished situations may come to trigger a negative anticipation. As a result, cues that seem totally nonthreatening to most people may come to elicit self-defensive responses in battered women. When safety depends on reading significant cues accurately, people become speed readers.

Back to Baby Albert: After he became permanently traumatized by the sight of the white rat, similar objects such as a fur coat or Santa Claus's beard also evoked a fear reaction. Baby Albert had learned to generalize (Watson & Raynor, 1920).

Case Study: Cheryl

Cheryl didn't risk much anymore. She knew that her husband got angry when she visited friends and family. She knew he didn't like her to change plans. She also knew that even though he said she was crazy, he wouldn't like her going to therapy for help.

Cheryl visited her family sometimes, and she took one night class, but her misgivings about his response restricted her activities. She was afraid to make new friends, to get a job, or to go out after class with other students. Her fear had generalized to almost everything.

Even though her husband told her she needed a shrink, she was afraid to contact a counselor. Cheryl's sister called a therapist specializing in spouse abuse and drove Cheryl to her first few appointments. Cheryl was never able to tell her husband that she was going to therapy, and she paid for it in cash so that her check register could not give her away.

Punishment Effects and Fear

The effects of abuse (i.e., a type of punishment) on battered women are quite variable. Several investigators have found a relationship between severity of abuse and the decision to leave. According to many researchers, women who returned to their violent mates were those who reported less intense violence than women who did not return (Gondolf, 1988a; Lawrence & Bradbury, 2001). A review of data from 293 shelter residents, however, contradicted these findings. The more severe a woman's injuries were, the longer she remained in the relationship. This was true even though the severity, frequency, and degree of pain suffered from the beatings increased over the duration of the relationship (Pagelow, 1981a). Finally, Schwartz's (1988) results did not agree with any of the others. He found that tolerance for injury in married, divorced, or separated women varied individually and was unrelated to women's decisions to stay or leave (see also Panchanadeswaran & McCloskey, 2007).

Some people think that leaving is easy and that abused women must like to be hit or they would leave. There is no indication that abused women enjoy a good beating. There was nothing about laboratory experiments that indicated that animals liked to be punished in order to obtain food. They just liked to eat! (See Appendix E.2 and Appendix F.3 for relevant experiments.)

Laboratory research can provide a model for understanding learned responses brought on by aggression. Violence in an abusive home can be seen as comparable to punishment in a Skinner box (Skinner, 1938). (See Appendix E.2 for a description of operant conditioning in the Skinner box.) Punishment is the presentation of an event that reduces (suppresses) responses. Commonly used punishments are shocks for animals or spankings for children. Experiments demonstrate that a number of variables, such as intensity and timing of punishers, modify their effectiveness. Severe punishment can function to greatly suppress behavior. (See Appendix E.4 for explanations about the effects of punishment on behavior.) Furthermore, later research has shown that punishment negatively alters the psychobiology of the brain (Watts-English, Fortson, Gibler, Hooper, & De Bellis, 2006). The following case history illustrates the long-term effects of intense punishment.

Punishment variables other than intensity also affect battered women's decision making. Findings on the effects of intermittent punishment and punishment plus reinforcement (i.e., rewards) form a foundation to explain battered women's persistence in their relationships (see Azrin, Holz, & Hake, 1963; Long & McNamara, 1989). Interpreting battering followed by contrition as equivalent to punishment followed by reinforcement suggests

Case Study: Julie and Mickey

Julie and Mickey were high school sweethearts. He was a popular football star. Although Julie also was well liked, she thought she was lucky to have Mickey. They married because she became pregnant. Julie believed her love would mold Mickey into the perfect husband.

He did not hit her until after they married. Julie says she will never forget the incident: "He balled up his fist and hit me in the mouth. My lip and chin opened up and there was blood all over my face. I remember seeing stars and thinking, 'This is what happens to Popeye in the cartoons.' I went numb. You never forget it when someone hits you that hard, and you never have to be hit that hard again to continue to be afraid. In fact, I don't think he ever hit me that hard again. But in the following years that we were together, I was always afraid that he would, and it kept me in line."

that the cyclical nature of battering actually increases the female partner's love and dependency.

The battering cycle in conjunction with imbalances in marital power bond the woman to her abuser, diminishing her resolve to leave (i.e., traumatic bonding) (D. Dutton & Painter, 1981). The effects of traumatic bonding are resistant to change (D. Dutton & Painter, 1993b). (See Dinsmoor [1952] and Holz and Azrin [1961] in Appendix F.3, Rosenblum and Harlow [1963] in Appendix F.4, and Azrin et al. [1963] in Appendix F.5.)

Animal research has established that the gradual escalation of punishment leads to continued responses rather than to suppression. Along the same lines, an initial intense shock followed by shocks of decreasing intensity will continue to suppress behavior (Sandler, Davidson, Greene, & Holzschuh, 1966). (See Appendix F.6 for a summary of this experiment.) Extrapolation of these findings to humans suggests that battered women subjected to escalation of abuse will adapt and remain in the relationship.

The significance of a gradual buildup of violence came to light primarily from anecdotal reports offered by shelter workers and Walker's (1979) Cycle of Violence theory. While scientific evidence supporting a pattern of escalating abuse has frequently been found, this pattern is not inevitable (Aldarondo, 1996; Keilitz, Davis, Eikeman, Flango, & Hannaford, 1998; Rand & Saltzman, 2003; Walker, 1979). Other patterns have occurred (see Aldarondo, 1996; D. Dutton, 1998; Follingstad, Hause, Rutledge, & Polek, 1992). Differences in the research participants tested and data collection methods employed may have caused these disparities.

There are, however, other credible interpretations for the inconsistent findings: (a) severe abuse early in a relationship may make later abuse unnecessary to obtain the same effects (see Church, 1969; Larkin & Popaleni, 1994); (b) abuse is triggered sporadically by factors such as unemployment and stress (Margolin, John, & Foo, 1998); (c) survivors have perfected their denial and minimization (D. L. R. Graham, Rawlings, & Rimini, 1988); and (d) escalation may characterize one pattern of abusive relationships while not precluding others (Aldarondo, 1996).

Another likely supposition is that the batterer is also affected by the gradual escalation of so-called punishment directed back at him (the battered woman's reactions to his abuse). The responsive punishments that he receives for his violent behavior probably also start out mildly. Her initial reaction to his abuse may include anger, shock, and withdrawal. Over time, she may add depression, silent suffering, her own angry outbursts, and leaving temporarily. Her behavior will probably occur along a continuum of increasing intensity over a period of time. With gradual, subtle changes in his aggression and her response, adjustments and adaptations in thinking occur. (See Appendix F.6 for an explanatory animal study by Sandler et al., 1966.) Battering couples stop believing each other. They begin to accept as fact that he is not going to stop and she is not going to leave.

Violent couples tend to think of the aggression in their relationship as an aberration and the noncrisis period as the norm and true state of their marriage (H. Douglas, 1991). The gradual buildup of intermittent punishment allows the partners (and children) in a violent family the opportunity to recuperate. With subtle adjustments, individuals may change their standards for judging the violence. What they previously thought of as severe punishment may now seem mild. The once severe punishment may become the new baseline.

Case Study: Kathy

"The first time I heard him say he felt like cutting my heart out with a knife, I was stunned. Nobody had ever said anything like that to me before. I had never been threatened before this relationship. I guess it just stopped meaning anything after I heard it over and over. It fell into the category of 'That's just the way he talks,' and then he beat me up. As I look back on it, the physical threats should have taken on new meaning, a greater significance, but they didn't. I couldn't sort it out or make sense of it. It was just one more thing."

The Nature of Gender Violence

The role gender plays in intimate violence has fueled a passionate controversy within the field of domestic violence. The primary point of debate revolves around the apparent mutuality of marital violence (i.e., comparable frequency rates) obtained with research based on the Conflict Tactics Scales (CTS) (M. A. Straus, 1979). The results of surveys of aggression using the CTS revealed that both men and women admit to initiating violent acts, including slapping, pushing, grabbing, kicking, and punching, at corresponding rates (M. A. Straus & Gelles, 1990). "The number of assaults by itself, however, ignores the context, meaning, and consequences of those assaults. The fact that women produce less injury than men is a critical difference" (M. A. Straus, 1991a, p. 11).

It is interesting to note that canvasses of the public using scales other than the CTS (i.e., the National Crime Victimization Survey or the National Survey of Families and Households), as well as one using a modified CTS (the National Violence Against Women Survey), have not exhibited gender equivalence (Bachman & Saltzman, 1995; Tjaden & Thoennes, 1998a; Zlotnick, Kohn, Peterson, & Pearlstein, 1998). Further disparities in findings have originated from research conducted in shelters, emergency rooms, and police departments. Frequency data provided by women in these settings diverge dramatically from responses of women in the general population. Family violence experts have ordinarily attributed these inconsistencies to the vast variations among the samples of women interviewed and to variations in the methods of collecting data (see Koss et al., 1994; M. A. Straus, 1993).

Against the historical backdrop of male privilege, a number of experts, most women, and women's advocates in particular perceive women to be the true victims of marital violence (see R. P. Dobash, Dobash, Wilson, & Daly, 1992; Seamans, Rubin, & Stabb, 2007). Conversely, some experts, some men, and most batterers assign a much more culpable role to women's actions in domestic violence (Graham-Kevan & Archer, 2005; M. A. Straus, 1997). Steinmetz's 1977 postulation of a "battered husband syndrome" in particular rankled feminists and helped spark a backlash, leading to articles such as "The Myth of Sexual Symmetry in Marital Violence" (R. P. Dobash et al., 1992) and "The Return of the 'Battered Husband Syndrome'" (Schwartz & DeKeseredy, 1993). Despite dissension, it is important to note that no one is proposing that violent females do not exist and that there are no assaulted men (Cook, 1997). A truly battered male in the physical sense, however, is rare (Hamberger, 1997; O'Leary, Slep, & O'Leary, 2007).

Murray Straus and his colleagues conducted two national surveys of family violence using the CTS (M. A. Straus, 1979). In the most recent survey, 3,520 currently or previously coupled men and women (either one or both members of the couple) described the actions they took (as perpetrators) during the course of a marital conflict. The interviewers did not ask the participants directly whether they had been violent or whether they saw themselves as having an abusive relationship. Instead, they asked 18 specific questions about individual acts of verbal, symbolic, and physical aggression that had occurred during the previous 12 months and over the lifetime of the relationship. (See Appendix A.1 for estimates of perpetration of assaults based on the M. A. Straus and Gelles [1986] study.)

Only later did a new study using a modified version of the same test (CTS) contradict the early findings from M. A. Straus and Gelles's two national surveys. The Center for Policy Research randomly sampled 8,000 men and 8,000 women between November 1995 and May 1996 for the National Violence Against Women Survey (NVAWS). The results indicated that 22.1% of women and 7.4% of men reported being physically assaulted by an intimate (current or former spouse, cohabiting partner, or date) (Tjaden & Thoennes, 1998a).

Opponents of the gender equivalence viewpoint have looked for and found a number of rationales for rejecting the conclusion that women are as maritally violent as men:

- *False assumptions about the context of abuse.* The CTS asks only about abuse during arguments and why the aggressive act occurred (e.g., self-defense, retaliation, attempt to control or intimidate) (Henderson, Bartholomew, Trinke, & Kwong, 2005; O'Leary et al., 2007).
- *Flaws in self-report data* (e.g., issues of honesty and completeness of respondents' reports for each sex) (e.g., Armstrong, Wernke, Medina, & Schafer, 2002; R. P. Dobash, Dobash, Cavanagh, & Lewis, 1998; Riggs, Murphy, & O'Leary, 1989; Szinovacz, 1983).
- *The selection of questions used in the CTS and other scales.* Some test items can be user-unfriendly because of their dependence on legal terminology (Koss, 1989). Merely redesigning the items for the National Crime Victimization Survey to inquire about more specific behaviors radically altered the results (Bachman & Taylor, 1994).
- *Lack of information on motivations for the violent act* (e.g., self-defense, control, intent to injure) (e.g., Barnett et al., 1997; Stuart, Moore, Hellmuth, Ramsey, & Kahler, 2006; Weston, Marshall, & Coker, 2007).
- *Little information about outcomes* (e.g., fear, end of argument, escape, injuries) (Temple, Weston, & Marshall, 2005).
- *Inadequate measures of chronicity of violence prior to or after the study's timeline* (see Hirschel & Buzawa, 2002; U.S. Department of Justice, Office for Victims of Crime, 2002).

- *Insufficient measures of the survivor's fear, isolation, and level of control* (Barnett et al., 1997; Lindgren & Renck, 2008).
- *False presumptions about gender equivalence of violent acts* (e.g., the ability to frighten others through aggression) (Hamberger, Lohr, Bonge, & Tolin, 1997; Henning & Holdford, 2006; Koss et al., 1994; Vivian & Langhinrichsen-Rohling, 1994).
- *False assumptions about the equality of an occasional act of aggression and a battering relationship* (Cavanaugh & Gelles, 2005; L. L. Marshall, 1992a; 1992b).
- *CTS measures isolated acts of aggression and not patterns of abuse* (Hirschel & Buzawa, 2002).

Several investigators examined possible distinctions in initiation and severity of the abuse. Although debatable, a number of reports, but not all, found that wives use severe violence less frequently (Browning & Dutton, 1986; Brush, 1990; Harris, 1991; Langhinrichsen-Rohling et al., 1995; Morse, 1995; Tjaden & Thoennes, 1998a). Furthermore, some comparisons have disclosed that men usually start the violence and are more likely than women to engage in multiple acts of assault (Saunders, 1989; see also Connelly et al., 2006).

In a study of more than 800 ethnically diverse women, researchers (Temple et al., 2005) found that when women participated in violent interactions with their male partners, the violence was more frequent and more severe than when females were the primary aggressors. When both partners were aggressive, health consequences were worse for women whether the female or male was the primary perpetrator. These authors found that mutual violence became more male dominated over time.

A number of investigators contend that when women react violently, it is more likely to be a product of the situation than when men react violently (e.g., Koss et al., 1994; Laner & Thompson, 1982). Saunders (1986) asked 56 battered women whether they used violence, and if so, under what circumstances. The women judged the percentage (0% to 100%) of time that their violent responses were self-defensive, retaliatory, and the first strike. Results revealed that self-defense was the most common motive for both severe and nonsevere violence (see J. C. Campbell, 2010, for a review).

Another evaluation of 482 battered women disclosed that 66% said their violence was self-defensive, and an additional 22% said it was fear-motivated (Gondolf, 1998a; see also Barnett, Keyson, & Thelen, 1992; Cascardi, Langhinrichsen-Rohling, & Vivian, 1992; Hamberger et al., 1997). Collectively, research strongly corroborates the judgment of L. L. Marshall and Rose (1990) that "the actions by a person of one sex cannot be considered the equivalent of the other sex engaging in the behavior" (p. 60).

In animal research, punishment leads to increased aggression, a phenomenon termed *elicited aggression*. A punished monkey will attack objects, other organisms not involved in the punishment, or even itself (Ulrich, Wolff, & Azrin, 1964). Humans also will become aggressive toward noninvolved individuals when shocked (Berkowitz & LePage, 1967). This finding helps explain battered women's self-defensive aggression, and it predicts outbursts of aggression toward others. Surprisingly, an extrapolation of the phenomenon of elicited aggression suggests that battered women's aggression toward their children may occur as one outcome of being battered themselves. Another possibility is Freudian displacement of aggression, the trickle-down theory, or that women themselves are violent.

Anger and fear emerge as the two predominant reactions to assault (Gore-Felton, Gill, Koopman, & Spiegel, 1999). Anger can be, and often is, a buffer against fear. In one English study, 62% of crime victims reported feeling angry because of their victimization (Shepherd, 1990; see also Stuckless, 1998). Similarly, battered women and those in shelters are significantly angrier than comparison groups of nonbattered women (see also Feindler, 1988; M. N. Russell et al., 1989).

Several experts have recognized this combination of anger and fear in victims (Blackman, 1988; Walker, 1984). Very likely, the motives of self-defense (fear motivated) and retaliation (anger motivated) become blended together for some battered women (Saunders, 1986). A comprehensive analysis of 23 research reports on women's motivations for violence against their male partners found that battered women frequently felt ignored, powerless, and angry. Other common rationales for abuse against males were self-defense and retaliation (Bair-Merritt et al., 2010). Legally, extreme rage mixed with extreme terror do not nullify self-defense pleas in homicide cases, because it is reasonable to combine anger and fear when attacked (Schneider & Jordan, 1978).

The Multidimensionality of Violence

It is important to note that physical abuse is more often in the less severe range (Holtzworth-Munroe & Stuart, 1994; Rand, 2009), and it occurs less often than psychological and verbal abuse (Vitanzas, Vogel, & Marshall, 1995). Episodes of marital violence usually include hitting, throwing things, slapping, and pushing. Ordinarily, the injuries are cuts and bruises, and they rarely require hospitalization (Tjaden & Thoennes, 2000). The level of fright engendered during a battering episode, however, does not parallel the degree of violence used or the seriousness of an injury inflicted (see Cohen, Forjuoh, & Gondolf, 1999; Muelleman, Lenaghan, & Pakieser, 1996). Even a nonphysical form of abuse can create a high level of foreboding (Heyman & Slep, 2006; Jacobson et al., 1996).

Isolated acts of aggression have not been distinguished from patterns of chronic abuse that weave a web, a context in which partners live and function. Too often, research and policy are based on a one-dimensional view of a one-dimensional batterer and his one-dimensional family. Researchers and advocates seek to describe batterers in profiles, descriptive lists, or personality traits.

As stated previously, there continues to be something of a battle of the sexes in terms of the role of women's behavior in domestic violence. Some view women's aggression as more aggravating than intimidating and more limit-setting than controlling. Others think women's violence is as intimidating and controlling as men's. When the debate gets noisy and angry, the result is the creation of something akin to a battering relationship between experts.

It is helpful to keep in mind that people on both sides of this argument do not believe that women are entitled to act out physically whenever they feel like it. Some women are abusive and some are downright violent. There is no research, however, that can say that the cost of women's violence—emotionally, physically, or in regard to property damage—in any way matches that same violence perpetrated by men. The body of evidence suggests that there should be nothing to argue about. Diffusing energy into an ongoing gender war takes away from the critical task of developing effective prevention and intervention strategies.

Issues concerning partner violence call attention to the role of patriarchy in marital violence (R. P. Dobash et al., 1998; Hunnicutt, 2009; Levesque, 2001). Male-dominated societies create a type of patriarchal pollution.

Case Study: Dan

"He came in not because he wanted to see a therapist, but because his wife encouraged it. They were both professionals, attractive, well dressed, and well paid. He was very depressed and reluctant to talk. He was ashamed and isolated. He had been called names and threatened with a knife. His good suits had been cut up. He lived in apprehension of the next violent outburst. I knew he was a battered husband, but I didn't learn that from him. He wouldn't talk about it. I learned it from his wife, the woman who loved and abused him."

Patriarchy is the smog we breathe, the pesticides we ingest, and the toxins that find a home in our bodies. We cannot necessarily taste it or feel it. Its effects may be subtle, but they are cumulative. The patriarchal structure of a society creates a mood that allows, encourages, and normalizes violence, particularly violence directed at the least powerful, safest targets (see Kandel-Englander, 1992).

A "single-bullet" theory in which patriarchy is the single bullet, however, does not adequately explain the existence of wife beating (D. Dutton, 1994). If patriarchy were the main factor contributing to wife assault, then a large percentage of men raised in that system should exhibit assaultive behavior (see also T. W. Julian & McKenry, 1993). Furthermore, patriarchy does not explain female violence in either heterosexual or lesbian relationships in which self-defense is not the impetus (Lie & Gentlewarrior, 1991; Renzetti, 1992).

A broader rationale for intimate violence that accounts for these more diverse types of violence is needed. One such theory, attachment theory, posits that intimacy has the potential for generating dependency, jealousy, and anger, which is sometimes expressed violently (D. Dutton et al., 1994; see also Fangundes, 2012; Kane, Staiger, & Ricciardelli, 2000). Some other theories highlight childhood exposure to violence and offender psychopathology (see Hamberger & Hastings, 1991; Widom & Maxfield, 2001). Other theories emphasize the contribution of personality traits (e.g., anger) to battering by both men and women (Slocum, Rengifo, & Carbone-Lopez, 2012; see also Eckhardt, Samper, Suhr, & Holtzworth-Munroe, 2012).

Any single-answer interpretation of the complex problem of partner violence would fail to do justice to the men and women for whom causation affects staying, leaving, and the nature of the assistance they receive. To accurately define partner abuse, all sides of the argument must be considered. One way of conceptualizing intimate partner abuse is to place it on a continuum. A continuum emphasizes the fact that anyone can, and many do, commit an act, or limited acts, of aggression. Very few, however, become involved in an escalating and/or chronic pattern of physical abuse and coercive control. A continuum also incorporates the notion that interpersonal violence normally occurring at a low level may erupt suddenly into severe violence with perilous repercussions.

A distinction can be made between common couple violence and patriarchal terrorism (M. P. Johnson, 1995). These two levels can serve as anchors at opposite ends of the continuum of spousal abuse. At the low end of the continuum, common couple violence, abuse may include relatively infrequent, noninjurious fighting that may occur in many intimate relationships. It may be mutual, does not tend to victimize the partners, and does not create fear. At the high end, patriarchal terrorism, abuse may cluster around a pattern of assaultive, fear-producing, controlling behaviors, both criminal (e.g., physical assaults, terrorist threats, stalking) and noncriminal (e.g., isolating the partner, jealous monitoring of the partner's friends and activities, humiliating the partner).

Patriarchal terrorism is rooted in the historical and cultural notions of male ownership and domination of female partners. It is simultaneously a mechanism of men's control over women and an escalating pattern of coercive violence. Patriarchal terrorism is most clearly typified by concomitant factors, such as chronic foreboding. As L. Gordon (1988) posits, "One assault does not make a battered woman; she becomes that because of her socially determined inability to resist or escape" (p. 285). Battering includes both physically violent acts and their political framework (the pattern of social, institutional, and interpersonal controls that entrap women and prevent them from determining their own destinies) (Stark, 2007).

Common couple violence is associated with conflict, which inevitably arises in relationships. It is less gendered than patriarchal terrorism and extremely prevalent. It is this type of interpersonal violence that population surveys tend to detect. While it often includes an element of partner control, it does not engender an alarm reaction. The terminology is meant to infer actions like yelling at a partner, a near-universal behavior that partners use during an argument when things get out of hand. Although this conflict may include psychological abuse or even an occasional push or shove, it rarely escalates into serious violence (see M. P. Johnson, 1995; Lupri, Grandin, & Brinkerhoff, 1994; O'Leary, 1999).

Separating the endpoints of the continuum into common couple violence and patriarchal terrorism has some advantages. Differentiating the two forms of abuse not only recognizes the validity of different kinds of findings, but it also sets the stage for different theoretical formulations and different types of interventions (M. P. Johnson, 1995; see also Adams, 1988; Hamberger et al., 1997; L. L. Marshall, 1996; O'Leary, 1999).

Inspired by M. P. Johnson's (1995) work, LaViolette (2009) developed a five-point continuum of aggression, which includes isolated acts of aggression that can occur in nonabusive relationships. (See Appendix C for an expanded table that encompasses exacerbating factors.)

Presumably, types of assaultive acts (physical, sexual, emotional, controlling) can interact with varying levels of apprehension, oppression, and control to designate different points on a continuum of abuse. Fear and balance of power are critical emotional components in defining marital violence. Once fear becomes part of the relationship, the relationship changes.

Common couple aggression denotes a generally healthy relationship that has included an isolated act or acts of aggression. The act of aggression is couched in a context of stress or escalation emotion; it is atypical of the relationship and occurs in a couple who are not emotionally or verbally abusive to each other. There is a balance of power between the individuals; the physical act can be initiated by one or both partners, and fear is not an outcome of the exchange. Neither party *believes* that aggression is a good or viable way to solve problems, so remorse is genuine.

It is also important to note that younger people are more likely to act out physically, even in a nonabusive context. Flash back to your early twenties and think about the nature, content, and length of arguments that you participated in with an intimate partner. Over time, as we age and develop experience and understanding, the arguments we have tend to be more constructive—and a lot shorter. We learn to examine our perceptions and gain perspective.

Highly conflicted relationships tend not to be healthy, but they are not *abusive*. Aggression is sporadic, does not create fear or apprehension, and the couple has an emotional balance of power. The couple is likely to have "anger problems" in that they do not solve their problems well and the friendship erodes over time. They may stop liking each other, and eventually, goodwill can become nonexistent. Fear, oppression, and control do not characterize the relationship.

According to Geffner and Rosenbaum (2001, p. 2),

> The term aggression should not be used as a synonym for abuse. Aggression is an action, abuse is a dynamic. Partners may be mutually aggressive, and the evidence overwhelmingly suggests that they are (Archer, 2000; Straus & Gelles, 1990), but they are rarely mutually abusive. Hitting by either partner is equally unacceptable, but not equally destructive. Women may hit their male partners, but infrequently batter them, because battering or abuse includes a pattern of coercion, intimidation and control, which is less frequently present in female-to-male aggression.

The first author of this book (A. L.) has divided violent behavior into three categories and the gray areas between them. Most of the men in perpetrators' groups tend to fall within the first two areas (abuse and battering). The famous one-dimensional batterer of *The Burning Bed* and *Sleeping With the Enemy* is not interested in changing, is in jail, or is smart enough to avoid being caught. This profile of a batterer does not describe most of the men who are seen in programs for men who behave abusively (G. Billings-Beck, K. Evans, & C. Morris, and D. Eddy, personal communication, March, 11, 2011). It is important to remember that these separations on the curve are contiguous and not linear.

Abusive men tend to use physical aggression sporadically, sometimes with long periods between outbursts. There tends to be physical aggression directed against objects, such as throwing things against a wall.

Threats in these relationships focus on the theme of abandonment as opposed to bodily harm. Threats to cheat, to leave, or to engage in some other hurtful behavior are not uncommon. Abusive individuals tend to be on the low end of the scale in terms of physical and psychological aggression. They do not isolate their partners or verbally assassinate their character. They may swear and shout obscenities. They may call their partners generic names, such as *bitch*, but they do not tell their partners what horrible people they are, how ugly they are, or how stupid they are. This low level of aggression does not necessarily correlate positively with the level of apprehension experienced by the victim.

Sexual abuse generally occurs as a byproduct of the perpetrator's fear. Once he has done something hurtful to his partner, he is afraid she will leave. To assuage that fear, he pushes to get close, to be sexual. His intention is not to humiliate or degrade her, but the result may be that she feels humiliated or degraded nevertheless. He is not as concerned with her feelings as he is with alleviating his own discomfort.

Emotional abuse (e.g., verbal outbursts, withdrawal, jealousy), rather than physical abuse, generates much of the apprehension in a battering relationship (Pico-Alfonso, 2005; Woods, 1999). Since emotional abuse seems objectively less potent and less tangible, it is difficult for a victim to justify making major life changes because of it. Giving up a home, financial security, intimacy, social support, and a job may seem disproportionately difficult in view of the enormity of the dread generated by the unknown.

Men in abusive relationships do not ordinarily respond the same way women do. In the Carmody and Williams (1987) study, men predicted that retaliatory physical assault by their wives was very unlikely, and they further judged the severity of their assaults to be very low. Men also reported that they could easily protect themselves against physical assaults: "She was easy to stop," "I just pushed her away," or "I restrained her." One important reason why few men fit into the category of "battered" is that, unless their mates have used an equalizer, such as a weapon, the men are just not afraid. This does not mean they are not assaulted or cannot be battered.

The combination of sporadic violence interspersed with kindness (as in the Stockholm syndrome) contributes to the development of hope and allows the battered woman to deny the side of the abuser that terrifies her (D. L. R. Graham et al., 1988). If she denies his violent side, she can deny that she is in danger. That is, battered women deny that their mates either intend to or actually do harm them. In fact, sometimes they deny being victimized altogether (Hebbert, Silverm, & Ellard, 1991). Batterers deny the abusive nature of their behavior as well (D. Dutton, 1998; Hamberger, 2005; Hamberger et al., 1997; Henning & Holdford, 2006). One of the authors (O. B.) encountered a man who characterized himself as unhappily married but nonviolent. Later inspection of his test data uncovered that he admitted to having choked his wife "several times a year"!

Professionals working with survivors may be fearful, themselves, and in danger of developing long-lasting anxiety reactions known as secondary traumas (Gore-Felton et al., 1999; V. C. Strand, 2000). According to Mary Ann Dutton (1992), work with victims of trauma is the most demanding of professional experiences, and it may have enduring psychological consequences. Several authors have described the effects of secondary trauma on therapists (as well as advocates and others working with survivors of violence). Judith Herman (1992) warns that repeated exposure to stories of human cruelty will eventually challenge a counselor's basic faith and trust in other people. Perhaps even more terrifying is identifying with the perpetrator, which can happen to any advocate for battered women. Empathy for a batterer feels like the ultimate betrayal of one's values and beliefs.

Case Study: Keith

Keith called his counselor early in the morning. She was already gone, but he talked to another therapist in the office. This therapist had had no previous connection with Keith, but the conversation made her anxious. When Keith's counselor returned, she received an urgent message from her associate to call Keith. Her previous experience with Keith and his impulsive anger created a strong emotional response of uneasiness and apprehension.

Keith was furious when his counselor called. He sarcastically thanked her for her help, and then said he was "leaving to kill his wife." Needless to say, the counselor was hooked; she believed that Keith would carry out his threat. The therapist worried that, as in the past, the criminal justice system would be unable to protect Keith's ex-wife. He had successfully violated a temporary restraining order at least three times and physically assaulted his ex-wife during several of these incidents. The counselor hoped that Keith had called so that he would not harm his ex-wife.

The therapist was unable to calm him down—and, in fact, felt an escalation of alarm and anxiety, herself. She called Keith's probation officer to warn her, and to have her call Keith's ex-wife. The probation officer and Keith's ex-wife lived six hours away.

What ensued were two hours of calls involving the therapist, the client, the probation officer, and the estranged spouse. The client's rage produced rapid results. The therapist and the probation officer contacted the ex-wife and acted as intermediaries. The ex-wife made contact with Keith, and a negotiation followed, which concluded with positive results: Keith's anger dissolved. His ex-wife was safe, and the problem was resolved, at least for the time.

(Continued)

(Continued)

It is interesting to observe the behavior of those involved in this particular situation and to hear about their reactions. First of all, everyone responded to the rage by moving in the direction that seemed most productive, but also in the direction pushed by the batterer—contact with his ex-wife. The threats produced immediate results, once again reinforcing the notion that violence works. The probation officer and the therapist talked about feeling manipulated, emotionally battered, and unable to slow down until the problem was resolved.

Keith sent the counselor a thank-you card and an apology. He talked about feeling appreciative of her efforts. The air was cleared; communication was open and honest. They had been through a crisis together and had come out of it with a positive resolution. A residue of misgiving and distrust remained, even though good feelings returned. The cycle of fear and hope had begun for the counselor.

If peripherally involved individuals react with fear to their minimal involvement with a batterer by changing their behaviors, why should one be surprised by the extreme behavior changes undergone by battered women and their children?

The vicariously traumatized helping professional can also experience an overidentification with the client or an emotional distancing. Self-care becomes extremely important for the counselor working with survivors of violence. Support from family and friends, exercise, play, rest, nutrition, peer support, and networking with others working in the field are essential for creating a balanced emotional environment (J. Zorza, 1998). Experiencing and expressing the feelings that this work elicits becomes critical to preserving mental health. Much like having the stomach flu, catharsis promotes healing (see Ben-Porat & Itzhaky, 2009).

When a family member is privy to the pain and danger of an abusive relationship, the traumatic effect is magnified.

Case Study: A Father's Choice

Dick had watched the transformation take place. Nina had been a successful engineer. She earned good money, had bought her own home, had friends all over the world, and had landed a great position working for Euro-Disney. His daughter, his baby, the child who had followed him everywhere and had learned to ride the big Harley motorcycles that he loved, had become anxious, jumpy, and isolated. She had recently borrowed money from her parents to buy baby furniture.

Dick was worried. Nina's marriage to a rugged, handsome rugby player she met in France seemed to change her. In Dick's mind, the most dramatic change came after the birth of his first grandson, who was the apple of his eye.

At first Nina seemed very happy, and her family was happy for her. Ned was charming and, by his own account, successful in business. Nina and Ned moved back to California after their marriage. It was after Tim's birth that Nina began to confide in her father. Nina told Dick that Ned was controlling and didn't seem to care much about Tim, who had been born two months prematurely and had some physical problems.

Dick had noticed a few things about Ned that had disturbed him. Ned was cocky, a braggart, and seemed to stretch the truth. He had talked about his love of motorcycles and his numerous experiences riding big bikes, but he really didn't know much about them and was uncomfortable on the long ride he took with Dick and his friends. Dick also noticed that Nina was dressing differently and seemed to look to Ned for approval of her clothing. Ned did not take Nina to the hospital during her pregnancy when she was experiencing difficulty. He also refused to come to the hospital when infant Tim had to have surgery.

One day Nina brought Tim to Dick's house, asking for her parents' help and a place to stay. She took her father aside and told him that she was leaving Ned. Everything seemed to pour out of her as she told her father of the constant criticism; the violence, mostly directed at property; and the restrictions that Ned placed on her contact with her friends. She had gotten over the fact that Ned had spent her money and had demanded that she return to work when Tim was very small and very ill, but she could not handle his lack of involvement and concern for Tim.

Dick became a focus of Ned's campaign to "get his wife and son back where they belonged." The phone calls and taped messages were ongoing. Ned was intimidating and screamed, "I'll be your worst Goddamned nightmare." He called the Department of Children and Family Services (DCFS) repeatedly, reporting his estranged wife and her family for child abuse and neglect. At one point, DCFS made a midnight visit with the intention of removing Dick's grandson from their home because of the frequency and severity of the reports. DCFS dismissed all of the allegations, as it found no evidence of abuse or neglect.

Visitations were uncomfortable to horrific. Ned was surly to the family and made numerous trips to hospital emergency rooms when Tim had mosquito bites, a rash, or a cough, attempting to gather evidence that Nina and her parents were unfit caretakers. He subjected Tim to blood tests, X-rays, and other procedures. Ned also became the perfect father at work, with neighbors, and even on the road, with personalized license plates proclaiming he was "TIMSDAD." It was a social worker from DCFS who told Nina that she was a battered woman and gave her a shelter hotline number. She began attending groups, and her father became her only confidant and protector. He took over the visitation transfers. Turning Tim over to Ned was painful. Watching his daughter become frightened and nervous was excruciating. Additionally, taking his own wife to the doctor, hearing that her blood

(Continued)

(Continued)

pressure was skyrocketing, and having the doctor tell him, "Dick, the stress is killing her; you have to do something" was unbearable.

And Ned had upped the ante. He was filing continuous court documents, screaming threats on the phone, and in person beating on Dick's front door to the point that neighbors got involved. Ned began to stalk Nina. He sat outside their house in his car to observe her comings and goings. On another occasion, in the emergency room, Ned pushed Dick into the wall. Dick, a former Japanese prisoner of war and survivor of the death march on Corregidor, began sleeping curled up in fetal position on the living room floor. He described himself as the "last wagon in the wagon train," the only defense for his wife, daughter, and grandson.

Dick secretly bought a gun to protect himself and his family. He carried it in the waistband of his pants when Ned came to pick up Tim. Ned's menacing behavior was escalating and the family's trepidation was escalating as well. Ned had begun to act out in front of other people in the neighborhood, and his harassing legal maneuvers were becoming more frantic.

Then, on a Saturday morning, Ned arrived at Dick's home for another visitation. He was belligerent and derogatory. Nina and her mother were in another room when they heard the first shot. Ned, wounded and bleeding, fled down the street of the quiet middle-class neighborhood in which Dick had lived for over 20 years. Neighbors reported that Dick walked down the street as if he were in a trance. He fired four more shots into Ned. Ned died on the street. Dick had believed that the nightmare would never end for his daughter, his grandson, his wife, and himself. In his fugue-like state, Dick had ended the nightmare.

Domestic violence perpetrators have gotten very creative. According to a 2009 report from the United States Department of Justice (Baum et al., 2009), more than 31,000 American adults are stalked or harassed (annually) using GPS technology. According to Cindy Southworth, founder of the Safety Net Project at the National Network to End Domestic Violence, survivors should "be weary of a gift of a phone from a controlling partner and know that an abuser may be able to turn on features of a phone on a shared plan" (Hallett, 2011, p. 16). JoAnna Davis of the California Partnership to End Domestic Violence says an abusive partner might hide a phone with a GPS turned on in a victim's car or activate the GPS tracking using a family phone plan (Barak, 2005; Finn & Banach, 2000; Spitzberg & Hoobler, 2002).

Summary

This chapter has pointed out that redefining partner violence to include its emotional contexts and outcomes is crucial to understanding why battered women stay. Fear, both objective and subjective, is an integral aspect of the meaning of male-to-female abuse. Fear actually causes enduring change in brain functions. In addition to fear, anger is a near-universal reaction to assault. Wife beating accounts for a large number of injuries to women and the murder of men, women, family members, and associates of the victim. Assaults are costly to society in terms of medical, legal, and criminal justice services.

Learning experiments on animals have provided a number of human analogs that furnish a useful framework for understanding the behavior of battered women. Learning theory offers information about a number of learned reactions: (a) the generalization of fear to other cues in the environment, (b) the effects of punishment variables on the extent of suppression of behavior (e.g., intermittent punishment), (c) the effects of a gradual buildup or decline of assaults, and (d) the creation of an atmosphere typified by chronic anxiety. Over time, couples learn to accept the battering in their relationship.

Research also portrays women's aggression as primarily self-defensive, while men's is power-oriented. Furthermore, men's aggression successfully intimidates their partners, while women's assaultive behavior usually does not. Men show little worry about criminal justice sanctions, one of the many factors alluding to the patriarchal nature of male-to-female violence. Some researchers and societal agents have implied gender equality in intimate partner violence and have even gone so far as to suggest a battered husband syndrome. Although there are clearly some aggressive and violent female partners, research has clearly contradicted the assumption that there are large numbers of battered male partners. Given the broad nature of learning principles and their applicability to behavior in general, becoming a battered woman could happen to anyone.

5

Meltdown

The Impact of Stress
and Learned Helplessness

She has lost her faith in the world's essential predictability, fairness and safety, and approaches even ordinary routines like driving with the hesitancy of an outsider, a foreigner in a hostile land.

—Jeffrey Jay (1991, p. 23)

Stress is part of everyday life and can result from either positive or negative events. Apparently, most individuals do not handle stress productively and pay a heavy price both physically and psychologically for chronic mismanagement. Individuals exposed to traumatic events, such as an assault or military combat, often develop posttraumatic stress disorder (PTSD). Both battered women and abused children who are exposed to the abuse develop PTSD. Learned helplessness is another significant condition brought about by violence, or more specifically, by the inability to stop it. Effects of PTSD and learned helplessness may eventually culminate in a cluster of cognitions, feelings, and behaviors that constitute the battered woman syndrome. The core of fear and paralysis typifying this syndrome helps to explain the inexplicable: why battered women stay and why they sometimes kill.

Violence-Induced Stress

In humans, a moderate amount of stress is essential to growth and development, but prolonged, intense stress debilitates the body and the soul. The concept of stress incorporates psychological reactions to stress(ors) as well as physiological ones. Loss of a job constitutes a negative stressor, while going on vacation constitutes a positive stressor. Psychological reactions to stress include cognitive impairment (e.g., confusion and poor test performance) and emotional responses (e.g., anxiety, anger, aggression, and depression). (Readers who enjoyed *Willard* and *Ben* will find an early experiment on stress in rats, conducted by Selye [1946], in Appendix F.8.)

Researchers experimentally, and clinicians anecdotally, have documented the physiological toll of chronic apprehension. A longitudinal study found that mental health and physical health varied with abuse levels (J. C. Campbell & Soeken, 1999; see also Follette, Polusny, Bechtle, &

Case Study: Nickie and Tom

To describe Nickie now is to describe her life with Tom, a successful businessman. Tom was obsessed with Nickie's life prior to their relationship. In particular, he wanted open disclosure of previous sexual experiences. His interrogation would sometimes last for hours. He read her private papers and journals and went through her picture album. He found pictures of her standing next to male friends and relatives. These pictures served as a basis for his distrust, even though he was aware that she had had no prior sexual experience. She had come to this relationship as a virgin.

When Nickie married Tom, she had not anticipated how much he would mistrust and control her. She had nearly earned her doctorate, and she wanted to keep things at home on an even keel until her qualifying exams were completed. She recognized that she had given up some important things to keep her relationship together. She had given up her friends and family, but only for a time, to make it easier for her husband to feel secure.

Nickie had known that Tom was jealous, but she expected it to diminish over time. She understood his jealousy and fear so well, in fact, that his frenzied fantasies of her infidelities became real to her. She began to wonder if she had repressed the memories of affairs she had never had. His reality had become hers. Her ability to define herself apart from him had become obscured.

Nickie didn't understand why she cried a lot, or why she was unable to concentrate. She didn't know why she shook when she talked or why she was afraid. She had not been physically abused. She had no idea how she had gotten from there to here, or when the change had begun—only that it seemed complete.

Naugle, 1996). Generally, the women in the Follingstad, Brennan, Hause, Polek, and Rutledge (1991) study reported that their physical and emotional health had been better before the violent relationship and also improved after it was over. One study of Nicaraguan battered women showed a clear relationship between the abuse of either the wife or her child and the woman's level of emotional distress (Ellsberg, Caldera, Herrera, Winkvist, & Kullgren, 1999). Similarly, a review and statistical analysis of a number of studies concerned with interpersonal violence identified a large number of violence-induced stress symptoms (Kiecolt-Glaser, 2009; Sledjeski, Speisman, & Dierker, 2008; Weaver & Clum, 1995).

There is ample evidence that the impulsive and unpredictable behavior of abusers produces stress and feelings of helplessness in the people most affected by that behavior (Barnett & Hamberger, 1992; Langford, 1996). Some batterers suffer from intermittent explosive disorder, and they are likely to fly into a rage (Gass, Stein, Williams, & Seedat, 2011; Kessler et al., 2006). Cole and Sapp (1988) found that the lower the level of internal control, the greater the level of stress (see Weaver & Clum, 1995, for a review).

Women in physically or emotionally destructive relationships can become hypersensitive to changes in their partners' eyes, speech, tone of voice, and facial expressions, as well as specific situations that may signal an onset of aggression. It seems that the battered women who can foresee a violent assault are so entrenched in this pattern that their greater exposure and familiarity have made them both more fearful and perhaps more accurate in predicting whether abuse will recur (Langford, 1996). Interestingly, battered women's ability to predict their male partner's violence is frequently more exact than researchers' statistical predictions (Heckert & Gondolf, 2004). No matter how practiced battered women may be, however, they can never predict when and how with exact precision.

As mentioned previously, laboratory research can provide a scientific basis for these findings about battered women (see Mineka & Zinbarg, 2006, for an application to human anxiety disorders). Seligman (1968)

Case Study: Mei

"I started having stomach pains the second year that we lived together, after the violence began. It was weird. I would be visiting a friend, and after I'd been there a few hours, I'd get a stabbing pain in my abdomen and feel sick. It was like the alarm ringing in the morning telling me that it was time to get up and go, and I would get up and go because I knew if I didn't, something bad would happen when I got home."

and Seligman and Meyer (1970) were able to demonstrate that rats that were unpredictably shocked developed a chronic state of fear and ulcers. In another study, college students obliged to view photographs of graphic crime scenes without control over the timing of the presentations reported much more stress than students who had control over the timing (Geer & Maisel, 1972; see also Abbot, Schoen, & Badia, 1984). Knowing what to expect seems to provide an illusion of control.

Posttraumatic Stress Disorder

Traumatic events are the most obvious sources of negative stress for anyone. Experiences such as earthquakes, nuclear accidents, plane crashes, and physical assaults produce severe stress reactions in almost everyone, sometimes called disaster syndromes (Atkinson, Atkinson, Smith, & Bem, 1990). A disaster syndrome encompasses three psychological stages: (a) shock, disorientation, and bewilderment; (b) passivity and lack of capacity to initiate tasks, accompanied by the inability to follow orders; and (c) anxiety and concentration difficulties. Recent evidence has revealed that experiencing PTSD is related to the degree of trauma exposure (Sledjeski et al., 2008).

When a traumatic event has a prolonged reaction, it is called posttraumatic stress disorder, a diagnosis first applied to Vietnam veterans (Gore-Felton, Gill, Koopman, & Spiegel, 1999; Kulka et al., 1990). Subsequent innovative research showed that the brain structure, known as the amygdala, is involved in a set of recurrent and long-lasting symptoms that occur in response to PTSD (Poulos et al., 2009; Rausch, van der Kolk, Fisler, & Alpert, 1996).

PTSD received medical status in 1979 (American Psychiatric Association, 1980). Similar symptoms, however, have been associated with war for more than a century. These symptoms have been classified, depending on the war they were associated with, as nostalgia, shell shock, and battle fatigue. Prior to the Vietnam War, medical professionals and others suspected that an individual who did not get over a traumatic experience in a reasonable amount of time was inherently disturbed or pathological. *Reasonable* was usually defined by the individuals who had a significant investment in the survivor's moving on emotionally.

The definition of the disorder is still evolving (J. L. Herman, 1992). PTSD is an anxiety disorder produced by an uncommon, extremely stressful event (e.g., assault, rape, military combat, death camp) and characterized by (a) reexperiencing the trauma in painful recollections or recurrent dreams; (b) diminished responsiveness (numbing), with disinterest in significant activities and feelings of detachment and estrangement from others; and (c) such symptoms as exaggerated startle response, disturbed sleep, difficulty in concentrating or remembering, guilt about surviving when others did not, and avoidance of activities that call the traumatic event to mind (Goldenson, 1984; see also Gore-Felton et al., 1999).

Living in a war zone caused PTSD in about 15% of Vietnam veterans (American Psychiatric Association, 1980). Overall, military personnel have significantly higher rates of PTSD than nonmilitary personnel (Kessler, Sonnega, Brommet, Hughes, & Nelson, 1995). A survey of 4,008 adult women revealed that 69% of them had been exposed to some type of traumatic event over their lifetimes. Exposure to sexual assaults, aggravated assaults, or homicides involving a close relative had occurred among 36% of the sample. Over a lifetime, the prevalence of PTSD was 12.3%. The rate of PTSD was significantly higher among crime victims (25.8%) than non–crime victims (9.4%). Historical factors most closely related to PTSD included a direct threat to life or an actual injury (Resnick, Kilpatrick, Dansky, Saunders, & Best, 1993; see also Zinzow, Grubaugh, Frueh, & Magruder, 2008).

Other studies have estimated even higher percentages of PTSD symptoms: (a) 24 of 30 rape victims (80%) (Kramer & Green, 1991); (b) 24 of 25 adult incest survivors (96%) (Donaldson & Gardner, 1985); and (c) 66% of family survivors of homicide victims (Amick-McMullen, Kilpatrick, Veronen, & Smith, 1989). Some experts consider female survivors of sexual assault and other assault survivors to be the largest major group of PTSD victims (R. Campbell, 2008). Astin, Lawrence, Pincus, and Foy (1990) demonstrated a significant relationship between childhood sexual victimization and PTSD (Berliner & Saunders, 2010; Polusny & Follette, 2008; Zinzow et al., 2008). In Amick-McMullen and colleagues' (1989) study of homicide victims' relatives, the more dissatisfied family members were with the criminal justice system (e.g., charges against the perpetrator were reduced), the worse their PTSD symptoms.

Some have argued that marital rape is not a serious crime, not as serious a crime as stranger-perpetrated rape. The research findings support a different conclusion. Sexually assaulted wives are just as traumatized, if not more so, than women assaulted by strangers (Monson, Byrd, & Langhinrichsen-Rohling, 1996; Riggs, Kilpatrick, & Resnick, 1992). As one court held, "When you are raped by a stranger you have to live with a frightening memory. When you are raped by your husband, you have to live with your rapist" (*Warren v. State*, 1985). Riggs and colleagues (1992) established that levels of PTSD symptomatology in women raped or assaulted by a husband were comparable to levels in women raped or assaulted by strangers (E. K. Martin, Taft, & Resnick, 2007).

In terms of physical and psychological injury, the effects of marital rape are extremely damaging and long-lasting (Riggs et al., 1992; Temple, Weston, Rodrigues, & Marshall, 2007). Sexually abused women report more physical health symptoms, including pain, and seek more medical care than women who have not been sexually abused (see Eby, Campbell, Sullivan, & Davidson, 1995; E. K. Martin et al., 2007). They also have poorer subjective health ratings (Golding, Cooper, & George, 1997; see also Nelson, Baldwin, & Taylor, 2011).

A childhood sexual assault is also a factor for soldiers who experience PTSD. Psychiatric studies undertaken by the Veterans Administration found evidence suggesting that soldiers physically or sexually abused as children had a greater sensitivity to developing PTSD than soldiers who did not have a history of childhood abuse (Bower, 1992; see also Rosen, Parmley, Knudson, & Fancher, 2002).

It can be challenging for PTSD sufferers to find support. One correlate of stress-related illness is having a network of close friends from whom the survivor feels she or he must hide a shameful trauma. In other words, the traumatized individual actively inhibits disclosure (Pennebaker & Susman, 1988). According to Jay (1991, p. 22), there is a "relentless external pressure on the survivor to maintain the breach between the private, ravaged self and the public, acquiescent persona." Listening to trauma survivors tell their stories creates stress because the listener sees the pain and empathizes with the fear (Kessler, McLeod, & Wethington, 1985). Trauma once or twice removed still shakes the security of those peripherally involved in the world of the traumatized.

Eight weeks after the Loma Prieta earthquake in San Francisco (October 1989), a study revealed that victims were still thinking about it. However, they had stopped talking about it because others did not want to listen. In another study, parents bereaved by a child's death discovered that many of their friends and relatives avoided them, thus reducing opportunities for them to talk out their feelings and sending a strong message that the time for being sad and the time for being heard were over (Pennebaker, 1991; see also Goodkind, Gillum, Bybee, & Sullivan, 2003).

Recognition of an external stressor as the precursor to PTSD produced a radical contrast to the innate character defects theory so frequently attributed to battered women (see T. Adler, 1990). "In short, the diagnosis tacitly recognizes that the world can drive a normal person crazy" (Jay, 1991, p. 22). One significant consequence of the PTSD diagnosis in war veterans has been the provision of an appropriate status for trauma survivors. In an effort to create an analogy between the experience of combat soldiers and those of battered women, we have inserted parallel wording in a quotation from J. Goodwin's (1987, p. 8) description of PTSD survivors:

> Due to circumstances of war [her married life], extended grieving was unproductive [and not allowed] and could become a liability [exacerbating her batterer's guilt could lead to increased anger]. Grief was handled as quickly as possible [to make way for the honeymoon stage]. Many soldiers [battered women] reported feeling numb. They felt depressed and unable to tell anyone. "How can I tell my wife [neighbor/friend/family member/pastor]? She'd never understand. How can anyone who has not been there understand?"

> Essentially, Vietnam-style combat [home-style combat] held no final resolution of conflict for anyone. Regardless of how one might respond, the overall outcome seemed to be an endless production of casualties with no perceivable positive results. They found little support from their friends and neighbors back home, the people in whose name so many people were drafted into military service [a battering relationship]. They felt helpless. They returned to the United States trying to put some positive resolution to this episode in their lives, but the atmosphere at home was hopeless. They were still helpless.

PTSD in battered women represents a configuration of factors: high arousal, high avoidance, intrusive memories, memory loss, and cognitive confusion. Houskamp and Foy (1991) indicated that 45% of their sample met full criteria in the *Diagnostic and Statistical Manual of Mental Disorders* (DSM-IV) for PTSD (see also Jones, Hughes, & Unterstaller, 2001; Kemp, Green, Hovanitz, & Rawlings, 1995). In two samples of battered women seeking treatment, over 60% experienced PTSD symptoms (Saunders, 1994). Prior to the research documenting PTSD, Painter and Dutton (1985, p. 366) described some abused women as having suffered an "emotional collapse indicative of extreme aversive, prolonged arousal similar to that experienced by disaster victims."

Sustained contact with the batterer through such events as court appearances, along with his continuing threats, "is likely to have significant influence on symptomology" (Houskamp & Foy, 1991, p. 374). Subjective factors, such as one's perception of the degree of threat and level of self-blame, contribute to the magnitude of psychological distress as well (Weaver & Clum, 1995; see also Temple et al., 2007). Kemp, Rawlings, and Green (1991) established that subjective abuse-related stress and actual assault level correlated positively with PTSD, anxiety, and depression. For the most part, the more severe and more chronic the trauma, the more extreme the symptoms (Follette et al., 1996; Sledjeski et al., 2008; see also van der Kolk, Roth, Pelcovitz, Mandel, & Spinazzola, 2005).

Case Study: Ginger and Fernando

Ginger went to counseling because her supervisor told her that "whatever it is that is bothering you is negatively affecting your work." Ginger's symptoms included emotional anesthesia (diminished responsiveness), inability to concentrate on or complete projects she had started, difficulty in getting to sleep, and having nightmares when she finally did sleep. She was a nurse and earned substantially more money than Fernando, who worked in a restaurant. They had been married for five years.

The beatings had been going on for the past three years, but the humiliation and emotional assaults had gone on longer than that. One night while she was making dinner, she heard Fernando muttering in the living room. She knew that he was angry. Then she heard something break. When she looked in the living room, her new coffee table had been flattened and her crystal bowl was flying into the wall. Ginger tried to calm him, but he stormed out of the apartment. She cleaned up the mess one more time.

On one occasion, Fernando screamed at her in front of her sister because "she thinks she is too important to do my laundry and is too busy with her important job to cook and clean for me." He called her *gorda* (fat) and told her she was ugly and disgusting, and no one would want her. Then, a week later, he beat her for coming on to a neighbor in the elevator.

The ultimate humiliation for Ginger was coming home from work and finding Fernando in bed with a prostitute. This time she did the screaming, and this time he beat her for embarrassing him. Later, he suggested that they both be tested for HIV.

Ginger closed herself off from friends and family. She lost interest in her life and avoided any situation that could put her in jeopardy. In fact, Ginger appeared more depressed and anxious than many of her clients in the psychiatric unit at the hospital.

Avoidance behavior is a central feature of PTSD and a basic coping strategy employed by Ginger and other battered women. In one study of battered women, physical arousal (i.e., hypersensitivity) was the most common symptom manifested, denial (i.e., avoidance) symptoms were second, and reexperiencing symptoms (i.e., intrusive thoughts) were third (Kemp et al., 1995). An earlier study showed similar results and that the levels of stress suffered by battered women were actually higher than those found in a community sample of Vietnam veterans (B. L. Green, Lindy, Grace, & Glese, 1989).

Learning experiments with animals offer an explanation for some of the PTSD-associated behaviors of battered women. Rats in a Skinner box learn to press a bar to escape from or avoid a shock. In escape and avoidance learning, the animal must learn to make a response (press the bar) to escape or avoid pain. (See Appendix F.10 and F.11 for a learning explanation of avoidance behavior.) A battered woman might learn to avoid battering through self-protective actions (Langford, 1996). For example, if she is talking to a friend on the phone when the threats occur, she may hang up and start dinner, move to what she considers to be a safe area of the house, or leave the area entirely. She may avoid going home or move out for a period of time, avoid intimacy, or withdraw from her partner emotionally (Wuest & Merritt-Gray, 1999).

One of the most remarkable aspects of responses learned through avoidance conditioning techniques is their persistence (failure to extinguish). In one experiment, dogs learned to avoid a traumatic shock by jumping over a barrier after a warning signal (tone). In a second phase, the experimenters turned off all the equipment so that the dogs were not shocked no matter what they did. When the investigators occasionally presented the tone during this period, the dogs continued jumping over the barrier. They continued jumping for over 200 trials! They never learned that they did not need to jump to avoid a painful shock. They seemed unwilling to take the risk of not jumping (Solomon, Kamin, & Wynne, 1953).

An extrapolation of the persistence of avoidance learning to battering relationships may help explain the inflexible behavior of some battered women. Battered women who have escaped beatings through some behaviors, such as being sexually available, compliant, or nonconfrontive with their partners, may come to rely on these behaviors and to use them even when no beating is imminent. The problem of persistent nonadaptive responding will also become apparent to therapists working with individuals conditioned in this manner. Battered women may feel unable to make changes in their behavior. Moreover, the extreme fear brought about by the abuse may not diminish (extinguish) for many years.

An investigation of the effects of abuse on attachment styles uncovered two results (Justice & Hirt, 1992). Compared to nonabused women, abused women scored significantly higher on emotional detachment, specifically on the factors of angry withdrawal and availability. Angry withdrawal reflects an avoidance coping style. Availability refers to the expectation that responses to one's needs will not be positive. PTSD in battered women represents this combination of high arousal and high avoidance.

Attachment

The attachment styles of both members of a couple profoundly influence their interactions. In Gordon and Christman's study (2008), individuals who had developed some form of fearful attachment were very likely to avoid intimacy by distancing themselves from their partner. A contemporary study of Israeli women compared battered women living in a shelter with a community sample of nonbattered women. The findings indicated that the battered women were significantly more anxious and avoidant than the nonbattered women. The battered women also had a lower level of romantic feelings for their partners (Shechory, 2012).

In an English study of male and female victims of violent assaults (including battered women), behavioral changes were apparent in 66% of the sample immediately after the assault. These changes remained for at least six months in 25% of the victims (Shepherd, 1990). The most common behavioral change was avoidance of the location where the attack had occurred. An individual who has been stalked at one location is very likely to move to avoid additional incidents (Spitzberg, 2002). Other symptoms were physical problems and emotional distress.

Amick-McMullen and colleagues (1989) introduced a learning conceptualization *(two-process avoidance theory)* to explain the occurrence and maintenance of PTSD. In this theory, two processes occur: classical conditioning (fear) and operant conditioning (avoidance response; e.g., run to a safe location) (Mowrer, 1947; Rescorla & Solomon, 1967). In the first process, an organism (i.e., a young woman) becomes classically conditioned to fear a stimulus, such as the ringing of the phone, paired with an aversive message (e.g., "Your brother has been killed in Afghanistan"). In the second process, the organism (she) becomes operantly conditioned to take the phone off the hook (avoidance behavior) to avoid the fear generated by the stimulus (ringing phone).

Preventing the fear associated with such a message is reinforcing and therefore maintains the avoidance behavior. Unfortunately, one core feature of PTSD is the constant cognitive reexperiencing of the stressful event. This recurrence helps to maintain a high level of anxiety. To counteract the anxiety generated by the mental replays, an individual must repeatedly expend energy to monitor his or her actions. Even when someone is feeling less stressed, the occurrence of a very similar event can elicit the fear all over again. In learning terms, experiencing the fear again after a respite is called spontaneous recovery (re-remembering the fear after a period of not responding with fear). (Refer to Appendix E.2 for an explanation of spontaneous recovery.)

Case Study: Wanda and Paul

Wanda paid a high price for having fun. Paul went through her closet, removing her fancy dresses and ripping them to shreds. He wanted to punish her for dancing with other men at her cousin's wedding. Actually, this was not the first time she had been punished for indiscretions. He had slapped her and had broken the phone because she had talked with her sister twice in one week.

Wanda spent a lot of time questioning her behavior. Activities that used to seem normal became distorted in her own mind: "Maybe I do spend too much time on the phone or with my family." "I shouldn't have danced with other men at my cousin's wedding."

A little at a time, Wanda withdrew and avoided contact with people who upset Paul. If she was on the phone and Paul entered the room, she jumped. She forgot what life before Paul had been like, and that she used to be happy.

Frustration, Problem Solving, Coping Skills, and Learned Helplessness

Frustration

For a battered woman, the desire to be close to a partner and to have a happy home is countered by the reality of her husband's violence. Frustration generated by this approach-avoidance conflict may diminish her ability to solve problems effectively (see Frye, 2011). For animals caught in an approach-avoidance situation, frustration develops when a problem leading to a reward becomes unsolvable and attempts at solution are painful and presumably create fear. Some of the consequences for the laboratory animals were the development of inflexible, rigid behavior, refusal to behave, and unsuccessful attempts to escape. (Turn to Appendix F.14 for an explanation of the N. R. F. Maier [1949] animal experiment on frustration.)

Effects of frustration vary, however, depending upon the design of the experiment. Amsel and Rousel (1972) rewarded rats twice, first after a short run and again after another run. After the animals adjusted to that pattern, the researchers removed the first reward. The animals began to run faster to get the second reward. In other words, the rats performed more but got less. Researchers interpreted this outcome as increased performance motivated by frustration. How is this animal research relevant to human behavior? Battered women may be willing to do more to get less. In their frustration, they may be willing to try harder to please a partner who gives them less. (See Appendix F.13 for an explanation of motivation following frustration.)

Increased performance as a consequence of frustration sharply contrasts with apathy and rigid responding as outcomes. That is, the differences in the outcomes of the two types of frustration experiments (inflexibility versus increased motivation) arise from differences generated by the dissimilarity between experimental procedures. The inflexibility outcome (as in N. R. F. Maier, 1949) arises from the frustration accompanied by pain and fear. The increased motivation (as in Amsel & Rousel, 1972) emanates from the desire to achieve a goal. It is possible to apply the findings of both of these studies to abusive relationships. The more a battered woman is frustrated by her inability to improve her relationship and to end the violence, the more motivated she is to continue trying (Amsel & Rousel, 1972). Nonetheless, as fear increases, active problem-solving behavior diminishes (N. R. F. Maier, 1949). (See Appendix F.13 and F.14 to review the animal research.)

Problem Solving

Crime victims experience severe symptoms, including an inability to perform ordinary tasks. Female assault survivors have demonstrated a vast range of impairments in cognitive processing, trauma memory, and decision making (Halligan, Michael, Clark, & Ehlers, 2003; Mather & Lighthall, 2012). In an early study, Launius and Jensen (1987) studied problem solving in three different groups of women: (a) nonbattered women in therapy for anxiety and depression, (b) nonbattered women who were not in therapy, and (c) battered women. All three groups received everyday problems to solve, such as: "You are in a long line in the theater and two people cut in ahead of you. You don't appreciate this. What can you do?" Battered women selected and generated fewer effective solutions to the situations presented than did the other groups.

Not every investigation indicates that battered women are poor problem solvers. In a test involving a hypothetical abuse situation, they showed no deficit. In fact, data indicated that battered women solved a higher number of relationship problems than did nonbattered women (J. C. Campbell, 1989; see also Shechory, 2012). Nonetheless, in situations with their male partners, they were more passive and less assertive than the other women (see also Claerhout, Elder, & Janes, 1982; Launius & Lindquist, 1988).

Problem-solving deficits seem to be situation-specific and an outcome of the cognitive distortions associated with PTSD. Survival mandates a focus of attention on the person who controls the situation. From this perspective, the battered woman's attention and problem-solving abilities seem to be pointed in the practical direction (J. C. Campbell, 1989). Trimpey (1989) speculates that a battered woman's inability to effectively generate solutions to some problems is the result of anxiety brought on by pervasive physical and psychological abuse (see also Clements, Sabourin, & Spilby, 2004). M. N. Russell, Lipov, Phillips, & White (1989) found that abused women were significantly more anxious, confused, and fatigued than nonbattered women. In an important longitudinal study, battered women's self-care was similar to that of other adult women, but worsened over the three-and-a-half-year duration of the study for those still involved in abusive relationships (J. C. Campbell & Soeken, 1999).

Depression, brain injury, and mental disorders are all possible consequences of abuse, and when they occur, they may in themselves contribute to problem-solving deficits in survivors (Deering, Templer, Keller, & Canfield, 2001; Lindgren & Renck, 2008; Seedat, Stein, & Forde, 2005; Strom & Kosciulek, 2007). Negative effects of extreme stress are not limited to battered women. Depressed and anxious individuals in other populations also manifest problem-solving deficits (Nezu, D'Zurilla, Zwick, & Nezu, 2004; Yang & Clum, 1994).

Coping Skills

Coping skills seem to overlap problem-solving skills, and the literature is somewhat inconsistent in its findings about battered women's coping skills. Coping refers to cognitive and behavioral strategies that people use to manage the demands of a situation when it is stressful or overwhelming; coping is a way of reducing the stress or making the situation feel less overwhelming (VandenBos, 2007, p. 232). The ability to cope with stress has generated a sizeable amount of research, especially by experts who study diseases and disorders (epidemiologists) (Clements & Sawhney, 2000; Penley, Tomaka, & Wiebe, 2002).

Coping ability has significant effects on health, and it is strongly correlated with both physical and mental health measures. Also, the use of coping skills overlaps a number of specialized research areas, such as problem solving, PTSD, and therapeutic practices. A battered woman's ability to cope is the subject of much ongoing research. Because of the stressful and overwhelming situations faced by battered women, they usually develop some explicit type of coping strategy.

Most investigations have established that battered women's coping strategies are less effective than the coping techniques of women who have

Table 5.1   Brief Findings Regarding Coping Strategies Among Battered Women

Findings	Researchers
Intimate partner violence (IPV) diminishes a victim's ability to cope effectively.	Anson & Sagy, 1995; Kemp, Rawlings, & Green, 1991.
IPV victims seem less apt to use active coping strategies but significantly more prone to using passive or avoidance strategies.	Bernhard, 2000; Finn, 1985; Nurius, Furrey, & Berliner, 1992; Valentiner, Foa, Riggs, & Gershuny, 1996; Waldrop & Resick, 2004
The use of avoidance coping actually generates stress.	Holahan, Moos, Holahan, Brennan, & Schutte, 2005
Problem-focused coping is associated with decreased hopelessness.	Clements, Sabourin, & Spilby, 2004 Clements & Sawhney, 2000;
Placating and resisting are the strategies used earliest and most often, but they are the least effective.	Goodman, Dutton, Weinfurt, & Cook, 2003
The characteristics of the situation and one's resources are associated with the specific stressor variables.	DeLongis & Holtzman, 2005; De Ridder, 1997
Stressor type is a predictor of the coping strategy selected.	Lee-Baggley, Preece, & DeLongis, 2004
Women with a high sense of coherence (SOC) cope more effectively than those with a lower SOC. (SOC is a tendency to view the world as comprehensible and manageable.)	Lindgren & Renck, 2008
Changes in coping strategies occur over time. If one coping method does not work, a battered woman might try a different strategy.	Bowker, 1983; Dougall, Hyman, Hayward, McFeely, & Baum, 2001
Leaving an abuser may lead to a change in a survivor's coping strategies. Emotionally focused coping may decrease, while problem-focused coping may increase.	Lerner & Kennedy, 2000
Couples tend to use similar coping styles, and their styles become more similar over 10 years.	Holahan et al., 2007
Racial minorities and subgroups, such as rural battered women, may use different coping strategies.	Greer, 2007; Shannon, Logan, Cole, & Medley, 2006
Religious coping reduces the impact of stress on depression.	Lee, B.-J., 2007

Source: Barnett, O. W., Miller-Perrin, C. L., & Perrin, R. D. (2011). *Family violence across the lifespan* (3rd ed., p. 374). Thousand Oaks, CA: Sage. Reprinted with permission.

not been abused (e.g., Goodman, Dutton, Weinfurt, & Cook, 2003; Kemp et al., 1995). Battered women are less apt to use *active* coping strategies (obtaining social support, reframing stressful events, and seeking spiritual support), but significantly more apt to use *passive* strategies (fantasizing) (e.g., Nurius, Furrey, & Berliner, 1992; Waldrop & Resick, 2004). One current comparison between a sample of sheltered battered women and a sample of nonbattered women living in the community, however, found different results. Battered women in this study actually used more problem-focused coping (Shechory, 2012). Most experts contend that any problem-solving deficits among battered women are the result of male assaults (DeLongis & Holtzman, 2005). See Table 5.1 for details about coping among battered women.

The use of wishful thinking is especially prevalent among battered women. In a group of violent crime victims (not only battered women), one investigator found a positive link between the severity of symptoms and both avoidance and active coping styles (Kemp et al., 1995). Walker (1984) conjectured that active coping behaviors, such as confrontation, might escalate the abuse. One study found that as stress levels increased, effective coping strategies decreased (Gellen, Hoffman, Jones, & Stone, 1984; see also Britz & Pappas, 2010).

Women who blame their abuser for the intimate partner violence (IPV) in their relationship develop more coping strategies than women who do not. Women who blame their abuser also use more active and public coping methods. These results suggest that it is advantageous for battered victims to blame their batterer (Meyer, Wagner, & Dutton, 2010). Future research should try to identify the coping strategies battered women and other trauma victims need to develop to maintain their safety.

Clinical experience supports the notion that while battered women are creative and tenacious problem solvers, they may be trying to solve the wrong problem. Most battered women are striving to stop the violence by focusing on changing the abuser's behavior. One therapeutic goal should be to help them refocus their efforts on their own safety and the safety of their children. Designing safety or temporary escape plans can be useful in this regard.

Learned Helplessness

Additional theoretical rationales help complete the picture of why battered women stay. Gerow (1989, p. 193) defines learned helplessness as "a condition in which a subject does not attempt to escape from a painful or noxious situation after learning in a previous, similar situation that escape is not possible." Hiroto (1974) empirically documented learned helplessness in humans using a sample of college students in an uncontrollable noise experiment. (See Appendix F.15 for a more detailed description of the original animal experiment by S. F. Maier and Seligman, 1976.)

According to Martin Seligman (1975), there are three components to learned helplessness: (a) motivational impairment (passivity), (b) intellectual impairment (poor problem-solving ability), and (c) emotional trauma (increased feelings of helplessness, incompetence, frustration, and depression). Seligman particularly emphasized the similarity between learned helplessness and clinical depression (Peterson & Seligman, 1984; see also Eagly & Johnson, 1990; Peterson, Maier, & Seligman, 1993).

Walker (1977) was the first researcher to apply the original learned helplessness findings to battered women. Both Walker and Hendricks-Matthews (1982) have suggested that learned helplessness causes battered women to make causal attributions that tend to keep them entrapped in the relationship, and one study detected higher levels of externality (attributing events to the outside world) in survivors than in nonvictims (Theodore, 1992). For example, a battered woman is likely to blame herself for the violence as though she had done something to provoke the attacks. Unfortunately, society tends to reinforce this view.

There has been continuing disagreement over the appropriateness of applying the learned helplessness model to battered women (see Rhodes & McKenzie, 1998, for a review). Investigators testing the model have examined depression, locus of control, coping styles, and helpseeking behavior. Walker (1984) used the Levenson Locus of Control Scale (Levenson, 1973) to measure three different types of control (internal, powerful others, and chance) in battered women. She tested the hypothesis that battered women would score high on the powerful others and chance dimensions. The women, however, scored high on all three scales. From these data, Walker suggested that battered women believe that they have a great amount of control over their lives. They think that they will eventually be able to change their batterer's behavior, a sort of illusion of control or learned hopefulness, as described previously (see also Arias, Lyons, & Street, 1997; Follingstad, Hause, Rutledge, & Polek, 1992).

Wauchope (1988) attempted to use the relationship between helpseeking behavior and severity of violence as a test of learned helplessness theory. Her findings indicated that as the severity of violence increased, women were more likely, rather than less likely, to seek help. She interpreted her findings as failing to support learned helplessness theory. Gondolf (1988a) developed an alternative model to learned helplessness. He based his "survivor theory" on the many helpseeking attempts made by battered women.

A later study found that severity of abuse was not only related to increased helpseeking behavior, but also to increased levels of helplessness. The researchers concluded that helpseeking behavior and helplessness are not equivalent or mutually exclusive. In fact, they theorized that women who are severely abused become helpless, believing that the only avenue of escape is through the assistance of others; thus, they seek help (K. Wilson, Vercella, Brems, Benning, & Renfro, 1992). Later research has confirmed that increased physical abuse is related to increased helpseeking efforts (Raghavan, Swan, Snow, & Mazur, 2005). Stalking is also associated with increased helpseeking (Flicker et al., 2011). Furthermore, L. L. Marshall (1996) discovered that different types of abuse, such as psychological, physical, or sexual abuse, are related to different ways of seeking help. Experts who tend to reject the application of learned helplessness to battered women's actions interpret the findings differently. They believe that battered women's many helpseeking attempts and their use of different types of coping strategies are behaviors that do *not* support a learned helplessness model (J. C. Campbell, Miller, Cardwell, & Belknap, 1994; Goodman, Bennett, & Dutton, 1999).

A 1996 national random telephone survey of 6,766 women identified 2,811 female survivors of partner violence, 226 of whom had been assaulted within the last five years. Of the assaulted group, 38% had contacted the police, 32% had sought a restraining order, and 31% had sought medical care. Many of these women (41%) had failed to access any services. Factors associated with failure to obtain help were as follows: (a) higher income; (b) no children in the house; (c) employment, homemaker, or school activities; (d) higher educational attainment; (e) nonminority racial status; and (f) youthfulness (J. Hathaway et al., 1998). Finally, in one study of battered women with protection orders, 78% had sought help other than emergency protection orders, but almost half (46%) had turned to neighbors and friends rather than to shelters (Keilitz, Davis, Eikerman, Flango, & Hannaford, 1998).

A cross-cultural study has shed additional light on dissimilar conceptions of learned helplessness versus agency by describing how battered women in Pakistan respond. Pakistani women in general live in a patriarchal society in which they are powerless along several dimensions, such as the availability of police protection and the availability of work. In the present qualitative study of 21 battered women, the women reported that the least desirable alternative for coping with battering was divorce. Although shelters for women were available, none of the women sought them out. Instead, they chose innovative solutions that yielded limited success within their culture. The creativity of their solutions may be viewed by many as support for an agency theory of battered women's actions.

A particularly interesting coping strategy was to pray to Allah. No person in Pakistan is allowed to interfere with another person's prayers; thus, women could often stop the abuse by falling into a prayerful state. Praying itself helped reduce the women's fear and stress. Another technique was to go on a trip to worship at a religious shrine, which might be quite distant. Taking a bus in a male-dominated society and leaving children behind for a day, however, was personally costly. The women took other actions, such as avoiding the batterer by going into another room and by seeking help from families and neighbors. Another move was to stay close to male children whom they believed would protect them if they were strong enough to do so (Zakar, R., Zakar, M. Z., & Krämer, 2012).

It seems probable that, like problem-solving deficits, learned helplessness may be situation-specific, a finding consistent with the animal studies (S. F. Maier & Seligman, 1976; see also DeLongis & Holtzman, 2005).

Case Study: Janice

Janice finally called the police, who arrested her violent boyfriend, Adam. The police officers were sensitive and supportive about her assault, and they gave her a shelter hotline number. The shelter advocate listened to Janice's story and made appropriate referrals to a battered women's group, a victim advocate in the courts, and a therapist.

The court advocate and the city prosecutor got Janice ready for her day in court, which occurred six weeks after the incident. She was not prepared, however, for the complexity of the system or the outcomes. Her injuries were tangible and substantial. Six weeks after her boyfriend had punched her in the face, her eyes were still bruised and swollen. The doctor had removed the stitches over her upper lip, but the scar was an angry red.

Janice was not emotionally ready to see Adam again. When he appeared in court, he was different. He seemed contrite, and the judge thought so too. The final results of Janice's hours of helpseeking ended this way:

- Adam had to attend an abusers' group counseling program.
- He had to pay restitution to Janice, which was supposed to be $100 a month for two years but totaled only $50. She received the money before Adam's records were buried in a probation bank caseload of 5,000.
- Janice's therapist advised her to make contact with Adam's therapist, but the therapist never returned the call.
- Janice lost her job because of time lost while she sought medical attention and made court appearances.
- Janice then lost her apartment because of her lost income and because Adam did not pay the restitution that she needed for her rent.

Janice, a 35-year-old professional woman, lost her home, her job, and her boyfriend. Adam kept his home and his job and found a new romantic interest while attending his recovery program.

A battered woman may acquire learned helplessness regarding certain areas of her life, but not all. Another possibility is that as the abuse occurs more frequently and the severity escalates, the learned helplessness generalizes. Consider the cases of battered women who believe that homicide or suicide are their only viable options.

Battered women are very focused on the abuse and the abuser. It becomes the predominant theme of family life and the pivotal feature around which everything else revolves. It would make sense that generalized problem solving and coping may be impaired, as energy goes primarily to problem solving and coping with the abuser. For the most part, the behavior of the battered woman has little long-term effect on what happens within the relationship. If she stops talking to friends on the phone because it upsets him, sooner or later something else will trigger the controlling behavior or the violent episode. Even her effective problem solving may only delay the abuse; it will not stop it. Support for the premise that battered women have little control over an abuser's behavior comes from a study of abusive couples' arguments. None of a wife's behaviors successfully suppressed a husband's violence once it began (Jacobson et al., 1994; see also Lindgren & Renck, 2008).

According to the model of social support provided by Dunkel-Schetter, Folkman, and Lazarus (1987), people need to have social support systems in place. The system needs to include a network of individuals who can function appropriately in times of stress. Seeking help is easier if there is someone tangible to seek it from. A number of battered women lack adequate and available social support systems. Unfortunately, having a support network in place may be a double-edged sword. For example, a friend may listen with concern to a neighbor's story of abuse but then insist that the neighbor's only answer is an immediate divorce (Kocot & Goodman, 2003; Postmus, Severson, Berry, & Yoo, 2009). Helpfulness and harmfulness may be independent dimensions that coexist. In other words, certain forms of social support are not necessarily helpful and may even increase PTSD or depression in victims (Kocot & Goodman, 2003).

The Battered Woman Syndrome

While the law specifically, and society in general, have offered little help to the battered wife, and indeed may be partially responsible for the actions of those who strike back violently, many of these women now face homicide charges brought by the same society and its legal system.

—Anonymous (cited in Nerney, 1987, p. 21)

There has been confusion concerning the definition of the battered woman syndrome (BWS). Some authors use the abusive acts committed against the woman as the defining aspects of BWS (e.g., severity, frequency of assaults) (see J. C. Campbell, 1990). Walker (1985a), in contrast, conceptualizes the syndrome as a severe stress reaction, a subcategory of PTSD. Basic personality components of BWS include fear, depression, guilt, passivity, and low self-esteem (M. A. Douglas, 1987; Lovik, 2011a). BWS may be conceptualized as a set of personality attributes brought on by abuse that render the victim more able to survive in the relationship and less able to escape it. The battered woman's belief that escape is impossible and her depression and fear accompanying this belief lead to her entrapment in the relationship. The three components of the syndrome include the following: (a) behaviors brought on by victimization, (b) learned helplessness behavior, and (c) self-destructive coping behaviors.

In 1992, M. A. Dutton developed a model of PTSD that suggested that battered women experience great stress from being battered that alters their cognitions. Disturbance in the woman's intimate relationships (e.g., attachment) is a factor as well. Not all women react to battering the same way because of several variables: (a) the levels of social support they receive, (b) the level of concurrent stress in their lives, (c) the level of premarital (e.g., childhood) abuse they have experienced, and (d) the severity of the current violence directed against them. Given the difficulties in defining BWS, Follingstad (1998) speculates that it might be best just to drop the BWS terminology and simply rely on the PTSD framework and the more specific definition by the American Psychiatric Society.

The Violence Against Women Act (VAWA) of 1994 (Public Law 103-322, Title IV) called for a report on a number of factors involving BWS: (a) medical and psychological bases; (b) the use of BWS in trials; and (c) the perceptions of judges, prosecutors, and defense attorneys regarding the effects of BWS evidence in criminal trials (U.S. Department of Justice, 1996). The report found the following:

1. The name *BWS* does not satisfactorily reflect the scientific knowledge accumulated, and it carries the implication of a malady or a single pattern of responses to battering. Also, there is no "battered woman's defense" per se, only expert testimony.

2. There is an extensive body of literature about the dynamics of battering and stress reactions to battering.

3. Expert testimony tends to increase knowledge about domestic violence and improves the ability of juries to reach decisions.

Gender differences in reasons for killing highlight the need for the "battered woman syndrome." In one study of over 1,600 homicides, self-defense characterized almost all killings by females but almost none by males. A number of other actions and motives typified male killers, but not females: (a) men often hunt down and kill spouses who have left them; (b) men kill as part of a planned murder-suicide; (c) men kill in response to revelations of wifely infidelity, although men are generally more adulterous than women; (d) men kill after subjecting their wives to lengthy periods of coercive abuse and assaults; and (e) men perpetrate family massacres (M. I. Wilson & Daly, 1992).

Contemporary research has established that battered women nearly always kill out of fear for their own lives or fear for their children's safety (Melbin, Sullivan, & Cain, 2003; W. Wells & DeLeon-Granados, 2002; see also Weizmann-Henelius et al., 2012). A battered woman may perceive homicide to be her only viable option. Defense attorney Leslie Abramson (cited in Gibbs, 1993, p. 43) has argued, "Morally and legally, she should not be expected to wait until his hands are around her neck." She believes that while men may kill out of wounded pride, women most often kill out of fear (see Abramson, 1994).

One reason a battered woman may come to believe that she has no option is that society has not protected women from intimate partner violence. The 1987 Committee on Domestic Violence and Incarcerated Women recognized that the criminal justice system does not act effectively to protect women from being beaten ("Panel Says," 1987). A battered woman may not be able to obtain a restraining order or keep it in effect. She may be unable to obtain even temporary financial support for a 30-day period. The court will most likely allow her abuser visitation with the children. In the end, no one can guarantee her safety ("Domestic Violence in the Courts," 1989).

The 1987 committee concluded that the criminal justice system's response was inconsistent and inadequate ("Panel Says," 1987). The New York Committee on Domestic Violence (Nerney, 1987) has concluded that killing an assaultive male should not be the only option left to battered women. When leaving is more dangerous than staying but staying amounts to living in daily terror, the battered woman's dilemma can reach its final, catastrophic climax. It remains an ongoing societal struggle to find a balance between expressing compassionate concern for survivors of marital violence and condoning violence as the justifiable response.

Most courts have gradually allowed expert testimony to explain why battered women kill. When accepted by the court, defense attorneys have used PTSD symptomatology to negotiate and diminish responsibility for a criminal act. The PTSD defense presents several challenges to defense attorneys. Primarily, a diagnosis of PTSD stems from subjective self-reports. Obviously, people striving to avoid criminal punishments might try to distort their symptoms. Furthermore, defense attorneys must show a causal connection between PTSD symptoms and the alleged criminal act. That is, something about the symptoms (e.g., a flashback) caused the defendant to commit the criminal act. Attorneys also must show that the defendant's PTSD stemmed from a specifiable stressor (e.g., rape) rather than from past childhood traumas or other stressful events (Sparr, 1996).

Some legal scholars use BWS to expand the concept of legal self-defense. This defense holds that a battered woman is virtually held hostage in a violent household by a man who isolates and terrorizes her, convincing her that if she leaves he will track her down and kill her. Violence and threats usually occur frequently, and even when there is a period of alleged non-violence, abused women do not feel safe. A mood of danger has been created that predisposes the survivor to an ongoing state of chronic fear and arousal (hypervigilance). DePaul (1992, p. 5) describes the syndrome as "the situation of a long-time victim of physical, sexual, and psychological abuse who loses self-confidence, feels trapped, and eventually strikes back, assaulting or killing the abuser" (see also Mones, 1992). At the very least, violence by a loved one can create what civil law calls "the exacerbation of a pre-existing condition."

The standard for assessing the nature of self-defense has been euphemistically called the reasonable man's defense. In other words, what would a reasonable man do in this situation? Reasonable women and children may have different perceptions about what is life threatening and react in different and distinct ways (see Osthoff, 1992). According to Schneider (1986), the reasonable man standard needs extension to a reasonable woman standard. Increasingly, this viewpoint is being heard.

Legal scholars and battered women's advocates argue that the experiences of battered women are unique and should be explained to a jury (Dodge & Greene, 1991). According to DePaul (1992, p. 5),

> Without expert testimony to explain how women come to feel so dependent or fearful that they cannot leave an abusive relationship, juries often are left to wonder why the woman did not walk out long before she felt compelled to retaliate.

One investigation studied jurors' knowledge about the experiences of battered women. Results indicated that jurors were relatively informed about the escalation of violence in a relationship. They also understood that women could be anxious, depressed, and fearful. Jurors had less understanding about self-blame, dependency, hopefulness that the partner would change, and victims' use of deadly force (Greene, Raitz, & Lindblad, 1989; see also Huss, Tomkins, Garbin, Schopp, & Kilian, 2006).

To offset jurors' lack of understanding, expert testimony should focus on the impact of violence and the woman's perception of threat. As an example, suppose a woman's husband indicates in obvious or subtle ways that he is going to give her "what for" when he gets up from his nap. Further suppose that he has beaten her previously under similar circumstances. She might believe the time has come to keep him from waking up. The threat, which has been paired with certain violence in the past, takes on a reality of its own. The nap itself can become a generalized cue that signals to a woman that danger lies ahead. The nap can become a blinking red light (Nerney, 1987; see also *State of Kansas v. Deborah Davis*, cited in Creach, 1982).

Researchers who have investigated the backgrounds of women incarcerated for murder have found that many were abused. A report of the Governor's Committee to Study Sentencing and Correctional Alternatives for Women Convicted of Crime (State of Maryland, 1988, cited in "Domestic Violence in the Courts," 1989) established that 43% of the incarcerated women in Maryland had been physically abused and 33% had been sexually abused. According to Sheila Kuehl (personal communication, April 16, 1992), who worked on the California Clemency Project for battered women who kill, 93% of the women imprisoned for homicide in California claim to have killed their batterers.

Case Study: Patricia

Patricia was the top student in her nursing program and a grandmother when she killed her husband. Her abuse had been primarily sexual (rape and sodomy with injury) and emotional (threats to kill her or her children). He had pushed her around for years, but she didn't even count that behavior as violent.

Her case was given to an overworked public defender, and the battered woman's expert received preparation for her testimony only one hour before she appeared on the stand. Even though there were several people who could have corroborated the deceased's abusive behavior, the only witness her attorney called in her defense was a teacher who had a love affair with Patricia and remained her friend.

Patricia was planning to leave her abusive husband when he threatened to sexually abuse her three-year-old grandson. She paid a neighbor $300 to kill her abuser. The prosecutor charged Patricia with murder for financial gain, as she was the beneficiary on her husband's $1,500 life insurance policy. She confessed to everything on the stand except wanting the money or wanting her husband dead. She wanted the jury, the judge, the attorneys, and everyone in the courtroom to understand that she just wanted to protect her grandson.

Patricia did not have the benefit of a fully developed battered woman's defense. The judge, using the reasonable man defense as a yardstick, found her guilty of murder with special circumstances. Patricia is serving a life sentence without the possibility of parole.

Advocates for battered women have raised the question about the fairness of these convictions and whether battered women who kill should be in prison. The battered woman syndrome as a defense, however, is controversial. A number of observers worry that husband killings will go unpunished: "What message are we giving women when they can kill their husbands and get away with it?" Across the years, the authors of this book have not seen or heard of any hesitation in utilizing the heat-of-passion defense. This defense is notoriously one-sided, a gendered defense for men who killed their wives or their wives' lovers when they found them *in flagrante delicto* (in the act of sexual intercourse). Its use has gradually expanded to include other female infractions (e.g., when a woman leaves her spouse).

Many states are reexamining cases in which females claimed they killed a spouse or lover who abused them. Several governors have commuted sentences or granted clemency (Gibbs, 1993; Jewett, 2011). Many more have not. In reality, most battered women who kill are no threat to society. Nonetheless, few women are acquitted at trials; most (72% to 80%) are convicted or accept a plea, and many receive very long sentences (Osthoff, 1991). To address this problem, various organizations have solicited funds to help imprisoned battered women. The California Habeas Project (n.d.) has worked with 80 incarcerated battered women and secured the release of 19.

The very good news is that the number of homicide victims across the United States fell 31% between 1992 and 2007. Intimate partner deaths declined 29% during the same period. While deaths of male intimates declined 36%, deaths of female intimates declined only 26% (Catalano, Smith, Snyder, & Rand, 2009).

Case Study: Barbara

On October 6, 2011, a jury in Queens, New York, acquitted Barbara Sheehan of murdering her husband of 24 years, Raymond Sheehan, a policeman. The jury reached this verdict despite the fact that Ms. Sheehan had fired 11 bullets at Mr. Sheehan while he was shaving. Some observers questioned the verdict on grounds that Mr. Sheehan did not seem to present an "imminent danger" to Ms. Sheehan at the time of the shooting.

Other information about Mr. Sheehan's chronic and vicious domestic violence explained the jury's verdict. Ms. Sheehan and her children testified that Mr. Sheehan had smashed Ms. Sheehan's head against a cinderblock wall during a vacation. He also had thrown boiling spaghetti sauce at her and punched her the evening before she shot him. She testified that when she started to leave him the next day, she took a gun with her for protection. When he saw it, he reached for his police revolver on the bathroom vanity.

The jury concluded that Ms. Sheehan did fear for her life when she shot him, a decision reflecting the jurors' acceptance of the battered woman's defense. A legal expert said the case represented the jury's belief that abuse influences a victim's decision to act in self-defense. (Bilefsky, 2011)

Summary

A woman's acceptance of responsibility for the violence in her home, coupled with her inability to stop it, creates confusion and frustration and obstructs certain forms of effective problem solving and coping. If she is unable to see any relationship between what she does and what happens to her, it is likely that she will feel helpless and depressed. Further complicating her options is the chronic fear resulting from her abuse. She may receive supportive responses from her family and friends but also some negative, hurtful, and nonsupportive comments. If she tries to leave, she may face a greater likelihood of continued assault or an increased possibility that she will be murdered.

Results from learning experiments have explained and simplified the mechanisms underlying the development of PTSD symptoms among battered women as well as their avoidance-motivated behaviors. While the concept of learned helplessness helps explain some aspects of her behavior, such as her problem-solving deficits and ineffective coping styles, PTSD provides a broader psychological and physiological framework. PTSD more fully documents the experiences of individuals exposed to chronic or severe trauma such as battering. If a battered woman cannot stop the violence and perceives that she has no other options, the day may come when she makes a lethal choice: to kill her abuser.

6

Catalysts for Change

This chapter is dedicated to the community-change agents of the 1970s who uncovered a problem that had been buried and unnamed. That problem is the violence directed against women in their homes, the places that have been synonymous with women's safety. Without the feminist movement, battered wives would still be deadbolted into their houses and manacled to their abusers. These grassroots pioneers began organizing to create solutions. "Catalysts for Change" is a chapter about those solutions and the solutions for the future.

The Importance of Prevention

The progressive nature of domestic violence, along with such consequences as substance abuse, depression, and attempted suicide, underscores the importance of early recognition and intervention.

—"The Battered Woman: Breaking the Cycle of Abuse"
(1989, p. 104; see also Flood & Pease, 2009;
C. E. Murray & Graybeal, 2007)

In addition to the life-altering consequences for women, exposure of children to family violence has profoundly negative effects. Children exposed to family violence suffer from increased anxiety, low self-esteem, truancy, low school achievement, and other behavioral problems (Finkelhor, Turner, Ormrod, Hamby, & Kracke, 2009; P. G. Jaffe, Hastings, & Reitzel, 1992).

Toddlers as young as three are affected (Main & George, 1985). Given the serious consequences to women, children, and society, steps to prevent battering are essential.

For change to happen, basic ideological transformations must occur, and "men have a particular role to play in educating other men about the nature of abuse and how men can change" (D. C. Adams & McCormick, 1982, p. 171; see also Bennett, Stroops, Call, & Flett, 2007). Glen Good, president of the Society for the Psychological Study of Men and Masculinity, a division of the American Psychological Association, has brought attention to the problems of masculine socialization. According to Good,

> Problems like violence, substance abuse, relationship issues, parenting problems, and poor health habits need attention. We also need to develop intervention for more recently identified masculinity-related problems, such as lack of emotional competence, defensive self-sufficiency, poor sexual integrity, and uninvolved fathers. (1998, p. 3)

Males are both killers and victims. Today's adolescents are in grave conflict about the masculine role, as is society. It is time for society to change its model of masculinity. "Men feel intense demands to uphold traditional gender roles. Aggressive behaviors may be reactions to the stress men experience in trying to abide by these expectations" (T. M. Moore et al., 2008, p. 83). People need to let real boys be diverse, loving, caring, and emotionally expressive (Good, 1998).

Society needs to change not only its model of masculinity, but also its treatment of women everywhere. Organizations that have traditionally championed human rights should recognize the inhumane treatment of women around the globe as a human rights issue (Howard-Hassman, 2011). Murphy and Meyer (1991, p. 99) proposed that "treatment in the area of spousal violence should be part of a larger movement designed to alter the social factors that contribute to violence against women and that keep women trapped in abusive relationships."

Children exposed to family violence suffer from increased anxiety, low self-esteem, truancy, low school achievement, and other behavioral problems (Bair-Merritt et al., 2008; Graham-Bermann & Howell, 2010; P. G. Jaffe et al., 1992; D. Russell, Springer, & Greenfield, 2010). Early and appropriate intervention with children can counteract the insidious consequences of exposure to parental violence. Interventions must be designed according to the emotional, behavioral, cognitive, social, and physiological functioning of the child.

Lynn Loar, a children's advocate, and Carol Rathmann, director of the Sonoma County Humane Society, have pioneered a program to teach

abused and neglected children gentleness with living things. The program facilitators introduce the children to gardening, instilling in them a sense that they can nurture and cause beautiful or edible things to grow. They start the children with plants, because they know that children who live with abuse might also perpetrate it when they became frustrated. Loar and Rathmann did not want the children in their program to hurt an animal or carry the guilt of having harmed a pet. Once the fledgling farmers have mastered the gentle caretaking of plants and flowers, they are promoted to playing with large, sturdy animals.

The volunteers and staff at the Humane Society of Sonoma County want to teach children that touch does not need to be frightening—that it can be healing, gentle, and loving. They want to promote trusting relationships between children and adults. The children learn both empathy and compassion through human interaction and by tending the animals. They learn to be patient, as the plants and animals have different schedules than the people who care for them. These traumatized children learn that they can be superheroes who nurture and protect other living creatures, and that they themselves are worthy of care and attention. They learn values that are incompatible with violence (Loar & Rathmann, 1994).

Children living in abusive families need to label and deal with their emotional reactions to the violence. They need to develop safety skills and learn how to develop social support networks. They also need to understand that they are not responsible for the violence in their families (Gruzinski, Brink, & Edleson, 1988). An exciting new treatment developed by Alicia Liberman and her associates (cited in J. Zorza, 1999) considers the mother and the child as dual victims of domestic violence and treats them both through a series of weekly home visits. The treatment has led to a dramatic reduction in PTSD symptomatology in both mother and child, a decrease in the number of mothers who returned to their abusers, and an amazing increase in children's tested IQs (10 to 25 points).

Education is an essential piece of primary prevention programs and has the potential to reach across generational and cultural differences. There is a great need for education that conveys the message that family violence will not be tolerated (Kaci, 1990). Evidence suggests that public service announcements and documentaries have been successful in that regard (Kaci, 1990). In New Jersey, advocates have initiated a program to offer information to battered women. The underlying philosophy is that knowledge about domestic violence and the belief that one is not alone will crack through denial and isolation and reinforce action. Some doctors allow educational films to be shown in their waiting rooms and in hospital lobbies. These films enlighten the public about the causes and effects of spouse abuse and its legal consequences and remedies, including emergency protective orders and local resources.

Prevention programs are also available in some schools. The Southern California Coalition on Battered Women and Barrie Levy developed a curriculum for junior and senior high school called Prevention Skills for Violence-Free Relationships (Levy, 1984). One outgrowth of the program was the development at Jordan High School in Long Beach, California, of a family support group for students who lived in violent households or who had experienced dating violence. Later, Peace Over Violence (POV), formerly the Los Angeles Commission on Assaults Against Women (LACAAW), developed its In Touch With Teens curriculum. This innovative program utilizes teens and adults as facilitators (Aldrige, Friedman, & Occhiuzzo Giggans, 1995). P. G. Jaffe, Suderman, Reitzel, and Killip (1992) documented favorable changes in attitudes, behavior, and intentions following a large-scale secondary school prevention program. Gender differences indicated that females had greater sensitivity to domestic violence and women's equality than males. Evidence is accumulating that education can change attitudes toward wife abuse (Fox & Cook, 2011; Wolfe et al., 1996). Even a 20-minute oral presentation to university students about domestic violence produced some changes (O'Neal & Dorn, 1998).

One area of concern is that teenagers do not define or recognize dating violence as a problem (Levy, 1993; Parrot & Bechhofer, 1991; U.S. Department of Health and Human Services, Centers for Disease Control and Prevention, 2010). Schools can become more involved in education and prevention (Krajewski, 1996). One program prepared teens to provide resources and referrals for abused peers (Creighton & Kivel, 1993). Another called Safe Dates has shown a 25% reduction in emotional abuse (Foshee et al., 1998; 2000). Programs such as Break the Cycle are now available on the Internet (Gallopin & Leigh, 2009). There is a clear need to design programs that attempt to reduce attitudes supportive of male violence (O'Keefe & Treister, 1998; Whitaker et al., 2006). It is also crucial to educate parents about how to help their teens avoid dating violence (Levy & Occhiuzzo Giggans, 1995; see also Chapter 6 in Barnett, Miller-Perrin, & Perrin, 2011).

P. G. Jaffe and his colleagues (1992) make several recommendations for schools: (a) train personnel to recognize the behavior of children exposed to domestic abuse, (b) teach children conflict resolution skills, (c) establish a board to enlist agency services for referrals, and (d) develop a school protocol for handling disclosures. Because of mandatory child abuse reporting laws in every state, the school may intervene in spouse abuse because of the possibility of child endangerment. Along similar lines, screening for violence can be expanded to schools and pediatricians' offices and parenting education can be provided (Freed, Gupta, Hynes, & Miller, 2003).

One societal change necessary to prevent the transmission of violence across generations is to attack the problem of children's exposure to violence more effectively. By 1998, the legal system had made some headway but still failed to safeguard children's physical and mental health needs in a number of critical situations (L. D. Johnson, 1998). Utah led the way to correcting some of these needs by including witnessing parental abuse two or more times as a form of child maltreatment chargeable as a misdemeanor (cited in Edleson, 1999). In 2003 the federal government enacted the Child Abuse Prevention and Treatment Act (CAPTA), which mandated early intervention for maltreated children (Stahmer, Sutton, Fox, & Leslie, 2008; see also C. M. Adams, 2006). It should be noted that poverty is the variable most strongly linked with maltreatment of children (see Guetzkow, 2010).

Responding to research indicating that children chronically exposed to violence at home or in their communities are at much higher risk of becoming juvenile delinquents and adult criminals, President Bill Clinton said that "children's exposure to violence has tremendous negative consequences . . . for them and for all the rest of us" (cited in "President Announces Crackdown," 1998, p. 6). Clinton further stated, "It's time to send a message through the court that when a man assaults or kills someone in the presence of a child, he has committed not one horrendous act, but two" (p. 7) (see also Osofsky, 1998). The old saying "An ounce of prevention is worth a pound of cure" has particular relevance when considering the consequences to future generations.

Empowerment of Battered Women

Empowerment strategies are an essential component of recovery for women already victimized by intimate violence (Busch & Valentine, 2000; Kulkarni, Bell, & Rhodes, 2012). Empowerment involves two major aspects: (a) gaining power, and (b) taking action along specific dimensions (e.g., personal/ interpersonal or social/collective levels). Individual empowerment incorporates the notion of intrapsychic change. Social or environmental empowerment refers to deficiencies in the structure of forces in society. A team of international researchers working in Vietnam defined women's empowerment as the "ability to exercise agency and make strategic choices in an environment where this ability is limited by norms related to gender inequity" (Schuler, Trang, Ha, & Anh, 2011, p. 1423). Newer biobehavioral evidence has shown that having a choice or even the anticipation of having a choice can be emotionally beneficial because it evokes pleasure responses in the brain (Leotti & Delgado, 2011).

Women often pass through several different empowerment stages before they are able to change their feelings and cognitions about being battered. During the first stage, women feel fearful, angry, and powerless. During the second stage, victims become more aware of the danger of being victimized, and they start to place the blame for battering on the abuser. In the last stage, the woman is able to be more assertive and self-determined. She is likely to escape through getting a job or going back to school (see Paquet, Damant, Beaudoin, & Proulx, 1998, for a review).

Conditions central to the maintenance of abusive home environments are the self-perpetuating nature of family violence and the isolation in which it thrives. "The negative cycle of psychological control, damage to self-esteem and subsequent ability to leave a relationship requires intense therapeutic intervention" (Lewis et al., 2006, p. 351). Battered women's programs can effect change by intervening in these processes. A number of studies have provided empirical evidence of favorable changes fostered by shelter programs. In one short-term outreach treatment, women reported a decrease in abuse and an increase in life satisfaction and perceived coping ability (McNamara, Ertl, Marsh, & Walker, 1997). A small study of 20 sheltered women showed that after three weeks in the shelter, the women were significantly less depressed, more hopeful, and had higher internal locus of control scores (Dziegielewski, Resnick, & Krause, 1996).

Shelters

Shelters also help women to seek appropriate support services in the community (Fleury-Steiner & Brady, 2011). An emerging trend is to provide transitional housing and other post-shelter services (Melbin, Sullivan, & Cain, 2003; Orava, McLeod, & Sharpe, 1996). Battered women generally have favorable opinions of staff and the shelter experience. When funding problems have forced staff into multiple roles and increased their workloads, however, some residents have voiced concerns about the lack of staff availability for one-on-one counseling (Goodman & Epstein, 2008; Tutty, Weaver, & Rothery, 1999).

Battered women in a shelter can begin a restoration process by virtue of being separated from their abusers, feeling safe, having people to talk with about their problems, and working at a practical level to solve some of these problems. Battered women who have formed close relationships with other shelter residents or shelter staff are more likely to leave their abusive relationships (Dalto, 1983; Wathen & MacMillan, 2002).

Hotline counselors and shelter staff are generally very creative and aware of community resources. Shelter workers explore options with a battered woman to help her devise a safety and housing plan. Referrals may include a funded after-hours hotel, another emergency shelter (mission or church), a 24-hour coffee shop, or a friend or relative's home. Usually, space in a battered women's program will become available within a week. For a safe space outside of the area, a battered woman can sometimes obtain a small financial grant through an agency such as Traveler's Aid, Catholic Charities, Lutheran Social Services, or the YWCA.

The role of shelters has expanded as the special needs of underserved populations have come to the forefront (see Huisman, 1996, about Asian women; Valencia & Van Hoorn, 1999, about Latinas). Shelters have begun training staff and upgrading facilities to accommodate disabled women (Reyna, 1995; see also Rand & Harrell, 2009). Many shelters are now wheelchair accessible (ramps, wider doors) and have connections with specialized agencies in the community to meet the needs of handicapped women. One point of progress has been the inclusion of special telecommunication devices for hearing-impaired callers (Danis, Lewis, Trapp, Reid, & Fisher, 1998; see also Cohen-Mansfield et al., 2005).

Shelter programs are becoming better prepared to meet the needs of older battered women (Vinton, 1998; see also Boudreau, 1993; Zink, Regan, Jacobson, & Pabst, 2003). Reingold (2006) described a successful project that converted an assisted living center into a shelter. The REACH program, for instance, enhanced community outreach methods by advertising support groups that discussed concerns of older women rather than advertising battered women's groups (Brandl, Hebert, Rozwadowski, & Spangler, 2003).

Wisconsin, one of the first states to implement special programs for abused older women, has assisted other states in the development of protocols and programming. In a 1992 Florida survey of 6,026 women who had been sheltered during the previous year, approximately 2% were over 60. In a five-year follow-up study of these shelters, special programming had increased, as had the percentage of older staff members, volunteers, and board members (Vinton, Altholz, & Lobell, 1997). About a third offered outreach services, and 19% offered individual interventions for older victims. Despite these improvements, a minority of older battered women refuse services from any agency or organization (A. Klein, Tobin, Salomon, & Dubois, 2008; see also Shilling, 2008).

At the national level, the Women's Initiative of the American Association of Retired Persons (AARP) convened a forum bringing together service providers working with the elderly, battered women's advocates, and researchers. The Administration on Aging, an agency of the federal government, funded six demonstration projects in 1994 and 1995 that focused on the protection of older women against partner abuse (AARP, 1993, 1994).

An AARP study recommended the utilization of safe houses, a type of sister-to-sister program for sheltering abused older women. Another innovative approach is the formation of multidisciplinary community teams (Hwalek, Williamson, & Stahl, 1991; Nachman, 1991; Nerenberg, 2008). Using a team approach not only improves victim identification but also allows for joint decision making about which agency and type of intervention is best suited to the task (Matlaw & Spence, 1994). An important update in the research has suggested that older battered women would be better served by having greater access to elder care facilities rather than to shelters. From this perspective, providing shelter care for aging battered women should be refocused on providing more elder care facilities (Dunlop, Rothman, Condon, Hebert, & Martinez, 2000).

Leaving/Staying: Helping on an Individual Level

Whether battered women choose to leave or stay in the relationship, either temporarily or permanently, appropriate counseling needs to be part of the package for real change to occur. Many professionals see the woman's choice as one between staying or leaving. In contrast, a battered woman often experiences the conflict as, "Don't help me end the relationship; help me end the abuse" (Landenburger, 1989).

Although abused women who have counseling are significantly more likely to leave than women who do not (Frisch & MacKenzie, 1991), leaving as the measure of success of counseling is an inaccurate and invalid criterion (J. Brown, 1998). Leaving is a process for most battered women. Counselors need to acknowledge a battered woman's psychological upheaval during the process of leaving and to help her regain an emotional balance. Women need to feel safe and to eliminate the chaos in their lives. They especially need to salvage some sense of self-confidence and to reclaim the self (J. Brown, 1997; J. C. Chang et al., 2006; Moss, Pitula, Campbell, & Halstead, 1997; Wuest & Merritt-Gray, 1999).

Battered women grieve not only their loss of self, but also the loss of their abusive partner. There are those who ask, "Where's the loss?" Most battered women, however, feel great deprivation and loss when their relationships end (Allison, Bartholomew, Mayseless, & Dutton, 2008; Walker, 1984). While some argue that battered women are grieving the loss of a relationship, others suggest they are grieving the loss of their dreams and hopes (see Landenburger, 1989; Wuest & Merritt-Gray, 1999). Negating that loss does not help the women. Assessing battered women's losses and dealing with them in a support group enables women to develop a new sense of self-determination and to avoid the immobilizing effects of grief (Varvaro, 1991).

Some intimate partner abuse survivors do not confront their partners' abusive behavior for fear of losing them (Roloff, Soule, & Carey, 2001). Usually, both the batterer and the battered woman are strongly attached to each other (Griffing et al., 2002). Such feelings of attachment cause emotional turmoil for most people after a breakup with a romantic partner (Fangundes, 2012). Consequently, attachment between couples in an abusive relationship has become an important research topic, particularly as it relates to leave/stay decisions. If a woman leaves, loneliness may be a major factor in pulling her back to her batterer. Even a threat to leave by the female partner may drive the batterer to violence. Counselors may help persons involved in battering relationships to understand their attachment to their partners (Allison et al., 2008; Gordon & Christman, 2008; Vazquez, 1996).

Some of the most important work with battered women is the remaking of their belief systems in counseling. To make this change, shelters, therapists, and battered women's support groups should help women to stop believing that they caused or can stop the abuse (Massad & Hulsey, 2006). One effective approach to changing beliefs is cognitive reappraisal. The woman must make some cognitive readjustments along the lines of defining the meaning of the violence, what caused it, and what role it plays in her life now (D'Zurilla, 1986; see also Enander, 2011).

There are several other ways to accomplish an attitudinal shift: (a) breaking the silence and isolation by confiding in someone else (Vaughn, 1987); (b) getting education regarding sex roles and their relationship to domestic violence and power inequality; (c) building resources outside the relationship (M. N. Wilson, Baglioni, & Downing, 1989); (d) developing empathy for other battered women and compassion for oneself; and (e) grieving the loss of the relationship and one's idealistic beliefs (B. Russell & Uhlemann, 1994; Schiff, Gilbert, & El-Bassel, 2006).

Appropriate counseling should address the very real restrictions that women face in the world, in their relationships, and in stereotypical roles. At a practical level, counselors can role play job-interviewing techniques, assertion skills, parenting skills, and even basic apartment- or house-hunting approaches. Some believe that self-defense training for women is critical. Self-defense training can tap into a woman's physical power. It offers her a constructive physical outlet for her emotions (N. Cummings, 1990; see also Greenfeld et al., 1998).

Cognitive behavioral problem-solving strategies used in a group setting can be effective in helping abused women restore independent decision making skills. Holiman and Schilit (1991) found that role playing, expressing feelings, and problem sharing assisted the women in altering their feelings of powerlessness. Women sexually abused as children and revictimized as adults may feel particularly powerless. Research-practitioners have suggested that it is imperative to help women understand the root cause of their emotions and the relationships between their emotions and their actions (Bair-Merritt et al., 2010). Current research has illuminated the value of understanding the brain as it impacts recovery from PTSD (Cappas, Andres-Hyman, & Davidson, 2005). Therapists should routinely refer clients to medical practitioners who are experienced in prescribing psychotropic drugs (Stein, van der Kolk, Austin, Fallad, & Clary, 2006).

Goodkind, Gillman, Bybee, and Sullivan (2003) have pinpointed the importance of social support in recovery from chronic abuse. In one review, 63% of battered women who had little or no support returned to their abusers. In contrast, of those who had strong support systems, only 19% returned (I. M. Johnson, 1988). One of the great assets of 12-step and other self-help programs is the abundance and continuity of support that they provide. Goodkind and her colleagues (2003) have pointed out that social support helps to offset the negative effects of battering. Empowerment approaches to the counseling of battered women may be the most effective methods in helping battered women recover from PTSD (Perez, Johnson, & Wright, 2012).

Leaving/Staying: Helping on a Community Level

Sullivan and her associates (Sullivan, Basta, Tan, & Davidson, 1992; Sullivan, Rumptz, Campbell, Eby, & Davidson, 1996) proposed an experimental longitudinal study to ascertain specific community resources that women perceived as empowering (see also Tan, Basta, Sullivan, & Davidson, 1995). Investigators assumed that the most effective interventions would be defined by the women themselves. This strategy also allowed the battered women to direct the intervention process.

An initial step was conducting a needs assessment survey of 141 sheltered women. The results indicated that over 60% of the women needed legal assistance and over half needed jobs, further education, transportation, material goods, health care, social support, financial assistance, child care, and resources for their children. Almost 40% of the women needed housing (Sullivan, Tan, Basta, Rumptz, & Davidson, 1992).

The findings laid the groundwork for the development of a post-shelter program that used female students as advocates. The advocates received training in the dynamics of woman battering, empathy and active listening skills, and strategies for generating and accessing community resources.

Once an advocate was assigned to a woman, she began working with her one on one for four to six hours a week for a period of 10 weeks. Interventions were varied, practical, and specific to the woman's situation.

One advocate accompanied her client to a divorce workshop to learn about her legal rights. Another met with the formerly battered woman and a police officer for coffee to discuss a safety plan. Some advocates helped women register for school, look for work, meet neighbors, and locate child care. In other words, the advocates offered more than referrals. They helped the women make the system work for them.

The researchers assessed the effectiveness of the individually tailored interventions by asking the battered women to respond to six interviews: the first one immediately upon leaving the shelter and successively at 10 weeks, 6 months, 12 months, 18 months, and 24 months. Some additional contacts also occurred between interviews. The results substantiated a strong relationship between social support and the psychological well-being of battered women. The participants who worked with advocates were significantly more effective in obtaining resources than those without advocates. Furthermore, these battered women reported less depression and more satisfaction with their quality of life. Most notably, they experienced less physical violence by the end of the two-year period (Sullivan & Bybee, 1999; see also Seidman, 2011).

Throughout the world, women are slowly making progress in ending domestic violence. One program in Iztacalco, Mexico, rechanneled its efforts from changing legislation to raising public awareness. They used small-scale media, such as buttons and posters, to change attitudes about the legitimacy of wife abuse (Fawcett, Heise, Isita-Espejel, & Pick, 1999). Some Ecuadorian villages assign a "compadre" to newlywed couples. The compadre's job is to intervene at the first sign of discord. The Marshall Islanders of Oceania use community chastisement provided by the village elders to confront and curtail the problem of spousal abuse (Counts, Brown, & Campbell, 1992). Other countries, such as Chile, Nicaragua, and Japan, also report renewed efforts and some progress in reducing wife abuse and other forms of family violence (e.g., Ellsberg, Caldera, Herrera, Winkvist, & Kullgren, 1999; Kozu, 1999; McWhirter, 1999).

Reducing Male Violence in Ongoing Relationships

When women choose to stay with their abusers, eliminating the abuse is critical. The use of counseling as one method of changing batterers' behavior has not produced universally satisfactory results, according to program evaluation studies of court-sponsored programs. Depending upon variables such as the number of counseling sessions, the length of the follow-up period, the measure of recidivism, and the type of counseling provided, effectiveness has varied. The majority of studies considered methodologically sound have found modest but statistically significant reductions in recidivism (Babcock, Green, & Robie, 2004; Healey, Smith, & O'Sullivan, 1998). Over the years, methodological problems such as small samples, no comparison groups, and high attrition rates have rendered judgments of effectiveness uncertain (see Tutty, Bidgood, Rothery, & Bidgood, 2001; see also Davis & Taylor, 1997; Feder & Wilson, 2005). Other experts still hold out hope that counseling might at least reduce the battering if not totally eliminate it (Bennett et al., 2007; see also Gondolf, 2001).

It is important to acknowledge, however, that counselors attempting to change chronic behaviors (e.g., substance abuse) and attitudes anticipate some form of recidivism. Men committing other crimes show recidivism rates of 62.5% to 67.5% (see Palermo, 2010). Many batterers' programs tend to take a resocialization stance, highlighting attitudinal and belief change as well as behavioral change. These programs do not refer to cure, but something more like recovery (G. Billings-Beck, K. Evans, & D. Eddy, personal communication, 2012). Increasingly, it has become clear that criminal justice agencies must become aware of the key components of an integrated criminal justice response. The system needs to develop a coordinated, systemwide response to battering that includes law enforcement, prosecutors, judges, probation offices, and victim advocates (Garner & Maxwell, 2009; Healey et al., 1998; Teichroeb, 2009).

The Michigan Domestic Violence and Prevention Board has funded a coalition of agencies to address domestic violence from a more holistic perspective. These agencies address victim safety, provide batterer intervention services with a focus on accountability, and have developed prevention programs (Lovik, 2011a).

International Catalysts for Change

The International Medical Corps (IMC) and ABAAD, also known as the Resource Center for Gender Equality, an international organization that is working to achieve gender equality and women's rights in Lebanon, have established a Men's Center to address gender-based violence. While men have long been addressed as perpetrators, they are now being addressed as "partners in prevention." With the support of the Arab Foundation for Freedom and Equality, ICM and ABAAD have launched a media campaign to advertise the Men's Center. The campaign slogan is "Mest'edeen Nesma' Haki," which translates to "We are willing and here to listen."

A spokeswoman for ABAAD, Ghida Anani, states that the slogan has another meaning as well: "Someone is speaking to you in an abusive manner." As an advocate for survivors of gender-based violence, Anani says women are asking, "Why are you only talking to me? Speak to him too!"

The Calgary Counseling Centre in Canada (with Dr. Robbie Babins-Wagner and program director Lynda Snyder) provides services to the community by continuing to evolve and adapt to the needs of the families and individuals who come to them for help. They reach out to people who feel marginalized and try to eliminate barriers to accessing services. Their program for victims of domestic violence is called "You Are Not Alone" and addresses the needs of female and male survivors. They do not label the perpetrators of abuse as "batterers," but as men or women who are abusive in their intimate relationships. They are open to innovative approaches and also involve themselves in developing empirical evidence to support and inform their work.

Nori Yamaguchi, a women's advocate in Japan, developed the concept of teen dating violence. There were no words for dating violence in Japan. Yamaguchi speaks on prevention. She has also developed a program called AWARE to work with abusive men. There are no laws in Japan mandating perpetrators of IPV to receive intervention services, but Yamaguchi works collaboratively with victim services to get the word out. These collaborations are essential to addressing the issues that abused women face with little institutional support.

A team of researchers developed a fresh approach to ending gender-based violence (GBV) at the community level in Vietnam. The team based its techniques on previous research showing that 37% of a community sample of 465 Vietnamese women had been beaten by their husbands (Luke, Schuler, Mai, Thein, & Minh, 2007). The team then hosted two workshops for research participants, representatives of mass organizations, and health service providers. After identifying several problem areas, the group developed a program containing several major components: sensitizing members of the criminal justice system to GBV; conducting public awareness campaigns; and establishing linkages between health systems, counseling centers, legal services, and the police.

The overall goal of the program was to empower battered women. Some of the results of this program were that community members realized they had the right and the obligation to intervene in GBV and that they did in fact intervene. Another improvement was that women more easily identified GBV and were more likely to obtain help. Finally, the women joined together to provide each other with support (Schuler et al., 2011).

Institutional Interventions

Society plays a critical role in empowering (or failing to empower) battered women. In fact, there may be no totally effective individual solutions to battering. It is society's (not a woman's) responsibility to change practices and policies to eliminate battering. Much of the intervention that occurs must happen at the most basic level. Society must change its view of women as subordinate to men and change the structure that imposes that subordination ("For Women," 2007).

A number of experts suggest that those interested in helping battered women should focus their efforts on a holistic community response networking with all of the systems that impact families. The actions of certain individuals, such as police officers, judges, emergency room personnel, employers, counselors, and clergy, all influence women's actions and ability to leave or stay away from their abusers (U. Douglas, Bathrick, & Perry, 2008; Wuest & Merritt-Gray, 1999).

Religious Institutions

Since religious institutions are the first place to which many women turn in a crisis, the religious community has an opportunity to make important contributions in assisting couples caught up in the cycle of violence. Thompson (1989) claims that clergy should help victims determine the best theological choices, yet realistically offer them a number of possible options. She goes so far as to advise victims "to shop around and get second or third opinions from religious helpers in the community" (p. 38). Others suggest that clergy include the topic of battering in their sermons and that they help congregants understand IPV (Neergaard, Lee, Anderson, & Wong Gengler, 2007; Neuger, 2002).

Some religious organizations have taken very active roles in aiding spouse-abuse victims by starting shelters or by designing and conducting training programs for shelter staff and the religious community (S. E. Martin, 1989). Clergy can take several helpful actions when a woman discloses her victimization: (a) consider her safety first, (b) believe her account, (c) talk about the violence directly, (d) encourage her to seek additional resources, (e) respect her need for self-determination, (f) be sensitive to cultural differences, and (g) give her spiritual support. It is likewise important to avoid common pitfalls: (a) believing that the problem has disappeared, (b) believing the denials or minimizations, (c) believing that an upstanding community member could not be assaultive, (d) suggesting forgiveness prematurely before any changes are made, (e) using a couples counseling approach, (f) conceptualizing marital violence as noncriminal, and (g) actively trying to "rescue" the woman (Cooper-White, 1996).

Researchers have increased their investigations of forgiveness and identified several functions that forgiveness serves (Riek & Mania, 2011). A 2012 study revealed that individuals are more likely to forgive for the sake of the self and for the sake of the relationship rather than for the sake of the offender. When applied to battered women, each of these motivations is associated with different survivor behaviors. First, if forgiveness occurs for the sake of the self, outcomes include less relationship satisfaction and fewer forgiving responses. Second, if forgiveness occurs for the sake of the relationship, outcomes include enhanced relationship quality and decreased behaviors of revenge and avoidance. Third, forgiveness occurring for the sake of the offender is associated with nonrevengeful behaviors (Strelan, McKee, Calic, Cook, & Shaw, 2012). Factors such as the perception that the offender is sincere directly influence the decision to forgive, while event severity and overall relationship satisfaction mediate the decision to forgive (Pansera & La Guardia, 2011). In another study, researchers found a direct correlation between the ability to forgive and good health (see also Lawler-Row, Hyatt-Edwards, Wuensch, & Karremans, 2011).

Garanzini (1988), a Jesuit priest with a doctorate in counseling and education psychology, addressed the appropriate role of pastors from a different perspective. First, he highlighted the legal obligations ministers have to report child abuse and neglect and how best to meet this requirement. Second, he summarized research-derived warning signs that pastors might use in identifying and helping at-risk families and called attention to several general problem areas that families are likely to face. Finally, he suggested a group of strategies pastors might adopt to combat family violence: (a) establish regular supportive relationships with trained professionals in counseling, services for families, and family medicine; (b) recognize family violence by founding peer support groups for families and by including family violence as a topic for sermons; and (c) establish pastoral teams or mobilize special ministries to assist at-risk families.

Fundamentalist clergy may be particularly unsupportive of battered women because of their ultraconservative attitudes about marriage and sex roles. It is appropriate to address all of these beliefs by questioning them or reinterpreting them, by reframing certain biblical writings, and by placing the situation within a broader context. Reframing can include highlighting the responsibilities of husbands and emphasizing the second account of Creation, which gives both males and females dominion over the Earth. This approach places many of the issues faced by a fundamentalist battered woman within her own framework (Whipple, 1987; see also McDonald, 1990).

Economic Independence

Helping battered women achieve economic independence also plays a pivotal role in avoiding victimization. Working away from home appears to be a crucial survival strategy, possibly because it lessens the battered woman's economic, social, and emotional dependence on her husband (M. N. Wilson et al., 1989). One qualitative study pinpointed six different ways that employment may help female IPV victims: It (a) improves finances, (b) promotes physical safety, (c) increases self-esteem, (d) enhances social connectedness, (e) provides a cognitive respite, and (f) provides a purpose in life (Rothman, Hathaway, Stidsen, & de Vries, 2007; see also Li, Mardhekar, & Wadkar, 2012).

Programs geared toward assisting battered women in finding employment should be sensitive to the women's possible lack of self-confidence and job skills and the effects of battering on work performance. Employers can play a key role in helping women escape from abusive relationships by boosting victims' self-confidence. Positive employer feedback makes battered women feel successful at work, which in turn implies to them that they are worth something. An employer who cuts a woman some slack or who allows her to have time off is profoundly influential in a woman's ability to take control of her life (Wuest & Merritt-Gray, 1999; Swanberg, Logan, & Macke, 2005).

Lowe and Prout (2011) argue that some perpetrators use an economic strategy of abuse. This tactic can have the same effects as violence in terms of control and manipulation. It can serve as an effective method of further isolating the victim and deepening her dependence upon her abuser. The victim can be dependent upon the abuser for basic needs such as food, clothing, and shelter, which helps explain why "domestic violence is the leading cause of homelessness in America" (p. 33).

Agencies, attorneys, and other court personnel can help victims to increase their access to public assistance, financial literature, judicial relief, and employment opportunities. A lawyer experienced with these issues is often the best chance a victim has in escaping her abuser, "primarily because the tools of economic stability lie within the family court system" (Lowe & Prout, 2011, p. 33).

An experienced and educated lawyer can help a victim achieve long-term economic stability and safety as opposed to short-term relief. Because public legal services often have limited access to resources, this is particularly relevant for private lawyers:

> Advocacy by trained lawyers from the private bar is essential to assisting domestic violence survivors to maintain long-term safety for themselves and their children by securing an appropriate division of the marital estate, protective orders,

public benefits, disentanglement of the financial relationship, and an equitable division of real property. (Lowe & Prout, 2011, p. 33)

Alicia Kelly (2012) has proposed ways to modernize and advance existing laws regulating economic relationships among couples. She advocates what she calls "partnership equals," a theory that calls for protecting each partner's economic rights regardless of whether the couple is married or cohabiting, heterosexual or homosexual. Her basic premise is that the "legal standard should be an assessment of economic interdependence in the relationship with resulting rules for sharing property and income streams that vary accordingly" (p. 258). Such forward thinking would go a long way in helping battered women leave abusive relationships.

Taking a broader, long-term view, economic equality for battered women may be an approach to interrupting the intergenerational transmission of abuse. When women leave their violent homes, they usually take their children with them. From Hackler's view, leaving is a prevention strategy for reducing future crime, as it removes the children from a violent environment (Hackler, 1991).

One growing solution to a combination of problems is the development of transitional housing. Transitional housing programs provide continued assistance in helping women find and participate in essential activities (e.g., vocational training, education, counseling) over a period of 3 to 18 months beyond the customary shelter stay (Loren, 1994; Tsesis, 1996). In addition, transitional housing is low-cost housing (Melbin et al. 2003).

Proactive Medical Care

The history of widespread medical proaction is short. In 1989, McLeer and Anwar (1989) reported that identification of battered women in the emergency room rose from 5.6% to 30% when protocols were in place that simply asked how injuries occurred. According to J. C. Campbell and Alford (1989), sexual abuse of battered women has been routinely ignored. In 1992, hospital accrediting bodies decreed that emergency room personnel must try to identify battered women and provide appropriate referrals (Joint Commission on Accreditation of Healthcare Organizations, 1992; Shepherd, 1990; J. Zorza & Schoenberg, 1995).

The American Medical Association (AMA) got on board by issuing a booklet to be used in detecting and treating victims of family abuse (Children's Safety Network, 1992; Schornstein, 1997). Because of these efforts, hospital employees became increasingly willing to screen patients and to attend training seminars (e.g., Hambleton, Clark, Sumaya, Weissman, & Horner, 1997; P. H. Smith, Danis, & Helmick, 1998). Moreover, medical schools began including domestic violence in their curriculum (Alpert & Cohen, 1997; J. R. Hill, 2005).

Although the AMA supports screening patients for domestic violence, educating medical staff, and carrying out appropriate interventions, it does not support mandatory reporting. The AMA's objections rest on well-established policies about confidentiality. Little research, if any, has systematically studied the effects of mandatory reporting laws (Lund, 1999). Reactions to the laws have been mixed. While some evidence suggests that the laws are protecting victims and dealing more effectively with offenders, some medical personnel and some victims have voiced complaints (J. C. Chang et al., 2003). Generally, battered women's advocates fear that mandatory reporting will discourage victims from seeking help and feel that it is too controlling, too intrusive, and even dangerous (Currens, 1998).

The Violence Against Women Act

Because of the $1.62 billion Violence Against Women Act (VAWA) (Biden, 1994), the criminal justice response to domestic violence and sexual assault has dramatically improved. A key provision of the bill was the $800 million funding of research grants. To identify areas where VAWA's impact was problematic, representatives of the Urban Institute visited a number of sites and interviewed battered women, shelter directors, and others (Urban Institute, 1998; see also C. F. Klein, 1995). Based on the institute's 1997 recommendations, the National Institute of Justice began soliciting grant proposals covering several areas, including the following: (a) judicial training, (b) interventions for domestic violence offenders, (c) mandatory reporting, and (d) mediation in domestic violence cases (U.S. Department of Justice, National Institute of Justice, 1999a). Another set of grants focused on interpersonal violence in the Native American community (U.S. Department of Justice, National Institute of Justice, 1999b). The reauthorization and extension of VAWA included relief to larger groups of family violence victims. (See Appendix D.1 for more details about VAWA.)

An example of grant money well spent involves the use of Internet-based preparation of court-acceptable protective orders and custody documents. When this computer program is made available in a safe and supportive location, such as a shelter, it allows victims and advocates to prepare complete petitions. Currently, advocates are modifying the program for non-English-speaking users and for application across state lines (R. Zorza & J. Klemperer, 1999; see also Shiemke, 2011).

Because antistalking legislation had received the least amount of attention, the Bureau of Justice Assistance convened a seminar of leading experts

to develop a model antistalking law. Participants also made recommendations concerning sentencing of stalkers, pretrial release provisions, strategies for implementing stalking statutes, and a national research agenda on
stalking (Tjaden & Thoennes, 1998b; U.S. Department of Justice, Office of
Justice Programs, Bureau of Justice Assistance, 1996). In 1996, Congress
enacted a federal law forbidding interstate stalking. (See Appendix A.9 for
statistical estimates of stalking of intimates.)

Additional areas of focus for helping battered women were as follows:
(a) waivers of fees for such documents as restraining orders; (b) interstate
enforcement of protective orders; (c) reformation of court procedures (e.g.,
plea bargaining); and (d) training of law enforcement personnel, particularly judges. Concerns regarding privacy and confidentiality have been scru-
tinized (J. Zorza, 1995). For example, mothers may face a double bind in
trying to obtain medical attention for their children, because abusers can get
legal access to their children's medical records. If a battered woman obtains
medical care, the abuser may be able to locate her through the addresses
provided to medical personnel. Another necessity for battered women is the
acknowledgment of privileged communication, the type honored between
doctor and patient or between attorney and client. Many states have upheld
victim-counselor privileges, but others have not.

Over time, there have been positive changes in restricting public access to
postal, motor vehicle, and voting records, particularly in regard to victims
of domestic violence. In many states, addresses and telephone numbers
that were previously easily obtained are now more difficult to access. In
November 1998, Vice President Al Gore announced that the federal government would make it easier for victims to change their Social Security
numbers with written evidence of domestic violence from a shelter, physician, or law enforcement agent ("Abuse Victims Get, 1998"; see also "Two
New York," 1999, for continuing problems).

In 2009, a project funded by the U.S. Department of Commerce developed and evaluated the results of using innovative technology for abuse
screening. In particular, the program screened clients for elder abuse, elder
self-neglect, and child abuse. Nurses used handheld computer devices and
recorded patients' answers to a set of questions When a patient screened
positive for domestic violence (or neglect), the health care provider was able
to take action immediately. The provider could mobilize available resources,
such as notification of the office of elder services or a police department,
by immediately sending the information electronically. The project called
for same-day follow-up by participating agencies. Initial information (e.g.,
name, address, description of injuries), obtained by the health care provider
and entered into the computer's database, had several benefits. Victims did
not have to repeat the same information over and over again to subsequent

service agency personnel, and records about abuse could be stored and retrieved when needed (Hawkins, Pearce, Skeith, & Roche, 2009).

Fortunately, the plight of crime victims in general has garnered increasing public support. While federal funding of crime victim compensation has increased, funding of victim service organizations is insufficient to assist victims over any extended period of time. Without community support, many women must return to their batterers because housing and child care are not available (Baker, Niolon, & Olyphant, 2009; C. F. Klein, 1995). All but one of the states has passed a Victims' Bill of Rights, and 22 states have passed constitutional amendments requiring certain crime victim services (Tomz & McGillis, 1997).

One outgrowth of VAWA's $1 million funding has been the establishment in Texas of the National Domestic Violence Hotline (NDVH) (1-800-799-SAFE), available 24 hours a day. During the first seven months of operation, the hotline received calls from all 50 states, averaging about 300 calls per day. Most callers had seen messages about the hotline in the media. About 50% of the calls originated from currently or formerly abused women; 14% came from family and friends of battered victims; almost 5% were from self-identified batterers; and the rest were from individuals such as service providers, professionals, and elected officials.

NDVH workers provided 24,441 referrals, primarily to shelters. They surmised that the greatest gap in services was inadequate shelter capacity, followed by lack of legal resources, criminal justice response, and housing. An analysis of calls to the hotline revealed some very important information. It became clear that a number of populations were underserved: foreign language speakers needing AT&T's translators, and women who were hearing disabled or had other disabilities. Another group with difficulty obtaining services was women in rural areas. Overall, the hotline has the potential to provide a vast amount of information relevant to understanding and intervening in domestic violence (Danis et al., 1998).

Battered Women and Child Protective Services (CPS)

The problem of conflicting interests of children and battered women spurred CPS agencies to consider ways to integrate both concerns into child welfare practice (Morris, 2009). Social workers are receiving training that directs them to see both the woman and her children as clients who need protection (S. P. Johnson & Sullivan, 2008; Stanley, Miller, & Foster, 2012). Thankfully, the newest articles appearing in social work journals specify exactly that—social workers must support the battered mother. A useful approach is to help her by using a stages-of-change approach. The goal is to help the mother find a way to keep her child safe (Melchiorre & Vis, 2012).

In an attempt to address some of these issues, the Los Angeles County Department of Children and Family Services (DCFS) has requested more training for its hotline, emergency response, and line workers. As of 2011, the University of Southern California's Center on Child Welfare has worked with one of the authors (A. L.) to develop a three-day, 15-hour training program. Currently, another group of social workers from DCFS have developed training modules to meet the specific needs of its staff. The ultimate goal is to create a group of domestic violence experts within the department.

The Detroit Center for Family Advocacy functions to prevent a common problem: placing children in foster care without proper justification when the mother is the victim of abuse. Instead, the center works toward providing support for the victim and her children by ensuring safety, finding legal assistance, and offering alternative housing options while making sure the child remains in the custody of the nonabusive parent (Sankaran, 2011). The Family Connection Center was established in Livingston County, Michigan, by a Safe Havens grant "to offer supervised parenting time and a safe exchange center for families with a history of domestic violence" (Church, 2011, p. 43). Child safety, familial health, and domestic abuse education are the main objectives of the center. Similar centers are planned for other counties as well (Church, 2011).

As urged by nearly every expert in the field, innovative approaches have increasingly included cross-agency collaborations (e.g., police, shelters, courts, CPS) (Brookoff, 1997; Davidson, 1995; see also L. C. Leung, 2011). Several recommendations affecting child custody emanated from these collaborations:

1. Attend to safety issues. See the nonabusing parent and child as one unit. Interventions (e.g., restraining orders, types of counseling recommended) should focus on the safety of both the child and the adult victim of abuse.

2. Hold the abuser, not the victim, accountable for his or her violence.

3. Set a context of domestic violence in the report to the court. Specify, for example, that the situation has occurred in the setting of long-standing spousal violence.

4. Keep the domestic violence victim and the child together and in their home unless there is a strong, compelling rationale not to do so.

5. Confront one's own stereotypes about mothers and fathers. One attorney reported that in 16 years of working in the courts, she had never seen a father charged with failure to protect when the child's abuser was the mother.

According to Minnesota law, a defense of the nonabusive parent is to determine whether, at the time of neglect (or abuse), there was reasonable apprehension in the mind of the battered victim that acting to stop or prevent neglect would result in substantial bodily harm to her or to her child. The American Bar Association's Center on Children created standards for evaluating failure to protect in the context of child sexual abuse, which also could be used in cases of spousal violence: (a) whether parents knew or had reasonable cause to believe their child had been abused and failed to take reasonable steps to prevent it; (b) the nature of the actions parents took to protect, following disclosure of the abuse or neglect; (c) whether parents voluntarily agreed to participate in specialized counseling programs and to accept other protective services.

Changing Legal Interventions in Child Custody

Some of the more innovative developments in the legal system have included family court interventions when child custody and domestic violence issues have collided. Prior to the increase in awareness of domestic violence and its effects on children and adult victims, mandatory mediation of custody and visitation disputes was the law of the land. As evidence has accumulated about domestic violence, credence for the superiority of joint custody over sole custody has slowly eroded (National Council of Juvenile and Family Court Judges, 1994).

Data from the California Family Law Court Snapshot Study, conducted in June 1991, revealed that of parents who use mediation services, 48% report high levels of interparental conflict (Depner, Canatta, & Ricci, 1995). In response to these problems and a request from the court, Margaret Little, director of family court services for the Los Angeles Superior Court, obtained funds in 1998 for the development of a parenting curriculum specifically for spouse abusers (and their victims).

Some studies have found that courts are very apt to consider alcohol or drug abuse as relevant to custody issues, but they are not inclined to perceive spouse abuse as an issue (National Center on Women and Family Law, 1994; cf. E. Sorensen et al., 1995). An appeals court in California reversed this trend by overturning the custody decision of Judge Nancy Wieben Stock in the case of O. J. Simpson's two minor children. Judge Wieben Stock had granted custody to O. J. Simpson, rather than to the children's grandparents, despite evidence indicating that he had beaten and possibly murdered his ex-wife, Nicole Brown Simpson. The appeals court was adamant in its decision that domestic violence and homicide (even alleged) of a parent are critical elements in determining whether the surviving parent should be awarded custody of his or her children (see Fields-Meyer, Benet, Berestein, & Dodd, 1998, for a review).

Experts in the field have increasingly called for proactive court approaches to mediation of custody. Guidelines for court intervention in domestic violence cases are available and should be followed, and sensitivity to cultural differences is imperative (see Duryee, 1995; B. Murray, 1999; Wong, 1995). Screening of client suitability for mediation is crucial. In one survey, 80% of mediation programs claimed to utilize screening procedures, but further analysis revealed that only half of them actually interviewed husbands and wives separately (Pearson, 1997; see also Davies, Ralph, Hawton, & Craig, 1995). Helpful approaches include the option to avoid face-to-face contact and the option to bring a support person or legal counsel to the meetings. Finally, all court-connected services should have access to referral information for parents, such as how shelters or abuser counseling programs can be contacted (Newmark, Harrell, & Salem, 1995). Overall, legal protections for domestic violence victims during divorce mediation have slowly been advancing ("Mediation Regulated," 1997).

By 1995, 44 states required courts to consider batterers' violence a factor in intrafamily custody cases (Hofford, Bailey, Davis, & Hart, 1995; see also P. G. Jaffe, Lemon, & Poisson, 2003). Now there are laws in every state aimed at protecting children from being in the custody of abusive fathers. Despite this apparent progress, batterers are still awarded custody in about half of the cases where the mother has been a victim of partner violence (Hanna & Goldstein, 2010; see also Dalton, Drozd, & Wong, 2006; N. S. Erickson, 2006). Advocates are actively working to change custody laws to protect children in every state.

Many different types of law cases either directly or indirectly involve domestic abuse. This makes access to adequate research and other community resources for all types of lawyers of paramount importance. The Internet has played an important role because it has allowed access to research and resources. Courts, municipalities, nonprofit organizations, and legal associations usually have their own up-to-date websites as well as links to other helpful online sources (Stevens, 2011; see also R. Chang, 2011).

Battered women often find themselves in a catch-22 situation if they are trying to discontinue contact with an abusive partner (e.g., leave the city) but the court mandates paternal visitation rights. Many battered women and children are terrified, because batterers often use visitation as an opportunity to continue their abuse (Hilton, 1992; P. G. Jaffe, & Geffner, 1998). It is important that guidelines for court-supervised visitation be developed and that funding of these services be made available (R. B. Straus, 1995). A 1997 survey of members of the National Coalition Against Domestic Violence (NCADV) found that their first legislative priority concerned child visitation and safety (NCADV, 1997).

The Criminal Justice System

According to P. G. Jaffe, Crooks, & Bala (2009), victims of domestic violence may face a less responsive system in family court than they do in criminal court (Lesher, 2009). "Growing support for coparenting and awareness" of domestic violence and its effects on children may be on a collision course (P. G. Jaffe et al., 2009, p. 170). P. G. Jaffe and colleagues (2009) suggest that domestic violence requires a paradigm shift, with a greater emphasis on a situation-specific parenting plan that protects adult and child victims. This plan would place less emphasis on reaching outcomes speedily and more emphasis on safe and effective outcomes. Adequate assessment that addresses the types of aggression that characterize the family being evaluated is a critical first step. It is important to differentiate between types of family violence, and between highly conflicted relationships and aggression that can occur in otherwise healthy families. Practitioners and researchers have developed useful approaches to assessment (J. C. Campbell, 2005; Geffner, Conradi, Geis, & Aranda, 2009; LaViolette, 2009).

Many states have passed statues requiring training for judges and child custody evaluators. Some jurisdictions (e.g., California) have prescribed mandatory training as a prerequisite for court-appointed child custody evaluators. Continuing education is also required annually. Guidelines have been established by the American Psychological Association (APA) for individuals conducting forensic evaluations involving child custody when domestic violence is an issue. The APA has also stressed the importance of identifying the impact of culture in child custody evaluations (APA, 1996, 2009; see also Stahl, 2004).

Police Training

Because police can play a pivotal role in interrupting the intergenerational cycle of violence, improving their training is a first step (Buchanan & Perry, 1985). In Hamberger's (1991) opinion, training of police should include their sensitization to the research on domestic violence—in particular, that violent women are rarely husband beaters or mutual combatants. At least 85% of the victims of spouse assaults and admissions to emergency rooms are women (Greenfeld et al., 1998). Officers can be trained to improve their investigatory work and their comprehension of the psychosocial context of abuse. Stubbing (1990), a police trainer and advocate for battered women, has promoted training that includes hearing battered women speak of their terror and inability to get out, and listening to batterers describe their out-of-control behavior and how an arrest started to turn their lives around. Police trainees have also heard the voices of children. According to one of the authors (A. L.), inclusion of battered women and children in police and probation training creates empathy, an effective tool for reaching the hearts of those who listen (see also Wuest & Merritt-Gray, 1999).

Currently, domestic violence training for police is readily available over the Internet. The National Institute of Crime Prevention (2012) holds multiple training conferences across the country. Some of the topics are as follows: (a) when women kill, (b) the primary aggressor, (c) stalking, (d) effects on children, (e) victim behaviors, (f) officer as abuser, (g) typologies of abusers, and (h) when women use violence. This program can radically alter officers' approaches to IPV.

The Military

Former domestic violence judge Pam Isles and her assistant Leslie Howard created the Family Violence Project, which gave birth to the Heroes and Healthy Families Program, a program for the Marine Corps. Kathy McCarroll became the executive director, with Judge Isles and Leslie Howard being actively involved. This program focuses on domestic violence, substance abuse, suicide, and other mental health issues. Marine culture is built around a deep, all-encompassing belief that translates into behavior. This philosophical reality is "Do not leave your buddy behind."

One of the most hopeful outcomes of the recent conflicts in Iraq and Afghanistan is the expansion of this concept to non–battlefield situations. Generals involved with the Heroes and Healthy Families team are providing inspirational leadership to create a new way of thinking in the corps. They train their corps members to include the importance of not leaving your male or female buddy behind if that buddy is drinking too much, abusing a partner, is suicidal, or has other mental health issues (McCarroll, K., 2010).

Case Study: Long Beach, California—A Creative Approach

Many cities and municipalities are developing creative, collaborative, and holistic approaches to the problems associated with spousal violence. Long Beach, California, a multiethnic seaport city of 450,000, people has a unique perspective and an effective collaboration of shelter advocates, police officers, and city prosecutors; a domestic-violence-dedicated court and follow-up team; probation officers; batterers' programs; child abuse agencies; and substance abuse programs.

Robbie Hill has been a member of the domestic violence unit of the Long Beach Police Department since 1993, and Nancy Rivera joined the team in 1994. Ruth Burton has been a battered women's advocate at WomenShelter of Long Beach since 1993. These three women are integral members of the Domestic Abuse Response Team (DART). Patrol units call DART to the scene of a domestic violence incident if any of the following criteria are met: (a) Department personnel are implicated; (b) there is serious injury, the victim refuses medical attention, or both; (c) there have been two or more prior incidents involving this family; (d) spousal rape has occurred; or (e) the case falls under the rubric of intimate relationships, past or present.

Robbie and Nancy handle the investigation, and they call Ruth only after the victim signs a consent form. On-call DART counselors will come out if the victim needs help, whether or not the victim meets DART criteria. According to Robbie, "sometimes we know just by reading the report that the victim needs to speak to a counselor." All three team members agree that most of the women feel more comfortable with a counselor present during the interview.

Robbie says that "the victim feels our true concern. It's not just a job to us. We're there for more than a criminal investigation. We're there for them. We give them information and provide options (e.g., shelter referrals, legal possibilities). We offer vertical prosecution all the way up the line. That is, victims and perpetrators see the same people. We follow through." Ruth and Nancy believe that it is this team approach that is so successful. "DART is 10% Rambette [Rambo's sisters], 10% maintaining perspective, 40% police work, and 40% social work. We are there for each other and have a common goal."

That statement could not have been made a decade ago. The relationship between the grassroots shelter movement and the traditionally hierarchical criminal justice system has been historically thorny. This recent marriage, however arranged, seems to be working.

A case moves from investigation to prosecution. Steve Shaw and Sharon Panian have been the consistent team representing victims in the city prosecutor's Domestic Violence Unit. The unit handles each case, from filing through arraignment, pretrial hearing, trial, and post-sentencing hearings.

Steve and Sharon both agree that working domestic violence misdemeanors does not appeal to many prosecutors because of the unusual difficulties associated with these cases. Steve says, "Misdemeanors are more difficult to prove because there is less evidence and juries take felonies more seriously. About 90% of the victims either recant or seriously minimize the incident. The victim who is bleeding and pleading for police protection on Friday night comes to court on Monday to tell the prosecutor that it was all just a misunderstanding. Victims and witnesses are often uncooperative and hostile. Most of the women say that their abuser is a good husband and father most of the time."

Both city prosecutors understand why this happens. From Sharon's point of view, "the prosecutor who keeps the defendant in jail may be revictimizing the victim. Many of the cases involve battered women who are financially dependent on their batterers. For these victims, a black eye once or twice a year may be a small price to pay for food and shelter for the victim and her children."

Sharon and Steve are willing to take a chance on what cases to file. They are committed to protecting the victim by making the best legal decision possible, even if they believe they will lose the case. Both are creative and see every situation, every victim, every perpetrator, every family as different. Both agree that prosecuting partner abuse is not a job for everyone; it is 20% law and 80% social work.

When a domestic violence case is successfully prosecuted, the defendant often completes a year-long counseling program. According to Steve, "these perpetrators frequently return to court saying they were glad they were forced to attend the group sessions. Sometimes the victims are grateful and things are better for them and for their families. Those are the moments that make the job worthwhile and keep us going."

The city prosecutors are able to work innovatively because they are working with a court that is also responsive to partner assault on a case-by-case basis. Deborah Andrews is one of the few judges who preside over a courtroom that exclusively handles domestic violence cases. The judge reflects, "The focus of my court is to treat each defendant individually, to provide logical consequences, and to give feedback that is often positive. I spend a lot of time explaining court orders. As a judge, I don't have to go into such detail, but it pays off. The defendants understand what is expected of them and what it means if they fail to comply. I see people over and over again during the process and I know their stories."

Judge Andrews works closely with the abusers' programs in the area and holds an annual meeting with the providers. She knows many of the facilitators personally and understands the relevance of these programs. When defendants return to court with their progress reports, she may ask them, "What's going on in group?" "What have you learned so far?" "What's a time-out?" "Why do you think you received a positive progress report?" She addresses issues directly and speaks directly to the perpetrators (not through their attorneys).

Judge Andrews will not issue a fee waiver. She believes that defendants should pay something for their counseling programs. She and her bailiff, Deputy Arnie Gonzales, believe that treating defendants disrespectfully gives them the wrong

(Continued)

(Continued)

message. "You can be respectful and still hold a defendant accountable for his behavior," she concludes.

Long Beach employs another arm of accountability in regard to the batterer as a program of the court. It is the only court in the state that utilizes domestic violence case monitoring. Elena Villacres and Joe Quick are part of the Court Referral Information Services Program (CRISP), which has been offering services since 1994. CRISP staff members are the administrative experts and liaisons between the court and the batterers' programs.

Defendants leave the courtroom and report to the CRISP office. Elena and Joe speak to the perpetrators, reinforcing Judge Andrews's orders. In brief, defendants are able to choose a program from the approved probation list. Batterers have 21 days to enroll in the selected group. After that time period, CRISP staff calls the offenders' programs to check on their enrollment status. If they have failed to comply, the court issues a bench warrant for their arrest. Now God speaks to the recalcitrant batterers through the CRISP office.

CRISP handles violations of court orders and notifies the court clerk. If there is a red item (serious infraction), the judge receives immediate notification. Elena states, "CRISP is like Switzerland. We're neutral, but our rules are not meant to be broken. The defendants have to respect the law, other individuals, and be responsible for their actions." Joe Quick describes CRISP as a work in progress.

In addition to the unified response of shelter staff, batterers' programs, and the criminal justice system, Paula Cohen, staff attorney for Long Beach Legal Aid's Domestic Violence Project, has coordinated the work of child and spouse-abuse advocates. These efforts have culminated in the development of the Long Beach Area Child Abuse and Domestic Violence Prevention Council. This coalition brings together former hesitant (at best) allies with ostensibly differing agendas—until they sit down together (See Witwer & Crawford, 1995, for a review of the literature; see this reference for recommendations on community coordination as well.)

Communication and respect between all of the cogs in the wheel have been critical to the success of the Long Beach model. There are several themes that are consistent throughout these programs:

1. Each member of this criminal justice team perceives him- or herself as part enforcer and part social worker, and considers each function necessary

2. Team members do not believe one size fits all. They look upon each victim and perpetrator as a distinctive individual. There is no simple formula.

3. This work is not for everyone.

4. Supportive interaction at every level in the system is crucial. Much as for the victims and perpetrators, isolation is an enemy. Unfortunately, the Long Beach community response, which operated very effectively for over a decade, has been negatively affected by leadership and budgetary constraints.

The Fast Track for Domestic Violence is a program that was established in 2006 in Michigan. Much like in Long Beach, the court officer follows the case through arraignment, pretrial, sentencing, and review hearings (Boyd, 2011).

Despite the efforts to improve criminal justice responses to battered women, the 2008–2012 economic recession fostered several setbacks. To save money, the city council in Topeka voted to repeal the city's law against IPV in order to force Shawnee County to bear the costs of criminal justice processing. Representatives from the National Coalition Against Domestic Violence condemned the action, but to no avail. The City and the County appear to be playing a game of brinkmanship over costs, with women's lives hanging in the balance ("Kansas' Capital City," 2011).

To really help battered women, the entire community needs to be involved. Shelters, medical personnel, employers, police, and members of society at large need to become involved. Although counseling and advocacy should work toward empowering survivors of abuse on an individual level, more emphasis should be placed on empowering women by changing the community (Barkley, 1997; Flaherty, 2010). Many small communities use creative interventions to confront violence between adult intimates. When the systems work together, safety and support are the possible outcomes. Margaret's case demonstrates a successful coupling of social services and the criminal justice system (see also Boles & Patterson, 1997).

Case Study: Margaret and Joe

Margaret was a teacher, a mother of four children, and the wife of an abusive husband. Joe was the stepfather of the three older children. The youngest child was a product of Joe and Margaret's seven-year marriage. Margaret and the children were becoming increasingly wary and fearful of Joe. His vicious verbal tirades had worsened over the years, and he had added hitting, choking, and throwing things to his repertoire.

Margaret's impetus to take action came from her oldest daughter's school counselor. Margaret's daughter had been an outstanding student, a member of the pep squad, and popular among her peers. The counselor was concerned because the girl was withdrawing from her friends, seemed depressed, and was failing in two classes. Did Margaret know of any reason for this? Was anything unusual happening at home? Margaret could truthfully answer, "No." What was happening at home was not unusual.

Margaret made contact with a local battered women's hotline. She decided she didn't need shelter, and she obtained a temporary restraining order with an

(Continued)

(Continued)

order for Joe to leave the house. Joe left, but not for long. He would park his car across the street and leave it there. Margaret and the kids were terrified. One night she came home from work to find the kids sitting in the living room very quietly. The lights were out. Joe came from out of the shadows and pinned Margaret against the wall. "Where's your protection now? Who's going to help you now?" Then he left.

Joe had intimidated Margaret and the kids before. It had worked. He was always able to return. This time, Margaret stood her ground. She again made contact with the local shelter. A shelter worker advised her over the phone and agreed to advocate for her when she returned to court.

The shelter worker suggested that Margaret get written statements from her neighbors about seeing Joe, as he was wise enough to leave before the police could arrive. She also suggested that Margaret take a close-up picture of the car (when he parked it across the street) with a dated newspaper on it, and then take a picture of the car and newspaper in relation to her house. These photographs and written statements would substantiate Margaret's allegations that Joe was violating the restraining order.

Armed with her evidence and her advocates, Margaret appeared in court. The judge issued a bench warrant for Joe's arrest, and he was picked up. Joe has stopped harassing Margaret and the kids. She made the system work.

7

Voices of Hope

Survivors Speak

As Simone de Beauvoir has said (cited in Steiner, 1966, p. xxii), "Heroism is not inherent in human nature. It is not their initial helplessness that must astonish us, but the way they finally overcame it."

Case Study: Gloria and Miles

Gloria is 44, has her Bachelor's degree and three children, and is an R.N. Her son will be graduating from Berkeley this year, and her daughters are in high school. Gloria is a devout Catholic, a dedicated mother, and an open-minded, free-thinking, compassionate human being. She is also a formerly battered woman who has spent the last decade pulling her life back together.

Gloria married her high school sweetheart, who was an athlete, popular, jealous, and abusive. She was pregnant before they got married and had to deal with the shame that engendered in her, but she thought that getting married would end the jealousy and violence, and the shame. Besides, she was in love.

They both attended college. He graduated, but didn't work regularly. She took early childhood education classes and worked in day care centers from the time she was 22 until she was 29 years old. She supported the family much of the time, but turned the money over to Miles. Miles had an economic principle upon which he operated: His money was his, and so was hers. Four months after they were married, James was born.

(Continued)

(Continued)

The first time Gloria left Miles was four months after they married. Miles hit her and threw her around. He accused her of "coming on" to his friends, dressing like a slut, not looking sexy enough, and on and on. The yelling, swearing, threats, name-calling, and beatings happened in front of her children. Gloria says that she never enjoyed being hit or thought it was sexually exciting. What she did feel was shame and hope. She thought that if she could just change a little, things would get better. "If I could have cooked better, looked better, or did what he wanted more often, things would improve. I even tried smoking marijuana with him. Hope kept me going."

"It is also important to know that I was coming from knowing nothing about battered women." The first time that she read anything on the subject, it was an article about Francine Hughes (*The Burning Bed*). She learned that Francine was appearing on television and asked a neighbor to watch the kids because she knew she would be upset.

One night, Miles came home angry and drunk. There was an argument, and he beat her with a soda bottle. "I don't know what I saw when I looked in the mirror afterward, but it scared me. I looked at the kids, looked in the mirror, and said to myself, "I'm going to die if I don't do something."

She started writing letters about what was happening to her. She wrote to the YWCA, NOW, Catholic Social Services, and the Salvation Army. While she was waiting for answers to the letters, Gloria went to Parents Anonymous (she didn't know what it was, and she wasn't abusing the kids) and to a group called Recovery (self-esteem). The only response that she received was from YWCA staff, who asked her to come in for a "talk." Later, Gloria found out that they wanted to know if she was crazy.

The Y took action. It set up three seminars on domestic violence to see who would show up. Of course, Gloria was there. From the meetings, a women's group evolved, and she was part of that program. The group was empowering, and Gloria also felt proud about having been an impetus for the YWCA involvement. Gloria began making plans to leave months before she actually left. She made a wheel with "things to take care of a day at a time." One of the tasks was to write letters to everyone who had helped her. She put them in the mailbox on her way out of town.

Gloria and her children trekked (by car) across the country to a shelter for battered women. It was 1977. She started college again in 1978. She put herself through school on welfare and side jobs (Avon, college work-study). She also went into therapy to get over Miles and the fantasies that she still had about building a life with him. She says that it's taken her 14 years to feel that she could be interested in another man, and she is still wary.

Gloria's son went away to college and wrote his first sociology paper on domestic violence. It gave Gloria and James a real opportunity to talk. Her children are doing well, and are proud of their mother. Gloria's daughter heard a lecture in school on spouse abuse. That evening she told her mother that she had lots of courage and that she was brave to leave. Gloria's eyes were full of emotion when she related that story.

Gloria has been a nurse at St. Mary's Hospital in Long Beach and has administered a hospice program for individuals suffering from AIDS. She is also the loving mother of her three grown children as well as a proud grandmother.

Case Study: Peggy

Peggy was married for 12 and a half years to the "All-American Boy." He was the guy other women wanted, and he was the guy who was going to protect her from her abusive stepfather. He was the father of their four children, and he was also the man who blackened her eye on their honeymoon. Peggy's husband was an alcoholic who continued to abuse her throughout their marriage. (His father had been an alcoholic and had beaten his mother.) When Peggy left him, her children ranged in age from five to nine. After he and Peggy separated, he neither supported the children financially nor visited them.

Peggy's second husband was charming, romantic, and more brutal than the first. She lived with him for four months and left after a beating. He followed her, promising her that things would change and that life would be wonderful once again. He was extremely romantic and affectionate. But very quickly, he began drinking and using drugs again, and Peggy left him in December 1975.

Peggy was terrified of her second husband, and although she left him, it took her five years to gather the courage to divorce him. Peggy had undergone corrective ear surgery because her husband had battered her to the point of deafness. Peggy was once asked if she went to therapy. She replied, "No, I went to school and that saved my life."

Peggy supported herself and her four daughters by tending bar until the gradual loss of hearing became a total loss of hearing. The only sounds she heard were the phantom noises in her head, typical for people who experience hearing loss. She utilized state vocational aid that paid for tuition, classes on deafness and sign language, and an interpreter. She also received Aid for Dependent Children. She completed her first semester with a 4.0 grade point average.

Peggy had a temporary restraining order, but her husband continued to harass her from the court-ordered distance. She changed her phone number and moved several times, but he would find her and drive around the neighborhood on his motorcycle. Peggy was often terrified but continued courageously to complete her schooling and to maintain a positive attitude.

(Continued)

(Continued)

Dr. Bud Martin of American River College in Sacramento was a major influence and source of support in Peggy's life during those difficult times. His class, Personal and Social Adjustment, was the beginning of her journey to healing. She wrote her first term paper in that class. It was an inspired autobiography called "A Case for the Battered Woman." Peggy took every course Dr. Martin taught, and he encouraged her to finish school.

In February 1979, Peggy and her family suffered a great personal tragedy. Her 17-year-old daughter passed away as the result of a brain tumor. Peggy's determined voice still breaks as she recalls her daughter's last day. Her resolve to graduate and to change her life probably gave Peggy the focus and resolve to complete her last semester.

Peggy became an expert in sign language and received her Bachelor of Arts in Special Education and Deafness in January 1980. She graduated with an overall grade point average of 3.5. Peggy volunteered for the Long Beach Police Department's emergency translation team. In 1986, she began working for Su Casa, a battered women's shelter in Southern California.

In 1988, Peggy was recruited by the daytime drama *Days of Our Lives* as a consultant, and later as a cast member. Peggy has become a national spokesperson for the problems of battered women and the double jeopardy experienced by battered women who are hearing impaired. Peggy was invited to sit on a panel at a conference at Gallaudet College (the only liberal arts college in the world for the deaf). Peggy spoke on deafness and domestic violence.

Peggy is currently the program director of deaf and disabled services for the nationally recognized nonprofit organization Peace Over Violence. Peggy has received numerous awards for her work, including the California Peace Prize.

Case Study: Ana

Ana was born in Sri Lanka. Her father hit her mother, and she believed that was a cultural norm. When Ana was 11, her mother died and her father raised her and her sisters. He did not abuse them and wanted them to have lots of experiences.

Ana was a tomboy and wanted to be independent. She left home at 28 against her father's wishes, after he tried to arrange a marriage for her.

She met her husband while living in Italy and working as a nanny. Ana fell in love with him. She was looking for a soul mate and he was looking for a good time. He was charming and charismatic. They met at a train station in Rome.

They dated for about three months and got married. She quit her full-time job after they got married, worked part-time at a coffee shop, and became pregnant a few months later. He wanted her to get an abortion, but Ana decided to carry the baby. She had been raised Roman Catholic and he had not.

He started pushing her around after she told him she was pregnant. He went to see her when she was four months pregnant and then went home to India. He returned to Ana when their son was 13 months old. He returned a kinder man, but that was short lived.

They moved to America, and they had lots of arguments. They didn't have much money, but he sent most of his money to his parents. This was a cultural expectation, as was her position in his family—subservient to his mother.

Ana's husband began to go to bars, come home drunk, drag her out of bed, and make her cook for him. He hit her on her body (not her face) with his fists, kicked her, called her names, cheated on her, and told her he had never loved her. He ran up the credit cards and called her a liar and bitch in front of their sons. He also told the boys she stole his money. He did not isolate her, but he sexually assaulted and humiliated her.

In 1987, Ana began to empower herself. She began to study and take odd jobs. She studied accounting but found her real passion as a skin care and massage therapist.

She stayed in her marriage for the boys, but was angry at herself for putting up with her husband's treatment of her. She stayed with him until she put both boys through college. Then she left.

She received support from the church and from her priests. Ana says it took her a few years to overcome her hatred and anger. She offers her own experience as advice: "I went to counseling for two and a half years; a women's support group sponsored by a battered women's shelter, Alanon; and a program called JOURNEY that worked on recovery from trauma."

Ana's sons are proud of her: "Mom, you never gave up." And Ana is feeling very good about herself—and radiates it. She says, "I am empowered, talented, beautiful, and have everything to look forward to. I am flying."

Do Women Remain in Abusive Relationships?

Generally, studies find that about a third of battered women fleeing to shelters return to their partners. Gondolf (1988b) discovered that 24% of shelter women planned to return, with an additional 7% being undecided. Strube and Barbour (1984) found that 62% of their sample were separated or divorced at a follow-up period 1 to 18 months post-shelter. Herbert, Silver, and Ellard (1991) found that 66% of a group of 132 battered community women had left. Of those remaining, 50% had left at least once. In a more current study, Zlotnick, Johnson, and Kohn (2006) disclosed that 43% of women in a community sample had left within five years (see Panchanadeswaran & McCloskey, 2007).

These findings indicate that leaving is often an ongoing process culminating in change, rather than a single event. According to Browne (1983), the average battering relationship lasts about six years, the same length of time as the average marriage. The findings of several researchers were that battered women leave and return about five to six times before actually leaving (R. E. Davis, 2002; Rhodes & McKenzie, 1998; Stroshine & Robinson, 2003). A number of experts have conceptualized leaving an abusive relationship as a process, perhaps with several stages (Merritt-Gray & Wuest, 1995). Basically, battered women must traverse several changes in beliefs: (a) acknowledging their relationship as unhealthy; (b) realizing it will not get better; (c) experiencing some catalyst (e.g., abuse of a child); (d) giving up the dream of an idealized, committed relationship; and (e) accepting that it will never be over (e.g., having to share child custody) (Moss et al., 1997).

Leaving an Abuser

What does it take for women to make a decision to take action? For the women interviewed by the first author (A. L.), breaking the isolation was a critical step. A second essential factor seemed to be the introduction of a person into the battered woman's life who was supportive and encouraging, and who somehow convinced her that she was important. Once she has taken little steps, she has tangible evidence that she can take bigger ones. A battered woman needs a new mirror on reality, and other human beings can hold the looking glass.

Karen's Catalysts for Change

We started our book with Karen Connell, and it seems appropriate to end with an update. What were Karen Connell's "catalysts for change"? During the later 1970s and early 1980s, the system was basically unresponsive to battered women, so Karen's catalysts did not come from the system. Karen's leaving was influenced by several factors. She saw her son, Ward, changing from a decent, fairly happy little boy into a person who screamed and swore at her, a person like her husband. A friend gave Karen a shelter hotline number. Finally, on the day she made up her mind to leave, her husband, Michael, raped her.

For the last three years of her marriage, Michael had not worked. He stayed home and virtually held her hostage. Her time and actions were monitored, and Michael placed a tap on the phone. Her "free" day was the morning she worked at Ward's co-op nursery. Karen planned her escape with a shelter advocate. On the day she worked at the co-op, she took Ward and went to the shelter. For the first time in years, she and Ward were safe. They never lived with Michael again.

Karen Revisited

Karen's surgery saved her life and her voice. Although her vocal cords were cut, she has miraculously been able to tell her story. Karen's whispering voice has screamed the plight of battered women to millions of people through radio and television interviews and speaking engagements. She served on the staff of the Sojourn shelter for battered women in Santa Monica, California, and worked as a victim advocate for the Los Angeles City Attorney's Domestic Violence Unit. Karen is currently self-employed as an accountant and financial planner. Ward continues to struggle with the abuse that he witnessed and directly experienced. In 1986, Karen received the Governor's Award for her work with survivors of spouse abuse.

Appendix A

Estimates of Intimate Partner Violence

A.1: NONFATAL PHYSICAL ASSAULTS OF INTIMATE PARTNERS

Researchers	Organization	Reported By	Sample Type	Sample Size	Assessment	Period of Time	Outcomes		
M. A. Straus and Gelles (1986)	Family Violence Laboratory	University	Married/divorced; males/females	3,500	Conflict Tactics Scales (CTS)[a]	Lifetime	*Percentage of perpetrators of abuse*	*Males*	*Females*
							Nonsevere abuse	1.3	12.1
							Severe abuse	3.0	4.4
Tjaden and Thoennes (1998a)	Center for Policy Research	National Institute of Justice (NIJ) and Centers for Disease Control and Prevention (CDC)	Married/divorced/cohabiting/dating; males/females	16,000 (8,000 males, 8,000 females)	Modified CTS	Lifetime	*Percentage of victims of abuse*	*Males*	*Females*
								7.4	22.1
Catalano, Smith, Snyder, & Rand (2009)	Census Bureau	Bureau of Justice Statistics (BJS)	Spouses, ex-spouses, common-law spouses, boyfriends or girlfriends	Not Provided	National Crime Victimization Survey (NCVS)[a]	2008	*Rate per 1,000 intimate partner victims*	*Males*	*Females*
							Overall	0.8	4.3
							Violent Crimes	0.1	0.3
							Rape/Sexual Assault	—	0.2
							Robbery	0.3	0.5
							Aggravated Assault	0.4	3.1
							Simple Assault		
E. L. Smith & Farole (2009)	State Court Processing Statistics	BJS	Spouses, ex-spouses, common-law spouses, boyfriends or girlfriends	3,750 IPV cases (physical violence or threat) in 16 large counties	NCVS	May 2002	*Percentage of IPV Violence . . .*	*Victims*	*Defendants*
							Male	14.0	83.6
							Female	86.0	13.7

[a]The CTS contains 18 self-report questions about abuse (perpetration and victimization). The NCVS contains approximately 10 items about crime victimization. Researchers conduct both surveys by telephone.

A.2: INJURIES OF INTIMATE PARTNERS

							Number of persons injured by gender		
							Males	*Females*	*Not Reported*
Rand (1997)	Consumer Product Safety Commission	BJS	Emergency room patients	1,417,600	National Electronic Injury Surveillance System (NEISS)	1 year	862,000	554,700	900

Number and percentage of injuries by relationship

	Males	*Females*
Current/ex-spouse	15,400 (1.80%)	88,400 (15.90%)
Current/ex-boyfriend/girlfriend	23,000 (2.75%)	116,000 (20.90%)

A.3: HOMICIDES OF INTIMATE PARTNERS

Greenfeld et al. (1998)	Police depts.	Supplemental Homicide Reports from the Federal Bureau of Investigation (FBI)	Murdered females/males 12+ years	446,370	Written reports	1976–1996	Average percentage of people killed by relationship to victim

Average percentage of people killed by relationship to victim

	Males	Females
Total Unknown	34.4	27.8
Total known to police	65.6	72.2
Spouse	3.7	18.9
Ex-spouse	0.2	1.4
Nonmarital partner	2.0	9.4
Other	59.6	42.5

Durose et al. (2005)	SHR	FBI and BJS	Family members, intimates, strangers	16,204 (relationship known = 56.2%)

Percentage of murders in which the victim was the offender's . . . . .

	Male	Female
Spouse	19.0	81.0
Boyfriend/girlfriend	29.0	71.0
Friend/acquaintance	83.4	16.6

A.4: RACIAL DIFFERENCES IN ASSAULTS OF AND BY INTIMATES

					Percentage of IPV violence . . .	
					Victims	*Defendants*
E. L. Smith & Farole (2009)	State Court Processing Statistics	BJS	3,750 IPV cases (physical violence or threat) in 16 large counties	Spouses, ex-spouses, common-law spouses, boyfriends or girlfriends	NCVS	May 2002
				White	37.1	33.6
				Black	26.4	33.5
				Hispanic	33.6	30.8
				Other	2.8	2.0

A.5: DATING VIOLENCE

						Percentage of victimization by current/ former dating partners		
							Males	Females
Bachman & Saltzman (1995)	Census Bureau	BJS	Dating males and females	Not provided	NCVS (assaults) FBI (murders)	1 year (1992–1993)		
						Simple assault	2.0	16.0
						Murder	1.4	10.3
						Percentage of simple assaults by nonfamily members		
Durose et al. (2005)	Census Bureau and police depts.	BJS and FBI	Nonfamily members	26,618,970	NCVS and FBI	1998–2002		
						Boyfriend/girlfriend	66.0	
						Friend/acquaintance	72.1	
						Stranger	59.4	

A.6: LESBIAN INTIMATE PARTNER VIOLENCE

							Percentage of female victims
Tjaden and Thoennes (1998a)	Center for Policy Research	NIJ and CDC	Cohabiting females	79 female cohabitants from a sample of 8,000 females	Modified CTS	Lifetime	11.4
National Coalition of Antiviolence Programs (NCAVI) (2010)	NCAVI	NCAVI	LGBTQH[b]	5,052	State databases	2010	*Percentage of IPV Survivors by Gender*

Identity

Female	45.7
Male	36.8
Transgender female	3.0
Transgender male	1.2
Questioning	0.0
Genderqueer	0.1
Not disclosed	11.0
Self-identified	1.7
Intersex	0.5

[b]Lesbian, gay, bisexual, transgendered, questioning, heterosexual (history).

A.7: ELDER ABUSE PREVALENCE AND IDENTITY OF ABUSERS

Tatara & Kuzmeskus (1997)	National Center on Elder Abuse	Males/ females 60+ years	293,000	Official records of states	FY95 & FY96	*Percentage of victims by gender*	
						Males	*Females*
						32.4	67.3
						Percentage of perpetrators by gender	
						Males	*Females*
						47.4	48.9
						Percentage of victims of abuse by relationship to victim	
						Adult child	36.7
						Spouse	12.6
						Other family	10.8
						Grandchild	7.7
						Sibling	2.7
						Service provider/Volunteer	3.5
						Other	13.4
						Unknown	5.1

A.8: SEXUAL ASSAULTS OF INTIMATE PARTNERS

Bachman and Saltzman (1995)	Census Bureau	BJS	Women	500,000	NCVS	1 year (1992–1993)	Percentage of sexual assaults by lone offenders	
							Stranger	23
							Friend/acquaintance	40
							Other relative	9
							Total intimates	29
							Husband	9
							Ex-husband	4
							Boyfriend/ex-boyfriend	16

A.9: STALKING OF INTIMATE PARTNERS

Basile, Swahn, Chen, and Saltzman (2006)	National Center for Injury Prevention and Control	CDC	Random sample	9,684 adults 18+ years	Injury Control and Risk Survey	2001–2003	*Percentage ever stalked*	
							Males	*Females*
							2	7
							Weighted percentage ever stalked by marital status	
							Never married	5.43
							Separated/widowed/ divorced	6.33
							Married/couple	3.86
Tjaden and Thoennes (1998b)	Center for Policy Research	NIJ and CDC	Married/ divorced/ cohabiting/ dating people	16,000 (8,000 males and 8,000 females)	Modified CTS	Lifetime	*Percentage ever stalked*	
							Males	*Females*
							2	8

Appendix B

Statistical Data About Violence Against Intimates

B.1: Homicides of and by Intimates

The U.S. Bureau of Justice Statistics (BJS) (2007) has reported on homicides among intimates (this includes all family members). Intimates killed 5.3% of male homicide victims, while intimates killed 30.0% of female homicide victims.

A number of statistics demonstrate the high incidence of homicide among intimates:

- *1976–1996*. During a 20-year period (1976–1996), male intimates killed approximately 30% of all women murdered each year. In contrast, female intimates murdered 5.9% of all males murdered (see Greenfeld et al., 1998).
- *2002*. In 2002, there were 9,102 murders of spouses. Of the relationships in which the murderers and victims were known, women committed 19.0% of the spousal murders and men committed 81.0% (Durose et al., 2005).
- *2006*. Data from the National Violent Death Reporting System (NVDRS) have provided more details of violent death incidents. One analysis of 209 homicide-suicide events revealed that 58% involved current or former partners (Bossarte, Simon, & Barker, 2006).
- *2011*. "Eighteen percent of all Michigan homicides in 2010 were related to domestic violence" (Boyd, 2011, p. 42). (See Appendix B.6 for a table of lifetime and 12-month abuses against women.)

B.2: Dating Violence

The BJS found that 86% of victims of dating partner abuse were female. Although individuals 18 to 24 years of age constitute only 11.7% of the population, they account for 17.6% of the cases of family violence victims (Durose et al., 2005). Federal Bureau of Investigation (FBI) data reveal that among boyfriends and girlfriends, 81.9% of assaults were male-to-female and 18.1% were female-to-male (U.S. Department of Justice, FBI, 2000).

B.3: A Comparison of Prevalence Estimates of Elder Abuse

Acierno, Hernandez-Tejada, Muzzy, and Steve (2009) 5,777 persons (random sample)	Teaster et al. (2006) 253,426 cases (adult protective services—substantiated elder abuse)
	Self-neglect 37.2%
Emotional abuse 4.6%	Emotional abuse 14.8%
Physical abuse 1.6%	Physical abuse 10.7%
Sexual abuse 0.6%	Sexual abuse 1.0%
Neglect.........................5.1%	Neglect.......................20.4%
Financial abuse 5.2%	Financial abuse 14.7%
	Other abuse 1.2%

Source: Barnett, O. W., Miller-Perrin, C. L., & Perrin, R. D. (2011). *Family violence across the lifespan* (3rd ed., p. 593). Thousand Oaks, CA: Sage. Adapted with permission.

B.4: Estimates of Costs of Intimate Partner Violence

Total Costs		*Medical Cost for Injuries*	
Rapes	$320 million	Hospital care	78.6%
Physical assaults	$4.2 billion	Physician care	51.5%
Stalking	$342 million	Ambulance/paramedics	14.9%
Murders	$893 million	Dental care	9.5%
		Physical therapy	8.9%

Source: Max, W., Rice, D. P., Finkelstein, E., Bardwell, R. A., & Leadbetter, S. (2004). The economic toll of intimate partner violence against women in the United States. *Violence and Victims*, 19, 259–272; Barnett, O.W., Miller-Perrin, C. L., & Perrin, R. D. (2011) *Family violence across the lifespan* (3rd ed., p. 25). Thousand Oaks, CA: Sage. Adapted with permission.

B.5: Sexual Assault Fact Sheet

1. 20% to 25% of women in college have experienced an attempted or completed rape.

2. Among 9,684 adults in one study:

   • 10.6% of the women had experienced forced sex sometime in their lives

   • 2.1% of the men had experienced forced sex sometime in their lives

3. In a nationally representative survey, victims' first rape experience was perpetrated by a/an:

   • Intimate partner   30.4%

   • Family member   23.7%

   • Acquaintance   20.0%

Source: "Sexual Violence Facts at a Glance," from Simon, T. R., Kresnow, M. J., & Bossarte, R. M. (2008). Self-reports of violent victimization among U.S. adults. *Violence and Victims, 23,* 711–726.

B.6: Lifetime and 12-Month Prevalence of Rape, Physical Violence, and Stalking Victimization by an Intimate Partner Among U.S. Women (NIPSVS, 2010)

	Lifetime		Last 12 Months	
	Weighted Percentage[a]	Estimated Number of Victims	Weighted Percentage[a]	Estimated Number of Victims
Rape	0.4	11,162,000	0.6	686,000
Physical Violence	32.9	39,167,000	4.0	4,741,000
Stalking	10.7	12,786,000	2.8	3,353,000

[a]A weighted percentage refers to an adjustment in calculations on the basis of the importance of the data.

Note: Researchers reached participants by telephone using a random digit dialing procedure. A total of 9,086 females and 7,421 males completed the questionnaire, which contained 58 questions.

Source: Black, M. C., et al. (2011, November). *The National Intimate Partner and Sexual Violence Survey (NIPSVS), 2010 summary report.* Atlanta, GA: National Center for Injury Prevention and Control, Centers for Disease Control and Prevention.

B.7: Estimates of Repeat Victimization or Assault

Offense	Repeat Offense	Repeat Victims	Data Source and Time Period
Assault	25%	11.4%	Emergency room reports, 25 years, the Netherlands
Sexual assault	85%	67%	Victim surveys, adult experience, Los Angeles, CA
Domestic Violence	90%	59%	Victimization survey, one year, Britain

Source: Weisel, D. L. (2005, August). *Problem-oriented guides for police: Analyzing repeat victimization* (problem-solving tools series no. 4.) Washington, DC: U.S. Department of Justice, COPS. Downloaded July 10, 2012, from www.cops.usdoj.gov. Adapted with permission.

Appendix C

A Context-Sensitive Aggression Scale

Common Couple Aggression	High Conflict	Abuse	Battering	Terrorism/Stalking
• Balance of power in the relationship	• Balance of power in the relationship	• Imbalance of power in the relationship	• Imbalance of power in the relationship	• Imbalance of power in relationship
• Aberrant act	• Poor problem solving	• Sporadic physical aggression	• Monopolization of perception	• Monopolization of perception
• Feels remorse	• Anger is an issue within the couple	• Name-calling, but not character assassination	• Generally, physical aggression is more regular, but can occur without physical aggression	• Insidious psychological abuse
• Does not cause fear, oppression, or feeling controlled	• May feel remorse	• Verbal abuse, but not psychological abuse	• Threats to victim's support system	• Well-planned threat to kill
• No injury	• May include sporadic physical aggression and/or destruction of property	• Develops apprehension	• Isolates victim	• Torturing of pets
• Derives from escalating conflict	• Not emotionally abusive	• May be remorseful	• Name-calling that attacks victim's character	• Extreme isolation
• Could happen in any couple	• No fear	• Threat of abandonment	• Threats to kill self or others	• Generally more regular physical aggression, but may occur without physical aggression
	• Derives from escalating conflict	• Aggression takes place without witnesses	• Jealousy	• Sexual humiliation and degradation
			• Putting down friends and family	
			• Destruction of property	
			• Self-absorbed	
			• Sexual abuse	
			• Change in victim's personality	
			• More generally violent	

Source: LaViolette, A. D. (2009). Assessing intimate partner violence: A context sensitive aggression scale. Journal of Child Custody, 6, 219–231. Reprinted with permission.

Appendix D

Miscellaneous Facts

D.1: VAWA Protections of Abused Women and Children

Some additional VAWA protections are as follows (U.S. Department of Justice, Office on Violence Against Women, n.d.):

- Protects child abuse and incest victims by allowing them to self-petition up to age 25
- Expands VAWA self-petitioning to elder abuse victims who have been battered or subjected to extreme cruelty by their adult U.S. citizen son or daughter
- Removes the two-year custody and residency requirement for abused adopted children
- Protects abused immigrant children and children of battered immigrants from being cut off from VAWA immigration protection because they turn 21
- Protects trafficking victims' family members living abroad and reunites family members
- Improves access to permanent residency for trafficking victims by providing a special visa
- Extends the duration of special visas
- Allows some trafficking victims earlier access to permanent residency
- Strengthens VAWA confidentiality enforcement
- Specifies that special immigrant juveniles shall not be compelled to contact the abusive family member
- Guarantees access to legal services for immigrant victims
- Allows for employment authorization for abused spouses of certain nonimmigrant professionals
- Creates a uniform definition of a "VAWA petitioner"

All VAWA cases are to be adjudicated at the specially trained VAWA unit at the Vermont Service Center.

D.2: Gendered Pattern of Injuries of Intimates

Current research has uncovered a gendered pattern of injuries. The most common injuries for women are blunt force trauma to the face and strangulation (D. J. Sheridan & Nash, 2007). Battered women suffer more complex fractures, orbital blowouts, and intracranial injuries than other crime victims (Arosarena, Fritsch, Hsueh, Aynehchi, & Haug, 2009).

Appendix E
General Learning Information

E.1: Understanding Divergence in Research Findings

In reading research results, one needs to bear in mind that a number of variables influence the findings. For example, the nature of the sample, the size of the sample, and the specific questions asked all determine the final outcome. Since investigators are prone to using different questionnaires and to focusing on particular problems, their results are likely to differ. Sometimes, apparently divergent results may not vary as much as a superficial reading leads one to believe.

E.2: Learning Research

A few basic assumptions govern learning research: (a) a similarity exists between human behavior and animal behavior; (b) the results of laboratory experiments with animals using reinforcement and punishment can be extrapolated to describe human behavior; and (c) it is necessary to postulate the effects of some nonobservable factors in humans, such as religious attitudes or beliefs in the traditional family, just as one postulates the existence of hunger as a motivation in food-deprived animals. Even when it is impossible to scientifically observe internal factors (e.g., sexist attitudes), it may be possible to verify them through empirically based research such as questionnaires. Furthermore, Follingstad, Hause, Rutledge, and Polek (1992) have asserted that "literature from the laboratory study of human aggression is particularly relevant for considering what happens in battering relationships" (p. 110).

This book incorporates several important experiments conducted on dogs and rats that have provided outcomes that seem to have significant applications for understanding why battered women may learn to stay with abusive husbands. Early researchers conducted a number of animal studies before newer guidelines governing animal research were enacted.

Classical Conditioning: Pavlov and His Dog

It is possible to condition emotional reactions. Laboratory experiments have demonstrated that human beings can learn to fear what they previously felt neutral about, liked, or even loved. The procedure used is called classical conditioning. Classical conditioning is simply pairing two stimuli to produce a response, such as in the famous case of Pavlov and his dog. Pavlov and his dog are the Jeff and Lassie of psychology. Pavlov sounded a tone, placed meat powder on the tongue of his hungry pet, and the dog salivated. After several pairings of the tone and the meat powder, the animal salivated after hearing the tone, before the meat powder arrived. That is, the dog salivated to the presentation of the tone by itself.

With classical conditioning, a reward (e.g., food) or aversive event (e.g., shock) occurs regardless of the subject's response. For example, Pavlov put the food in the dog's mouth whether or not the dog salivated. Pavlov, not the dog, controlled the presentation of the food.

Extinction and Spontaneous Recovery

Extinction refers to the decrease in responses when no reinforcement follows the designated response. Research has shown that when learning takes place under intermittent reinforcement schedules (occasional rewards), it takes animals longer to stop responding (resistance to extinction).

Pavlov also noted an interesting side effect of his learning experiments. If he continued to sound the tone but failed to present the food, the salivation diminished slowly; it was extinguished. If he waited a few days to present the tone (without the food) to the dog again, the dog once again salivated (spontaneous recovery). This pattern went on for days and did not seem to extinguish completely. The dog had to learn that the tone was no longer significant and did not mean food was on the way.

Operant Conditioning: Skinner and His Rat

Operant conditioning refers to a basic form of learning primarily covering voluntary behaviors such as driving a car or swimming. In contrast to classical, or Pavlovian, conditioning, operant conditioning requires the individual to earn a reward, or to work to eliminate a painful circumstance. B. F. Skinner, the famous behaviorist, developed the operant paradigm. In Skinner's (1938) experiments, behavior is shaped by rewarding (reinforcing) responses in a step-by-step manner as the animal approximates the desired behavior (successive approximation). Skinner's classic work involved putting a rat in a box containing a bar. Skinner has retained immortality with psychology students, not just for his research, but also because the box was given his name, the Skinner box.

In a Skinner box, the animal receives rewards (food pellets) as it slowly learns the desired behavior, the bar-press. As the rat stands on its hind legs near the bar, a food pellet arrives in the food dish. When the rat touches the bar, another food pellet arrives, and so on until the rat presses the bar and receives food regularly. This process is called *shaping*. The animal learns that the reward is dependent upon its own behavior, that it has control over the outcome of its behavior. The consequences of behavior (getting food or avoiding pain) control the animal's rate of lever-pressing.

E.3 Reinforcement

Definitions

Reinforcers: Reinforcers are events that increase responding.

1. *Positive reinforcer:* A positive reinforcer is any event that, when added to a situation, increases the probability that an organism will make a behavioral response.

   <u>Animal Examples</u>

   Primary (unlearned) reinforcers: food and water

   Secondary (learned) reinforcers: sound of a bell signifying food is coming

   Secondary reinforcers have previously been paired with a primary reinforcer.

   <u>Human Examples</u>

   Primary (unlearned) reinforcers: food and water

   Secondary (learned) reinforcers: smile, money, praise, approval, sexual contact, affection

2. *Negative reinforcer:* A negative reinforcer is any event that, when taken away, increases a behavioral response.

   <u>Animal Examples</u>

   Primary (unlearned) negative reinforcer: shock

   Secondary (learned) negative reinforcer: sound of a bell signifying that a shock is coming

<u>Human Examples</u>

Primary (unlearned) negative reinforcer: shock

Secondary (learned) negative reinforcer: frown, criticism, name-calling

Additional Facts About Reinforcement

1. Reinforcers greatly enhance learning, but learning can take place without reinforcement.

2. In general, the larger the reinforcer, the greater (or faster) the learning.

3. When reinforcement is not given after a response, the number of responses declines (extinction occurs).

4. Contingent (earned, dependent, or related) reinforcement produces much better learning than noncontingent reinforcement. A rat that must lever-press to earn food will learn to lever-press far better than a rat that is given the food without having to lever-press.

5. Delaying the presentation of the reinforcer retards learning.

6. Presenting the reinforcement on every trial in classical conditioning speeds up learning, while intermittent reinforcement (IR schedule) retards learning.

7. Presenting the reinforcement intermittently in operant conditioning will still induce learning, but the schedule of reinforcers (IR) will help maintain the behavior longer than if every trial were rewarded.

8. If motivation (e.g., hunger) is increased, learning occurs more rapidly.

9. Enjoyable activities (e.g., watching TV) can act as reinforcers as much as can stimuli such as food and water.

10. After a behavior is learned, it is harder to extinguish it, if intermittent reinforcement had been used.

E.4 Punishment

Definitions

Punishers: Punishers are events that decrease responding.

1. *Positive punisher:* A positive punisher is any event that, when added to a situation, decreases a behavioral response.

   <u>Animal Examples</u>

   Primary (unlearned) positive punisher: bar slap (shock for pressing a bar to obtain food)

   Secondary (unlearned) positive punisher: tone signifying that bar slap will occur

Human Examples

    Primary (unlearned) positive punisher: spanking, beating

    Secondary (learned) positive punisher: pouting, disapproval, swearing

2. *Negative punisher:* A negative punisher is any event that, when taken away, decreases a behavioral response.

Animal Examples

    Primary (unlearned) negative punisher: removal of water when the animal eats

    Secondary (learned) negative punisher: bell signaling that food is turned off when the animal presses the bar for food

Human Examples

    Primary (unlearned) negative punisher: taking away dessert after a meal

    Secondary (learned) negative punisher: deprivation of TV privileges; time-out (removal from others)

Additional Facts About Punishment

1. Punishment is not the opposite of reinforcement. A noxious event like a shock does not always decrease responding (Skinner, 1938). "Punishment typically produces a change in behavior much more rapidly than other forms of instrumental conditioning, such as positive reinforcement or avoidance" (Domjan & Burkhard, 1989, p. 259).

2. The less intense and briefer the duration of the punishment, the less the suppression (Karsh, 1962). Mildly punished behaviors will recover (Appel, 1963).

3. Severity of punishment = duration × intensity.

4. If the first punishment is severe but successive punishments are milder, the punished behavior will be inhibited (Sandler, Davidson, Greene, & Holzschuh, 1966).

5. If the first punishment is mild and successive punishments become more severe, behavioral suppression will usually not occur (Sandler et al., 1966). An animal continues to adjust and respond for the reward that is also present in the situation.

6. If punishment is discontinued, recovery may occur (Catania, 1984).

7. If the punishment is contingent upon the animal's behavior, the animal will learn to eliminate the response (Camp, Raymond, & Church, 1967).

8. If the punishment is not contingent upon the organism's response, the organism will probably not learn to inhibit the undesirable responses (Hunt & Brady, 1955).

9. Punishment is more effective if given immediately after the undesirable behavior. If the punishment is delayed, the animal probably will not learn to suppress the undesirable behavior (Kamin, 1959).

10. The more consistent the punishment, the greater the decrement in the number of responses. Intermittent punishment does not maintain suppression of the punished behavior (Azrin, Holz, & Hake, 1963). (Note that, in contrast, intermittent reinforcement schedules are very effective.)

11. If alternative, rewarded responses are available, the animal will inhibit the punished behavior more readily (R. L. Herman & Azrin, 1964).

12. A behavior that is both reinforced and punished is likely to recur (Azrin & Holz, 1966). If an animal receives both a mild shock and a pellet of food for a response, it will continue responding.

13. If a cue such as a light is used to signal forthcoming punishment, future presentations of the light will reduce behavior (Dinsmoor, 1952).

14. When punishment of a certain response is used as a discriminative stimulus (a signal) to indicate that a reinforcer will follow, the punished behavior will not be inhibited but probably will be increased (Azrin & Holz, 1961).

15. Higher levels of shock generally lead to more aggression by the punished organism toward objects or other people (Ulrich, Wolff, & Azrin, 1964) or toward oneself (Logan & Wallace, 1981).

16. Inescapable shock leads to a general inhibition of responding, which implies that the organism has developed a conditioned emotional response (CER) of "fear" (Estes & Skinner, 1941).

17. Inescapable punishment works proactively to prevent responding (Klee, 1944) and to reduce future problem solving. Dogs exposed to inescapable shock suffered from "learned helplessness" (S. F. Maier, Seligman, & Solomon, 1969).

18. Exposure to prior shock enhances the effects of mild punishment but decreases the effects of intense punishment (Church, 1969).

Note: The above terms, examples, and definitions appear in Willet and Barnett (1987).

Appendix F

Specific Learning Experiments

F.1: The Use of Both Punishment and Reinforcement in Humans

Ayllon and Azrin (1966) conditioned schizophrenics to respond to a punishment (noxious noise) coupled with reinforcement (token) and not to respond to a no-punishment, no-reinforcement condition. When the time between reinforcements lengthened, schizophrenics continued to select a punished response even without the accompanying reinforcement.

F.2: Conflict in Animals

J. S. Brown (1948) and N. E. Miller (1959) used rats to demonstrate several different types of conflict (approach-approach, approach-avoidance, avoidance-avoidance, and double approach–avoidance). For example, one goal consisted of water and shock while the other consisted of food and shock. An animal faced with such a dilemma often runs halfway toward one of the goals and then retreats. Momentarily, it runs toward the other goal, and then it returns. Presumably, its approach behavior represents its desire for the positive goal (food or water), while its avoidance behavior reflects its fear of the shock. The animal's degree of vacillation assesses its level of conflict or ambivalence.

F.3: Punishment as a Discriminative Cue for Reinforcement

When a cue (e.g., a tone) serves as a signal for forthcoming punishment, that same cue will reduce future behavior (Dinsmoor, 1952). Experiments by Holz and Azrin (1961) using pigeons indicated that if punishment was necessary to obtain a reward, the animal would accept the punishment. Pigeons learned to respond (on a variable interval schedule) to punishment (shock) coupled with reinforcement (food) and not to respond to punishment alone (extinction). Since getting food depended upon getting shocked, the pigeons increased their pecking even though they had to endure shocks. Punishment became a discriminative stimulus (cue) for a reward (i.e., signaled forthcoming food reinforcement).

F.4: Punishment-Facilitated Attachment

Rosenblum and Harlow (1963) detected significant variations between baby monkeys in their attachment behavior with surrogate mothers who differed in terms of their aversiveness. Babies that were given an opportunity to cling to a terry cloth "mother" in a situation involving the delivery of air blasts (punishment) spent more time with her than did a comparison group of monkey given access to a "mother" without the punishment. These findings suggest that punishment enhances the baby's responsiveness to the mother.

F.5: Extinction Failure: Responses Fixated Through Punishment

When rats receive punishment that is not sufficient to suppress their behavior, their behavior may become almost impossible to extinguish (Azrin, Holz, & Hake, 1963). In a human example, a child who is inconsistently punished for throwing tantrums may continue throwing the tantrums for a very long time, even when the parents walk away (i.e., remove the reinforcement of attention). In other words, if a parent reacts to a child's tantrum by giving him or her attention such as, "Don't cry. We're going to the park later. Come on, now, this isn't worth crying about," the attention serves as a reward for throwing the tantrum.

F.6: The Gradual Buildup of Punishment

Using an increasing level of shock to punish a rat for pressing a lever does not lead to suppression of lever-pressing. Instead, the rat learns to adjust to the ever-increasing level of shock; it continues to press the lever (Sandler, Davidson, Greene, & Holzschuh, 1966).

F.7: Matching Behavior

The Matching Law states that the relative frequency of responding on an alternative (e.g., choice A [highly rewarded] or choice B [less rewarded]) matches the relative frequency of reinforcement for responses on that alternative. Interpreted, this statement implies that an animal will work harder on one alternative if it receives a higher reward (e.g., A) than it will for another alternative of lesser reward (e.g., B). That is, the organism matches its responses to the frequency (amount, value) of a reward.

It may be possible to apply the matching behavior seen in animal experiments to the escalation of abuse in marital violence (Herrnstein, 1970). (In learning theory, noxious events such as electrical shocks for animals or physical violence for humans can be used either as punishers [to decrease behavior] or as negative reinforcers [to increase behavior through avoidance].) First, assume that various forms of abuse, such as threats or swearing, function as negative reinforcers. Since negative reinforcers increase the probability of future responses, one abusive behavior (e.g., swearing) might lead to responsive threats by the partner (a matching response), leading to shoving by the first partner (matching), and so forth. Each abuse (negative reinforcer) serves to increase the other partner's abusive response (which serves as a negative reinforcer) such that, overall, the abuse escalates.

F.8: Stress

Hans Selye (1946) was the first to offer a relatively complete picture of the devastating effects of response-based stress on rats. Different stressors, such as infection and heat, caused a nonspecific response of the body that went through three stages: (a) alarm (the body mobilizes its defenses, pushing energy use to the limit), (b) resistance (the body returns to normal and copes with the stressor), and (c) exhaustion (the body can no longer adapt to the stressor; symptoms occur, and death may follow). Human bodies may well go through similar stages when the stressor is emotional. If so, the experiments explain psychosomatic illnesses—real physical illnesses whose origin lies in emotional stress.

F.9: Predictable and Unpredictable Shock

Abbot, Schoen, and Badia (1984) gave rats a choice between a signaled and nonsignaled shock. The animals could not avoid the shock; they could only control their own ability to predict it. If the rat bar-pressed at the beginning of a sequence of trials, it earned a warning tone before every shock. If it did not bar-press at the beginning, it received no warning signal. All of the rats showed a marked preference for the signaled shock as reflected in their rapid learning of the bar-press. The construct of control might be implied here.

F.10: Signaled Avoidance: Use of a Warning Signal

Bolles, Stokes, and Younger (1966) performed an experiment designed to examine escape and avoidance. In *avoidance*, rats learned to perform a task such as running to the other ("safe") side of a box at the sound of a tone (a learned signal) that signified that a shock was imminent. In *escape*, the animals could get away only after receiving the shock. They could not prevent it by performing a learned task (e.g., moving to the other side of a shuttle box).

F.11: Nonsignaled Avoidance: The Use of Temporal Cues to Know When to Make an Avoidance Response

Work with laboratory animals in nonsignaled avoidance experiments also appears to be pertinent to control issues raised in battering relationships. In a series of studies, Sidman (1953) placed rats in precarious situations that required them to respond (almost continuously at certain points during the experiment) to avoid the pain of being shocked. In these experiments, there was no handy signal such as a tone to warn the animal of the forthcoming shock. To a certain extent, the rat had to estimate the time when a response was necessary by paying attention to time (temporal cues).

A clock was set to deliver shocks to an animal, provided it made no response. If the animal made an appropriate response (such as pressing a bar), the clock was reset, allowing the animal to rest before the clock was reactivated to deliver another shock. In other words, the rat could adjust its behavior to avoid or minimize the shock.

Actually, Sidman used two clocks in his experiment. The shock-shock (S-S) clock's timer was set to control the interval between shocks (e.g., 2 seconds) if the animal made no response (e.g., pressing a lever). In other words, an animal that did nothing or did the *wrong* thing would receive a shock every 2 seconds ad infinitum until a power failure brought temporary relief.

The other clock was called the response-shock (R-S) clock. This clock controlled the elapsed time between a response and delivery of a shock. To activate this clock, the animal had to make the appropriate response. If the R-S clock was set for 4-second intervals, the rat could "relax" for 4 seconds before responding again (pressing the lever). This behavior prevented the shock and reset the clock for another 4-second safe period. If the animal did not respond appropriately, the 2-second S-S clock took over again, and the animal was shocked every 2 seconds.

Although there was no tangible cue that a shock was coming—no loud noise, light, or other event (conditioned stimulus) to warn the rats that a shock was "just around the corner"—they apparently learned to avoid shocks by attending to temporal cues: that is, to anticipate and to respond at specific time intervals.

This two-clock procedure was one of the most demanding schedules ever devised by research psychologists. It required constant vigilance and rapid response. It also took a long time to learn. The animals virtually lived "on the edge." For animals tested over several days, fatigue made it impossible for them to avoid all shocks, and in fact to attend to the time interval cues. The rats could learn to avoid shocks, even most shocks, but they were never able to avoid *all* shocks.

F.12: A Warning Signal Generates Fear

J. S. Brown and Jacobs (1949) exposed rats to different fear experiences. The first group of rats received a warning signal that ended with a shock. The second group received the same "warning" signal, but no shock. Later, both groups experienced the opportunity to turn off the warning signal by crossing from one side of a shuttle box to the other. The light remained on until the rats crossed over. The results indicated that the first group, the group that received the warning signal followed by the shock, learned to make the shuttle response significantly faster than the second group. The researchers interpreted these findings as signifying that the first group learned the shuttle response to reduce the fear generated by the warning signal. The incentive to terminate fear is reinforcing.

F.13: Motivation Following Frustration by Nonreward

Amsel and Rousel (1972) allowed rats to run in a straight runway first to one goal box for food, and then onward in the alley to a second goal box for additional food. After the animals learned this procedure, the researchers frustrated them by not providing them with any food in the first goal box. When this occurred, the frustrated rats ran even faster than they had originally to the second goal box. They also ran faster than a control group of rats that continued to receive the food reward in the first goal box. Apparently, frustration produced by the absence of the anticipated reward in the first goal box intensified the rats' motivation to reach the second goal box.

F.14: Frustration and Its Consequences

Animals caught in an approach-avoidance situation develop "frustration" (N. R. F. Maier, 1949). One outcome of their frustration is stereotyped responses. For example, N. R. F. Maier, Glazer, and Klee (1940) trained rats to jump from a jumping stand into a slightly closed door. Food was behind the door as a reinforcer for jumping to the correct color (e.g., white rather than black). Later, after the jumping was well established, the problem was made insolvable. For a number of trials, the animals received reinforcement on half of their jumps to the formerly correct color (i.e., white) and on half of their jumps to the formerly incorrect color (i.e., black). After this frustration training, the animals exhibited a number of unusual behaviors: (a) rigid responses—for example, only jumping to the right; (b) apathy—refusal to jump at all; (c) peculiar postures that seemed catatonic; and (d) attempts to get out of the test situation altogether by jumping over the test apparatus into the laboratory area.

One of the most fascinating occurrences was that the animals "walked" to the correct door if the experimenter placed a little bridge between the jumping stand and the door. If the bridge was removed and the door was opened so that the animal could actually see the food, it still would *not* jump to obtain it. Its behavior was inflexible and self-defeating. The rat did not perform the correct response even when it knew what it was. This compulsive behavior is labeled *fixated*.

F.15: Learned Helplessness in Dogs

Researchers subjected one of three groups of dogs to inescapable shock trials (S. F. Maier Seligman, 1976). A second group could escape, and a third comparison group received no shocks at all. Later, the experimenters tried to teach the dogs a new task: how to jump over a barrier to avoid a shock. The dogs that had been given inescapable shocks were almost unable to learn the new task. The other two groups of dogs learned to avoid shocks in the new task quickly. The shocked dogs had apparently learned, "Nothing I do makes a difference" (learned helplessness).

References

Abbot, B. B., Schoen, L. S., & Badia, P. (1984). Predictable and unpredictable shock: Behavioral measures of aversion and physiological measures of stress. *Psychological Bulletin, 96,* 45–71.

Abraham, M. (2000). Isolation as a form of marital violence: The South Asian immigrant experience. *Journal of Social Distress and the Homeless, 9,* 221–236.

Abramson, L. (1994, July 25). Unequal justice. *Newsweek, 124,* 25.

Abuse victims get new federal cards. (1998, November 5). *Daily News,* p. 12.

Abusive relationships and Stockholm syndrome. (1991, September 23). *Behavior Today, 22*(39), 6–7.

Acierno, R., Hernandez-Tejada, M., Muzzy, W., & Steve, K. (2009). *The national elder mistreatment study* (NCJ Pub. No. 226456). Washington, DC: U.S. Department of Justice.

Ackerman, M. J., & Ackerman, M. C. (1996). Child custody evaluation practices: A 1996 survey of psychologists. *Family Law Quarterly, 30,* 565–586.

Adams, C. M. (2006). The consequences of witnessing family violence on children and implications for family counselors. *Family Journal, 14,* 334–341.

Adams, D. C. (1984, August). *Stages of anti-sexist awareness and change for men who batter.* Paper presented at the annual meeting of the American Psychological Association, Toronto, Ontario, Canada.

Adams, D. C. (1988). Treatment models of men who batter: A profeminist analysis. In K. A. Yllö & M. Bograd (Eds.), *Feminist perspectives on wife abuse* (pp. 176–199). Newbury Park, CA: Sage.

Adams, D. C., & McCormick, A. J. (1982). Men unlearning violence: A group approach based on the collective model. In M. Roy (Ed.), *The abusive partner: An analysis of domestic battering* (pp. 170–197). New York, NY: Van Nostrand Reingold.

Adler, A. (1927). *Practice and theory of individual psychology.* New York, NY: Harcourt, Brace & World.

Adler, T. (1990, May). PTSD linked to stress rather than character. *APA Monitor, 21*(5), 12.

Afifi, T. O., Brownridge, D. A., Cox, B. J., & Sareen, J. (2006). Physical punishment, childhood abuse and psychiatric disorders. *Child Abuse & Neglect, 30,* 1093–1103.

Agoff, C., Herrera, C., & Castro, R. (2007). The weakness of family ties and their perpetuating effects on gender violence. *Violence Against Women, 13,* 1206–1220.

Aguirre, B. E. (1985). Why do they return? Abused wives in shelters. *Social Work, 30,* 350–354.

Aldarondo, E. (1996). Cessation and persistence of wife assault: A longitudinal analysis. *American Journal of Orthopsychiatry, 66,* 141–151.

Aldrige, L., Friedman, C., & Occhiuzzo Giggans, P. (1995). *In touch with teens: A relationship violence prevention curriculum for youth ages 12 to 19.* Los Angeles, CA: Los Angeles Commission on Assaults Against Women.

Allen, D. M. (1988). *Unifying individual and family therapies.* San Francisco, CA: Jossey-Bass.

Allen, M. (2011). Is there gender symmetry in intimate partner violence? *Child and Family Social Work, 16,* 245–254.

Allison, C. J., Bartholomew, K., Mayseless, O., & Dutton, D. G. (2008). Love as a battlefield: Attachment and relationship dynamics in couples identified for male partner violence. *Journal of Family Issues, 29,* 125–150.

Al-Modallal, H., Sowan, A. K., Hamaideh, S., Peden, A. R., Al-Omari, H., & Al-Rawashdeh, A. B. (2012). Psychological outcomes of intimate partner violence experienced by Jordanian working women. *Health Care for Women International, 33,* 217–227.

Alpert, E. J., & Cohen, S. (1997). Educating the nation's physicians about family violence and abuse. *Academic Medicine, 71*(Suppl.1), S3–S110.

Alsaker, K., Kristoffersen, K., Moen, B. E., & Baste, V. (2011). Threats and acts of intimate partner violence reported by users at Norwegian women's shelters. *Journal of Interpersonal Violence, 26,* 950–970.

Alsdurf, J. M. (1985). Wife abuse and the church: The response of pastors. *Response, 8*(1), 9–11.

American Association of Retired Persons. (1993). *Abused elders or older battered women? Report on the AARP forum.* Washington, DC: Author.

American Association of Retired Persons. (1994, January 12). *Survey of services for older battered women.* Unpublished final report.

American Psychiatric Association. (1980). *Diagnostic and statistical manual of mental disorders* (3rd ed.). Washington, DC: Author.

American Psychological Association. (1996). *Report of the APA presidential task force on violence and the family.* Washington, DC: Author.

American Psychological Association. (2006). Evidence-based practice in psychology: APA presidential task force on evidence-based practice. *American Psychologist, 61,* 271–285.

American Psychological Association. (2009). *Guidelines for child custody evaluations in family law proceedings.* Washington, DC: Author. Retrieved April 25, 2009, from the American Psychological Association website: www.apa.org/practice/childcustody.pdf

Amick-McMullen, A., Kilpatrick, D., Veronen, L. J., & Smith, S. (1989). Family survivors of homicide victims: Theoretical perspective and an exploratory study. *Journal of Traumatic Stress, 2,* 21–35.

Ammar, N. H. (2006). Beyond the shadows: Domestic spousal violence in a "democratizing" Egypt. *Trauma, Violence, & Abuse, 7,* 244–259.

Amowitz, L. L., Kim, G., Reis, C., Asher, J. L., & Iacopino, V. (2004). Human rights abuses and concerns about women's health and human rights in Southern Iraq. *Journal of the American Medical Association, 291,* 1471–1479.

Amsel, A., & Rousel, J. (1972). Behavior habituation, counter-conditioning, and a general theory of persistence. In A. H. Black & W. F. Prokasy (Eds.), *Classical conditioning II: Current research and theory* (pp. 409–426). New York, NY: Appleton-Century-Crofts.

Andelin, H. B. (1963). *Fascinating womanhood.* New York, NY: Bantam Books (Pacific Press ed.).

Anderson, D. K., Saunders, D. G., Yoshihama, M., Bybee, D. I., & Sullivan, C. M. (2003). Long-term trends in depression among women separated from abusive partners. *Violence Against Women, 9,* 807–838.

Anderson, K. L. (1997). Gender, status and domestic violence: An integration of feminist and family violence approaches. *Journal of Marriage and the Family, 59,* 655–669.

Andrews, B., & Brewin, C. R. (1990). Attributions of blame for marital violence: A study of antecedents and consequences. *Journal of Marriage and the Family, 52,* 757–767.

Anitha, S. (2011). Legislating gender inequalities: The nature and patterns of domestic violence experienced by South Asian women with insecure immigration status in the United Kingdom. *Violence Against Women, 17,* 1260–1285.

Anson, O., & Sagy, S. (1995). Marital violence: Comparing women in violent and nonviolent unions. *Human Relations, 48,* 285–305.

Appel, J. B. (1963). Punishment and shock intensity. *Science, 141,* 528–529.

Apsler, R., Cummins, M. R., & Carl, S. (2003). Perceptions of the police by female victims of domestic partner violence. *Violence Against Women, 9,* 1318–1335.

Archer, J. (2000). Sex differences in aggression between heterosexual partners: A meta-analytic review. *Psychological Bulletin, 126,* 651–680.

Archer, J. (2006). Cross-cultural differences in physical aggression between partners: A social-role analysis. *Personality and Social Psychology Review, 10,* 133–153.

Arias, I., Lyons, C. M., & Street, A. E. (1997). Individual and marital consequences of victimization: Moderating effects of relationship efficacy and spouse support. *Journal of Family Violence, 12,* 193–210.

Arias, I., & Pape, K. T. (1999). Psychological abuse: Implications for adjustment and commitment to leave violent partners. *Violence and Victims, 14*(Special issue), 55–67.

Armstrong, T. G., Wernke, J. Y., Medina, K. L., & Schafer, J. (2002). Do partners agree about the occurrence of intimate partner violence? *Trauma, Violence, & Abuse, 3,* 181–193.

Arosarena, O. A., Fritsch, T. A., Hsueh, Y., Aynehchi, A., & Haug, R. (2009). Maxillofacial injuries and violence against women. *Facial Plastic Surgery, 11,* 48–52.

Arriaga, X. B., & Capezza, N. M. (2005). Targets of partner violence: The importance of understanding coping trajectories. *Journal of Interpersonal Violence, 20,* 89–99.

Asher, S. J. (1990, August). *Primary, secondary, and tertiary prevention of violence against women.* Paper presented at the annual meeting of the American Psychological Association, Boston, MA.

Astin, M. C., Lawrence, K. J., Pincus, G., & Foy, D. W. (1990, October). *Moderator variables of post-traumatic stress disorder among battered women.* Paper presented at the Society for Traumatic Stress Studies, New Orleans, LA.

Atkinson, R. L., Atkinson, R. C., Smith, E. E., & Bem, D. J. (1990). *Introduction to psychology* (10th ed.). New York, NY: Harcourt Brace Jovanovich.

Avakame, E. F., & Fyfe, J. J. (2001). Differential police treatment of male-on-female spousal violence. *Violence Against Women, 7,* 22–45.

Avni, N. (1991). Battered wives: The home as a total institution. *Violence and Victims, 6,* 137–149.

Ayllon, T., & Azrin, N. H. (1966). Punishment as a discriminative stimulus and conditioned reinforcer with humans. *Journal of the Experimental Analysis of Behavior, 9,* 411–419.

Azrin, N. H., & Holz, W. C. (1961). Punishment during fixed-interval reinforcement. *Journal of Experimental Analysis of Behavior, 4,* 343–347.

Azrin, N. H., & Holz, W. C. (1966). Punishment. In W. R. Honig (Ed.), *Operant behavior: Areas of research and application.* New York, NY: Appleton-Century-Crofts.

Azrin, N. H., Holz, W. C., & Hake, D. F. (1963). Fixed-ratio punishment. *Journal of Experimental Analysis of Behavior, 6,* 141–148.

Babcock, J. C., Green, C. E., & Robie, C. (2004). Does batterers' treatment work? A meta-analytic review of domestic violence treatment. *Clinical Psychology Review, 23,* 1023–1053.

Babinski, L. M., Hartsough, C. S., & Lambert, N. M. (2001). A comparison of self-report of criminal involvement and official arrest records. *Aggressive Behavior, 27,* 44–54.

Bachman, R., & Coker, A. L. (1995). Police involvement in domestic violence: The interactive effects of victim injury, offender's history of violence, and race. *Violence and Victims, 10,* 91–106.

Bachman, R., & Saltzman, L. E. (1995). *Violence against women: Estimates from the redesigned survey* (NCJ Pub. No. 154348). Rockville, MD: U.S. Department of Justice.

Bachman, R., & Taylor, B. M. (1994). The measurement of family violence and rape by the redesigned National Crime Victimization Survey. *Justice Quarterly, 11,* 499–512.

Bair-Merritt, M. H, Crowne, S. S., Thompson, D. A., Sibinga, E., Trent, M., & Campbell, J. (2010). Why do women use intimate partner violence?

A systematic review of women's motivations. *Trauma, Violence, & Abuse, 11,* 178–189.

Bair-Merritt., M. H., Feudtner, C., Localio, A. R., Feinstein, J. A., Rubin, D., & Holmes, W. C. (2008). Health care use of children whose female caregivers have intimate partner violence histories. *Archives of Pediatrics and Adolescent Medicine, 162,* 134–139.

Baker, C. K., Niolon, P. H., & Olyphant, H. (2009). Descriptive analysis of transitional housing programs for survivors of partner violence in the United States. *Violence Against Women, 15,* 460–481.

Bancroft, L. (2011). Representing protective mothers in custody and visitation litigation. *Michigan Bar Journal, 90,* 28–30.

Bancroft, L., & Silverman, J. (2002). *The batterer as parent: Assessing the impact of domestic violence on family dynamics.* Newbury Park, CA: Sage.

Bandura, A. (1971). *Social learning theory.* Morristown, NJ: General Learning.

Barak, A. (2005). Sexual harassment on the Internet. *Social Science Computer Review, 23,* 77–92.

Barkley, K. M. (1997). *Social change and social service: A case study of a feminist battered women's shelter* [CD-ROM]. Abstract retrieved from ProQuest, Dissertation Abstracts Item 9638071.

Barner, J. R., & Carney, M. M. (2011). Interventions for intimate partner violence: A historical review. *Journal of Family Violence, 26,* 235–244.

Barnett, O. W. (1990). *Forms and frequencies of abuse.* Unpublished manuscript, Pepperdine University, Malibu, CA.

Barnett, O. W., & Fagan, R. W. (1993). Alcohol use in male spouse abusers and their female partners. *Journal of Family Violence, 8,* 1–25.

Barnett, O. W., & Hamberger, L. K. (1992). The assessment of maritally violent men on the California Psychological Inventory. *Violence and Victims, 7,* 15–28.

Barnett, O. W., Haney-Martindale, D. J., Modzelewski, C. A., & Sheltra, E. M. (1991, April). *Reasons why battered women feel self-blame.* Paper presented at the annual meeting of the Western Psychological Association, San Francisco, CA.

Barnett, O. W., Keyson, M., & Thelen, R. E. (1992, August). *Battered women's responsive violence.* Paper presented at the annual meeting of the American Psychological Association, Washington, DC.

Barnett, O. W., Lee, C. Y., & Thelen, R. E. (1997). Differences in forms, outcomes, and attributions of self-defense and control in interpartner aggression. *Violence Against Women, 3,* 462–481.

Barnett, O. W., & Lopez-Real, D. I. (1985, November). *Women's reactions to battering and why they stay.* Paper presented at the annual meeting of the American Society of Criminology, San Diego, CA.

Barnett, O. W., Martinez, T. E., & Keyson, M. (1996). The relationship between violence, social support, and self-blame in battered women. *Journal of Interpersonal Violence, 11,* 221–233.

Barnett, O. W., Miller-Perrin, C. L., & Perrin, R. D. (2011). *Family violence across the lifespan* (3rd ed.). Thousand Oaks, CA: Sage.

Barshis, V. R. G. (1983). The question of marital rape. *Women's Studies International Forum, 6,* 383–393.

Basile, K. C., & Smith, S. G. (2011). Sexual violence victimization of women: Prevalence, characteristics, and the role of public health and prevention. *American Journal of Lifestyle Medicine, 5,* 407–417.

Basile, K. C., Swahn, M. H., Chen, J., & Saltzman, L. E. (2006). Stalking in the United States: Recent national prevalence estimates. *American Journal of Preventive Medicine, 31,* 172–175.

Basow, S. A., & Thompson, J. (2012). Service providers' reactions to intimate partner violence as a function of victim sexual orientation and type of abuse. *Journal of Interpersonal Violence, 27,* 1225–1241.

Bassuk, E. L., Weinreb, L. F., Buckner, J. C., Browne, A., Salomon, A., & Bassuk, S. S. (1996). The characteristics and needs of sheltered homeless and low-income housed mothers. *Journal of the American Medical Association, 276,* 640–646.

The battered woman: Breaking the cycle of abuse. (1989, June 15). *Emergency Medicine, 15,* 104–115.

Baum, K., Catalano, S., Rand, M., & Rose, K. (2009). *Stalking victimization in the United States* (NCJ Pub. No. 224527). U.S. Department of Justice, NCVS.

Baumeister, R. F., Stillwell, A., & Wotman, S. R. (1990). Victim and perpetrator accounts of interpersonal conflict: Autobiographical narratives about anger. *Journal of Personality and Social Psychology, 59,* 994–1005.

Bauserman, S. A. K., & Arias, I. (1992). Relationships among marital investment, marital satisfaction, and marital commitment in domestically victimized and nonvictimized wives. *Violence and Victims, 7,* 287–296.

Beach, S. R. H., Kim, S., Cercone-Keeney, J., Gupta, M., Arias, I., & Brody, G. H. (2004). Physical aggression and depressive symptoms: Gender asymmetry in effects. *Journal of Social and Personal Relationships, 21,* 341–360.

Bechtel, K. A., Alarid, L. F., Holsinger, A., & Holsinger, K. (2012). Predictors of domestic violence prosecution in a state court. *Victims and Offenders, 7,* 143–160.

Bedi, G., & Goddard, C. (2007). Intimate partner violence: What are the impacts on children? *Australian Psychologist, 42,* 66–77.

Belknap, J. (2000). *Factors related to domestic violence court dispositions in a large urban area: The role of victim/witness reluctance and other variables* (NCJ Pub. No. 184232). Washington, DC: National Institute of Justice.

Belknap, J., & Melton, H. (2005). *Are heterosexual men also victims of intimate partner abuse?* (NCJ Pub. No. 213556). Washington, DC: U.S. Department of Justice.

Belle, D. (1990). Poverty and women's mental health. *American Psychologist, 45,* 385–389.

Belmore, M. F., & Quinsey, V. P. (1994). Correlates of psychopathy in a non-institutional sample. *Journal of Interpersonal Violence, 9,* 339–349.

Bemiller, M. (2008). When battered mothers lose custody: A qualitative study of abuse at home and in the courts. *Journal of Child Custody, 5*(3/4), 228–255.

Bennett, L. W., Stroops, C., Call, C., & Flett, H. (2007). Program completion and re-arrest in a batterer intervention system. *Research and Social Work Practice, 17,* 42–54.

Bennett, L. W., Tolman, R. M., Rogalski, C. A., & Srinivasaraghavan, J. (1994). Domestic abuse by male alcohol and drug addicts. *Violence and Victims, 9,* 359–368.

Ben-Porat, A., & Itzhaky, H. (2009). Implications of treating family violence for the therapist: Secondary traumatization, vicarious traumatization, and growth. *Journal of Family Violence, 24,* 507–515.

Bent-Goodley, T. B. (2001). Eradicating domestic violence in the African-American community: A literature review and action agenda. *Trauma, Violence, & Abuse, 2,* 316–330.

Bergen, R. K. (1995). *Wife rape: Understanding the response of service providers.* Thousand Oaks, CA: Sage.

Bergen, R. K., & Bukovec, P. (2006). Men and intimate partner rape. *Journal of Interpersonal Violence, 21,* 1375–1384.

Berger, P. J., & Berger, B. (1979). *Becoming a member of society.* In P. I. Rose (Ed.), *Socialization and the life cycle* (pp. 4–20). New York, NY: St. Martin's Press.

Berger, R., & Rosenberg, E. (2008). The experience of abused women with their children's law guardians. *Violence Against Women, 14,* 71–92.

Berk, R. A., Fenstermaker, S., & Newton, P. J. (1988). *An empirical analysis of police responses to incidents of wife battery.* In G. T. Hotaling, D. Finkelhor, J. T. Kirkpatrick, & M. A. Straus (Eds.), *Coping with family violence* (pp. 158–168). Newbury Park, CA: Sage.

Berkowitz, L., & LePage, A. (1967). Weapons as aggression-eliciting stimuli. *Journal of Personality and Social Psychology, 7,* 202–207.

Berliner, L. (1998). Battered women and abused children: The question of responsibility. *Journal of Interpersonal Violence, 13,* 287–289.

Berliner, L., & Saunders, B. (2010). Child sexual abuse: Definitions, prevalence, and consequences. In J. E. B. Myers (Ed.), *APSAC handbook on child maltreatment* (3rd ed., pp. 215–231). Thousand Oaks, CA: Sage.

Bernard, C., & Schlaffer, E. (1992). *Domestic violence in Austria: The institutional response.* In E. C. Viano (Ed.), Intimate violence: An interdisciplinary perspective (pp. 243–254). Bristol, PA: Taylor & Francis.

Bernhard, L. A. (2000). Physical and sexual violence experienced by lesbian and heterosexual women. *Violence Against Women, 6,* 68–79.

Betz, C. L. (2007). Editorial: Teen dating violence: An unrecognized health care need. *Journal of Pediatric Nursing, 22,* 427–429.

Biden, J. R., Jr. (1994). *Turning the act into action: The violence against women law.* Washington, DC: U.S. Senate (Committee on the Judiciary).

Bilefsky, D. (2011, October 6). Wife who fired 11 shots is acquitted of murder. *New York Times.* Retrieved December 2, 2011, from www.nytimes.com/2011/10/07/nyregion/barbara-sheehan-who-killed-husband-found-not-guilty

Birns, B., Cascardi, M., & Meyer, S. L. (1994). Sex-role socialization: Developmental influences on wife abuse. *American Journal of Orthopsychiatry, 64,* 50–59.

Black, M. C., Basile, K. C., Breiding, M. J., Smith, S. G., Walters, M. L., Merrick, M. T., . . . Stevens, M. R. (2011, November). *The National Intimate Partner and Sexual Violence Survey, 2010 summary report* (NIPSVS). Atlanta, GA: U.S. Department of Health and Human Services, Centers for Disease Control and Prevention, National Center for Injury Prevention and Control.

Blackman, J. (1988, August). *Exploring the impacts of poverty on battered women who kill their abusers.* Paper presented at the annual meeting of the American Psychological Association, Atlanta, GA.

Blau, F. D., & Kahn, L. M. (2007). The gender pay gap: Have women gone as far as they can? *Academy of Management Perspectives, 21,* 7–23.

Block, C. R. (2003, November). How can practitioners help an abused woman lower her risk of death? (NCJ Pub. No. 196545). *NIJ Journal, 250,* 4–7.

Blowers, A. N., Davis, B., Shenk, D., Kalaw, K., Smith, M., & Jackson, K. (2012). A multidisciplinary approach to detecting and responding to elder mistreatment: Creating a university community partnership. *American Journal of Criminal Justice, 37,* 276–290.

Blumenthal, D. R., Neeman, J., & Murphy, C. M. (1998). Lifetime exposure to interparental physical and verbal aggression and symptom expression in college students. *Violence and Victims, 13,* 175–196.

Bodenmann, G., Pihet, S., & Kayser, K. (2006). The relationship between dyadic coping and marital quality: A 2-year longitudinal study. *Journal of Family Psychology, 20,* 485–493.

Bograd, M. (1992). Values in conflict: Challenges to family therapists' thinking. *Journal of Marital and Family Therapy, 18,* 245–256.

Boles, A. B., & Patterson, J. C. (1997). *Improving community response to crime victims: An eight-step model for developing protocol.* Thousand Oaks, CA: Sage.

Bolles, R. C., Stokes, L. W., & Younger, M. S. (1966). Does CS termination reinforce avoidance behavior? *Journal of Comparative and Physiological Psychology, 62,* 201–207.

Borochowitz, D. Y., & Eisikovits, Z. (2002). To love violently: Strategies for reconciling love and violence. *Violence Against Women, 8,* 476–494.

Bossarte, R. M., Simon, T. R., & Barker, L. (2006). Characteristics of homicide followed by suicide in multiple states, 2003–2004. *Injury Prevention, 2006, 12*(Suppl. 11), ii33–ii38.

Boudreau, F. A. (1993). Elder abuse. In R. L. Hampton, T. P. Gullotta, G. R. Adams, E. H. Potter, III, & R. P. Weissberg (Eds.), *Family violence: Prevention and treatment* (pp. 142–158). Newbury Park, CA: Sage.

Bourg, S., & Stock, H. V. (1994). A review of domestic violence arrest statistics in a police department using a pro-arrest police: Are pro-arrest policies enough? *Journal of Family Violence, 9,* 177–192.

Bower, B. (1992). Prior abuse stokes combat reactions. *Science News, 141,* 332.

Bowes, N., McMurran, M., Williams, B., David, S., & Zammit, I. (2012). Treating alcohol-related violence: Intermediate outcomes in a feasibility study for a randomized controlled trial in prison. *Criminal Justice and Behavior, 39,* 333–344.

Bowker, L. H. (1983). *Beating wife beating.* Lexington, MA: Lexington.

Bowker, L. H. (1984). Battered wives and the police: A national study of usage and effectiveness. *Police Studies, 7,* 84–93.

Boyd, T. P. (2011). Domestic violence court—55th district court. *Michigan Bar Journal, 90,* 42.

Braidbill, K. (1997, October). A deadly force. *Los Angeles Magazine,* pp. 68–69, 71, 130–132.

Brandl, B., Hebert, M., Rozwadowski, J., & Spangler, D. (2003). Feeling safe, feeling strong: Support groups for older abused women. *Violence Against Women, 9,* 1490–1503.

Brandt, M. J. (2011). Sexism and gender inequality across 57 societies. *Psychological Science.* doi: 10.1177/0956797611420445

Brandwein, R. A. (2003). *The use of public welfare by family violence victims: Implications of new federal welfare "reform."* Newbury Park, CA: Sage.

Brenner, J. (1991). Feminization of poverty. In J. Lorber & S. A. Farrell (Eds.), *The social construction of gender* (pp. 193–209). Newbury Park, CA: Sage.

Brines, J. (1994). Economic dependency, gender, and the division of labor at home. *American Journal of Sociology, 100,* 652–688.

Britz, J., & Pappas, E. (2010). Sources and outlets of stress among university students: Correlations between stress and unhealthy habits. *Undergraduate Research Journal for the Human Sciences, 9.*

Brookoff, D. (1997, October). *Drugs, alcohol, and domestic violence in Memphis.* Washington, DC: National Institute of Justice.

Broverman, I. K., Vogel, S. R., Broverman, D. M., Clarkson, F. E., & Rosenkrantz, P. S. (1972). Sex-role stereotypes: A current appraisal. *Journal of Social Issues, 28,* 59–78.

Brown, C. (2008). Gender-role implications on same-sex intimate partner violence. *Journal of Family Violence, 23,* 457–462.

Brown, J. (1997). Working toward freedom from violence: The process of change in battered women. *Violence Against Women, 3,* 5–26.

Brown, J. (1998, July). *The Process of Change in Abused Women Scale (PROCAWS): Stage of change, pros & cons, and self-efficacy as measurable outcomes.* Paper presented at Program Evaluation and Family Violence Research: An International Conference, Durham, NH.

Brown, J. K. (1992). Introduction: Definitions, assumptions, themes, and issues. In D. A. Counts, J. K. Brown, & J. C. Campbell (Eds.), *Sanctions and sanctuary: Cultural perspectives on the beating of wives* (pp. 1–18). Boulder, CO: Westview Press.

Brown, J. S. (1948). Gradients of approach and avoidance responses and their relation to motivation. *Journal of Comparative and Physiological Psychology, 41,* 450–465.

Brown, J. S., & Jacobs, A. (1949). The role of fear in the motivation and acquisition of responses. *Journal of Experimental Psychology, 39,* 747–759.

Brown, L. K., Puster, K. L., Vazquez, E. A., Hunter, H. L., & Lescano, C. M. (2007). Screening practices for adolescent dating violence. *Journal of Interpersonal Violence, 22,* 456–464.

Browne, A. (1983). *Self-defensive homicides by battered women: Relationships at risk*. Paper presented at the meeting of the American Psychology-Law Society, Chicago, IL.

Browne, A., & Bassuk, B. A. (1997). Intimate violence in the lives of homeless and poor housed women: Prevalence and patterns in an ethnically diverse sample. *American Journal of Orthopsychiatry, 67*, 261–278.

Browning, J., & Dutton, D. (1986). Assessment of wife assault with the Conflict Tactics Scale: Using couple data to quantify the differential reporting effect. *Journal of Marriage and the Family, 48*, 375–379.

Brownridge, D. A., & Halli, S. S. (2001). Marital status as differentiating factor in Canadian women's coping with partner violence. *Journal of Comparative Family Studies, 32*, 117–125.

Bruch, C. (2001). Parental alienation syndrome and parental alienation: Getting it wrong in child custody cases. *Family Law Quarterly, 35*, 527.

Brush, L. D. (1990). Violent acts and injurious outcomes in married couples: Methodological issues in the National Survey of Families and Households. *Gender and Society, 4*, 56–67.

Brustin, S. L. (1995). Legal responses to teen dating violence. *Family Law Quarterly, 29*, 331–356.

Buchanan, D. C., & Perry, P. A. (1985). Attitudes of police recruits towards domestic disturbances: An evaluation of family crisis intervention training. *Journal of Criminal Justice, 13*, 561–572.

Bulman, P. (2010, April). Elder abuse emerges from the shadows of public consciousness. *NIJ Journal, 265*, 4–7.

Burke, A. (1995, July 31). Valley needs more shelter beds. *Daily News*, p. 6.

Burt, M. R., Newmark, L. C., Olson, K. K., Aron, L. Y., & Harrell, A. V. (1997, March). *1997 report: Evaluation of the STOP formula grants under the Violence Against Women Act of 1994*. Washington, DC: Urban Institute.

Busch, N. B., & Valentine, D. (2000). Empowerment practice: A focus on battered women. *Affilia, 15*(1), 82–95.

Bush, G. W. (2002, February 26). *President announces welfare reform agenda*. Retrieved June, 25, 2004, from www.whitehouse.gov/news/release/2002/02/20020226-11.html

Buzawa, E. S., Austin, T. L., & Buzawa, C. G. (1995). Responding to crimes of violence against women: Gender differences versus organizational imperatives. *Crime and Delinquency, 41*, 443–466.

Buzawa, E. S., & Buzawa, C. G. (2003). *Domestic violence: The criminal justice response* (3rd ed.). Thousand Oaks, CA: Sage.

Byrne, C. A., Resnick, H. S., Kilpatrick, D., Best, C. L., & Saunders, B. E. (1999). The socioeconomic impact of interpersonal violence on women. *Journal of Consulting and Clinical Psychology, 67*, 362–366.

California Habeas Project. (n.d.). Retrieved from www.habeaasproject.org/faq.htm

California panel urges reforms to curb gender bias in courts. (1990, May, 1). *Criminal Justice Newsletter, 21*(9), 4–5.

Camp, D. S., Raymond, G. A., & Church, R. M. (1967). Temporal relationship between response and punishment. *Journal of Experimental Psychology, 74,* 114–123.

Campbell, J. C. (1989). A test of two explanatory models of women's responses to battering. *Nursing Research, 38*(1), 18–24.

Campbell, J. C. (1990, December). Battered woman syndrome: A critical review. *Violence Update, 1*(4), 1, 4, 10–11.

Campbell, J. C. (2005). Assessing dangerousness in domestic violence: History, challenges, and opportunities. *Criminology & Public Policy, 4,* 653–672.

Campbell, J. C. (2010). Why do women use intimate partner violence? A systematic review of women's motivations. *Trauma, Violence, & Abuse, 11,* 178–179.

Campbell, J. C., & Alford, P. (1989). The dark consequences of marital rape. *American Journal of Nursing, 87,* 946–949.

Campbell, J. C., Kub, J., Belknap, R. A., & Templin, T. N. (1997). Predictors of depression in battered women. *Violence Against Women, 3,* 271–293.

Campbell, J. C., Miller, P., Cardwell, M. M., & Belknap, R. A. (1994). Relationship status of battered women over time. *Journal of Family Violence, 9,* 99–111.

Campbell, J. C., & Soeken, K. L. (1999). Women's responses to battering over time. *Journal of Interpersonal Violence, 14,* 21–40.

Campbell, R. (2008). The psychological impact of rape victims' experiences with the legal, medical, and mental health systems. *American Psychologist, 63,* 702–717.

Cantos, A. L., Neidig, P. H., & O'Leary, K. D. (1994). Injuries of women and men in a treatment program for domestic violence. *Journal of Family Violence, 9,* 113–124.

Capezza, N. M., & Arriaga, X. B. (2008). Why do people blame victims of abuse? The role of stereotypes of women on perceptions of blame. *Sex Roles, 59,* 839–850.

Caplan, P. J. (1984). The myth of women's masochism. *American Psychologist, 39,* 130–139.

Cappas, N. M., Andres-Hyman, R., & Davidson, L. (2005). What psychotherapists can begin to learn from neuroscience: Seven principles of a brain-based psychotherapy. *Psychology, Theory, Research, Practice, Training, 42,* 374–383.

Carlisle-Frank, P. (1991, July). Do battered women's beliefs about control affect their decisions to remain in abusive environments? *Violence Update, 1*(11), 1, 8, 10–11.

Carlson, B. E., McNutt, L. A., Choi, D. Y., & Rose, I. M. (2002). Intimate partner abuse and mental health: The role of social support and other protective factors. *Violence Against Women, 8,* 720–745.

Carlson, C., & Nidey, F. J. (1995). Mandatory penalties, victim cooperation, and the judicial processing of domestic abuse assault cases. *Crime and Delinquency, 41,* 132–149.

Carlson, M. J., Harris, S. D., & Holden, G. W. (1999). Protective orders and domestic violence: Risk factors for re-abuse. *Journal of Family Violence, 14,* 205–226.

Carmody, D. C., & Williams, K. R. (1987). Wife assault and perceptions of sanctions. *Violence and Victims, 2,* 25–38.

Carr, J. L., & VanDeusen, K. M. (2002). The relationship between family of origin violence and dating violence in college men. *Journal of Interpersonal Violence, 17,* 630–646.

Cascardi, M., Langhinrichsen-Rohling, J., & Vivian, D. (1992). Marital aggression: Impact, injury, and health correlates for husbands and wives. *Archives of Internal Medicine, 152,* 1178–1184.

Cascardi, M., & O'Leary, K. D. (1992). Depressive symptomatology, self-esteem, and self-blame in battered women. *Journal of Family Violence, 7,* 249–259.

Castro, T. (2010, December 30). New laws and how they will affect you. *Daily News, A1,* p. 53.

Catalano, S., Smith, E., Snyder, H., & Rand, M. (2009). *Female victims of violence, selected findings* (NCJ Pub. No. 228356). Washington, DC: Bureau of Justice Statistics.

Catania, C. (1984). *Learning.* Englewood Cliffs, NJ: Prentice Hall.

Cater, A., & Forssell, A. M. (2012). Descriptions of fathers' care by children exposed to intimate partner violence (IPV)—relative neglect and children's needs. *Child and Family Social Work.* doi: 10.1111/j.1365-2206.00892.x

Cavanagh, K. (2003). Understanding women's responses to domestic violence. *Qualitative Social Work, 2,* 229–249.

Cavanaugh, M. M., & Gelles, R. J. (2005). The utility of male violence offender typologies: New directions for research, policy, and practice. *Journal of Interpersonal Violence, 20,* 155–166.

Cercone-Keeney, J. J., Beach, S. R. H., & Arias, I. (2005). Gender asymmetry in dating intimate partner violence: Does similar behavior imply similar constructs? *Violence and Victims, 20,* 207–218.

Chalk, R., & King, P. A. (Eds.). (1998). *Violence in families: Assessing prevention and treatment programs.* Washington, DC: National Academy Press.

Chamberland, C., Fortin, A., Turgeon, J., & Laport, L. (2007). Men's recognition of violence against women and spousal abuse: Comparison of three groups of men. *Violence and Victims, 22,* 419–436.

Chambers, A. L., & Wilson, M. N. (2007). Assessing male batterers with the personality assessment inventory. *Journal of Personality Assessment, 88,* 57–65.

Chan, K. L., Tiwari, A., Fong, D. Y. T., Leung, W. C., Brownridge, D. A., & Ho, P. C. (2009). Correlates of in-law conflict and intimate partner violence against Chinese pregnant women in Hong Kong. *Journal of Interpersonal Violence, 24,* 97–110.

Chang, J. C., Dado, D., Ashton, S., Hawker, L., Cluss, P. A., Buranosky, R., & Scholle, S. H. (2006). Understanding behavior change for women experiencing intimate partner violence: Mapping the ups and downs using the stages of change. *Patient Education and Counseling, 62,* 330–339.

Chang, J. C., Decker, M., Moracco, K. E., Martin, S. L., Petersen, R., & Frasier, P. Y. (2003). What happens when health care providers ask about intimate partner violence? A description of consequences from the perspective of female survivors. *Journal of the American Women's Medical Association, 58,* 76–81.

Chang, J. J., Theodore, A. D., Martin, S. L., & Runyan, D. K. (2008). Psychological abuse between parents: Associations with child maltreatment from a population-based sample. *Child Abuse & Neglect, 32,* 819–829.

Chang, R. (2011, August 4). New bill would target domestic violence. *Ventura County Star,* p. 4.

Chapple, C. L. (2003). Examining intergenerational violence: Violent role modeling or weak parental controls? *Violence and Victims, 18,* 142–162.

Chavez, V., et al. (2005, September). *Cultural perspectives on domestic violence.* Symposium presented at the Tenth International Conference on Family Violence, San Diego, CA.

Chawla, N., & Solinas-Saunders, M. (2011). Supporting military parent and child adjustment to deployment and separations with filial therapy. *American Journal of Family Therapy, 39,* 179–192.

Chesler, P. (2009). Are honor killings simply domestic violence? *Middle East Quarterly, Spring,* 61–69.

Chester, B., Robin, R. W., Koss, M. P., Lopez, M. P., & Goldman, D. (1994). Grandmother dishonored: Violence against women by male partners in American Indian communities. *Violence and Victims, 9,* 249–258.

Children's Safety Network. (1992). *Domestic violence: A directory of protocols for health care providers.* Newton, MA: Education Development Center.

Chrisler, J. C., & Ferguson, S. (2006). Violence against women as a public health issue. *Annals of the New York Academy of Sciences, 1087,* 235–249.

Church, C. (2011). The family connection center supports safe parenting in Howell. *Michigan Bar Journal, 90,* 43.

Church, R. M. (1969). *Response suppression.* In B. A. Campbell & R. M. Church (Eds.), Punishment and aversive behavior (pp. 111–156). New York, NY: Appleton-Century-Crofts.

City receives grant to combat abuse. (1996, December 21). *Daily News,* p. 8.

Claerhout, S., Elder, J., & Janes, C. (1982). Problem-solving skills of rural battered women. *American Journal of Community Psychology, 10,* 605–612.

Clarke, P. N., Pendry, N. C., & Kim, Y. S. (1997). Patterns of violence in homeless women. *Western Journal of Nursing Research, 19,* 490–500.

Clarke, R. L. (1986). *Pastoral care of battered women.* Philadelphia, PA: Westminster Press.

Clements, C. M., Sabourin, C. M., & Spilby, L. (2004). Dysphoria and hopelessness following battering: The role of perceived control, coping, and self-esteem. *Journal of Family Violence, 19,* 25–36.

Clements, C. M., & Sawhney, D. K. (2000). Coping with domestic violence: Control attributions, dysphoria, and hopelessness. *Journal of Traumatic Stress, 13,* 221–240.

Clemmons, J. C., Walsh, K., DiLillo, D., & Messman-Moore, T. L. (2007). Unique and combined contributions of multiple child abuse types and abuse severity to adult trauma symptomatology. *Child Maltreatment, 12,* 172–181.

Coan, J., Gottman, J. M., Babcock, J., & Jacobson, N. (1997). Battering and the male rejection of influence from women. *Aggressive Behavior, 23,* 375–388.

Cohen, J. H., Forjuoh, S. N., & Gondolf, E. W. (1999). Injuries and health care use in women with partners in batterer intervention programs. *Journal of Family Violence, 14,* 83–94.

Cohen-Mansfield, J., Creedon, M. A., Malone, T. B., Kirkpatrick, M. J., III, Dutra, L. A., & Herman, R. P. (2005). Electronic memory aids for community-dwelling elderly persons: Attitudes, preferences, and potential utilization. *Journal of Applied Gerontology, 24,* 3–20.

Cole, T., & Sapp, G. (1988). Stress, locus of control, and achievement of high school seniors. *Psychological Reports, 63,* 355–359.

Coleman, D. H., & Straus, M. A. (1986). Marital power, conflict, and violence in a nationally representative sample of American couples. *Violence and Victims, 1,* 141–157.

Connelly, C. D., Hazen, A. L., Cohen, J. H., Kelleher, K. J., Barth, R. P., & Landsverk, J. A. (2006). Persistence of intimate partner violence among families referred to child welfare. *Journal of Interpersonal Violence, 21,* 774–797.

Conrad, S. D., & Morrow, R. S. (2000). Borderline personality organization, dissociation, and willingness to use force in intimate relationships. *Psychology of Men and Masculinity, 1*(1), 37–48.

Cook, P. W. (1997). *Abused men: The hidden side of domestic violence.* Westport, CT: Praeger.

Cooper-White, P. (1996). An emperor without clothes: The church's views about treatment of domestic violence. *Pastoral Psychology, 45,* 3–20.

Counts, D. A., Brown, J. K., & Campbell, J. C. (Eds.). (1992). *Sanctions and sanctuary: Cultural perspectives on the beating of wives.* Boulder, CO: Westview.

Craft, S. M., & Serovich, J. M. (2005). Family-of-origin factors and partner violence in the intimate relationships of gay men who are HIV positive. *Journal of Interpersonal Violence, 20,* 777–791.

Creach, D. L. (1982). Partially determined imperfect self-defense: The battered wife kills and tells why. *34 Stanford Law Review,* 615–638.

Creighton, A., & Kivel, P. (1993). *Helping teens stop violence: A practical guide to counselors.* Alameda, CA: Hunter House.

Crittenden, P. M., Kozlowska, K., & Landini, A. (2010). Assessing attachment in school-age children. *Clinical Child Psychology and Psychiatry, 15,* 185–208.

Cucio, W. (1997). *The Passaic County study of AFDC recipients in a welfare-to-work program: A preliminary analysis.* Patterson, NJ: Passaic County Board of Social Services.

Cummings, E. M. (1998). Children exposed to marital conflict and violence: Conceptual and theoretical directions. In G. W. Holden, R. Geffner, & E. N. Jouriles (Eds.), *Children exposed to marital violence* (pp. 55–93). Washington, DC: American Psychological Association.

Cummings, N. (1990). Issues of the 1990s. *Response, 13*(1), 4.

Cunradi, C. B., Bersamin, M., & Ames, G. (2009). Agreement on intimate partner violence among a sample of blue-collar couples. *Journal of Interpersonal Violence, 24,* 551–568.

Currens, S. (1998, April/May). Kentucky coalition's concerns about mandatory reporting. *Domestic Violence Report, 3,* 49–50.

Dallam, S. J., & Silberg, J. L. (2006). Myths that place children at risk during custody disputes. *Sexual Assault Report, 9*(3), 33–47.

Dalto, C. A. (1983). Battered women: Factors influencing whether or not former shelter residents return to the abusive situation. *Dissertation Abstracts International, 44,* 1277B. (UMI No. 8317463)

Dalton, C., Drozd, L. M., & Wong, F. Q. F. (2006). *Navigating custody and visitation evaluation in cases with domestic violence: A judge's guide.* Reno, NV: National Council of Juvenile and Family Court Judges.

Danis, F. S., Lewis, C. M., Trapp, J., Reid, K., & Fisher, E. R. (1998, July). *Lessons from the first year: An evaluation of the National Domestic Violence Hotline.* Paper presented at Program Evaluation and Family Violence Research: An International Conference, Durham, NH.

Davidson, H. A. (1995). Child abuse and domestic violence: Legal connections and controversies. *Family Law Quarterly, 29*(2, Special issue), 357–373.

Davies, B., Ralph, S., Hawton, M., & Craig, L. (1995). A study of client satisfaction with family court counseling in cases involving domestic violence. *Family and Conciliation Courts Review, 33,* 324–341.

Davis, L. V. , & Srinivasan, M. (1995). Listening to the voices of battered women: What helps them escape the violence. *Affilia, 10,* 49–69.

Davis, M. H., & Morris, M. M. (1998). Relationship-specific and global perceptions of social support: Associations with well-being and attachment. *Journal of Personality and Social Psychology, 74,* 468–481.

Davis, R. C., & Erez, E. (1998, May). *Immigrant populations as victims: Toward a multicultural criminal justice system* (NCJ Pub. No. 167571). Washington, DC: U.S. Department of Justice.

Davis, R. C., & Taylor, B. G. (1997). A proactive response to family violence: The results of a randomized experiment. *Criminology, 35,* 307–333.

Davis, R. E. (2002). "The strongest women": Exploration of the inner resources of abused women. *Qualitative Research, 12,* 1248–1263.

Davis, R. L. (1998). *Domestic violence: Facts and fallacies.* Westport, CT: Praeger.

Deering, C., Templer, D. I., Keller, J., & Canfield, M. (2001). Neuropsychological assessment of battered women: A pilot study. *Perceptual and Motor Skills, 92,* 682–686.

DeJong, C., Burgess-Proctor, A., & Elis, L. (2008). Police officer perceptions of intimate partner violence: An analysis of observational data. *Violence and Victims, 23,* 683–696.

DeKeseredy, W. S. (1990). Male peer support and woman abuse: The current state of knowledge. *Sociological Focus, 23,* 129–139.

DeKeseredy, W. S., & Schwartz, M. D. (2006). An economic exclusion/male peer support model looks at "wedfare" and woman abuse. *Critical Criminology, 14,* 23–41.

DeKeseredy, W. S., & Schwartz, M. D. (2008). *Escaping abusive relationships in rural America.* New Jersey: Rutgers University Press.

DeKeseredy, W. S., Schwartz, M. D., Fagen, D., & Hall, M. (2006). Separation/divorce sexual assault: The contribution of male support. *Feminist Criminology*, *1*, 228–250.

DeLongis, A., & Holtzman, S. (2005). Coping in context: The role of stress, social support, and personality in coping. *Journal of Personality*, *73*, 1633–1656.

DePaul, A. (1992, January). New laws in California aid women victimized by violence. *Criminal Justice Newsletter*, *23*(2), 5–6.

Depner, C. E., Canatta, K., & Ricci, I. (1995). Report 4: Mediated agreements on child custody and visitation—1991 California family court services snapshot study. *Family and Conciliation Courts Review*, *33*, 87–109.

De Ridder, D. (1997). What is wrong with coping assessment? A review of conceptual and methodological issues. *Psychological Health*, *12*, 417–431.

Dersch, C. A., Harris, S. M., & Rappleyea, D. L. (2006). Recognizing and responding to partner violence: An analog study. *American Journal of Family Therapy*, *34*, 317–331.

Dethier, M., Counerotte, C., & Blairy, S. (2011). Marital satisfaction in couples with an alcoholic husband. *Journal of Family Violence*, *26*, 151–162.

DeValve, B. (2004, January/February). Repeat victimization: An overview and assessment of its usefulness for crime. *ACJS Today*, pp. xxix, 1, 5–6, 9.

Dinsmoor, J. A. (1952). A discrimination based on punishment. *Quarterly Journal of Experimental Psychology*, *4*, 27–45.

Dobash, R. E., & Dobash, R. P. (1979). *Violence against wives: A case against patriarchy*. New York, NY: Free Press.

Dobash, R. P., Dobash, R. E., Cavanagh, K., & Lewis, R. (1998). Separate and intersecting realities: A comparison of men's and women's accounts of violence against women. *Violence Against Women*, *4*, 382–414.

Dobash, R. P., Dobash, R. E., Wilson, M., & Daly, M. (1992). The myth of sexual symmetry in marital violence. *Social Problems*, *39*, 71–91.

Dodge, M., & Greene, E. (1991). Juror and expert conceptions of battered women. *Violence and Victims*, *6*, 271–282.

d'Olivera, A. F., & Schraiber, L. B. (2005). *Violence against women in Brazil: Overview, gaps and challenges*. Geneva: WHO (UN Division for the Advancement of Women).

Domestic violence conviction bars gun possession by officers. (1997, January 2). *Criminal Justice Newsletter*, pp. 2–3.

Domestic violence in the courts [Excerpted from *Gender Bias in the Courts, Report of the Maryland Special Joint Committee on Gender Bias in the Courts*, 1989, Annapolis, MD]. (1989). *Response*, *12*(4), 3–6.

Domjan, M., & Burkhard, B. (1989). *The principles of learning and behavior*. Monterey, CA: Brooks/Cole.

Donaldson, M., & Gardner, R. (1985). Diagnosis and treatment of traumatic stress among women after childhood incest. In C. R. Figley (Ed.), *Trauma and its wake* (Vol. 1, pp. 356–377). New York, NY: Bruner/Mazel.

Donovan, R., & Williams, M. (2002). Living at the intersection: The effects of racism and sexism on Black rape survivors. *Women and Therapy*, *25*, 95–105.

Dougall, A. L., Hyman, K. B., Hayward, M. C., McFeeley, S., & Baum, A. (2001). Optimism and traumatic stress: The importance of social support and coping. *Journal of Applied Social Psychology, 31,* 223–245.

Douglas, H. (1991). Assessing violent couples. *Families in Society: The Journal of Contemporary Human Services, 72,* 525–534.

Douglas, H., & Walsh, T. (2010). Mothers, domestic violence, and child protection. *Violence Against Women, 16,* 489–508.

Douglas, M. A. (1987). *The battered woman syndrome.* In D. J. Sonkin (Ed.), Domestic violence on trial: Psychological and legal dimensions of family violence (pp. 39–54). New York, NY: Springer.

Douglas, M. A., & Colantuono, A. (1987, July). *Cluster analysis of MMPI scores among battered women.* Paper presented at the Third National Family Violence Research Conference, Durham, NH.

Douglas, U., Bathrick, D., & Perry, P. A. (2008). Deconstructing male violence against women. *Violence Against Women, 14,* 247–261.

Dowd, M. (2005). *Are men necessary? When sexes collide.* New York, NY: Putnam.

Downs, W. R., & Miller, B. A. (1998). Relationship between experiences of parental violence during childhood and women's self-esteem. *Violence and Victims, 13,* 63–77.

Dragiewicz, M. (2010). Gender bias in the courts: Implications for battered mothers and their children. In M. Hanna & B. Goldstein (Eds.), *Domestic violence, abuse, and child custody: Legal strategies and policy issues* (§5.1–5.18). Kingston, NJ: Civic Research Institute.

Drozd, L. M., & Oleson, N. W. (2004). Is it abuse, alienation, and/or estrangement? A decision tree. *Journal of Child Custody, 1,* 65–106.

Dube, S. R., Anda, R. F., Felitti, V. J., Croft, J. B., Edwards, V. J., & Giles, W. H. (2001). Growing up with parental alcohol abuse: Exposure to childhood abuse, neglect, and household dysfunction. *Child Abuse & Neglect, 25,* 1627–1640.

Dunford, F. W., Huizinga, D., & Elliott, D. S. (1990). The role of arrest in domestic assault: The Omaha police experiment. *Criminology, 28,* 183–206.

Dunkel-Schetter, C., Folkman, S., & Lazarus, R. S. (1987). Correlates of social support receipt. *Journal of Personality and Social Psychology, 53,* 71–80.

Dunlop, B. D., Rothman, M. B., Condon, K. M., Hebert, K. S., & Martinez, I. L. (2000). Elder abuse: Risk factors and use of case data to improve policy and practice. *Journal of Elder Abuse and Neglect, 12*(3/4), 95–122.

Durfee, A. (2012). Situational ambiguity and gendered patterns of arrest for intimate partner violence. *Violence Against Women, 18,* 64–84.

Durose, M., Harlow, C. W., Langan, P. A., Motivans, M., Rantala, R. R., & Smith, E. L. (2005). *Family violence statistics: Including statistics on strangers and acquaintances* (NCJ Pub. No. 207846). Washington, DC: Bureau of Justice Statistics.

Duryee, M. A. (1995). Guidelines for family court services intervention when there are allegations of domestic violence. *Family and Conciliation Courts Review, 33,* 79–86.

Dutton, D. (1994). Patriarchy and wife assault: An ecological fallacy. *Violence and Victims, 9*, 167–182.

Dutton, D. (1998). *The abusive personality.* New York, NY: Guilford.

Dutton, D., Fehr, B., & McEwen, H. (1982). Severe wife battering as deindividuation violence. *Victimology: An International Journal, 7*(1–4), 13–23.

Dutton, D., & Haring, M. (1999). Perpetrator personality effects on post-separation victim reactions in abusive relationships. *Journal of Family Violence, 14,* 193–204.

Dutton, D., & Painter, S. (1981). Traumatic bonding: The development of emotional attachments in battered women and other relationships of intermittent abuse. *Victimology: An International Journal, 6*(1–4), 139–155.

Dutton, D., & Painter, S. L. (1993a). The battered woman syndrome: Effects of severity and intermittency of abuse. *American Journal of Orthopsychiatry, 63,* 614–622.

Dutton, D., & Painter, S. L. (1993b). Emotional attachments in abusive relationships: A test of traumatic bonding theory. *Violence and Victims, 8,* 105–120.

Dutton, D., Saunders, K., Starzomski, A., & Bartholomew, K. (1994). Intimacy-anger and insecure attachment as precursors of abuse in intimate relationships. *Journal of Applied Social Psychology, 24,* 1367–1386.

Dutton, M. A. (1992). *Empowering and healing the battered woman: A model of assessment and intervention.* New York, NY: Springer.

Dutton, M. A. (2009). Pathways linking intimate partner violence and posttraumatic disorder. *Trauma, Violence, & Abuse, 10,* 211–224.

Dutton, M. A., Goodman, L. A., & Bennett, L. (1999). Court-involved battered women's responses to violence: The role of psychological, physical, and sexual abuse. *Violence and Victims, 14,* 89–104.

Dziegielewski, S. F., Resnick, C., & Krause, N. B. (1996). Shelter-based crisis intervention with battered women. In A. R. Roberts (Ed.), *Helping battered women* (pp. 159–171). New York, NY: Oxford University Press.

D'Zurilla, T. J. (1986). *Problem-solving therapy: A social competence approach to clinical intervention.* New York, NY: Springer.

Eagly, A. H., & Johnson, B. T. (1990). Gender and leadership style: A meta-analysis. *Psychological Bulletin, 108,* 233–256.

Eby, K. K., Campbell, J. C., Sullivan, C. M., & Davidson, W. S. (1995). Health effects of experiences of sexual violence for women with abusive partners. *Health Care for Women International, 16,* 563–576.

Eckhardt, C. I., Samper, R., Suhr, L., & Holtzworth-Munroe, A. (2012). Implicit attitudes toward violence among male perpetrators of intimate partner violence: A preliminary investigation. *Journal of Interpersonal Violence, 27,* 471–491.

Edleson, J. L. (1999). The overlap between child maltreatment and woman battering. *Violence Against Women, 5,* 134–154.

Edwards, J. N., Fuller, T. D., Vorakitphokatom, S., & Sermsi, S. (1994). *Household crowding and its consequences.* Boulder, CO: Westview.

Ehrensaft, M. K., Cohen, P., Brown, J., Smailes, E. M., Chen, H., & Johnson, J. G. (2003). Intergenerational transmission of partner violence: A 20-year prospective study. *Journal of Consulting and Clinical Psychology, 71,* 741–753.

Ehrensaft, M. K., Cohen, P., & Johnson, J. G. (2006). Development of personality disorder symptoms and the risk for partner violence. *Journal of Abnormal Psychology, 115,* 474–483.

Eisenberger, N. I. (2012). Broken hearts and broken bones: A neural perspective on the similarities between social and physical pain. *Current Directions in Psychological Science, 21,* 42–47.

Eisikovits, Z., & Buchbinder, E. (1996). Pathways to disenchantment: Battered women's views of their social workers. *Journal of Interpersonal Violence, 11,* 425–440.

Ellard, J. H., Herbert, T. B., & Thompson, L. J. (1991). Coping with an abusive relationship: How and why do people stay? *Journal of Marriage and the Family, 53,* 311–325.

Ellsberg, M., Caldera, T., Herrera, A., Winkvist, A., & Kullgren, G. (1999). Domestic violence and emotional distress among Nicaraguan women. *American Psychologist, 54,* 30–36.

Emery, R. E., Otto, R. K., & O'Donohue, W. T. (2007). Custody evaluations: Limited science and a flawed system. *Psychological Science in the Public Interest, 6*(1), 1–29.

Enander, V. (2011). Leaving Jekyll and Hyde: Emotion work in the context of intimate partner violence. *Feminism and Psychology, 21,* 29–48.

Epidemiology of domestic violence. (1984, September). *Criminal Justice Newsletter, 16*(17), 4.

Erez, E., Adelman, M., & Gregory, C. (2009). Intersection of immigration and domestic violence: Voices of battered immigrant women. *Feminist Criminology, 4,* 32–56.

Erez, E., & Belknap, J. (1998). In their own words: Battered women's assessment of the criminal processing system's response. *Violence and Victims, 13,* 251–268.

Erickson, M. F., & Egeland, B. (2010). Child neglect. In J. E. B. Myers (Ed.), *APSAC handbook on child maltreatment* (3rd ed., pp. 103–124). Thousand Oaks, CA: Sage.

Erickson, N. S. (2006). Problems with custody evaluations. (2006, June/July). *Domestic Violence Report, 11,* 67.

Estes, W. K., & Skinner, B. F. (1941). Some quantitative properties of anxiety. *Journal of Experimental Psychology, 29,* 390–400.

Evans, G. W., Gonnella, C., Marcynszyn, L. A., Gentile, L., & Salpekar, N. (2005). The role of chaos in poverty and children's socio-emotional adjustment. *Psychological Science, 16,* 560–565.

Ewing, C. P., & Aubrey, M. (1987). Battered women and public opinion: Some realities about myths. *Journal of Family Violence, 2,* 257–264.

Ezechi, O. C., Kalu, B. K., Ezechi, L. O., Nwokoro, C. A., Nduduba, V. L., & Okeke, G. C. E. (2004). Prevalence and pattern of domestic violence against pregnant women. *Journal of Obstetrics and Gynaecology, 24,* 652–656.

Fals-Stewart, W. (2003). The occurrence of partner physical aggression on days of alcohol consumption: A longitudinal diary study. *Journal of Consulting and Clinical Psychology, 71,* 41–52.

Faludi, S. (1991). *Backlash.* New York, NY: Crown.

Family Violence Prevention Fund. (2002, April 19). *Coercing marriage among welfare recipients*. Retrieved from www.endabuse.org

Fangundes, C. P. (2012). Getting over you: Contributions of attachment theory for postbreakup emotional adjustment. *Personal Relationships, 19,* 37–50.

Farberman, R. A. (2007, March). Empowerment through inclusions. *APA Monitor on Psychology, 38,* 36–38.

Farrell, G., & Sousa, W. (2001). Repeat victimization and hot spots: The overlap and its implications for crime control and problem-oriented policing. In G. Farrell & K. Pease (Eds.), *Repeat victimization*. Monsey, NY: Criminal Justice Press.

Farrington, D. P. (2000). Psychosocial predictors of adult antisocial personality and adult convictions. *Behavioral Sciences and the Law, 18,* 605–622.

Fawcett, G. M., Heise, L. L., Isita-Espejel, L., & Pick, S. (1999). Changing community responses to wife abuse. *American Psychologist, 54,* 41–49.

Feder, L. (1997). Domestic violence and police response in a pro-arrest jurisdiction. *Women and Criminal Justice, 8*(4), 79–97.

Feder, L. (1998). Police handling of domestic and nondomestic assault calls: Is there a case for discrimination? *Crime and Delinquency, 44,* 335–349.

Feder, L., & Wilson, D. B. (2005). A meta-analytic review of court-mandated batterer intervention programs: Can courts affect abusers' behavior? *Journal of Experimental Criminology, 1,* 239–262.

Federal court finds no protection against dismissal from employment due to spousal violence. (1996, February/March). *Domestic Violence Report, 1,* 7.

Federal sex discrimination lawsuit settled, company agrees to end housing discrimination against battered women. (2001). *Family Violence and Sexual Assault Bulletin, 17*(7), 42.

Feindler, E. L. (1988, August). *Cognitive-behavioral analysis of anger in abused women*. Paper presented at the annual meeting of the American Psychological Association, Atlanta, GA.

Felix, A. C., III, & McCarthy, K. F. (1994). *An analysis of child fatalities, 1992.* Boston: Commonwealth of Massachusetts Department of Social Services.

Felson, R. B. (1992). "Kick 'em when they're down": Explanation of the relationship between stress and interpersonal aggression and violence. *Sociological Quarterly, 33,* 1–16.

Felson, R. B., Messner, S. F., Hoskin, A. W., & Deane, G. (2002). Reasons for reporting and not reporting domestic violence to the police. *Criminology, 40,* 617–647.

Ferguson, K. E. (1980). *Self, society, and womankind: The dialectic of liberation.* Westport, CT: Greenwood.

Ferraro, K. J. (1981). Battered women and the shelter movement. *Dissertation Abstracts International, 42,* 879A. (UMI No. 8115605)

Fields-Meyer, T., & Benet, L. (1998, November 16). Speaking out. *People, 50*(18), 232, 234.

Fields-Meyer, T., Benet, L., Berestein, L., & Dodd, J. (1998, November 30). Upfront. *People, 50*(20), 66–68.

Fighting discrimination against battered victims. (1996, May). *Merritt Insurance Pro,* pp. 1–3.

Finkelhor, D., Ormrod, R. K., & Turner, H. A. (2007). Re-victimization patterns in a national longitudinal sample of children and youth. *Child Abuse & Neglect, 31,* 479–502.

Finkelhor, D., Turner, H., Ormrod, R., & Hamby, S. L. (2010). Trends in childhood violence and abuse exposure: Evidence from 2 national surveys. *Archives of Pediatric and Adolescent Medicine, 164,* 238–242.

Finkelhor, D., Turner, H., Ormrod, R., Hamby, S., & Kracke, K. (2009, October). *Children's exposure to violence: A comprehensive national survey.* Washington, DC: U.S. Department of Justice.

Finkelhor, D., & Yllö, K. (1982). Forced sex in marriage: A preliminary research report. *Crime & Delinquency, 82,* 459–478.

Finn, J. (1985). The stresses and coping behavior of battered women. *Social Casework: The Journal of Contemporary Social Work, 66,* 341–349.

Finn, J., & Banach, M. (2000). Victimization online: The downside of seeking services for women on the Internet. *Cyberpsychology and Behavior, 3,* 776–785.

Flaherty, M. P. (2010). Constructing a world beyond intimate partner abuse. *Affilia, 25,* 224–235.

Flanzer, J. P. (1993). Alcohol and other drugs are key causal agents of violence. In R. J. Gelles & D. R. Loseke (Eds.), *Current controversies on family violence* (pp. 171–181). Newbury Park, CA: Sage.

Fleury, R. E., Sullivan, C. M., & Bybee, D. I. (2000). When ending the relationship does not end the violence: Women's experiences of violence by former partners. *Violence Against Women, 6,* 1363–1383.

Fleury-Steiner, R. E., & Brady, L. T. (2011). The importance of resources and information in the lives of battered mothers. *Violence Against Women, 17,* 882–903.

Flicker, S. M., Cerulli, C., Zhao, X., Tang, W., Watts, A., Xia, Y., & Talbot, N. L. (2011). Concomitant forms of abuse and help-seeking behavior among White, African American and Latina women who experience intimate partner violence. *Violence Against Women, 17,* 1067–1085.

Flood, M., & Pease, B. (2009). Factors influencing attitudes to violence against women. *Trauma, Violence, & Abuse, 10,* 125–142.

Flynn, C. P. (1996). Normative support for corporal punishment: Attitudes, correlates, and implications. *Aggression and Violent Behavior, 1,* 47–55.

Follette, V. M., Polusny, M. A., Bechtle, A. E., & Naugle, A. E. (1996). Cumulative trauma: The impact of child sexual abuse, adult sexual assault, and spouse abuse. *Journal of Traumatic Stress, 9,* 25–35.

Follingstad, D. R. (1998, March 5–7). *Battered woman syndrome and rape trauma syndrome: How exactly are they defined and what definitions can we actually state in court?* Paper presented at the American Psychology-Law Society 1998 Biennial Conference, Redondo Beach, CA.

Follingstad, D. R., Brennan, A. F., Hause, E. S., Polek, D. S., & Rutledge, L. L. (1991). Factors moderating physical and psychological symptoms of battered women. *Journal of Family Violence, 6,* 81–95.

Follingstad, D. R., Hause, E. S., Rutledge, L. L., & Polek, D. S. (1992). Effects of battered women's early responses on later abuse patterns. *Violence and Victims, 7,* 109–128.

Follingstad, D. R., Runge, M. M., Ace, A., Buzan, R., & Helff, C. (2001). Justifiability, sympathy level and internal/external locus of the reasons battered women remain in abusive relationships. *Violence and Victims, 16,* 621–643.

Follingstad, D. R., Rutledge, L. L., Berg, B. J., Hause, E. S., & Polek, D. S. (1990). The role of emotional abuse in physically abusive relationships. *Journal of Family Violence, 5,* 107–120.

For women, equal pay? No way. (2007, May 7). *Time, 169,* 20.

Foran, H. M., & O'Leary, K. D. (2008). Problem drinking, jealousy, and anger control: Variables predicting physical aggression against a partner. *Journal of Family Violence, 23,* 141–148.

Ford, D. A. (1999, July). *Coercing victim participation in domestic violence prosecutions.* Paper presented at the Sixth International Family Violence Research Conference, Durham, NH.

Fortune, M. (1987). *Keeping the faith.* San Francisco, CA: Harper & Row.

Foshee, V. A., Bauman, K. E., Arriaga, X. R., Helms, R. W., Koch, G. G., & Linder, G. F. (1998). An evaluation of Safe Dates, an adolescent prevention program. *American Journal of Public Health, 88,* 45–50.

Foshee, V. A., Bauman, K. E., Greene, W. F., Koch, G. G., Linder, G. F., & MacDougall, J. E. (2000). The Safe Dates program: 1-year follow-up results. *American Journal of Public Health, 90,* 1619–1622.

Fox, K. A., & Cook, C. L. (2011). Is knowledge power? The effects of a victimology course on victim blaming. *Journal of Interpersonal Violence, 26,* 3407–3427.

Freed, L. H., Gupta, R., Hynes, C., & Miller, E. (2003). Detecting adolescent dating violence in the clinical setting. *Journal of Adolescent Health, 32,* 151–152.

Freud, A. (1942). *The ego and the mechanisms of defense.* New York, NY: International Universities Press.

Frisch, M. B., & MacKenzie, C. J. (1991). A comparison of formerly and chronically battered women on cognitive and situational dimensions. *Psychotherapy, 28,* 339–344.

Fry, P. S., & Barker, L. A. (2001). Female survivors of violence and abuse: Their regrets of action and inaction in coping. *Journal of Interpersonal Violence, 16,* 320–342.

Frye, N. E. (2011). Responding to problems: The roles of severity and barriers. *Personal Relationships, 18,* 471–478.

Fyfe, J. J., Klinger, D. A., & Flavin, J. M. (1997). Differential police treatment of male-on-female spousal violence. *Criminology, 35,* 455–473.

Gabbidon, S. L., & Greene, H. T. (Eds.). (2005). *Race, crime, and justice: A reader.* New York, NY: Routledge.

Gager, C. T., & Sanchez, L. (2003). Two as one? Couples' perceptions of time spent together, marital quality, and the risk of divorce. *Journal of Family Issues, 24,* 21–50.

Gallopin, C., & Leigh, L. (2009). Teen perceptions of dating violence, help-seeking, and the role of schools. *Prevention Researcher, 16,* 17–20.

Garanzini, M. J. (1988). Troubled homes: Pastoral responses to violent and abusive families. *Pastoral Psychology, 36,* 218–229.

Garber, B. D. (2011). Parental alienation and the dynamics of the enmeshed parent-child dyad: Adultification, parentification, and infantilization. *Family Court Review, 49,* 322–335.

Garcia-Moreno, C., Jansen, H., Ellsberg, M., Heise, L., & Watts, C. H. (2006). Prevalence of intimate partner violence: Findings from the WHO multi-country study on women's health and domestic violence. *Lancet, 386,* 1260–1269.

Gardner, R. A. (1987). *The parental alienation syndrome and the differentiation between fabricated and genuine child sex abuse.* Creskill, NJ: Creative Therapeutics.

Garner, J., & Clemmer, E. (1986). *Danger to police in domestic disturbances—a new look.* Washington, DC: U.S. Department of Justice, National Institute of Justice.

Garner, J. H., & Maxwell, C. D. (2009). *Prosecution and conviction rates for intimate partner violence.* Shepherdstown, WV: Joint Centers for Justice Studies.

Gass, J. D, Stein, D. J., Williams, D. R., & Seedat, S. (2011). Gender differences in risk for intimate partner violence among South African adults. *Journal of Interpersonal Violence, 26,* 2764–2789.

Gauthier, D. K., & Bankston, W. B. (1997). Gender equality and the sex ratio of intimate killings. *Criminology, 35,* 577–600.

Gay, W. C. (1997). The reality of linguistic violence against women. In L. L. O'Toole & J. R. Schiffman (Eds.), *Gender violence: Interdisciplinary perspectives* (pp. 467–473). New York, NY: New York University Press.

Geer, J., & Maisel, E. (1972). Evaluating the effects of the prediction-control confound. *Journal of Personality and Social Psychology, 23,* 314–319.

Geffner, R., Conradi, L., Geis, K., & Aranda, B. (2009). Conducting child custody evaluations in the context of family violence allegations: Practical techniques and suggestions for ethical practice. *Journal of Child Custody, 6,* 232–257.

Geffner, R. A., & Rosenbaum, A. (2001). Domestic violence offenders: Treatment and intervention standards. In R. A. Geffner and A. Rosenbaum (Eds.), *Domestic violence offenders: Current interventions, research and implications for policies and standards* (pp. 1–10). New York, NY: Haworth Maltreatment and Trauma Press.

Gellen, M. I., Hoffman, R. A., Jones, M., & Stone, M. (1984). Abused and nonabused women: MMPI profile differences. *Personnel and Guidance Journal, 62,* 601–604.

Gerow, J. R. (1989). *Psychology: An introduction* (2nd ed.). Glenville, IL: Scott, Foresman.

Gershoff, E. T. (2008). *Report on physical punishment in the United States: What research tells us about its effects on children.* Columbus, OH: Center for Effective Discipline.

Gibbs, N. (1993, January 18). "Til death do us part." *Time Magazine, 141*(2), 38, 40–45.

Gibson, J. W., & Gutierrez, L. (1991). A service program for safe-home children. *Families in Society, 72*(Special issue: Family violence), 554–562.

Gilbert, L., & Webster, P. (1982). *Bound by love, the sweet trap of daughterhood.* Boston, MA: Beacon.

Gilligan, C. (1982). *In a different voice.* Boston, MA: Harvard University Press.

Gillum, T. L. (2009). Improving services to African American survivors of IPV. *Violence Against Women, 15,* 57–80.

Givertz, M., & Segrin, C. (2005). Explaining personal and constraint commitment in close relationships: The role of satisfaction, conflict responses, and relational bond. *Journal of Social and Personal Relationships, 22,* 757–775.

Gleason, W. J. (1995). Children of battered women: Developmental delays and behavioral dysfunction. *Violence and Victims, 10,* 153–160.

Goelman, D. M., Lehrman, F. L., & Valente, R. L. (Eds.). (1996). *The impact of domestic violence on your legal practice: A lawyer's handbook* (No. 5480001). Chicago, IL: American Bar Association.

Goelman, D. M., & Valente, R. L. (1997). *When will they ever learn? Education to end domestic violence: A law school report* [American Bar Association Commission on domestic Violence] (NCJ Pub. No. 168098). Washington, DC: U.S. Department of Justice, Office for Victims of Crime.

Goldenson, R. M. (1984). *Longman dictionary of psychology and psychiatry.* New York, NY: Longman.

Golding, J. M. (1999). Intimate partner violence as a risk factor for mental disorders: A meta-analysis. *Journal of Family Violence, 14,* 99–132.

Golding, J. M., Cooper, M. L., & George, L. K. (1997). Sexual assault history and health perceptions: Seven general populations studied. *Health Psychology, 16,* 417–425.

Goldner, V., Penn, P., Sheinberg, M., & Walker, G. (1990). Love and violence: Gender paradoxes in volatile attachments. *Family Process, 29,* 343–364.

Gondolf, E. W. (1988a). *Battered women as survivors: An alternative to treating learned helplessness.* Lexington, KY: Lexington Books.

Gondolf, E. W. (1988b). The effect of batterer counseling on shelter outcome. *Journal of Interpersonal Violence, 3,* 275–289.

Gondolf, E. W. (1995). Alcohol abuse, wife assault, and power needs. *Social Service Review, 18,* 274–284.

Gondolf, E. W. (1998a). *Assessing woman battering in mental health services.* Newbury Park, CA: Sage.

Gondolf, E. W. (1998b). Service contract and delivery of a shelter outreach project. *Journal of Family Violence, 13,* 131–145.

Gondolf, E. W. (1998c). The victims of court-ordered batterers. *Violence Against Women, 4,* 659–676.

Gondolf, E. W. (2001). *Batterer intervention systems.* Thousand Oaks, CA: Sage.

Gondolf, E. W., & Shestakov, D. (1997). Spousal homicide in Russia. *Violence Against Women, 3,* 533–546.

Good, G. E. (1998). Men & masculinities: The good, the bad, and the ugly. *SPSMM Bulletin, 3*(4), 1–3.

Goodkind, J. R., Gillum, T. L., Bybee, D. I., & Sullivan, C. M. (2003). The impact of family and friends' reactions on the well-being of women with abusive partners. *Violence Against Women, 9,* 347–373.

Goodman, L. A., Bennett, L., & Dutton, M. A. (1999). Obstacles women face in prosecuting their batterers: The role of social support. *Violence and Victims, 14,* 427–444.

Goodman, L. A., Dutton, M. A., Weinfurt, K., & Cook, S. (2003). The Intimate Partner Violence Strategies Index. *Violence Against Women, 9,* 163–186.

Goodman, L. A., & Epstein, D. (2008). *Listening to battered women: A survivor-centered approach to advocacy, mental health and justice.* Washington, DC: American Psychological Association.

Goodman, L. A., Koss, M. P., Fitzgerald, L. F., Russo, N. F., & Puryear-Keita, G. P. (1993). Male violence against women. *American Psychologist, 48,* 1054–1058.

Goodwin, J. (1987). The etiology of combat-related posttraumatic stress disorders. In T. Williams (Ed.), *Post-traumatic stress disorders: A handbook for clinicians* (pp. 1–18). Cincinnati, OH: Disabled American Veterans.

Goodwin, S. N., Chandler, S., &. Meisel., J. (2003). *Violence against women: The role of welfare reform* (NCJ Pub. No. 205792). Final report to the National Institute of Justice.

Gordon, K. C., & Christman, J. A. (2008). Integrating social information processing and attachment style research with cognitive-behavioral couples therapy. *Journal of Contemporary Psychotherapy, 38,* 129–138.

Gordon, L. (1988). *Heroes of their own lives: The politics and history of family violence, Boston 1880–1960.* New York, NY: Viking.

Gore-Felton, C., Gill, M., Koopman, C., & Spiegel, D. (1999). A review of acute stress reactions among victims of violence: Implications for early intervention. *Aggression and Violent Behavior, 4,* 293–206.

Gracia, E., Garcia, F., & Lila, M. (2011). Police attitudes toward policing partner violence against women: Do they correspond to different psychosocial profiles? *Journal of Interpersonal Violence, 26,* 189–201.

Graham, C. M., Tsuge, M., & Soucar, E. (1998). Cultural considerations: A reply to Eisikovits and Buchbinder (1996) [Letter to the editor]. *Journal of Interpersonal Violence, 13,* 299–304.

Graham, D. L. R., Rawlings, E. I., Ihms, K., Latimer, D., Foliano, J., Thompson, A., . . . Hacker, R. (1995). A scale for identifying "Stockholm syndrome" reactions in young dating women: Factor structure, reliability, and validity. *Violence and Victims, 10,* 3–22.

Graham, D. L. R., Rawlings, E. I., & Rigsby, R. (1994). *Loving to survive: Sexual terror, men's violence, and women's lives.* New York, NY: New York University Press.

Graham, D. L. R., Rawlings, E. I., & Rimini, N. (1988). Survivors of terror: Battered women, hostages and the Stockholm syndrome. In K. Yllö &

M. Bograd (Eds.), *Feminist perspectives on wife abuse* (pp. 217–233). Newbury Park, CA: Sage.

Graham-Bermann, S. A. (1998). The impact of woman abuse on children's social development: Research and theoretical perspectives. In G. W. Holden, R. Geffner, & E. N. Jouriles (Eds.), *Children exposed to marital violence* (pp. 21–54). Washington, DC: American Psychological Association.

Graham-Bermann, S. A., & Howell, K. H. (2010). Child maltreatment in the context of intimate partner violence. In J. E. B. Myers (Ed.), *APSAC handbook on child maltreatment* (3rd ed., pp. 167–179). Thousand Oaks, CA: Sage.

Graham-Kevan, N., & Archer, J. (2005). Investigating three explanations of women's relationship aggression. *Psychology of Women Quarterly, 29,* 270–277.

Green, A. H. (1998). Factors contributing to the generational transmission of child maltreatment. *Journal of the American Academy of Child and Adolescent Psychiatry, 37,* 1334–1336.

Green, B. L., Lindy, J., Grace, M., & Glese, G. (1989). Multiple diagnoses in posttraumatic stress disorder: The role of war stressors. *Journal of Nervous and Mental Disorders, 177,* 329–335.

Green, R. L. (1991). *MMPI-2/MMPI: An interpretive manual.* Boston, MA: Allyn & Bacon.

Greene, E., Raitz, A., & Lindblad, H. (1989). Jurors' knowledge of battered women. *Journal of Family Violence, 4,* 105–125.

Greenfeld, L. A., Rand, M. R., Craven, D., Klaus, P. A., Perkins, C. A., Ringel, C., . . . Fox, J. A. (1998, March). *Violence by intimates* (NCJ Pub. No. 167237). Washington, DC: U.S. Department of Justice, Bureau of Justice Statistics.

Greer, T. M. (2007). Measuring coping strategies among African Americans: An exploration of the latent structure of the COPE inventory. *Journal of Black Psychology, 33,* 260–277.

Griffing, S., Ragin, D. F., Sage, R. E., Madry, L., Bingham, L. E., & Primm, B. J. (2002). Domestic violence survivors' self-identified reasons for returning to abusive relationships. *Journal of Interpersonal Violence, 17,* 306–319.

Grigsby, N., & Hartman, B. (1997). The barriers model: An integrated strategy for intervention with battered women. *Psychotherapy, 31,* 485–497.

Grossman, S. F., & Lundy, M. (2008). Double jeopardy: A comparison of persons with and without disabilities who were victims of sexual abuse and/or sexual assault. *Journal of Social Work in Disability and Rehabilitation, 7,* 19–46.

Gruzinski, R. J., Brink, J. C., & Edleson, J. L. (1988). Support and education groups for children of battered women. *Child Welfare, 67,* 431–444.

Guetzkow, J. (2010). Beyond deservingness: Congressional discourse on poverty, 1964–1996. *The Annals of the American Academy of Political and Social Science, 629,* 173–197.

Guns and dolls. (1990, May 28). *Newsweek, 115*(23), 58–62.

Hackler, J. (1991). The reduction of violent crime through economic equality for women. *Journal of Family Violence, 6,* 199–216.

Haj-Yahia, M. M. (1999). Wife abuse and its psychological consequences as revealed by the First Palestinian National Survey on Violence Against Women. *Journal of Family Psychology, 13,* 642–662.

Haj-Yahia, M. M. (2000). Implications of wife abuse and battering for self-esteem, depression, and anxiety as revealed by the Second Palestinian National Survey on Violence Against Women. *Journal of Family Issues, 21,* 435–463.

Haj-Yahia, M. M., & Uysal, A. (2011). Toward an integrated theory for explaining beliefs about wife beating: A study among students from Turkey. *Journal of Interpersonal Violence, 26,* 1401–1431.

Hale, M. (1874). *The history of the pleas of the crown.* Philadelphia, PA: Robert H. Small. [Original work published 1736.]

Hall, J. E., Walters, M. L., & Basile, K. C. (2012). Intimate partner violence perpetrations by court-ordered men: Distinctions among subtypes of physical violence sexual violence, psychological abuse, and stalking. *Journal of Interpersonal Violence, 27,* 1374–1395.

Hallett, S. (2011, Winter). High tech stalking. *Ms. Magazine,* p. 16.

Halligan, S. L., Michael, T., Clark, D. M., & Ehlers, A. (2003). Posttraumatic stress disorder following assault: The role of cognitive processing, trauma memory, and appraisals. *Journal of Consulting and Clinical Psychology, 71,* 419–431.

Halloran, R. (2011). Statewide domestic violence initiatives. *Michigan Bar Journal, 90,* 40.

Halperin, J. M., Newcorn, J. H., Matier, K., Bedi, G., Hall, S., & Sharma, V. (1995). Impulsivity and the initiation of fights in children with disruptive behavioral disorders. *Journal of Child Psychology and Psychiatry, 36,* 1199–1211.

Hamberger, L. K. (1991, August). *Research concerning wife abuse: Implications for training physicians and criminal justice personnel.* Paper presented at the annual meeting of the American Psychological Association, San Francisco, CA.

Hamberger, L. K. (1997). Cognitive behavioral treatment of men who batter their partners. *Cognitive and Behavioral Practice, 4,* 147–169.

Hamberger, L. K. (2005). Men's and women's use of intimate partner violence in clinical samples: Toward a gender-sensitive analysis. *Violence and Victims, 20,* 131–151.

Hamberger, L. K., & Arnold, J. (1991). The impact of mandatory arrest on domestic violence perpetrator counseling services. *Family Violence Bulletin, 6*(1), 11–12.

Hamberger, L. K., & Guse, C. (2002). Men's and women's use of intimate partner violence in clinical samples. *Violence Against Women, 8,* 1301–1331.

Hamberger, L. K., & Hastings, J. E. (1991). Personality correlates of men who batter and nonviolent men: Some continuities and discontinuities. *Journal of Family Violence, 6,* 131–147.

Hamberger, L. K., Lohr, J. M., Bonge, D., & Tolin, D. F. (1997). An empirical classification of motivation for domestic violence. *Violence Against Women, 3,* 401–423.

Hambleton, B. B., Clark, G., Sumaya, C. V., Weissman, G., & Horner, J. (1997). HRSA's strategies to combat family violence. *Academic Medicine, 72*(Suppl.1), S110–S115.

Hamby, S. L. (1996). The Dominance Scale: Preliminary psychometric properties. *Violence and Victims, 11,* 199–212.

Hampton, R. L., LaTaillade, J. J., Dacey, A., & Marghi, J. R. (2008). Evaluating domestic violence interventions for Black women. *Journal of Aggression, Maltreatment and Trauma, 16,* 330–353.

Hanks, S. E. (1992). Translating theory into practice: A conceptual framework for clinical assessment, differential diagnosis, and multi-modal treatment of maritally violent individuals, couples, and families. In E. C. Viano (Ed.), *Intimate violence: Interdisciplinary perspectives* (pp. 157–176). Washington, DC: Hemisphere (Taylor & Francis).

Hanna, M., & Goldstein, B. (Eds.). (2010). *Domestic violence, abuse, and child custody: Legal strategies and policy issues.* Kinston, NJ: Civic Research Institute.

Hanneke, C. R., Shields, N. M., & McCall, G. J. (1986). Assessing the prevalence of marital rape. *Journal of Interpersonal Violence, 1,* 350–362.

Hansen, M., Harway, M., & Cervantes, N. (1991). Therapists' perceptions of severity in cases of family violence. *Violence and Victims, 6,* 225–235.

Harlow, C. W. (1991). *Female victims of violence crime* (NCJ Pub. No. 126826). Rockville, MD: U.S. Department of Justice, Bureau of Justice Statistics.

Harper, D. W., & Voigt, L. (2007). Homicide followed by suicide: An integrated theoretical perspective. *Homicide Studies, 11,* 295–318.

Harpo Productions. (1992, May 22). *Learning to be assertive [Oprah Winfrey Show].* New York.

Harris, M. B. (1991). Effects of sex of aggressor, sex of target, and relationship on evaluations of physical aggression. *Journal of Interpersonal Violence, 6,* 174–186.

Harrison, L. A., & Esqueda, C. W. (1999). Myths and stereotypes of actors in domestic violence: Implications for domestic violence culpability. *Aggression and Violent Behavior, 4,* 129–138.

Hart, S. N., & Brassard, M. R. (1990). *Psychological maltreatment of children.* In R. T. Ammerman & M. Hersen (Eds.), *Children at risk: An evaluation of factors contributing to child abuse and neglect* (pp. 109–140). New York, NY: Plenum.

Harway, M. (1993). Battered women: Characteristics and causes. In M. Hansen & M. Harway (Eds.), *Battering and family therapy: A feminist perspective* (pp. 82–92). Newbury Park, CA: Sage.

Hastings, J. E., & Hamberger, L. K. (1988). Personality characteristics of spouse abusers: A controlled comparison. *Violence and Victims, 3,* 31–48.

Hathaway, J., Silverman, J., Brooks, D., Mucci, L., Tavares, B., Keenan, H., & Cordeiro, L. (1998, July). *Utilization of police, civil restraining order and medical care services by female survivors of partner violence.* Paper presented at the Program Evaluation and Family Violence Research: An International Conference, Durham, NH.

Hathaway, S. R., & McKinley, J. C. (1967). *Minnesota Multiphasic Personality Inventory manual.* New York, NY: Psychological Corporation.

Hawkins, J. W., Pearce, C. W., Skeith, J., & Roche, R. (2009). Using technology to expedite screening and intervention for domestic abuse and neglect. *Public Health Nursing, 26,* 58–69.

Hays, D. G., & Emelianchik, K. (2009). A content analysis of intimate partner violence assessments. *Measurement and Evaluation in Counseling and Development, 42,* 139–153.

Hazen, A. L., & Soriano, F. I. (2007). Experiences with intimate partner violence among Latina women. *Violence Against Women, 13,* 562–582.

Healey, K. M. (1995). *Victim and witness intimidation: New developments and emerging responses* (NCJ Pub. No. 156555). Rockville, MD: U.S. Department of Justice.

Healey, K. M., & Smith, C. (1998, July). *Batterer programs: What criminal justice agencies need to know* (NCJ Pub. No. 171683). Washington, DC: U.S. Department of Justice, National Institutes of Health.

Healey, K. M., Smith, C., & O'Sullivan, C. (1998, February). *Batterer intervention: Program approaches and criminal justice strategies* (NCJ Pub. No. 168638). Washington, DC: U.S. Department of Justice, National Institute of Justice.

Hebbert, T. B., Silverm, R. C., & Ellard, J. H. (1991). Coping with an abusive relationship: I. How and why do women stay? *Journal of Marriage and the Family, 53,* 311–325.

Heckert, D. A., & Gondolf, E. W. (2004). Battered women's perceptions of risk versus risk factors and instrument in predicting repeat reassault? *Journal of Interpersonal Violence, 19,* 778–800.

Heise, L. L., Ellsberg, M., & Gottemoeller, M. (1999). Ending violence against women. *Population Reports, Series L, No. 11.* Baltimore, MD: Johns Hopkins University School of Public Health.

Heiskanen, M., & Pilspa, M. (1998*). Faith, hope, battering: A survey of men's violence against women in Finland.* Helsinki: Statistics Finland/Council for Equality Between Women and Men.

Henderson, A. J. Z., Bartholomew, K., & Dutton, D. (1997). He loves me; he loves me not: Attachment and separation resolution of abused women. *Journal of Family Violence, 12,* 169–191.

Henderson, A. J. Z., Bartholomew, K., Trinke, S. J., & Kwong, M. J. (2005). When loving means hurting: An explanation of attachment and intimate abuse in a community sample. *Journal of Family Violence, 20,* 219–230.

Hendricks-Matthews, M. (1982). The battered woman: Is she ready for help? *Journal of Contemporary Social Work, 63,* 131–137.

Henning, K., & Connor-Smith, J. (2011). Why doesn't he leave? Relationship continuity and satisfaction among male domestic violence offenders. *Journal of Interpersonal Violence, 28,* 1366–1387.

Henning, K. R., & Holdford, R. (2006). Minimization, denial, and victim blaming by batterers. *Criminal Justice and Behavior, 33,* 110–130.

Herbert, T. B., Silver, R. C., & Ellard, J. H. (1991). Coping with an abusive relationship: How and why do women stay? *Journal of Marriage and the Family, 53,* 311–325.

Herman, J. L. (1992). *Trauma and recovery.* New York, NY: Basic Books.

Herman, R. L., & Azrin, N. H. (1964). Punishment by noise in an alternative response situation. *Experimental Analysis of Behavior, 7,* 16–26.

Herrnstein, R. J. (1970). On the law of effect. *Journal of Experimental Analysis of Behavior, 13,* 243–266.

Hettrich, E. L., & O'Leary, K. D. (2007). Females' reasons for their physical aggression in dating relationships. *Journal of Interpersonal Violence, 23,* 1131–1143.

Heyman, R. E., & Neidig, P. H. (1999). A comparison of spousal aggression prevalence rates in U.S. Army and civilian representative samples. *Journal of Consulting and Clinical Psychology, 67,* 239–242.

Heyman, R. E., & Slep, A. M. S. (2006). Creating and field-testing diagnostic criteria for partner and child maltreatment. *Journal of Family Psychology, 20,* 397–408.

Hill, J. R. (2005). Teaching about family violence: A proposed model curriculum. *Teaching and Learning in Medicine, 17,* 169–178.

Hill, S. A. (2006). Marriage among African American women: A gender perspective. *Journal of Comparative Family Studies, 37,* 421–440.

Hilton, N. Z. (1992). Battered women's concerns about their children witnessing wife assault. *Journal of Interpersonal Violence, 7,* 77–86.

Hilton, N. Z., Harris, G. T., Rice, M. E., Houghton, R. E., & Eke, A. W. (2008). An in-depth actuarial assessment for wife assault recidivism: *The Domestic Violence Risk Appraisal Guide. Law and Human Behavior, 32,* 150–163.

Hiroto, D. S. (1974). Locus of control and learned helplessness. *Journal of Experimental Psychology, 102,* 187–193.

Hirschel, J. D., & Buzawa, E. S. (2002). Understanding the context of dual arrest with directions for future research. *Violence Against Women, 8,* 1449–1473.

Hirschel, J. D., Buzawa, E., Pattavina, A., & Faggiani, D. (2007, April). *Explaining the prevalence, context, and consequences of dual arrest in intimate partner cases* (NCJ Pub. No. 218355). Washington, DC: U. S. Department of Justice, National Institute of Justice.

Hirschel, J. D., Dean, C. W., & Lumb, R. C. (1994). The relative contribution of domestic violence to assault and injury of police officers. *Justice Quarterly, 11,* 99–117.

Hirschel, J. D., & Hutchison, I. W. (2011). Unraveling the relative contributions of his, her, and their drinking to the likelihood of arrest in intimate partner violence cases. *Journal of Interpersonal Violence, 26,* 3050–3079.

Hirschel, J. D., Hutchison, I. W., & Dean, C. W. (1992). The failure of arrest to deter spouse abuse. *Journal of Research in Crime and Delinquency, 29,* 7–33.

Hirschel, J. D., Hutchison, I. W., Dean, C. W., & Mills, A. M. (1992). Review essay on the law enforcement response to spouse abuse: Past, present, and future. *Justice Quarterly, 9,* 247–283.

Hoffman, K. L., Demo, D. H., & Edwards, J. N. (1994). Physical wife abuse in a non-Western society: An integrated theoretical approach. *Journal of Marriage and the Family, 56,* 131–146.

Hofford, M., Bailey, C., Davis, J., & Hart, B. (1995). Family violence in child custody statutes: An analysis of state codes and legal practice. *Family Law Quarterly, 29,* 197–224.

Hofling, C. K., Brotzman, E., Dalrymple, S., Graves, N., & Pierce, C. M. (1966). An experimental study in nurse-physician relationships. *Journal of Nervous and Mental Disease, 143,* 171–180.

Holahan, C. J., Moos, R. H., Holahan, C. K., Brennan, P. L., & Schutte, K. K. (2005). Stress generation, avoidance coping, and depressive symptoms: A 10 year model. *Journal of Consulting and Clinical Psychology, 73,* 658–666.

Holahan, C. J., Moos, R. H., Moerkbak, M. L., Cronkite, R. C., Holahan, C. K., & Kenney, B. A. (2007). Spousal similarity in coping and depressive symptoms over 10 years. *Journal of Family Psychology, 21,* 551–559.

Holden, G. W. (2003). Children exposed to domestic violence and child abuse: Terminology and taxonomy. *Clinical Child and Family Psychology Review, 6,* 151–160.

Holden, G. W., Geffner, R., & Jouriles, E. N. (1998a). Appraisal and outlook. In G. W. Holden, R. Geffner, & E. N. Jouriles (Eds.), *Children exposed to marital violence* (pp. 409–421). Washington, DC: American Psychological Association.

Holden, G. W., Geffner, R., & Jouriles, E. N. (Eds.). (1998b). *Children exposed to marital violence.* Washington, DC: American Psychological Association.

Holiman, M. J., & Schilit, R. (1991). Aftercare for battered women: How to encourage the maintenance of change. *Psychotherapy, 28,* 345–353.

Holtzworth-Munroe, A. (1988). Causal attribution in marital violence: Theoretical and methodological issues. *Clinical Psychology Review, 8,* 331–344.

Holtzworth-Munroe, A., Smutzler, N., & Sandin, E. (1997). A brief review of the research on husband violence: Part II. The psychological effects of husband violence on battered women and their children. *Aggression and Violent Behavior, 2,* 179–213.

Holtzworth-Munroe, A., & Stuart, G. L. (1994). Typologies of male batterers: Three subtypes and the differences among them. *Psychological Bulletin, 116,* 476–497.

Holz, W. C., & Azrin, N. H. (1961). Discriminative properties of punishment. *Journal of Experimental Analysis of Behavior, 4,* 225–232.

Horne, S. (1999). Domestic violence in Russia. *American Psychologist, 54,* 55–61.

Horner, M. S. (1972). Toward an understanding of achievement-related conflicts in women. *Journal of Social Issues, 28,* 157–175.

Hornung, C. A., McCullough, B. C., & Sugimoto, T. (1981). Status relationships in marriage: Risk factors in spouse abuse. *Journal of Marriage and the Family, 43,* 675–692.

Horton, A. L., & Johnson, B. L. (1993). Profile and strategies of women who have ended abuse. *Families in Society, 74,* 481–492.

Horton, A. L., Wilkins, M. M., & Wright, W. (1988). Women who ended abuse: What religious leaders and religion did for these victims. In A. L. Horton & J. A. Williamson (Eds.), *Abuse and religion* (pp. 235–245). Lexington, MA: Lexington Books.

Hotaling, G. T., & Sugarman, D. B. (1986). An analysis of risk markers in husband to wife violence: The current state of knowledge. *Violence and Victims, 1,* 101–124.

Hotaling, G. T., & Sugarman, D. B. (1990). A risk marker analysis of assaulted wives. *Journal of Family Violence, 5,* 1–13.

Houry, D., Kaslow, N. J., & Thompson, M. P. (2005). Depressive symptoms in women experiencing intimate partner violence. *Journal of Interpersonal Violence, 20,* 1467–1477.

Houskamp, B. M., & Foy, D. W. (1991). The assessment of post-traumatic stress disorder in battered women. *Journal of Interpersonal Violence, 6,* 367–375.

Howard-Hassman, R. E. (2011). Universal women's rights since 1970: The centrality of autonomy and agency. *Journal of Human Rights, 10,* 433–449.

Hoyle, C., & Sanders, A. (2000). Police response to domestic violence: From victim choice to victim empowerment? *British Journal of Criminology, 40,* 14–36.

Huisman, K. A. (1996). Wife battering in Asian American communities. *Violence Against Women, 2,* 260–283.

Hulbert, S. N. (2008). Children exposed to violence in the child protection system: Practice-based assessment of the system process can lead to practical strategies for improvement. *Journal of Emotional Abuse, 6,* 217–234.

Human Rights Watch. (1992). *Double jeopardy: Police abuse of women in Pakistan.* New York, NY: Author.

Humphreys, C., & Absler, D. (2011). History repeating: Child protection responses to domestic violence. *Child and Family Social Work, 16,* 464–473.

Hunnicutt, G. (2009). Varieties of patriarchy and violence against women. *Violence Against Women, 15,* 553–573.

Hunt, H. F., & Brady, J. V. (1955). Some effects of punishment and intercurrent anxiety on a simple operant. *Journal of Comparative and Physiological Psychology, 48,* 305–310.

Hurlburt, M. S., Zhang, J., Barth, R. P., Leslie, L. K., & Burns, B. J. (2010). Posttraumatic stress symptoms in children and adolescents referred for child welfare investigation. *Child Maltreatment, 15,* 48–63.

Huss, M. T., Tomkins, A. J., Garbin, C. P., Schopp, R. F., & Kilian, A. (2006). Battered women who kill their abusers: An examination of commonsense notions, cognitions, and judgments. *Journal of Interpersonal Violence, 21,* 1063–1080.

Husso, M., Virkki, T., Notko, M., Holma, J., Laitila, A., & Mäntysaari, M. (2012). Making sense of domestic violence intervention in professional health care. *Health and Social Care in the Community, 20,* 347–355.

Hutchison, I. W. (1999). *Influence of alcohol and drugs on women's utilization of the police for domestic violence* (NCJ Pub. No. 179277). Washington, DC: U.S. Bureau of Justice Statistics.

Hutchison, I. W., Hirschel, J. D., & Pesackis, C. E. (1994). Family violence and police utilization. *Violence and Victims, 9,* 299–313.

Hwalek, M., Williamson, D., & Stahl, C. (1991). Community-based M-team roles: A job analysis. *Journal of Elder Abuse and Neglect, 3*(3), 45–71.

Hydén, M. (1999). The world of the fearful: Battered women's narratives of leaving abusive husbands. *Feminism and Psychology, 9,* 449–469.

Hydén, M. (2005). "I must have been an idiot to let it go on": Agency and positioning in battered women's narratives of leaving. *Feminism and Psychology, 15,* 169–188.

"I'm supposed to be safe . . . Oh my God." (1992, April 23). *Tribune Newspapers of Arizona, 2*(162), A6. (Cox Arizona Publications, Inc.)

Institute for Women's Policy Research. (2012, Winter). *Promoting economic security for low-income women through STEM education at community colleges.* Washington, DC: Author.

Irvine, J. (1990). Lesbian battering: The search for shelter. In P. Elliott (Ed.), *Confronting lesbian battering* (pp. 25–30). St. Paul: Minnesota Coalition for Battered Women.

Jackson, S. M. (1998). Issues in the dating violence research: A review of the literature. *Aggression and Violent Behavior, 4,* 233–247.

Jacobson, N. S., Gottman, J. M., Gortner, E., Berns, S., & Shortt, J. W. (1996). Psychological factors in the longitudinal course of battering. *Violence and Victims, 11,* 625–629.

Jacobson, N. S., Gottman, J. M., Waltz, J., Rushe, R., Babcock, J. C., & Holtzworth-Munroe, A. (1994). Affect, verbal content and psychophysiology in the arguments of couples with a violent husband. *Journal of Consulting and Clinical Psychology, 62,* 982–988.

Jaffe, E. (2007, May). Mirror neurons. *Observer, 20,* 20–23, 25.

Jaffe, P. G., Crooks, C. V., & Bala, N. (2009). A framework for addressing allegations of domestic violence in child custody disputes. *Journal of Child Custody, 6,* 169–188.

Jaffe, P. G., & Geffner, R. (1998). Child custody disputes and domestic violence: Critical issues for mental health, social service, and legal professionals. In G. W. Holden, R. Geffner, & E. N. Jouriles (Eds.), *Children exposed to marital violence* (pp. 371–396). Washington, DC: American Psychological Association.

Jaffe, P. G., Hastings, E., & Reitzel, D. (1992). Child witnesses of woman abuse: How can schools respond? *Response, 79*(2), 12–15.

Jaffe, P. G., Lemon, N., & Poisson, S. (2003). *Child custody and domestic violence: A call for safety and accountability.* Thousand Oaks, CA: Sage.

Jaffe, P. G., Suderman, M., Reitzel, D., & Killip, S. M. (1992). An evaluation of a secondary school primary prevention program on violence in intimate relationships. *Violence and Victims, 7,* 129–146.

Jaffe, P. G., Wolfe, D. A., & Wilson, S. K. (1990). *Children of battered women.* Newbury Park, CA: Sage.

Jay, J. (1991, November—December). Terrible knowledge. *Family Therapy Networker,* pp. 18–29.

Jenkins, E. L. (1996). Homicide against women in the workplace. *Journal of the American Medical Women's Association, 51,* 118–119, 122.

Jerome, R., Grisby, L., Esselman, M., Klise, K., Free, C., Porterfield, E., . . . Dagostino, M. (1998, August 17). Growing up gay. *People, 50*(5), 44–51.

Jewett, C. (2011, January 4). Mercy for women who killed their abusers. *California Watch, Health & Welfare/Daily Report.*

Johnson, I. M. (1988). Wife abuse: Factors predictive of the decision-making process of battered women. *Dissertation Abstracts International, 48,* 3202A. (UMI No. 8803369)

Johnson, I. M. (1992). Economic, situational, and psychological correlates of the decision-making process of battered women. *Families in Society: The Journal of Contemporary Human Services, 73,* 168–176.

Johnson, J. M., & Bondurant, D. M. (1992). Revisiting the 1982 church response survey. *Studies in Symbolic Interaction, 13,* 287–293.

Johnson, L. D. (1998). Caught in the crossfire: Examining legislative and judicial response to the forgotten victims of domestic violence. *Law and Psychology Review, 22,* 271–286.

Johnson, M., & Elliott, B. A. (1997). Domestic violence among family practice patients in midsized and rural communities. *Journal of Family Practice, 44,* 391–400.

Johnson, M. P. (1995). Patriarchal terrorism and common couple violence: Two forms of violence against women. *Journal of Marriage and the Family, 57,* 283–294.

Johnson, S. P., & Sullivan, C. M. (2008). How child protection workers support or further victimize battered mothers. *Affilia, 23,* 242–258.

Joint Commission on Accreditation of Healthcare Organizations. (1992). *Accreditation manual for hospitals* (Vol. 1). Oakbrook Terrace, IL: Author.

Jones, L., Hughes, M., & Unterstaller, U. (2001). Post-traumatic stress disorder (PTSD) in victims of domestic violence: A review of the research. *Trauma, Violence, & Abuse, 2,* 99–119.

Josephs, R. A., Markus, H. R., & Tafarodi, R. W. (1992). Gender and self-esteem. *Journal of Personality and Social Psychology, 63,* 391–402.

Jouriles, E. N., McDonald, R., Slep, A. M. S., Heyman, R. E., & Garrido, E. (2008). Child abuse in the context of domestic violence: Prevalence, explanations, and practice implications. *Violence and Victims, 23,* 221–235.

Julian, J., & Kornblum, W. (1983). *Social problems.* Englewood Cliffs, NJ: Prentice Hall.

Julian, T. W., & McKenry, P. C. (1993). Mediators of male violence toward female intimates. *Journal of Family Violence, 8,* 39–56.

Justice, A., & Hirt, M. H. (1992, August). *Attachment styles of women with histories of abusive relationships.* Paper presented at the annual meeting of the American Psychological Association, Washington, DC.

Kaci, J. H. (1990). Issues of the 1990s. *Response, 13*(1), 4.

Kahn, M. W. (1980). Wife beating and cultural context: Prevalence in an aboriginal and islander community in Northern Australia. *American Journal of Community Psychology, 8,* 727–731.

Kalmuss, D. S. (1984). The intergenerational transmission of marital aggression. *Journal of Marriage and the Family, 46,* 11–19.

Kamin, L. J. (1959). The delay-of-punishment gradient. *Journal of Comparative and Physiological Psychology, 52,* 44–51.

Kandel-Englander, E. (1992). Wife battering and violence outside the family. *Journal of Interpersonal Violence, 7,* 462–470.

Kane, T. A., Staiger, P. K., & Ricciardelli, L. A. (2000). Male domestic violence: Attitudes, aggression, and interpersonal dependency. *Journal of Interpersonal Violence, 15,* 16–29.

Kann, M. E. (1998). Similarity and political patriarchy during the American founding. *Men and Masculinities, 1,* 193–219.

Kansas' capital city repeals domestic violence law. (2011, October 12). Associated Press. Retrieved October 13, 2011, from www.msnbc.msm.com/id/ 44868091 /ns/us_news-crime_and_courts/t/kansas-capital-city-repeals-domestic

Karsh, E. B. (1962). Effects of number of rewarded trials and intensity of punishment on running speed. *Journal of Comparative and Physiological Psychology, 55,* 44–51.

Kaslow, N. J., Thompson, M. P., Meadows, L. A., Jacobs, D., Chance, S., Gibb, B., . . . Phillips, K. (1998). Factors that mediate and moderate the link between partner abuse and suicidal behavior in African American women. *Journal of Consulting and Clinical Psychology, 66,* 533–540.

Kateiva, J., & Bowker, L. H. (2010). Trigger mechanisms in lethal counter-violence by battered women. *Family and Intimate Partner Violence Quarterly, 3,* 175–180.

Katz, J., Arias, I., Beach, S. R. H., & Roman, P. (1995). Excuses, excuses: Accounting for the effects of partner violence on marital satisfaction and stability. *Violence and Victims, 10,* 315–326.

Kaukinen, C. (2002). The help-seeking decisions of violent crime victims: An examination of the direct and conditional effects of gender and the victim-offender relationship. *Journal of Interpersonal Violence, 17,* 432–456.

Keilitz, S. L., Davis, C., Eikeman, H. S., Flango, C., & Hannaford, P. L. (1998, January). *Civil protection orders: Victims' views on effectiveness.* Washington, DC: U.S. Department of Justice, National Institute of Justice.

Kelly, A. B. (2012). Actualizing intimate partnership theory. *Family Court Review, 50,* 258–272.

Kemp, A., Green, B. L., Hovanitz, C., & Rawlings, E. I. (1995). Incidence and correlates of posttraumatic stress disorder in battered women: Shelter and community samples. *Journal of Interpersonal Violence, 10,* 43–55.

Kemp, A., Rawlings, E. I., & Green, B. L. (1991). Post-traumatic stress disorder (PTSD) in battered women: A shelter sample. *Journal of Traumatic Stress, 4,* 137–148.

Kernic, M. A., Holt, V. L., Stoner, J. A., Wolf, M. E., & Rivara, F. P. (2003). Resolution of depression among victims of intimate partner violence: Is cessation of violence enough? *Violence and Victims, 18,* 115–129.

Kernsmith, P. (2005a). Exerting power or striking back: A gendered comparison of motivations for domestic violence perpetration. *Violence and Victims, 20,* 173–185.

Kernsmith, P. (2005b). Treating perpetrators of domestic violence: Gender differences in the applicability of the theory of planned behavior. *Sex Roles, 52,* 757–770.

Kesner, J. E., Julian, T., & McKenry, P. C. (1997). Application of attachment theory to male violence toward female intimates. *Journal of Family Violence, 12,* 211–228.

Kessler, R. C., Coccaro, E. F., Fava, M., Jaeger, S., Jin, R., & Walters, E. (2006). The prevalence and correlates of DSM-IV intermittent explosive disorder in the National Comorbidity Survey replication. *Archives of General Psychiatry, 63,* 669–678.

Kessler, R. C., McGonagle, K. A., Zhao, S., Nelson, C. B., Hughes, M., Eshelman, S., . . . Kendler, K. S. (1994). Lifetime and 12-month prevalence of *DSM-III-R* psychiatric disorders in the United States: Results from the National Comorbidity Survey. *Archives of General Psychiatry, 51,* 8–19.

Kessler, R. C., McLeod, J. D., & Wethington, E. (1985). The costs of caring: A perspective on the relationship between sex and psychological distress. In I. G. Sarason & B. R. Sarason (Eds.), *Social support: Theory, research, and applications* (pp. 491–506).

Kessler, R. C., Molnar, B. E., Feurer, I. D., & Appelbaum, M. (2001). Patterns and mental health predictors of domestic violence in the United States: Results from the National Comorbidity Survey. *International Journal of Law and Psychology, 24,* 487–508.

Kessler, R. C., Sonnega, A., Brommet, E., Hughes, M., & Nelson, C. B. (1995). Posttraumatic stress disorder in the National Comorbidity Survey. *Archives of General Psychiatry, 52,* 1048–1060.

Khan, F. I., Welch, T. L., & Zillmer, E. A. (1993). MMPI-2 profiles of battered women in transition. *Journal of Personality Assessment, 60,* 100–111.

Kiecolt-Glaser, J. K. (2009). Psychoneuroimmunology: Psychology's gateway to the biomedical future. *Perspectives on Psychological Science, 4,* 367–369.

Killcross, S., Robbins, T. W., & Everitt, B. J. (1997). Different types of fear-conditioned behaviour by separate nuclei within amygdala. *Nature, 338,* 377–380.

Kilpatrick, K. L., Litt, M., & Williams, L. M. (1997). Post-traumatic stress disorder in child witnesses to domestic violence. *American Journal of Orthopsychiatry, 67,* 639–644.

Kim-Goodwin, Y. S., Clements, C., McCuiston, A. M., & Fox, J. A. (2009). Dating violence among high school students in Southeastern North Carolina. *Journal of School Nursing, 25,* 141–151.

Kimmerling, R. E., Alvarez, J., Pavao, J., Mack, K. P., Smith, M. W., & Baumrind, N. (2009). Unemployment among women: Examining the relationship of physical and psychological intimate partner violence and posttraumatic stress disorder. *Journal of Interpersonal Violence, 24,* 450–463.

King, A. (2009). Islam, women and violence. *Feminist Theology, 17,* 292–328.

Klee, J. B. (1944). The relation of frustration and motivation to the production of abnormal fixations in the rat. *Psychological Monographs, 56*(4).

Kleim, B., Wilhelm, F. H., Glucksman, E., & Ehlers, A. (2010). Sex differences in heart rate responses to scrip-driven imagery soon after trauma and risk of posttraumatic stress disorder. *Psychosomatic Medicine, 72,* 917–924.

Klein, A., Tobin, T., Salomon, A., & Dubois, J. (2008). *A statewide profile of abuse of older women and the criminal justice response* (NCJ Pub. No. 222459). Washington, DC: U.S. Department of Justice.

Klein, C. F. (1995). Full faith and credit: Interstate enforcement of protection orders under the Violence Against Women Act of 1994. *Family Law Quarterly, 29*(2, Special issue), 253–271.

Klein, E., Campbell, J. C., Soler, E., & Ghez, M. (1997). *Ending domestic violence.* Newbury Park, CA: Sage.

Klein, J. (2006). An invisible problem: Everyday violence against girls in schools. *Theoretical Criminology, 10,* 147–177.

Klevens, J., & Leeb, R. (2010). Child maltreatment fatalities in children under 5: Findings from the National Violent Death Reporting System. *Child Abuse & Neglect, 34,* 262–266.

Kocot, T., & Goodman, L. (2003). The roles of coping and social support in battered women's mental health. *Violence Against Women, 9,* 323–346.

Koepsell, J. K., Kernic, M. A., & Holt, V. (2006). Factors that influence battered women to leave their abusive relationships. *Violence and Victims, 21,* 31–147.

Kohl, P. L., & Macy, R. J. (2008). Profiles of victimized women among the child welfare population: Implications for targeted child welfare policy and practices. *Journal of Family Violence, 23,* 57–68.

Koss, M. P. (1989). Hidden rape: Sexual aggression and victimization in a national sample of students in higher education. In M. A. Pirog-Good & J. E. Stets (Eds.), *Violence in dating relationships: Emerging social issues* (pp. 145–168). New York, NY: Praeger.

Koss, M. P. (1990). The women's mental health research agenda. *American Psychologist, 45,* 374–380.

Koss, M. P., Goodman, L. A., Browne, A., Fitzgerald, L. F., Puryear-Keita, G., & Russo, N. F. (1994). *Male violence against women at home, at work, and in the community.* Washington, DC: American Psychological Association.

Kotch, J. B., Lewis, T., Hussey, J. M., English, D., Thompson, R., Litrownik, A. J., ... Dubowitz, H. (2008). Importance of early neglect for childhood aggression. *Pediatrics, 121,* 725–732.

Kovan, N. M., Chung, A. L., & Sroufe, L. A. (2009). The intergenerational continuity of observed early parenting: A prospective, longitudinal study. *Developmental Psychology, 45,* 1205–1213.

Kozu, J. (1999). Domestic violence in Japan. *American Psychologist, 54,* 50–54.

Kracke, K., & Hahn, H. (2008). The nature and extent of childhood exposure to violence: What we know, why we don't know more, and why it matters. *Journal of Emotional Abuse, 8,* 29–49.

Krajewski, S. S. (1996). Results of a curriculum intervention with seventh graders regarding violence in relationships. *Journal of Family Violence, 11,* 93–112.

Kramer, T. L., & Green, B. L. (1991). Post-traumatic stress disorder as an early response to sexual assault. *Journal of Interpersonal Violence, 6,* 160–173.

Krishnan, S. P., Hilbert, J. C., McNeil, K., & Newman, I. (2004). From respite to transition: Women's use of domestic violence shelters in rural New Mexico. *Journal of Family Violence, 19,* 165–173.

Kross, E., Berman, M. G., Mischel, W., Smith, E. E., & Wager, T. D. (2011). *Proceedings of the National Academy of Sciences.* Retrieved April 19, 2012, from pnas.org/cgi/doi/10.1073/pnas.1102693108

Krugman, S. D., Witting, M. D., Furuno, J. P., Hirshon, J. M., Limcangco, M. R., Perisse, A. R., & Rasch, E. K. (2004). Perceptions of help resources for victims of intimate partner violence. *Journal of Interpersonal Violence, 19,* 766–777.

Kuehl, S. J. (1991). Legal remedies for teen dating violence. In B. Levy (Ed.), *Dating violence: Young women in danger* (pp. 209–220). Seattle, WA: Seal Press.

Kugel, C., Retzlaff, C., Hopfer, S., Lawson, D. M., Daley, E., Drewes, C., & Freedman, S. (2009). Familias con Voz: Community survey results from an intimate partner violence (IPV) prevention projects with migrant workers. *Journal of Family Violence, 24,* 649–660.

Kuleshnyk, I. (1984). The Stockholm syndrome: Toward an understanding. *Social Action and the Law, 10*(2), 37–42.

Kulka, R., Schlenger, W., Fairbank, J., Hough, R., Jordan, B., Marmar, C., & Weiss, D. (1990). *Trauma and the Vietnam war generation: Report and findings from the National Vietnam Veterans Readjustment Study.* New York, NY: Bruner/ Mazel.

Kulkarni, S. J., Bell, H., & Rhodes, D. M. (2012). Back to basics: Essential qualities of services for survivors of intimate partner violence. *Violence Against Women, 18,* 85–101.

Kulwicki, A. D. (2002). The practice of honor crimes: A glimpse of domestic violence in the Arab world. *Issues in Mental Health Nursing, 23,* 77–87.

Kury, H., & Ferdinand, T. (1997). The victim's experience and fear of crime. *International Review of Victimology, 5,* 93–140.

Labi, N. (1998, June 28). For the next generation, feminism is being sold as glitz and image. But what to girls really want? *Time Magazine, 151*(25), 60–61.

Lamb, M. E. (2012). A wasted opportunity to engage with the literature on the implications of attachment research for family court professionals. *Family Court Review.* doi: 10.1111/j.1744-1617.2012.01463.x

Landenburger, K. (1989). A process of entrapment in and recovery from an abusive relationship. *Issues in Mental Health Nursing, 10,* 209–227.

Laner, M. R. (1990). Violence or its precipitators: Which is more likely to be identified as a dating problem? *Deviant Behavior, 11,* 319–329.

Laner, M. R., & Thompson, J. (1982). Abuse and aggression in courting couples. *Deviant Behavior, 3,* 229–244.

Lang, D. (1974, November 25). A reporter at large: The bank drama. *New Yorker,* pp. 56–126.

Langford, D. R. (1996). Predicting unpredictability: A model of women's processes of predicting battering men's violence. *Scholarly Inquiry for Nursing Practice: An International Journal, 10,* 371–385.

Langhinrichsen-Rohling, J., Neidig, P., & Thorn, G. (1995). Violent marriages: Gender differences in levels of current violence and past abuse. *Journal of Family Violence, 10,* 159–176.

Langley, P. A. (1991). Family violence: Toward a family-oriented public policy. *Families in Society: The Journal of Contemporary Human Services, 72,* 574–576.

Larkin, J., & Popaleni, K. (1994). Heterosexual courtship violence and sexual harassment: The private and public control of young women. *Feminism and Psychology, 4,* 213–237.

Latta, R. E., & Goodman, L. A. (2005). Considering the interplay of cultural context and service provision in intimate partner violence. *Violence Against Women, 11*,1441–1464.

Laumann, E. O., Leitsch, S. A., & Waite, L. J. (2008). Elder mistreatment in the United States: Prevalence estimate from a nationally representative study. *Journal of Gerontology: Journal of Gerontology B, Psychological Science Social Science, 63,* S248–S254.

Launius, M. H., & Jensen, B. L. (1987). Interpersonal problem-solving skills in battered, counseling, and control women. *Journal of Family Violence, 2,* 151–162.

Launius, M. H., & Lindquist, C. U. (1988). Learned helplessness, external locus of control, and passivity in battered women. *Journal of Interpersonal Violence, 3,* 307–433.

Lauritsen, J. L., Owens, J. G., Planty, M., Rand, M. R., & Truman, J. L. (2012). *Methods for counting high-frequency repeat victimizations in the National Crime Victimization Survey.* Washington, DC: U.S. Department of Justice, Bureau of Justice Statistics.

LaViolette, A. L. (1991). *Battered women, power, and family systems therapy.* Garden Grove, CA: Newman.

LaViolette, A. L. (2009). Assessing intimate partner violence: A context sensitive aggression scale. *Journal of Child Custody, 6,* 219–231.

Lawler-Row, K. A., Hyatt-Edwards, L., Wuensch, K. L., & Karremans, J. C. (2011). Forgiveness and health: The role of attachment. *Personal Relationships, 18,* 170–183.

Lawrence, E., & Bradbury, T. N. (2001). Physical aggression and marital dysfunction: A longitudinal analysis. *Journal of Family Psychology, 15,* 135–154.

Lawrence, E., Yoon, J., Langer, A., & Ro, E. (2009). Is psychological aggression as detrimental as physical aggression? The independent effects of psychological aggression. *Violence and Victims, 24,* 20–35.

Lazarus, R. S., & Folkman, S. (1984). *Stress, appraisal, and coping.* New York, NY: Springer.

Lee, B.-J. (2007). Moderating effects of religious/spiritual coping in the relation between perceived stress and psychological well-being. *Pastoral Psychology, 55,* 751–759.

Lee, J., & Trauth, D. (2009, October). *Domestic violence assaults in the workplace study.* Raleigh, NC: Peace at Work.

Lee-Baggley, D., Preece, M., & DeLongis, A. (2005). Coping with interpersonal stress: Role of big five traits. *Journal of Personality, 73,* 1141–1180.

Leotti, L. A., & Delgado, M. R. (2011). The inherent reward of choice. *Psychological Science, 22,* 1310–1318.

Lerner, C. F., & Kennedy, L. T. (2000). Stay-leave decision making in battered women: Trauma, coping and self-efficacy. *Cognitive Therapy and Research, 24,* 215–232.

Lesher, M. (2009). Justice for child victims of incest. *Family and Intimate Partner Violence Quarterly, 3,* 245–258.

Leung, L. C. (2011). Gender sensitivity among social workers handling cases of domestic violence: A Hong Kong case. *Affilia, 26,* 291–303.

Leung, P., & Cheung, M. (2008). A prevalence study on partner abuse in six Asian American ethnic groups in the USA. *International Social Work, 51,* 635–649.

Levant, R. F. (1995). *Masculinity reconstructed.* New York, NY: Dutton (Penguin Books).

Levenson, H. (1973). Activism and powerful others. Distinctions within the concept of internal-external control. *Journal of Personality Assessment, 38,* 377–383.

Levesque, R. J. R. (2001). *Culture and family violence.* Washington, DC: American Psychological Association.

Levitt, H. M., & Ware, K. N. (2006). Religious leaders' perspectives on marriage, divorce, and intimate partner violence. *Psychology of Women Quarterly, 30,* 212–222.

Levy, B. (1984). *Prevention skills for violence-free relationships* [Curriculum for young people ages 13–18]. Long Beach, CA: Southern California Coalition for Battered Women.

Levy, B. (1990). Abusive teen dating relationships: An emerging issue for the '90s. *Response, 13*(1), 5.

Levy, B. (1993). *In love and in danger: A teen's guide to breaking free of abusive relationships.* Seattle, WA: Seal Press.

Levy, B. (1997, Winter/Spring). Common stereotypes contribute to invisibility of battered lesbians. *Update: Newsletter of the Southern California Coalition on Battered Women, Winter/Spring*(1), 1, 6.

Levy, B., & Occhiuzzo Giggans, P. (1995). *What parents need to know about dating violence.* Seattle, WA: Seal Press.

Lewis, C. S., Griffing, S., Chu, M., Sage, R. E., Madry, L., & Primm, B. J. (2006). Coping and violence exposure as predictors of psychological functioning in domestic violence survivors. *Violence Against Women, 12,* 340–354.

Li, M., Mardhekar, V., & Wadkar, A. (2012). Coping strategies and learned helplessness of employed and nonemployed educated married women from India. *Health Care for Women International, 33,* 495–508.

Lie, G., & Gentlewarrior, S. (1991). Intimate violence in lesbian relationships: Discussion of survey findings and practical implications. *Journal of Social Service Research, 15,* 41–59.

Lindgren, S., & Renck, B. (2008). "It is still so deep-seated, the fear": Psychological stress reactions as a consequence of intimate partner violence. *Journal of Psychiatric and Mental Health Nursing, 15,* 219–228.

Lindhorst, T., Meyers, M., & Casey, E. (2008). Screening for domestic violence in public welfare offices: An analysis of case manager and client interactions. *Violence Against Women, 14,* 5–28.

Lloyd, S. A. (1988, November). *Conflict and violence in marriage.* Paper presented at the annual meeting of the National Council on Family Relations, Philadelphia, PA.

Loar, L. (1997, September). *Batterers and victims: When spousal and child abuse collide.* In R. Vaselle-Augenstein and M. Fraga (Chairs), Symposium conducted at the California Association of Batterers' Intervention Programs Semi-annual Conference, Oak.

Loar, L., & Rathmann, C. (1994, Spring). A humane garden of children, plants, and animals grows in Sonoma County, California. *Latham Letter*, pp. 6–9.

Logan, F. A., & Wallace, W. C. (1981). *Fundamentals of learning and motivation* (3rd ed.). Dubuque, IA: William C. Brown.

Long, G. M., & McNamara, J. R. (1989). Paradoxical punishment as it relates to the battered woman syndrome. *Behavior Modification, 13,* 192–205.

Lorber, J., & Farrell, S. A. (Eds.). (1991). *The social construction of gender.* Newbury Park, CA: Sage.

Loren, W. (1994). Surviving domestic violence. *Violence Update, 4*(12), 3, 10.

Los Angeles County Department of Probation. (2010). *Los Angeles Department of Probation approved batterers' programs.* Los Angeles, CA: Author.

Lovik, M. M. (2011a). If my spouse ever hit me, I'd just leave. *Michigan Bar Journal, 90,* 24–26.

Lovik, M. M. (2011b). Specialized services for survivors and perpetrators of battering. *Michigan Bar Journal, 90,* 44.

Lovik, M. M., & Shiemke, R. E. (2011). Theme introduction. *Michigan Bar Journal, 90,* 23.

Lowe, A., & Prout, S. R. (2011). Economic justice in domestic violence litigation. *Michigan Bar Journal, 90,* 32–34.

Lowenberg, K., & Fulcher, J. (2008). Thoughts on designing domestic violence laws and services to protect teens. *Family and Intimate Partner Violence Quarterly, 1,* 115–125.

Luke, N., Schuler, S. R., Mai, B. T. T., Thein, P. V., & Minh, T. H. (2007). Exploring couple attributes and attitudes and marital violence in Vietnam. *Violence Against Women, 13,* 5–27.

Luna-Firebaugh, A. M. (2006). Violence against American Indian women and the Services-Training-Officers-Prosecutors Violence Against Indian Women (STOP VAIW) program. *Violence Against Women, 12,* 125–136.

Lund, L. E. (1999). What happens when health practitioners report domestic violence injuries to the police? A study of the law enforcement response to injury reports. *Violence and Victims, 14,* 203–214.

Lupri, E., Grandin, E., & Brinkerhoff, M. B. (1994). Socioeconomic status and male violence in the Canadian home: A re-examination. *Canadian Journal of Sociology, 19,* 47–73.

Lytle, M. C., Foley, P. F., & Aster, A. M. (2012). Adult children of gay and lesbian parents: Religion and the parent-child relationship. *Counseling Psychologist.* doi: 0011000012449658

Maccoby, E. E., & Jacklin, C. N. (1974). *The psychology of sex differences.* Stanford, CA: Stanford University Press.

MacNair, R. R., & Elliott, T. R. (1992). Self-perceived problem-solving ability, stress appraisal, and coping over time. *Journal of Research in Personality, 26,* 150–164.

Maertz, K. F. (1990). Self-defeating beliefs of battered women (Unpublished doctoral dissertation, University of Alberta, Canada). *Dissertation Abstracts International, 51,* 5580B.

Magee, R., & Hampton, S. (1993). Family violence and the workplace: The role of employee assistance programs. *Family Violence and Sexual Assault Bulletin, 9*(1), 19–20.

Maier, N. R. F. (1949). *Frustration: The study of behavior without a goal.* New York, NY: McGraw-Hill.

Maier, N. R. F., Glazer, N. M., & Klee, J. B. (1940). Studies of abnormal behavior in the rat: III. The development of behavior fixations through frustration. *Journal of Experimental Psychology, 26,* 521–546.

Maier, S. F., & Seligman, M. E. P. (1976). Learned helplessness: Theory and evidence. *Journal of Experimental Psychology: General, 105,* 3–46.

Maier, S. F., Seligman, M. E. P., & Solomon, R. L. (1969). Pavlovian fear conditioning and learned helplessness. In B. A. Campbell & R. M. Church (Eds.), *Punishment and aversive behavior.* New York, NY: Appleton-Century-Crofts.

Main, M., & George, C. (1985). Responses of abused and disadvantaged toddlers to distress in age mates: A study in a day care setting. *Developmental Psychology, 21,* 407–412.

Mankowski, E. S., Haaken, J., & Silvergleid, C. S. (2002). Collateral damage: An analysis of the achievements and unintended consequences of batterer intervention programs and discourse. *Journal of Family Violence, 17,* 167–184.

Marano, H. E. (1997, November/December). A new focus on family values. *Psychology Today, 30*(6), 52–55, 78.

Margolies, L., & Leeder, E. (1995). Violence at the door: Treatment of lesbian batterers. *Violence Against Women, 1,* 139–157.

Margolin, G., John, R. S., & Foo, L. (1998). Interactive and unique risk factors for husbands' emotional and physical abuse of their wives. *Journal of Family Violence, 13,* 315–344.

Marshall, A. D., Panuzio, J., & Taft, C. T. (2005). Intimate partner violence among military veterans and active duty servicemen. *Clinical Psychology Review, 25,* 862–876.

Marshall, L. L. (1992a). Development of the Severity of Violence Against Women Scales. *Journal of Family Violence, 7,* 103–121.

Marshall, L. L. (1992b). The Severity of Violence Against Men Scales. *Journal of Family Violence, 7,* 189–203.

Marshall, L. L. (1996). Psychological abuse of women: Six distinct clusters. *Journal of Family Violence, 11,* 379–409.

Marshall, L. L., & Rose, P. (1990). Premarital violence: The impact of family of origin violence, stress, and reciprocity. *Violence and Victims, 5,* 51–64.

Martin, E. K., Taft, C. T., & Resnick, P. A. (2007). A review of marital rape. *Aggression and Violent Behavior, 12,* 329–347.

Martin, M. E. (1997). Double your trouble: Dual arrest in family violence. *Journal of Family Violence, 12,* 139–157.

Martin, S. E. (1989). Research note: The response of the clergy to spouse abuse in a suburban county. *Violence and Victims, 4,* 217–225.

Martin, S. L., Gibbs, D. A., Johnson, R. E, Rentz, E. D., Clinton-Sherrod, M., & Hardison, J. (2007). Spouse abuse and child abuse by army soldiers. *Journal of Family Violence, 22,* 587–595.

Mary Kay Foundation. (2012). *Truth about abuse survey.* Dallas, TX: Author.

Maslow, A. H. (1970). *Motivation and personality* (2nd ed.). New York, NY: Harper and Row.

Massad, P. M., & Hulsey, T. L. (2006). Causal attributions in posttraumatic stress disorder: Implications for clinical research and practice. *Psychotherapy: Theory, Research, Practice, Training, 43,* 201–215.

Mastrofski, S. D., Parks, R. B., Reiss, A. J., & Worden, R. E. (1998). *Policing neighborhoods: A report from Indianapolis.* Washington, DC: U.S. Department of Justice.

Mather, M., & Lighthall, N. R. (2012). Risk and reward are processed differently in decisions made under stress. *Current Directions in Psychological Science, 21,* 36–41.

Matlaw, J. R., & Spence, D. M. (1994). The hospital elder assessment team: A protocol for suspected cases of elder abuse and neglect. *Journal of Elder Abuse and Neglect, 6,* 23–37.

Matud, M. P. (2005). The psychological impact of domestic violence on Spanish women. *Journal of Applied Social Psychology, 35,* 2310–2322.

Max, W., Rice, D. P., Finkelstein, E., Bardwell, R. A., & Leadbetter, S. (2004). The economic toll of intimate partner violence against women in the United States. *Violence and Victims, 19,* 259–272.

May, D. C., Rader, N. E., & Goodrum, S. (2010). A gendered assessment of the "threat of victimization": Examining gender differences in fear of crime, perceived risk, avoidance, and defensive behaviors. *Criminal Justice Review, 35,* 159–182.

McCarroll, J. E., Castro, S., Nelson, M. E., Fan, Z., Evans, K. P., & Rivera, A. (2008). Characteristic of domestic violence incidents reported at the scene by volunteer victim advocates. *Military Medicine, 173,* 865–870.

McCarroll, K. (2010, February). *Heroes and Healthy Families Conference.* Atlanta, GA.

McCauley, J., Kern, D. E., Kolodner, K., Dill, L., Schroeder, A. F., DeChant, H., Ryder, J., . . . Derogotis, L. (1995). The "battering syndrome": Prevalence and clinical characteristics of domestic violence in primary care internal medicine practices. *Annals of Internal Medicine, 123,* 737–746.

McCloskey, L. A. (1996). Socioeconomic and coercive power within the family. *Gender and Society, 10,* 449–463.

McCloskey, L. A., & Lichter, E. L. (2003). The contribution of marital violence to adolescent aggression across different relationships. *Journal of Interpersonal Violence, 18,* 390–412.

McDonald, K. A. (1990). Battered wives, religion, & law: An interdisciplinary approach. *Yale Journal of Law and Feminism, 2,* 251–298.

McDowell, J., & Park, A. (1998, June 29). Feminism. *Time Magazine, 151*(25), 63.

McFarlane, J. M. , Campbell, J. C., & Watson, K. (2002). Intimate partner stalking and femicide: Urgent implications for women's safety. *Behavioral Sciences and the Law, 20,* 51–68.

McGreevy, P. (1997, July 19). LAPD called lax on violence by its own. *Daily News,* p. 3.

McGuire, P. A. (1999, April). Psychologists key in O. J. custody case. *APA Monitor*, *30*(4), 21.

McKay, M. M. (1994). The link between domestic violence and child abuse: Assessment and treatment considerations. *Child Welfare*, *73*, 29–39.

McLeer, S. V., & Anwar, R. (1989). A study of battered women presenting in an emergency department. *American Journal of Public Health*, *79*, 65–66.

McMullan, E. C., Carlan, P. E., & Nored, L. S. (2010). Future law enforcement officers and social workers: Perceptions of domestic violence. *Journal of Interpersonal Violence*, *29*, 1367–1387.

McMurray, A. (1997). Violence against ex-wives: Anger and advocacy. *Health Care for Women International*, *18*, 543–556.

McNamara, J. R., Ertl, M. A., Marsh, S., & Walker, S. (1997). Short-term response to counseling and case management intervention in a domestic violence shelter. *Psychological Reports*, *81*, 1243–1251.

McWhirter, P. T. (1999). La violencia privada. *American Psychologist*, *54*, 37–40.

Mediation regulated for benefit of domestic violence victims. (1997, June/July). *Domestic Violence Report*, *2*, 70.

Mega, L. T., Mega, J. L., Mega, B. T., & Harris, B. M. (2000). Brainwashing and battering fatigue: Psychological abuse in domestic violence. *North Carolina Medical Journal*, *61*, 260–265.

Melbin, A., Sullivan, C. M., & Cain, D. (2003). Transitional supportive housing programs: Battered women's perspectives and recommendations. *Affilia*, *18*, 445–460.

Melchiorre, R., & Vis, J. A. (2012). Engagement strategies and change: An intentional practice response for the child welfare worker in cases of domestic violence. *Child and Family Social Work*. doi: 10.1111/j.1365- 2206.2012.00868x

Melton, H. C., & Belknap, J. (2003). He hits, she hits: Assessing gender differences and similarities in officially reported intimate partner violence. *Criminal Justice and Behavior*, *30*, 328–348.

Merchant, M. (2000). A comparative study of agencies assisting domestic violence victims: Does the South Asian community have special needs? *Journal of Social Distress and Homelessness*, *9*, 249–259.

Merritt-Gray, M., & Wuest, J. (1995). Counteracting abuse and breaking free: The process of leaving revealed through women's voices. *Health Care for Women International*, *16*, 399–412.

Messner, M. A. (1997). *Politics of masculinities*. Thousand Oaks, CA: Sage.

Meyer, A., Wagner, B., & Dutton, M. A. (2010). The relationship between battered women's causal attributions for violence and coping efforts. *Journal of Interpersonal Violence*, *25*, 900–918.

Mickelson, R. A. (1989). Why does Jane read and write so well? The anomaly of women's achievement. *Sociology of Education*, *62*, 47–63.

Mihalic, S. W., & Elliott, D. (1997). A social learning theory model of marital violence. *Journal of Family Violence*, *12*, 21–47.

Milgram, S. (1963). Behavioral studies of obedience. *Journal of Abnormal and Social Psychology*, *67*, 371–378.

Miller, J. B. (1976). *Toward a new psychology of women.* Boston, MA: Beacon.

Miller, L. (2010, April 12). A woman's place in the church. *Newsweek, 36–41.*

Miller, N. E. (1959). Liberalization of basic S-R concepts: Extensions to conflict behavior, motivation, and social learning. In S. Koch (Ed.), *Psychology: A study of science* (Vol. 2, pp. 196–292). New York, NY: McGraw-Hill.

Miller, S. L., & Meloy, M. L. (2006). Women's use of force: Voices of women arrested for domestic violence. *Violence Against Women, 12,* 89–115.

Mills, L. G. (1998). Mandatory arrest and prosecution policies for domestic violence: A critical literature review and the case for more research to test victim empowerment approaches. *Criminal Justice and Behavior, 25,* 306–318.

Mills, T. (1985). The assault on the self: Stages in coping with battering husbands. *Qualitative Sociology, 8,* 103–123.

Mineka, S., & Zinbarg, R. (2006). A contemporary learning theory perspective on the etiology of anxiety disorders: It's not what you thought it was. *American Psychologist, 61,* 10–26.

Mladjenovic, L., & Libriein, V. (1993). Belgrade feminists 1992: Separation, guilt and identity crisis. *Feminist Review, 45,* 113–119.

Model police protocol on interstate orders. (1999, February/March). *Domestic Violence Report, 4,* 37.

Moe, A. M., & Bell, M. P. (2004). Abject economics: The effects of battering and violence on women's work and employability. *Violence Against Women, 10,* 29–55.

Moffitt, T. E., & Caspi, A. (1999, July). *Findings about partner violence from the Dunedin multidisciplinary health and development study* (NCJ Pub. No. 170018). Washington, DC: U.S. Department of Justice, National Institute of Justice.

Mondor, J., McDuff, P., Lussier, Y., & Wright, J. (2011). Couples in therapy: Actor-partner analyses of the relationships between adult romantic attachment and marital satisfaction. *American Journal of Family Therapy, 39,* 112–123.

Mones, P. A. (1992). Battle cry for battered children. *California Lawyer, 12*(5), 58.

Monson, C. M., Byrd, G. R., & Langhinrichsen-Rohling, J. (1996). To have and to hold: Perceptions of marital rape. *Journal of Interpersonal Violence, 11,* 410–424.

Mookherjee, H. (1997). Marital status, gender, and perception of well-being. *Journal of Social Psychology, 137,* 95–105.

Moore, A. R. (2008). Types of violence against women and factors influencing intimate partner violence in Togo (West Africa). *Journal of Family Violence, 23,* 777–783.

Moore, T. M., Stuart, G. L., McNulty, J. K., Addis, M. E., Cordova, J. V., & Temple, J. R. (2008). Domains of masculine gender role stress and intimate partner violence in a clinical sample of violent men. *Psychology of Men and Masculinity, 9,* 82–89.

Mordini, N. M. (2004). Mandatory state interventions for domestic abuse cases: An examination of the effects on victim safety and autonomy. *Drake Law Review, 52,* 295–306.

Morgan, R. (2011, Spring). Women of the Arab Spring. *Ms. Magazine,* pp. 20–22.

Morris, A. (2009). Gendered dynamics of abuse and violence in families: Considering the abusive household gender regime. *Child Abuse Review, 18,* 414–427.

Morrow, M., Hankivsky, O., & Varcoe, C. (2004). Women and violence: The effects of dismantling the welfare state. *Critical Social Policy Limited, 24,* 358–384.

Morse, B. J. (1995). Beyond the Conflict Tactics Scale: Assessing gender differences in partner violence. *Violence and Victims, 10,* 251–272.

Morton, E., Runyan, C. W., Moracco, K. E., & Butts, J. (1998). Partner homicide-suicide involving female homicide victims: A population-based study in North Carolina, 1988–1992. *Violence and Victims, 13,* 91–106.

Moss, V. A., Pitula, C. R., Campbell, J. C., & Halstead, L. (1997). The experience of terminating an abusive relationship from an Anglo and African American perspective: A qualitative descriptive study. *Issues in Mental Health Nursing, 18,* 433–454.

Mowrer, O. H. (1947). On the dual nature of learning: A reinterpretation of "conditioning" and "problem solving." *Harvard Educational Review, 17,* 102–148.

Mrsevic, Z., & Hughes, D. M. (1997). Violence against women in Belgrade, Serbia: SOS hotline 1990–1993. *Violence Against Women, 3,* 101–128.

Muelleman, R. L., Lenaghan, P. A., & Pakieser, R. A. (1996). Battered women: Injury locations and types. *Annals of Emergency Medicine, 28,* 486–492.

Muldary, P. S. (1983). Attribution of causality of spouse assault. *Dissertation Abstracts International, 44,* 1249B. (UMI No. 8316576)

Murphy, C. M., & Meyer, S. L. (1991). Gender, power, and violence in marriage. *Behavior Therapist, 14,* 95–100.

Murray, B. (1999, October). Cultural insensitivity leads to unfair penalties. *APA Monitor on Psychology.* Retrieved October 4, 2002, from http://apa.org/monitor/oct99/mv2.html

Murray, C. E., & Graybeal, J. (2007). Methodological review of intimate partner violence prevention research. *Journal of Interpersonal Violence, 22,* 1250–1269.

Myers, D. A. (1995). Eliminating the battering of women by men: Some considerations for behavior analysis. *Journal of Applied Behavioral Analysis, 28,* 493–507.

Myers, J. E. B., Tikosh, M. A., & Paxson, M. A. (1992). Domestic violence prevention statutes. *Violence Update, 3*(4), 3, 5–9.

Nachman, S. (1991). Community-based M-team roles: A job analysis. *Journal of Elder Abuse and Neglect, 3*(3), 45–71.

National Center on Women and Family Law. (1994). *The effects of woman abuse on children: Psychological and legal authority* (2nd ed.). New York, NY: Author.

National Center on Women and Family Law. (1995). *Same-sex provisions of state domestic violence laws.* New York, NY: Author.

National Coalition Against Domestic Violence. (1997, Spring/Summer). NCADV reports on annual member survey. *Update: Newsletter of the Southern California Coalition on Battered Women, 3*(2), 10.

National Council of Juvenile and Family Court Judges. (1994). *Model code on domestic and family violence*. Reno, NV: Author.

National Institute of Crime Prevention. (2012). *Domestic violence and sexual assault training*. Retrieved from http:domesticviolencetraining.com/?page_id=18

National Scientific Council on the Developing Child. (2006). *Children's emotional development is built into the architecture of their brains* (Working Paper No. 2). Retrieved from www.developingchild.net/pubs/wp/Childrens_Emotional_ Development_ Architecture_Brains.pdf

National Sexual Violence Resource Center. (2000). *Sexual assault in Indian country*. Retrieved from www.VAW.UMN.edu

Neergaard, J. A., Lee, J. W., Anderson, B., & Wong Gengler, S. (2007). Women experiencing intimate partner violence: Effects of confiding in religious leaders. *Pastoral Psychology, 55*, 773–787.

Neff, J. A., Holamon, B., & Schluter, T. D. (1995). Spousal violence among Anglos, blacks, and Mexican Americans: The role of demographic variables, psychosocial predictors, and alcohol consumption. *Journal of Family Violence, 10*, 1–21.

Nelson, S., Baldwin, N., & Taylor, J. (2011). Mental health problems and medically unexplained physical symptoms in adult survivors of childhood sexual abuse: An integrative literature review. *Journal of Psychiatric and Mental Health Nursing, 19*, 211–220.

Nerenberg, L. (2008). *Elder abuse prevention: Emerging trends and promising strategies*. New York, NY: Springer.

Nerney, M. (1987). *Battered women and criminal justice*. New York, NY: STEPS to End Family Violence.

Neuger, C. C. (2002). Premarital preparation: Generating resistance to marital violence. *Journal of Religion and Abuse, 4*(3), 43–59.

New York Commission. (1998, December/January). New York Commission on domestic fatalities. *Domestic Violence Report, 3*, 27–30.

Newcomb, M. D., & Locke, T. F. (2001). Intergenerational cycle of maltreatment: A popular concept obscured by methodological limitations. *Child Abuse & Neglect, 25*, 1219–1240.

Newmark, L., Harrell, A., & Salem, P. (1995). Domestic violence and empowerment in custody and visitation cases. *Family and Conciliation Courts Review, 33*, 30–62.

Nezu, A. M., D'Zurilla, T. J., Zwick, M. L., & Nezu, C. M. (2004). Problem-solving therapy for adults. In E. C. Chang, T. J. D'Zurilla, & L. J. Sanna (Eds.), *Social problem solving: Theory, research, and training* (pp. 171–191). Washington, DC: American Psychological Association.

Nichols, L., & Feltey, K. M. (2003). "The woman is not always the bad guy": Dominant discourse and resistance in the lives of battered women. *Violence Against Women, 9*, 784–806.

Nielsen, J. M., Endo, R. K., & Ellington, B. L. (1992). Social isolation and wife abuse: A research report. In E. C. Viano (Ed.), *Intimate violence: Interdisciplinary perspectives* (pp. 40–59). Bristol, PA: Taylor & Francis.

Norman, P., & Finan, E. (2001, November 12). Veil of tears. *People, 56,* 107–110.

Nurius, P. S., Furrey, J., & Berliner, L. (1992). Coping capacity among women with abusive partners. *Violence and Victims, 7,* 229–243.

O'Brien, M., John, R. S., Margolin, G., & Erel, O. (1994). Reliability and diagnostic efficacy of parents' reports regarding children's exposure to marital aggression. *Violence and Victims, 9,* 45–62.

O'Donnell, C. J., Smith, A., & Madison, J. R. (2002). Using demographic risk factors to explain variations in the incidence of violence against women. *Journal of Interpersonal Violence, 17,* 1239–1262.

O'Keefe, M., & Treister, L. (1998). Victims of dating violence among high school students. *Violence Against Women, 4,* 195–223.

Okun, L. E. (1986). *Woman abuse: Facts replacing myths.* Albany: State University of New York Press.

O'Leary, K. D. (1996). Physical aggression in intimate relationships can be treated within a marital context under certain circumstances. *Journal of Interpersonal Violence, 11,* 450–452.

O'Leary, K. D. (1999). Psychological abuse: A variable deserving critical attention in domestic violence. *Violence and Victims, 14,* 1–23.

O'Leary, K. D., Slep, A. M. S., & O'Leary, S. G. (2007). Multivariate models of men's and women's partner aggression. *Journal of Consulting and Clinical Psychology, 75,* 752–764.

Olson, L. N., & Lloyd, S. A. (2005). "It depends on what you mean by starting": An exploration of how women define initiation of aggression and their motives for behaving aggressively. *Sex Roles, 53,* 603–617.

O'Neal, M. F., & Dorn, P. W. (1998). Effects of time and an educational presentation on student attitudes toward wife beating. *Violence and Victims, 13,* 149–157.

Orava, T. A., McLeod, P. J., & Sharpe, D. (1996). Perceptions of control, depressive symptomatology, and self-esteem of women in transition from abusive relationships. *Journal of Family Violence, 11,* 167–186.

Orloff, L. E., & Kelly, N. (1995). A look at the Violence Against Women Act and gender-related political asylum. *Violence Against Women, 1,* 380–400.

Orlov, R. (1997, July 24). Violence may cost officers. *Daily News,* p. 4.

Osofsky, J. D. (1998). Children as invisible victims of domestic and community violence. In G. W. Holden, R. Geffner, & E. N. Jouriles (Eds.), *Children exposed to domestic violence* (pp. 95–117). Washington, DC: American Psychological Association.

Osthoff, S. (1991). Restoring justice: Clemency for battered women. *Response, 14*(2), 2–3.

Osthoff, S. (2002). But, Gertrude, I beg to differ, a hit is not a hit is not a hit. *Violence Against Women, 8,* 1521–1544.

Ostrom, B., & Kauder, N. (Eds.). (1997). *Examining the work of state courts, 1996: A national perspective from the court statistics project* (National Center for State Courts 1997). Washington, DC: State Justice Institute and the Bureau of Justice Statistics.

O'Toole, L. L., & Schiffman, J. R. (Eds.). (1997). *Gender violence: Interdisciplinary perspectives.* New York, NY: New York University Press.

Ott, B. J., Graham, D. L. R., & Rawlings, E. I. (1990, August). *Stockholm syndrome in emotionally abused adult women.* Paper presented at the annual meeting of the American Psychological Association, Boston, MA.

Overholser, J. C. (1993). Idiographic, quantitative assessment of self-esteem. *Personality and Individual Differences, 14,* 639–646.

Pagelow, M. D. (1981a). Factors affecting women's decisions to leave violent relationships. *Journal of Family Issues, 2,* 391–414.

Painter, S. L., & Dutton, D. (1985). Patterns of emotional bonding in battered women: Traumatic bonding. *International Journal of Women's Studies, 57,* 101–110.

Palermo, G. B. (2010). Editorial: Parricide. *International Journal of Offender Therapy and Comparative Criminology, 54,* 3–5.

Panchanadeswaran, S., & McCloskey, L. A. (2007). Predicting the timing of women's departure from abusive relationships. *Journal of Interpersonal Violence, 22,* 50–65.

Panel says battered women may have no choice but retaliation. (1987, August 3). *Criminal Justice Newsletter, 18*(15), 6–7.

Pansera, C., & La Guardia, J. (2011). The role of sincere amends and perceived partner responsiveness in forgiveness. *Personal Relationships.* doi: 10.1111/j.1475-6811.2011.01386.x

Paquet, J., Damant, D., Beaudoin, G., & Proulx, S. (1998, July). *Domestic violence: Legal process and process of empowerment.* Paper presented at Program Evaluation and Family Violence Research: An International Conference, Durham, NH.

Parrot, A., & Bechhofer, L. (1991). *Acquaintance rape: The hidden crime.* New York, NY: Wiley.

Parrott, D. J., & Zeichner, A. (2003). Effects of hypermasculinity on physical aggression against women. *Psychology of Men and Masculinity, 4*(1), 70–78.

Pearson, J. (1997). Mediating when domestic violence is a factor: Policies and practices in court-based divorce mediation programs. *Mediation Quarterly, 14,* 319–335.

Pearson, J., Thoennes, N., & Griswold, E. A. (1999). Child support and domestic violence: The victims speak out. *Violence Against Women, 5*(Special issue), 427–448.

Pecora, P. J., Whitaker, J. K., Maluccio, A. N., Barth, R. P., & Plotnick, R. D. (1992). *The child welfare challenge: Policy, practice, and research.* Hawthorne, NY: Aldine.

Peled, E. (1993). Children who witness women battering: Concerns and dilemmas in the construction of a social problem. *Children and Youth Services Review, 15,* 43–52.

Pence, E. & Paymar, M. (1986). *Power and control: Tactics of men who batter.* Duluth: Minnesota Program Development.

Penley, J. A., Tomaka, J., & Wiebe, J. S. (2002). The association of coping to physical and psychological health outcomes: A meta-analytic review. *Journal of Behavioral Medicine, 25,* 551–603.

Pennebaker, J. W. (1991). Inhibition as the linchpin of health. In H. S. Friedman (Ed.), *Hostility coping and health* (pp. 127–140). Washington, DC: American Psychological Association.

Pennebaker, J. W., & Susman, J. R. (1988). Disclosure of traumas and psychosomatic process. *Social Stress and Medicine, 26,* 327–332.

Perez, S., Johnson, D. M., & Wright, C. V. (2012). The attenuating effect of empowerment on IPV-related PTSD symptoms in battered women living in domestic violence shelters. *Violence Against Women, 18,* 102–117.

Perry, B. D. (1994). Neurobiological sequelae of childhood trauma: Post-traumatic stress disorders in children. In M. Murberg (Ed.), *Catecholamines in post-traumatic stress disorder: Emerging concepts* (pp. 253–276).Washington, DC: American Psychiatric Press.

Perry, B. D. (1995). Incubated in terror: Neurodevelopmental factors in the cycle of violence. In J. Osofsky (Ed.), *Children, youth and violence: Searching for solutions.* New York, NY: Guilford.

Perry, B. D. (1996). *Maltreated children: Experience, brain development, and the next generation.* New York, NY: W. W. Norton.

Peterson, C., Maier, S. F., & Seligman, M. E. P. (1993). *Learned helplessness: A theory for the age of personal control.* New York, NY: Oxford University Press.

Peterson, C., & Seligman, M. E. P. (1984). Causal explanations as a risk factor for depression: Theory and evidence. *Psychological Review, 91,* 347–374.

Petretic-Jackson, P. A., & Jackson, T. (1996). Mental health interventions with battered women (pp. 188–221). In A. R. Roberts (Ed.), *Helping battered women: New perspectives and remedies.* New York, NY: Oxford.

Pharaon, N. A. (2004). Saudi women and the Muslim state in the twenty-first century. *Sex Roles, 51,* 349–366.

Phelan, M. B., Hamberger, L. K., Guse, C. E., Edwards, S., Walczak, S., & Zosel, A. (2005). Domestic violence among male and female patients seeking emergency medical services. *Violence and Victims, 20,* 187–206.

Pico-Alfonso, M. A. (2005). Psychological intimate partner violence: The major predictor of posttraumatic stress disorder in abused women. *Neuroscience, 29,* 181–193.

Pillemer, K. A., & Finkelhor, D. (1989). Causes of elder abuse: Caregiver stress versus problem relatives. *American Journal of Orthopsychiatry, 59,* 179–187.

Pipher, M. (1994). *Reviving Ophelia.* New York, NY: Ballantine.

Polusny, M. A., & Follette, V. M. (2008). Long-term correlates of child sexual abuse: Theory and review of the empirical literature. *Applied and Preventive Psychology, 4,* 143–166.

Postmus, J. L., Severson, M., Berry, M., & Yoo, J. A. (2009). Women's experiences of violence and seeking help. *Violence Against Women, 15,* 852–868.

Potter, H., & Thomas, D. T. (2012). "We told you that's how they are": Responses to white women in abusive intimate relationships with men of color. *Deviant Behavior, 33,* 469–491.

Poulos, A. M., Li, V., Sterlace, S. S., Tokushige, F., Ponnusamy, R., & Fanselow, M. S. (2009). Persistence of fear memory across time requires the basolateral amygdala complex. *Proceedings of the National Academy of Science, 106,* 11737–11741.

Powers, A., & Ryan, H. (2008, December). Sentencing reveals a contrite Simpson. *Los Angeles Times.*

Prange, R. C. (1985). Battered women and why they return to the abusive situation: A study of attribution-style, multiple-dimensional locus of control and social-psychological factors. *Dissertation Abstracts International, 46,* 4026B. (UMI No. 8522840)

Prasad, B. D. (1994). Dowry-related violence: A content analysis of news in selected newspapers. *Journal of Comparative Family Studies, 25*(1), 71–89.

President announces crackdown on violence against children. (1998, October 1). *Criminal Justice Newsletter, 29*(19), 6–7.

Procci, W. R. (1990). *Medical aspects of human sexuality* [Cited in *Behavior Today,* April 30, 1990, pp. 2–5]. New York, NY: Cahners.

Ptacek, J. (1988). Why do men batter their wives? In M. Bograd & K. Yllö (Eds.), *Feminist perspectives on wife abuse* (pp. 133–157). Beverly Hills, CA: Sage.

Pyles, L. (2007). The complexities of the religious response to domestic violence. *Affilia, 22,* 281–291.

Quindlen, A. (1992, February, 4). Editorial. *Long Beach Press Telegram,* p. 10.

Rabasca, L. (1999, February). Women addicts vulnerable to trauma. *APA Monitor, 30*(2), 32.

Radutsky, M. (1999, January 17). The war at home. In D. Hewitt (Producer), *60 minutes.* New York, NY: Columbia Broadcasting System.

Ragg, D. M., Sultana, M., & Miller, D. (1999, July). *The situational appraisals scales (SAS): Initial findings in the development of a measure of minimization for battered women.* Paper presented at the Sixth Family Violence Research Conference, Durham, NH.

Raghavan, C., Swan, S. C., Snow, D. L., & Mazur, C. M. (2005). The mediational role of relationship efficacy and resource utilization in the link between physical and psychological abuse and relationship termination. *Violence Against Women, 11,* 65–88.

Ramsey-Klawsnik, H. (2004, July/August). Clinical practice: Alleged victimization. *Victimization of the Elderly and Disabled, 7,* 17, 31–32.

Rand, M. R. (1997). *Violence-related injuries treated in hospital emergency departments* (NCJ Pub. No. 156921). Rockville, MD: U.S. Department of Justice, Bureau of Justice Statistics.

Rand, M. R. (2009, September). *National Crime Victimization Survey, criminal victimization, 2008* (NCJ Pub. No. 227777). U.S. Department of Justice, Bureau of Justice Statistics.

Rand, M. R., & Harrell, E. (2009). *Crime against people with disabilities, 2007* (NCJ Pub. No. 227814). U.S. Department of Justice, NCVS.

Rand, M. R., & Saltzman, L. E. (2003). The nature and extent of recurring intimate partner violence against women in the United States. *Journal of Comparative Family Studies, 34,* 137–149.

Raphael, J. (1999). The family violence option: An early assessment. *Violence Against Women, 5,* 449–466.

Raphael, J., & Tolman, R. M. (1997). *Trapped by poverty/trapped by abuse: New evidence documents the relationship between domestic violence and welfare.* Ann Arbor, MI: Taylor Institute and the University of Michigan.

Rastogi, M., & Therly, P. (2006). Dowry and its link to violence against women in India. *Trauma, Violence, & Abuse, 7,* 66–77.

Rausch, S. L., van der Kolk, B. A., Fisler, R. F., & Alpert, N. M. (1996). A symptom provocation study of posttraumatic stress disorder using positron emission tomography and script-driven imagery. *Archives of General Psychiatry, 53,* 380–387.

Rawlings, E. I., Allen, G., Graham, D. L. R., & Peters, J. (1994). Chinks in the prison wall: Applying Graham's Stockholm syndrome theory in the treatment of battered women. In L. Vandecreek, S. Knapp, & T. Jackson (Eds.), *Innovations in clinical practice: A source book* (Vol. 13, pp. 401–417). Sarasota, FL: Professional Resource Press.

Reingold, D. A. (2006). An elder abuse shelter program: Build it and they will come, a long term care based program to address elder abuse in the community. *Journal of Gerontological Social Work, 46,* 123–135.

Reis, M. (2000). The IOA Screen: An abuse-alert measure that dispels myths. *Generations, 24*(6), 13–16.

Rennison, C. M., & Welchans, S. (2000). *Intimate partner violence* (NCJ Pub. No. 178247). Washington, DC: U.S. Department of Justice.

Renzetti, C. M. (1989). Building a second closet: Third party responses to victims of lesbian partner abuse. *Family Relations, 38,* 157–163.

Renzetti, C. M. (1992). *Violent betrayal: Partner abuse in lesbian relationships.* Newbury Park, CA: Sage.

Rescorla, R. A., & Solomon, R. L. (1967). Two-process learning theory: Relations between Pavlovian conditioning and instrumental learning. *Psychological Review, 74,* 151–182.

Resnick, H. S., Kilpatrick, D., Dansky, B. S., Saunders, B. E., & Best, C. L. (1993). Prevalence of civilian trauma and posttraumatic stress disorder in a representative national sample of women. *Journal of Consulting and Clinical Psychology, 61,* 984–991.

Reyes, K. (1999, Spring). Domestic violence prevention for clergy proves slow-going. *Focus, 4,* 1–3.

Reyna, P. (1995, Fall). Underserved populations have critical needs. *Update: Newsletter of the Southern California Coalition on Battered Women, 1*(5), 6.

Rhatigan, D. L., Moore, T. M., & Stuart, G. L. (2005). An investment model analysis of relationship stability among women court-mandated to violence interventions. *Psychology of Women Quarterly, 29,* 313–322.

Rhatigan, D. L., & Nathanson, A. M. (2010). The role of female behavior and attributions in predicting behavioral responses to hypothetical male aggression. *Violence Against Women, 16,* 621–637.

Rhodes, N. R. (1992). Comparison of MMPI Psychopathic Deviate scores of battered and nonbattered women. *Journal of Family Violence, 7,* 297–307.

Rhodes, N. R., & McKenzie, E. B. (1998). Why do battered women stay? Three decades of research. *Aggression and Violent Behavior, 3,* 391–406.

Rich, A. (1976). *Of woman born.* New York, NY: W. W. Norton.

Riek, B. B., & Mania, E. W. (2011). The antecedents and consequences of interpersonal forgiveness: A meta-analytic review. *Personal Relationships, 76,* 677–685.

Rigakos, G. S. (1995). Constructing the symbolic complainant: Police subculture and the nonenforcement of protection orders for battered women. *Violence and Victims, 10,* 227–247.

Riger, S., & Kreglstein, M. (2000). The impact of welfare reform on men's violence against women. *American Journal of Community Psychology, 28,* 631–647.

Riger, S., Raja, S., & Camacho, J. (2002). The radiating impact of intimate partner violence. *Journal of Interpersonal Violence, 17,* 184–205.

Riggs, D. S., Kilpatrick, D., & Resnick, H. S. (1992). Long-term psychological distress associated with marital rape and aggravated assault: A comparison to other crime victims. *Journal of Family Violence, 7,* 283–296.

Riggs, D. S., Murphy, C. M., & O'Leary, K. D. (1989). Intentional falsification in reports of interpartner aggression. *Journal of Interpersonal Violence, 4,* 220–232.

Rodriguez, M., Valentine, J. M., Son, J. B., & Muhammad, M. (2009). Intimate partner violence and barriers to mental health care for ethnically diverse populations of women. *Trauma, Violence, & Abuse, 10,* 358–374.

Rogers, P., Krammer, L., Podesta, J. S., & Sellinger, M. (1998, August 31). Angry and hurt, but no quitter. *People Weekly, 50*(7), 61–62, 64.

Rogers, S. J. (1999). Wives' income and marital quality: Are there reciprocal effects? *Journal of Marriage and the Family, 61,* 123–132.

Roiphe, A. (1986, September). Women who make sacrifices for their men. *Cosmopolitan, 201,* 308–313, 319.

Roloff, M. E., Soule, K. P., & Carey, C. M. (2001). Reasons for remaining in a relationship and responses to relational transgressions. *Journal of Social and Personal Relationships, 18,* 362–385.

Rosen, L. N., Parmley, A. M., Knudson, K. H., & Fancher, P. (2002). Intimate partner violence among married male U.S. Army soldiers: Ethnicity as a factor in self-reported perpetration and victimization. *Violence and Victims, 17,* 607–622.

Rosenblum, L. A., & Harlow, H. F. (1963). Approach-avoidance conflict in the mother surrogate situation. *Psychological Reports, 12,* 83–85.

Rossman, B. B. R. (1998). Descartes' error and posttraumatic stress disorder: Cognition and emotion in children who are exposed to parental violence. In Holden (Ed.), *Children exposed to marital violence* (pp. 223–256). Washington, DC: American Psychological Association.

Rotheram-Bokes, M. J., Rosario, N., & Koopman, C. (1991). Minority youths at high risk: Gay males and runaways (pp. 181–200). In M. E. Colton & S. Gore (Eds.), *Adolescent stress: Causes and consequences* (pp. 181–200). New York, NY: Aldine de Gruyter.

Rothman, E. F., Hathaway, J., Stidsen, A., & de Vries, H. F. (2007). How employment helps female victims of intimate partner violence: A qualitative study. *Journal of Occupational Health Psychology, 12,* 136–143.

Rowe, B. R., & Lown, J. M. (1990). The economics of divorce and remarriage for rural Utah families. *Journal of Contemporary Law, 16,* 301–332.

Ruether, R. R. (1983). *Sexism and God-talk: Toward a feminist theology.* Boston, MA: Beacon Press.

Rusbult, C. E. (1980) Commitment and satisfaction in romantic associations: A test of the investment model. *Journal of Experimental Social Psychology, 45,* 101–117.

Russell, B., & Uhlemann, M. R. (1994). Women surviving an abusive relationship: Grief and the process of change. *Journal of Counseling and Development, 72,* 362–367.

Russell, D., Springer, K. W., & Greenfield, E. A. (2010). Witnessing domestic abuse in childhood as an independent risk factor for depressive symptoms in young adulthood. *Child Abuse & Neglect, 34,* 448–453.

Russell, D. E. H. (1983). The prevalence and incidence of forcible rape and attempted rape of females. *Victimology: An International Journal, 7,* 81–93.

Russell, M. N., Lipov, E., Phillips, N., & White, B. (1989). Psychological profiles of violent and nonviolent maritally distressed couples. *Psychotherapy, 26,* 81–87.

Sabina, C., & Straus, M. A. (2008). Polyvictimization by dating partners and mental health among U.S. college students. *Violence and Victims, 23,* 667–682.

Saewyc, E. M., Pettingell, S., & Magee, L. L. (2003). The prevalence of sexual abuse among adolescents in school. *Journal of School Nursing, 19,* 266–272.

Samp, J. A., & Abbott, L. (2011). Help-seeking in a national sample of victimized Latino women: The influence of victimization types. *Journal of Interpersonal Violence, 27,* 40–61.

Sanders, B., & Moore, D. L. (1999). Childhood maltreatment and date rape. *Journal of Interpersonal Violence, 14,* 115–124.

Sanders, L. (2011, May 7). Shocked to learn that talk is cheap. *Science News, 179,* 18.

Sandler, J., Davidson, R. S., Greene, W. E., & Holzschuh, R. D. (1966). Effects of punishment intensity on instrumental avoidance behavior. *Journal of Comparative and Physiological Psychology, 61,* 212–216.

Sankaran, V. (2011). Preventing the unnecessary entry of children into foster care. *Michigan Bar Journal, 90,* 41.

Sansone, R. A., Wiederman, M. W., & Sansone, L. A. (1997). Health care utilization and history of trauma among women in a primary care setting. *Violence and Victims, 12,* 165–172.

Sapiente, A. A. (1988). Locus of control and causal attributions of maritally violent men. *Dissertation Abstracts International, 50,* 758B. (UMI No. 8822697)

Saunders, D. (1986). When battered women use violence: Husband-abuse or self-defense? *Violence and Victims, 1,* 47–60.

Saunders, D. (1989, November). *Who hits first and who hurts most? Evidence for the greater victimization of women in intimate relationships.* Paper presented at the annual meeting of the American Society of Criminology, Reno, NV.

Saunders, D. (1994). Posttraumatic stress symptom profiles of battered women: A comparison of survivors in two settings. *Violence and Victims, 9,* 31–44.

Saunders, D., Hamberger, L. K., & Hovey, M. (1993). Indicators of woman abuse based on a chart review at a family practice center. *Archives of Family Medicine, 2,* 537–543.

Schiff, M., Gilbert, L., & El-Bassel, N. (2006). Perceived positive aspects of intimate relationships among abused women in methadone maintenance treatment programs (MMTP). *Journal of Interpersonal Violence, 21,* 121–138.

Schindehette, S. (1998, September 7). High infidelity. *People Weekly, 50*(8), 52–59.

Schneider, E. M. (1986). Describing and changing: Women's self-defense work and the problem of expert testimony on battering. *Women's Rights Law Reporter, 9*(3&4), 195–222.

Schneider, E. M., & Jordan, S. B. (1978). Representation of women who defend themselves in response to physical or sexual assault. *Family Law Review, 1,* 118–132.

Schornstein, S. L. (1997). *Domestic violence and health care: What every professional needs to know.* Thousand Oaks, CA: Sage.

Schuler, S. R., Hashemi, S. M., Riley, A. P., & Akhter, S. (1996). Credit programs, patriarchy and men's violence against women in rural Bangladesh. *Social Science and Medicine, 43,* 1729–1742.

Schuler, S. R., Trang, Q. T., Ha, V. S., & Anh, H. T. (2011). Qualitative study of an operations research project to engage abused women, health providers, and communities in responding to gender-based violence in Vietnam. *Violence Against Women, 17,* 1421–1441.

Schuller, R. A., & Vidmar, N. (1992). Battered woman syndrome evidence in the courtroom: A review of the literature. *Law and Human Behavior, 16,* 273–291.

Schumacher, J. A., Homish, G. G., Leonard, K. E., Quigley, B. M., & Kearns-Bodkin, J. N. (2008). Longitudinal moderators of the relationship between excessive drinking and intimate partner violence in the early years of marriage. *Journal of Family Psychology, 22,* 894–904.

Schwartz, M. D. (1988). Marital status and woman abuse theory. *Journal of Family Violence, 3,* 239–248.

Schwartz, M. D., & DeKeseredy, W. S. (1993). The return of the "battered husband syndrome" through typification of women as violent. *Crime, Law and Social Change, 20,* 249–265.

Seamans, C. L., Rubin, L. J., & Stabb, S. D. (2007). Women domestic violence offenders: Lessons of violence and survival. *Journal of Trauma and Dissociation, 8,* 47–68.

Sedlak, A. J. (1988). The effects of personal experiences with couple violence on calling it "battering" and allocating blame. In G. T. Hotaling, D. Finkelhor, J. T. Kirkpatrick, & Straus (Eds.), *Coping with family violence* (pp. 31–59). Newbury Park, CA: Sage.

Sedlak, A. J., Mettenberg, J., Basena, M., Petta, I., McPherson, K., Greene, A., & Li, S. (2010). *Fourth National Incidence Study of Child Abuse and Neglect (NIS-4): Report to Congress, executive summary.* Washington, DC: U.S. Department of Health and Human Services, Administration for Children and Families.

Seedat. S., Stein, M. B., & Forde, D. (2005). Association between physical partner violence, posttraumatic stress, childhood trauma, and suicide attempts in a community sample of women. *Violence and Victims, 20,* 87–98.

Seidman, G. (2011). Positive and negative: Partner derogation and enhancement differentially related to relationship satisfaction. *Journal of Personality, 70,* 1079–1112.

Seligman, M. E. P. (1968). Chronic fear produced by unpredictable electric shock. *Journal of Comparative and Physiological Psychology, 66,* 402–411.

Seligman, M. E. P. (1975). *Helplessness: On depression, development and death.* San Francisco, CA: Freeman.

Seligman, M. E. P., & Meyer, B. (1970). Chronic fear and ulcers in rats as a function of the unpredictability of safety. *Journal of Comparative and Physiological Psychology, 73,* 202–207.

Selye, H. (1946). The general adaptation syndrome. *Journal of Clinical Endocrinology, 6,* 117–230.

Shannon, L., Logan, T., Cole, J., & Medley, K. (2006). Helpseeking and coping strategies for intimate partner violence in rural and urban women. *Violence and Victims, 21,* 167–181.

Sharps, P., Campbell, J. C., Campbell, D., Gary, F., & Webster, D. (2003). Risky mix: Drinking, drug use, and homicide. *National Institute of Justice Journal, 250,* 8–12.

Sharps, P., McLain, J., Campbell, J., McFarlane, J., Sachs, C., & Xu, X. (2001). Health care providers' missed opportunities for preventing femicide. *Journal of Preventive Medicine, 33*(11), 373–380.

Shechory, M. (2012). Attachment styles, coping strategies, and romantic feelings among battered women in shelters. *International Journal of Offender Therapy and Comparative Criminology.* doi: 10.1177/0306624X11434917

Shepherd, J. (1990). Victims of personal violence: The relevance of Symonds' model of psychological response and loss theory. *British Journal of Social Work, 20,* 309–332.

Sheridan, D. J., & Nash, K. R. (2007). Acute injury patterns of intimate partner violence victims. *Trauma, Violence, & Abuse, 8,* 281–289.

Sheridan, L. P., Gillett, R., Blaauw, E., Davies, G. M., & Patel, D. (2003). "There's no smoke without fire": Are male ex-partners perceived as more "entitled" to stalk than stranger or acquaintance stalkers? *British Journal of Psychology, 94,* 87–98.

Sheriff won't contest domestic violence law. (1996, December 29). *Daily News,* p. 16.

Sherman, L. W. (1992). *Policing domestic violence: Experiments and dilemmas.* New York, NY: Free Press.

Sherman, L. W., Schmidt, J. D., Rogan, D. P., Gartin, P. R., Cohn, E. G., Collins, D. J., & Bacich, A. R. (1991). From initial deterrence to long-term escalation: Short-custody arrest for poverty ghetto domestic violence. *Criminology, 29,* 821–850.

Shiemke, R. E. (2011). Domestic violence legal remedies in others states. *Michigan Bar Journal, 90,* 36–38.

Shilling, D. (2008, November/December). Improving the court system's response to elder abuse. *Victimization of the Elderly and Disabled, 11,* 49, 51–52, 59, 62–63.

Shir, J. S. (1999). Battered women's perceptions and expectations of their current and ideal marital relationship. *Journal of Family Violence, 14,* 71–82.

Shortt, J. W., Capaldi, D. M., Kim, H. K., & Owen, L. D. (2006). Relationship separation for young, at-risk couples: Prediction from dyadic aggression. *Journal of Family Psychology, 20,* 624–631.

Sidman, M. (1953). Two temporal parameters of the maintenance of avoidance behavior by the white rat. *Journal of Comparative and Physiological Psychology, 46,* 253–261.

Sierra, L. (1997, December). Representing battered women charged with crimes for failing to protect their children from abusive partners. *Double-Time, 5*(1&2), 1, 4–7.

Sigler, R. T., & Lamb, D. (1995, June). Community-based alternatives to prison: How the public and court personnel view them. *Federal Probation,* pp. 3–9.

Silverstein, L. B. (1996). Fathering is a feminist issue. *Psychology of Women Quarterly, 20,* 3–37.

Simon, T. R., Kresnow, M. J., & Bossarte, R. M. (2008). Self-reports of violent victimization among U.S. adults. *Violence and Victims, 23,* 711–726.

Simoneti, S., Scott, E. C., & Murphy, C. M. (2000). Dissociative experiences in partner-assaultive men. *Journal of Interpersonal Violence, 15,* 1262–1283.

Simons, R. L., Wu, C.-I., Johnson, C., & Conger, R. D. (1995). A test of various perspectives on the intergenerational transmission of domestic violence. *Criminology, 33,* 141–170.

Simpson, L. E., Atkins, D. C., Gattis, K. S., & Christensen, A. (2008). Low-level relationship aggression and couple therapy outcomes. *Journal of Family Psychology, 22,* 102–111.

Sirles, E. A., Lipchik, E., & Kowalski, K. (1993). A consumer's perspective on domestic violence intervention. *Journal of Family Violence, 8,* 267–276.

Skinner, B. F. (1938). *The behavior of organisms.* New York, NY: Appleton-Century-Crofts.

Sledjeski, E. M., Speisman, B., & Dierker, L. C. (2008). Does the number of lifetime traumas explain the relationship between PTSD and chronic medical conditions? Answers from the National Comorbidity Survey-Replication (NCS-R). *Central European Journal of Medicine, 31,* 341–349.

Slocum, L. A., Rengifo, A. F., & Carbone-Lopez, K. (2012). Specifying the strain-violence link: The role of emotions in women's descriptions of violent incidents. *Violence and Victims, 7,* 1–29.

Small, M. A., & Tetreault, P. A. (1990). Social psychology, "marital rape exemptions," and privacy. *Behavioral Sciences and the Law, 8,* 141–149.

Smeal, E. (2011, Winter). The gender gap lives. *Ms. Magazine,* p. 15.

Smith, C. (1988). *Status discrepancies and husband-to-wife violence.* Durham, NH: University of New Hampshire, Family Violence Research Program.

Smith, E. L., & Farole, D. J., Jr. (2009). *Profiles of intimate partner violence cases in large urban counties* (NCJ Pub. No. 228193). Washington, DC: U.S. Department of Justice, Bureau of Justice Statistics.

Smith, M. D. (1990). Patriarchal ideology and wife beating: A test of a feminist hypothesis. *Violence and Victims, 5,* 257–273.

Smith, P. H., Danis, M., & Helmick, L. (1998). Changing the health care response to battered women: A health education approach. *Family and Community Health, 20*(4), 1–18.

Smith, S. (1984). The battered woman: A consequence of female development. *Women and Therapy, 3*(2), 3–9.

Snodgrass, S. E. (1990, August). *Sex role stereotypes are alive and well.* Paper presented at the meeting of the American Psychological Association, Boston, MA.

Snyder, H. N., & McCurley, C. (2008). *Domestic assaults by juvenile offenders.* Washington, DC: Office of Juvenile Justice, Delinquency Prevention.

Solomon, R. L., Kamin, L. J., & Wynne, L. C. (1953). Traumatic avoidance learning: The outcomes of several extinction procedures with dogs. *Journal of Abnormal and Social Psychology, 48,* 291–302.

Somer, E., & Braunstein, A. (1999). Are children exposed to interparental violence being psychologically maltreated? *Aggression and Violent Behavior, 4,* 449–456.

Sorensen, D. D. (2004, July/August). Invisible victims 2003. *Victimization of the Elderly and Disabled, 7,* 17–18, 28–30.

Sorensen, E., Goldman, J., Ward, M., Albanese, I., Graves, L., & Chamberlain, C. (1995). Judicial decision-making in contested custody cases: The influence of reported child abuse, spouse abuse, and parental substance abuse. *Child Abuse & Neglect, 19,* 251–260.

Sorenson, S. B., & Telles, C. A. (1991). Self-reports of spousal violence in a Mexican-American and non-Hispanic white population. *Violence and Victims, 6,* 3–15.

Southworth, C., Finn, J., Dawson, S., Fraser, C., & Tucker, S. (2007). Intimate partner violence, technology, and stalking. *Violence Against Women, 13,* 842–856.

Sparr, L. E. (1996). Mental defense and posttraumatic stress disorder: Assessment of criminal intent. *Journal of Traumatic Stress, 9,* 405–425.

Spitzberg, B. H. (2002). The tactical topography of stalking victimization and management. *Trauma, Violence, & Abuse, 30,* 261–288.

Spitzberg, B. H., & Hoobler, G. (2002). Cyberstalking and the technologies of interpersonal terrorism. *New Media and Society, 4,* 71–92.

Stacey, W. A., & Shupe, A. (1983). *The family secret.* Boston, MA: Beacon Press.

Stahl, P. (2004). A historical perspective on child custody evaluations. *Journal of Child Custody, 1,* 9–18.

Stahmer, A. C., Sutton, D. T., Fox, L., & Leslie, L. K. (2008). State Part C agency practices and the Child Abuse Prevention and Treatment Act (CAPTA). *Topics in Early Childhood Special Education, 28,* 99–108.

Stalans, L. J., & Ritchie, J. (2008). Relationship of substance use/abuse with psychological and physical intimate partner violence: Variations across living situations. *Journal of Family Violence, 23*, 9–24.

Stanko, E. A. (1988). Fear of crime and the myth of the safe home: A feminist critique of criminology. In K. Yllö & M. Bograd (Eds.), *Feminist perspectives on wife abuse* (pp. 75–88). Newbury Park, CA: Sage.

Stanley, N., Miller, P., & Richardson-Foster, H. (2012). Engaging with children's and parents' perspectives on domestic violence. *Child and Family Social Work.* doi: 10.1111/j.1365-2206.2012.00832.x

Stanton, E. C., Anthony, S. B., & Gage, M. J. (Eds.). (1889). *History of women suffrage* (Vol. 1, pp. 1848–1861). New York, NY: Fowler & Wells. (Original work published 1881)

Stark, E. (1993). Mandatory arrest of batterers. *American Behavioral Scientist, 36*, 651–680.

Stark, E. (2007). *Coercive control: How men entrap women in personal life.* New York, NY: Oxford University Press.

Starkey, J. (2009). Afghan leader accused of bid to "legalise rape." *Independent.* Retrieved from www.independent.co.uk/news

Stein, D. J., van der Kolk, B., Austin, C., Fallad, R., & Clary, C. (2006). Efficacy of sertraline in posttraumatic stress disorder secondary to interpersonal trauma or childhood abuse. *Annals of Clinical Psychiatry, 18*, 243–249.

Steiner, J. (1966). *Treblinka.* New York, NY: New American Library.

Steinmetz, S. K. (1977). The battered husband syndrome. *Victimology: An International Journal, 2*(3&4), 499–509.

Stenius, V. M., & Veysey, B. M. (2005). "It's the little things": Women, trauma, and strategies for healing. *Journal of Interpersonal Violence, 20*, 1153–1174.

Stevens, R. S. (2011). Domestic violence research resources for Michigan attorney. *Michigan Bar Journal, 90*, 52–53.

Stickley, A., Kislitsyna, O., Timofeeva, I., & Vågerö, D. (2008a). Attitudes toward intimate partner violence against women in Moscow, Russia. *Journal of Family Violence, 23*, 447–456.

Stiegel, L. A. (2001). *Financial abuse of the elderly: Risk factors, screening techniques, and remedies.* Chicago: American Bar Association, Commission on Legal Problems of the Elderly. Retrieved December 8, 2003, from www.abanet .org/elderly/financial_abuse_of_the_elderly.doc

Stith, S. M., Rosen, K. H., Middleton, K. A., Busch, A. L., Lundberg, K., & Carlton, R. P. (2000). The intergenerational transmission of spouse abuse: A meta-analysis. *Journal of Marriage and the Family, 62*, 640–654.

Stokoe, E. (2010). "I'm not gonna hit a lady": Conversation analysis, membership categorization and men's denials of violence towards women. *Discourse and Society, 21*, 59–82.

Stone, A. E., & Fialk, R. J. (1999, December/January). Backlash against the abused victim in custody disputes. *Domestic Violence Report, 4*, 1, 26–27.

Strand, S. (2012). Using a restraining order as a protective risk management strategy to prevent intimate partner violence. *Police Practice and Research: An International Journal, 13*(Special issue), 254–266.

Strand, V. C. (2000). *Treating secondary victims: Intervention with the nonoffending mother in the incest family*. Thousand Oaks, CA: Sage.

Straus, M. A. (1979). Measuring intrafamily conflict and aggression: The Conflict Tactics scale (CT). *Journal of Marriage and the Family, 41,* 75–88.

Straus, M. A. (1991a, July). *Incidence and chronicity of assaults by wives on husbands: Implications for primary prevention of wife-beating* (VB33. P2,VB131.24). Durham, NH: University of New Hampshire. (Unpublished manuscript)

Straus, M. A. (1991b, September). *Children as witnesses to marital violence: A risk factor for lifelong problems among a nationally representative sample of American men and women*. Paper presented at the Ross Roundtable on Children and Violence, Washington, DC.

Straus, M. A. (1993). Physical assaults by wives: A major social problem. In R. J. Gelles & D. J. Loseke (Eds.), *Current controversies on family violence* (pp. 67–87). Newbury Park, CA: Sage.

Straus, M. A. (1997). Physical assaults by women partners: A major social problem. In M. R. Walsh (Ed.), *Women, men, and gender: Ongoing debates* (pp. 210–221). New Haven, CT: Yale University Press.

Straus, M. A., & Gelles, R. J. (1986). Societal change and change in family violence from 1975 to 1985 as revealed by two national surveys. *Journal of Marriage and the Family, 48,* 465–479.

Straus, M. A., & Gelles, R. J. (1990). *Physical violence in American families: Risk factors and adaptations to violence in 8,145 families*. New Brunswick, NJ: Transaction.

Straus, R. B. (1995). Supervised visitation and family violence. *Family Law Quarterly, 29*(Special issue), 229–252.

Strelan, P., McKee, I., Calic, D., Cook, L., & Shaw, L. (2012). For whom do we forgive? A functional analysis of forgiveness. *Personal Relationships.* doi: 10.1111/j.1475-6811.2012.01400.x

Strentz, T. (1979, April). Law enforcement policy and ego defenses of the hostage. *FBI Law Enforcement Bulletin,* pp. 2–12.

Strom, T. O., & Kosciulek, J. (2007). Stress, appraisal and coping following mild traumatic brain injury. *Brain Injury, 21,* 1137–1145.

Stroshine, M. S., & Robinson, A. L. (2003). The decision to end abusive relationships: The role of offender characteristics. *Criminal Justice and Behavior, 30,* 97–117.

Strube, M. J., & Barbour, L. S. (1984). Factors related to the decision to leave an abusive relationship. *Journal of Marriage and the Family, 46,* 837–844.

Stuart, G. L., Moore, T. M., Hellmuth, J. C., Ramsey, S. E., & Kahler, C. W. (2006). Reasons for intimate partner violence perpetration among arrested women. *Violence Against Women, 12,* 609–621.

Stubbing, E. (1990). Police who think family homicide is preventable are pointing the way. *Response, 13*(1), 8.

Stuckless, N. (1998). *The influence of anger, perceived injustice, revenge, and time on the quality of life of survivor-victim* [CD-ROM]. Abstract retrieved from ProQuest, Dissertation Abstracts Item No. NN20428.

Suarez, K. E. (1994). Teenage dating violence: The need for expanded awareness and legislation. *California Law Review, 82,* 423–471.

Suh, E. K., & Abel, E. M. (1990). The impact of spousal violence on the children of the abused. *Journal of Individual Social Work, 4,* 27–34.

Sullivan, C. M., Basta, J., Tan, C., & Davidson, W. S., II. (1992). After the crisis: A needs assessment of women leaving a domestic violence shelter. *Violence and Victims, 7,* 271–280.

Sullivan, C. M., & Bybee, D. I. (1999). Reducing violence using community-based advocacy for women with abusive partners. *Journal of Consulting and Clinical Psychology, 67,* 43–53.

Sullivan, C. M., Rumptz, M. H., Campbell, R., Eby, K., & Davidson, W. S., II. (1996). Retaining participants in longitudinal community research: A comprehensive protocol. *Journal of Applied Behavioral Science, 32,* 262–276.

Sullivan, C. M., Tan, C., Basta, J., Rumptz, M., & Davidson, W. S., II. (1992). An advocacy intervention program for women with abusive partners: Initial evaluation. *American Journal of Community Psychology, 30,* 309–332.

Swan, S. C., & Snow, D. L. (2002). A typology of women's use of violence in intimate relationships. *Violence Against Women, 8,* 286–319.

Swanberg, J. E., Logan, T. K., & Macke, C. (2005). Intimate partner violence, employment, and the workplace. *Trauma, Violence, & Abuse, 6,* 286–312.

Sweeny, K., Carroll, P. J., & Shepperd, J. A. (2006). Is optimism always best? Future outlooks and preparedness. *Current Directions in Psychological Science, 15,* 302–306.

Swenson, S. V. (1984). Effects of sex-role stereotypes and androgynous alternatives in mental health judgments of psychotherapists. *Psychological Reports, 54,* 475–481.

Syers, M., & Edleson, J. L. (1992). The combined effects of coordinated criminal justice intervention in woman abuse. *Journal of Interpersonal Violence, 7,* 490–502.

Symonds, A. (1979). Violence against women: The myth of masochism. *American Journal of Psychotherapy, 23,* 161–173.

Szinovacz, M. E. (1983). Using couple data as a methodological tool: The case of marital violence. *Journal of Marriage and the Family, 45,* 633–644.

Taft, C. T., O'Farrell, T. K., Torres, S. E., Panuzio, J., Monson, C. M., Murphy, M., & Murphy, C. M. (2006). Examining the correlates of psychological aggression among a community sample of couples. *Journal of Family Psychology, 20,* 581–588.

Taft, C. T., Street, A. E., Marshall, A. D., Dowdall, D. J., & Riggs, D. S. (2007). Posttraumatic stress disorder, anger, and partner abuse among Vietnam combat veterans. *Journal of Family Psychology, 21,* 270–277.

Tan, C., Basta, J., Sullivan, C. M., & Davidson, W. S. (1995). The role of social support in the lives of women exiting domestic violence shelters. *Journal of Interpersonal Violence, 10,* 437–451.

Tatara, T., & Kuzmeskus, L. (1999). *Types of elder abuse in domestic settings.* Washington, DC: National Center on Elder Abuse.

Tavris, C. (1992). *The mismeasure of woman.* New York, NY: Simon and Schuster.

Teaster, P. B., Otto, J. M., Dugar, T. A., Mendiondo, M. S., Abner, E. L., & Cecil, K. A. (2006). *Abuse of adults age 60+: The 2004 survey of state adult protective services*. Retrieved from National Center on Elder Abuse website: www .elderabusecenter.org

Teichroeb, R. (2009, January 7). McKenna targets repeat batterers. *Seattle Post-Intelligencer*, p. A8.

Temple, J. R., Weston, R., & Marshall, L. L. (2005). Physical and mental health outcomes of women in non-violent, unilaterally violent, and mutually violent relationships. *Violence and Victims, 20*, 335–359.

Temple, J. R., Weston, R., Rodrigues, B. F., & Marshall, L. L. (2007). Differing effects of partner and nonpartner sexual assault on women's mental health. *Violence Against Women, 13*, 285–297.

Thapar-Björkert, S., & Morgan, K. J. (2010). "But sometimes I think . . . they put themselves in the situation": Exploring blame and responsibility in interpersonal violence. *Violence Against Women, 16*, 32–59.

Theodore, R. M. (1992). The relationship between locus of control and level of violence in married couples. In E. C. Viano (Ed.), *Intimate violence: Interdisciplinary perspectives* (pp. 37–48). Bristol, PA: Taylor & Francis.

Thoits, P. A. (1982). Conceptual, methodological, and theoretical problems in studying practical implications. *Journal of Personality and Social Psychology, 52*, 813–832.

Thompson, C. (1989). Breaking through walls of isolation: A model for churches in helping victims of violence. *Pastoral Psychology, 38*, 35–38.

Thompson-McCormick, J., Jones, L., & Livingston, G. (2009). Medical students: Recognition of elder abuse. *International Journal of Geriatric Psychiatry, 24*, 770–777.

Three deputies get domestic violence convictions sealed. (1997, May 1). *Daily News*, p. 6.

Tiefenthaler, J., Farmer, A., & Sambria, A. (2005). Services and intimate partner violence in the United States: A county-level analysis. *Journal of Marriage and Family, 67*, 565–578.

Tierney, K. J. (1982). The battered women movement and the creation of the wife beating problem. *Social Problems, 29*, 207–220.

Tinsley, C. A., Critelli, J. W., & Ee, J. S. (1992, August). *The perception of sexual aggression: One act, two realities*. Paper presented at the annual meeting of the American Psychological Association, Washington, DC.

Tjaden, P., & Thoennes, N. (1998a, November). *Prevalence, incidence, and consequences of violence against women: Findings from the National Violence Against Women Survey* (NCJ Pub. No. 172837). Washington, DC: U.S. Department of Justice, National Institute of Justice.

Tjaden, P., & Thoennes, N. (1998b). *Stalking in America: Findings from the National Violence Against Women Survey* (NCJ Pub. No. 169592). Washington, DC: U.S. Department of Justice.

Tjaden, P., & Thoennes, N. (2000). *Extent, nature, and consequences of intimate partner violence* (NCJ Pub. No. 181867). Washington, DC: U.S. Department of Justice.

Todahl, J. L., Linville, D., Bustin, A., Wheeler, J., & Gau, J. (2009). Sexual assault support services and community systems: Understanding critical issues and needs in the LGBTQ community. *Violence Against Women, 15,* 952–976.

Toews, M. L., McHenry, P. C., & Catless, B. S. (2003). Male-initiated partner abuse during marital separation prior to divorce. *Violence and Victims, 18,* 387–402.

Tollefson, D. R. (2002, March). Factors associated with batterer treatment success and failure. *Dissertation Abstracts International, 62,* 3191A. (UMI No. 3026165)

Tolman, R. M. (1999). Guest editor's introduction. *Violence Against Women, 5*(4, Special issue), 355–369.

Tomkins, A. J., Mohamed, S., Steinman, M., Macolini, R. M., Kenning, M. K., & Afrank, J. (1994). The plight of children who witness woman battering: Psychological knowledge and policy implications. *Law and Psychology Review, 18,* 137–187.

Tomz, J. E., & McGillis, D. (1997, February). *Serving crime victims and witnesses* (2nd ed.) (NCJ Pub. No. 163174). Washington, DC: U.S. Department of Justice.

Towns, A., & Adams, P. (2000). "If I really loved him enough, he would be okay." *Violence Against Women, 6,* 558–585.

Trimpey, M. L. (1989). Self-esteem and anxiety: Key issues in an abused women's support group. *Issues in Mental Health Nursing, 10,* 297–308.

Trull, T. J. (2001). Structural relations between borderline personality disorder features and putative etiological correlates. *Journal of Abnormal Psychology, 110,* 471–481.

Tsesis, A. V. (1996). Preventing homelessness by empowering battered women through vocational opportunities. *Domestic Violence Report, 1*(5), 3, 12–13.

Tucker, N. (1999, April 14). Zimbabwe women stripped of rights. *Press-Telegram,* pp. A13–A14.

Tuel, B. D., & Russell, R. K. (1998). Self-esteem and depression in battered women: A comparison of lesbian and heterosexual survivors. *Violence Against Women, 4,* 344–362.

Turkat, I. D. (1995). Divorce-related malicious mother syndrome. *Journal of Family Violence, 10,* 253–264.

Turkat, I. D. (1999). Divorce-related malicious parent syndrome. *Journal of Family Violence, 14,* 95–97.

Turner, H. A., Finkelhor, D., & Ormrod, R. (2010). Child mental health problems as risk factors for victimization. *Child Maltreatment, 15,* 132–143.

Turque, B., Murr, A., Miller, M., Foote, D., Fleming, C., Biddle, N. A., . . . Namuth, T. (1994, June). He could run . . . but he couldn't hide. *Newsweek, 123*(26), 12–27.

Tutty, L. M., Bidgood, B. A., Rothery, M. A., & Bidgood, P. (2001). An evaluation of men's batterer treatment groups. *Research on Social Work Practice, 11,* 645–670.

Tutty, L. M., Weaver, C., & Rothery, M. A. (1999). Residents' views of the efficacy of shelter services for assaulted women. *Violence Against Women, 5,* 898–925.

Two New York lower court welfare-related confidentiality decisions troubling for battered women. (1999, February/March). *Domestic Violence Report, 4,* 41.

Ulrich, R. E., Wolff, P. C., & Azrin, N. H. (1964). Shock as an elicitor of intra- and inter-species fighting behavior. *Animal Behavior, 12,* 14–15.

Ulrich, Y. C., Cain, K. C., Sugg, N. K., Rivara, F. P., Rubanovice, D. M., & Thompson, R. S. (2003). Medical care utilization patterns in women with diagnosed domestic violence. *American Journal of Preventive Medicine, 24,* 9–15.

UNICEF. (2006). *Behind closed doors: The impact of domestic violence on children.* New York, NY: Author.

Urban Institute. (1998). *Evaluation of the STOP formula grants to combat violence against women.* Washington, DC: Author.

U.S. Department of Commerce, Bureau of the Census. (2008a). *Current population survey, 2008 annual social and economic supplement.*

U.S. Department of Commerce, Bureau of the Census. (2008b, August 14). *An older and more diverse nation by mid-century.* Retrieved from www.census.gov/popest/archives/files/MRSF-01-US1.html

U.S. Department of Health and Human Services, Centers for Disease Control and Prevention. (2006). *Youth risk behaviors surveillance—United States, 2005.* Surveillance Summaries, 2006. *Morbidity and Mortality Weekly Report, 55,* SS-5.

U.S. Department of Health and Human Services, Centers for Disease Control and Prevention. (2010, March). *Warning signs and excuses.* Washington, DC: Author.

U.S. Department of Health and Human Services, Office of the Inspector General (2008). *Child maltreatment.* Washington, DC: Author.

U.S. Department of Justice. (1996, May). *The validity and use of evidence concerning battering and its effects in criminal trials* (NCJ Pub. No. 160972). Washington, DC: Author.

U.S. Department of Justice, Bureau of Justice Statistics. (1994, November). *Violence between intimates* (NCJ Pub. No. 149259). Washington, DC: Author.

U.S. Department of Justice, Bureau of Justice Statistics. (2007). *Homicide trends in the U.S.* Retrieved from www.ojp.usdoj.gov.bjs/homicide/intimates.html

U.S. Department of Justice, Bureau of Justice Statistics. (2011, November). *Homicide trends in the United States, 1980–2008.* (NCJ Pub. No. 236018). Washington, DC: Author.

U.S. Department of Justice, Federal Bureau of Investigation. (1984). *Reporting handbook.* Washington, DC: Government Printing Office.

U.S. Department of Justice, Federal Bureau of Investigation. (2000). *National Incident-Based Reporting System (NIBRS).*

U.S. Department of Justice, National Institute of Justice. (1999a, March). *Evaluation of policies, procedures and programs addressing violence against women.* Washington, DC: Author.

U.S. Department of Justice, National Institute of Justice. (1999b, July). *Research on violence against Indian women.* Washington, DC: Author.

U.S. Department of Justice, Office for Victims of Crime. (2002). *Strengthening anti-stalking statutes* (NCJ Pub. No. 189192). Washington, DC: Author.

U.S. Department of Justice, Office of Justice Programs, Bureau of Justice Assistance. (1996, June). *Regional seminar series on developing and implementing antistalking codes* [Monograph] (NCJ Pub. No. 156836). Washington, DC: Author.

U.S. Department of Justice, Office on Violence Against Women. (n.d.). *The Violence Against Women Act of 2000, 2005 (VAWA 2000, 2005)*. Retrieved from www .ojp.usdoj.gov/vawo/laws/vawa_summary2.htm

U.S. Department of Labor, Bureau of Labor Statistics. (1999). *Usual weekly earnings of wage and salary workers*. Washington, DC: Author.

U.S. Government Accounting Office. (1998, November). *Domestic violence: Prevalence and implications for employment among welfare recipients (HEHS-12)*. Washington, DC: Author.

U.S. Preventative Services Task Force. (2004). Screening for family and intimate partner violence: Recommendation statement. *American Family Physician, 70,* 747–751.

Valencia, A., & Van Hoorn, J. (1999). La Isla Pacifico: A haven for battered Mexican American women. *American Psychologist, 54,* 62–63.

Valentiner, D. P., Foa, E. B., Riggs, D. S., & Gershuny, B. S. (1996). Coping strategies and posttraumatic stress disorder in female victims of sexual and non-sexual assault. *Journal of Abnormal Psychology, 105,* 455–458.

Valentino, K., Nuttall, A. K., Comas, M., Borkowski, J. G., & Akai, C. E. (2012). Intergenerational continuity of child abuse among adolescent mothers: Authoritarian parenting, community violence, and race. *Child Maltreatment, 17,* 172–181.

Vandello, J. A., & Cohen, D. (2003). Male honor and female fidelity: Cultural scripts that perpetuate domestic violence. *Journal of Personality and Social Psychology, 84,* 997–1010.

Vandello, J. A., Cohen, D., Grandon, R., & Franiuk, R. (2009). Stand by your man: Indirect prescriptions for honorable violence and feminine loyalty in Canada, Chile, and the United States. *Journal of Cross-Cultural Psychology, 40,* 81–104.

VandenBos, G. R. (2007). *APA dictionary of psychology*. Washington, DC: American Psychological Association.

van der Kolk, B. A., Roth, S., Pelcovitz, D., Mandel, F. S., & Spinazzola, J. (2005). Disorders of extreme stress: The empirical foundation of complex adaptation to trauma. *Journal of Traumatic Stress, 18,* 425–436.

Van Parys, H., & Rober, P. (2011). Micro-analysis of a therapist-generated metaphor referring to the position of a parentified child in the family. *Journal of Family Therapy*. doi: 10.1111/j.1467-6427.2011.00551.x

Varvaro, F. F. (1991). Using a grief response assessment questionnaire in a support group to assist battered women in their recovery. *Response, 13*(4), 17–20.

Vaughn, D. (1987, July). The long goodbye. *Psychology Today*, pp. 37–38, 42.

Vazquez, C. I. (1996). Spousal abuse and violence against women: The significance of understanding attachment. *Annals of the New York Academy of Sciences, 789,* 119–128.

Veltishchev, D. Y. (2004). *Violence and health in Russia: Statistical review.* Moscow, Russia: Moscow Research Institute of Psychiatry and the World Health Organization.

Victim agencies struggle with domestic violence and DUI cases. (1992, June 15). *Criminal Justice Newsletter, 23*(19), 5–7.

Vinton, L. (1991). Abused older women: Battered women or abused elders. *Journal of Women and Aging, 3,* 5–19.

Vinton, L. (1998). A nationwide survey of domestic violence shelters' programming for older women. *Violence Against Women, 4,* 559–571.

Vinton, L., Altholz, J. A., & Lobell, T. (1997). A five-year follow-up study of domestic violence programming for battered older women. *Journal of Women and Aging, 9,* 3–15.

Violence and women offenders. (1990). *Response, 13*(1), 7.

Virginia Coalition for the Homeless. (1995). *1995 shelter provider survey.* Richmond, VA: Virginia Coalition for the Homeless.

Vitanzas, S., Vogel, L. C., & Marshall, L. L. (1995). Distress and symptoms of post-traumatic stress disorder in abused women. *Violence and Victims, 10,* 23–34.

Vivian, D., & Langhinrichsen-Rohling, J. (1994). Are bi-directionally violent couples mutually victimized? A gender-sensitive comparison. *Violence and Victims, 9,* 107–124.

Von Eye, A., & Bogat, G. A. (2006). Mental health in women experiencing intimate partner violence as the efficiency goal of social welfare functions. *International Journal of Social Welfare, 15*(Suppl.1), S31–S40.

Waaland, P., & Keeley, S. (1985). Police decision making in wife abuse: The impact of legal and extralegal factors. *Law and Human Behavior, 9,* 355–366.

Waldman, S. (1992, May 4). Deadbeat dads. *Newsweek, 119,* 46–52.

Waldrop, A. E., & Resick, P. A. (2004). Coping among adult female victims of domestic violence. *Journal of Family Violence, 19,* 291–302.

Walker, L. E. (1977). Battered women and learned helplessness. *Victimology: An International Journal, 2,* 525–534.

Walker, L. E. (1979). *The battered woman.* New York, NY: Harper & Row.

Walker, L. E. (1984). *The battered woman syndrome.* New York, NY: Springer.

Walker, L. E. (1985a). Psychological impact of the criminalization of domestic violence on victims. *Victimology: An International Journal, 10,* 281–300.

Walker, L. E. (1985b, June 7). *Psychology of battered women.* Symposium conducted at the Laguna Human Options Conference, Laguna Beach, CA.

Walker, L. E. (1999). Psychology and domestic violence. *American Psychologist, 54,* 21–29.

Walker, L. E., & Browne, A. (1985). Gender and victimization by intimates. *Journal of Personality, 53,* 179–194.

Waltermaurer, E. (2012). Public justification of intimate partner violence: A review of the literature. *Trauma, Violence, & Abuse.* doi: 10.1177/1524838012447699

Warchol, G. (1998, July). *Workplace violence, 1992–1996* (NCJ Pub. No.168634). Washington, DC: U.S. Department of Justice, Bureau of Justice Statistics.

Warren v. State, 255 Ga. 151, 336 S.E.2d 221 (1985).

Wathen, C. N., & MacMillan, H. (2002). Interventions for violence against women. *Journal of the American Medical Association, 289,* 589–600.

Watson, J. B., & Raynor, R. (1920). Conditioned emotional reactions. *Journal of Experimental Psychology, 3,* 1–14.

Washington State Coalition Against Domestic Violence. (2000). *Honoring their lives, learning from their deaths.* Seattle, WA: Author.

Watts-English, T., Fortson, B. L., Gibler, N., Hooper, S. R., & De Bellis, M. D. (2006). The psychobiology of maltreatment in childhood. *Journal of Social Issues, 62,* 717–736.

Wauchope, B. A. (1988). *Help-seeking decisions of battered women: A test of learned helplessness and two stress theories.* Durham, NH: University of New Hampshire, Family Violence Research Program.

Waxman, L., & Trupin, R. (1997). *A status report on hunger and homelessness in America's cities: 1997.* Washington, DC: U.S. Conference of Mayors.

Weaver, T. L., & Clum, G. A. (1995). Psychological distress associated with interpersonal violence: A meta-analysis. *Clinical Psychology Review, 15,* 115–140.

Websdale, N. (1995a). An ethnographic assessment of the policing of domestic violence in rural eastern Kentucky. *Social Justice, 22,* 102–122.

Websdale, N. (1995b). Rural woman abuse: The voices of Kentucky women. *Violence Against Women, 1,* 309–338.

Weir, K. (2012). The pain of social rejection. *Science Watch.* Retrieved April 19, 2012, from www.apa.org/monitor/2012/04/rejection.aspx

Weisel, D. L. (2005, August). *Problem-oriented guides for police: Analyzing repeat victimization* (Problem-Solving Tools Series No. 4.). U.S. Department of Justice, COPS. Retrieved July 10, 2012, from www.cops.usdoj.gov

Weisz, A. N., & Wiersma, R. (2011). Does the public hold abused women responsible for protecting children? *Affilia, 26,* 419–430.

Weizmann-Henelius, G., Grönroos, L. M., Putkonen, H., Eronen, M., Lindberg, N., & Häkkänen-Nyholm, H. (2012). Gender-specific risk factors for intimate partner homicide: A nationwide register-based study. *Journal of Interpersonal Violence, 27,* 1519–1539.

Wells, K. (2012a, May 18). *CAEPV Newsletter.* Chicago, IL.

Wells, K. (2012b, June 1). *CAEPV Newsletter.* Chicago, IL.

Wells, W., & DeLeon-Granados, W. (2002). *Analysis of unexamined issues in the intimate partner homicide decline: Race, quality of victim services, offender accountability, and system accountability, final report* (NCJ Pub. No. 196666). Washington, DC: National Criminal Justice Reference Service.

West, C., & Zimmerman, D. H. (1987). Doing gender. *Gender and Society, 1,* 125–151.

Weston, R., Marshall, L. L., & Coker, A. L. (2007). Women's motives for violent and nonviolent behaviors in conflicts. *Journal of Interpersonal Violence, 22,* 1043–1065.

Weston, R., Temple, J. R., & Marshall, L. L. (2005). Gender symmetry and asymmetry in violent relationships: Patterns of mutuality among racially diverse women. *Sex Roles, 53,* 553–571.

Whatley, M. A., & Riggio, R. E. (1992). Attributions of blame for female and male victims. *Family Violence and Sexual Assault Bulletin, 8,* 16–18.

Whipple, V. (1987). Counseling battered women from fundamentalist churches. *Journal of Marital and Family Therapy, 13,* 251–258.

Whitaker, D. J., Haileyesusm, T., Swahn, M., & Saltzman, L. S. (2007). Differences in frequency of violence and reported injury between relationships with reciprocal and nonreciprocal intimate partner violence. *American Journal of Public Health, 97,* 941–947.

Whitaker, D. J., Morrison, S., Lindquist, C., Hawkins, S. R., O'Neil, J. A., Nesius, A. M., . . . Reese, L. R. (2006). A critical review of interventions for the primary prevention of perpetration of partner violence. *Aggression and Violent Behavior, 11,* 151–166.

Widom, C. S., & Maxfield, M. G. (2001). *An update on the "Cycle of Violence"* (NCJ Pub. No. 184894). Washington, DC: U.S. Department of Justice.

Willet, S. L., & Barnett, O. W. (1987, April). *Relational consequences of wife beating for violent husbands.* Paper presented at the meeting of the Western Psychological Association, Long Beach, CA.

Williams, C. J. (1999, May 27). In Kosovo, rape seen as awful as death. *Los Angeles Times,* pp. A1, A18–A19.

Williams, K. R., & Hawkins, R. (1989). The meaning of arrest for wife assault. *Criminology, 1,* 163–181.

Williams, S. L., & Frieze, I. H. (2005). Patterns of violent relationships, psychological distress, and marital satisfaction in a national sample of men and women. *Sex Roles, 52,* 771–784.

Williams, S. L., & Mickelson, K. D. (2004). The nexus of domestic violence and poverty: Resilience in women's anxiety. *Violence Against Women, 10,* 283–293.

Wilson, K., Vercella, R., Brems, C., Benning, D., & Renfro, N. (1992). Levels of learned helplessness in abused women. *Women and Therapy, 13,* 53–67.

Wilson, M. I., & Daly, M. (1992). Who kills whom in spouse killings? On the exceptional sex ratio of spousal homicides in the United States. *Criminology, 30,* 189–215.

Wilson, M. N., Baglioni, A. J., Jr., & Downing, D. (1989). Analyzing factors influencing readmission to a battered women's shelter. *Journal of Family Violence, 4,* 275–284.

Wilt, S., Illman, S., & Field, M. B. (1997, March). *Female homicide victims in New York City 1990–1994.* New York, NY: Department of Health Inquiry Prevention Program.

Winner, K. (1996). *Divorced from justice: The abuse of women and children by divorce lawyers and judges.* New York, NY: HarperCollins.

Wirtz, P. W., & Harrell, A. V. (1987). Effects of postassault exposure to attack—similar stimuli on long-term recovery of victims. *Journal of Consulting and Clinical Psychology, 55,* 10–16.

Witwer, M. B., & Crawford, C. A. (1995, October). *A coordinated approach to reducing family violence: Conference highlights* (NCJ Pub. No. 155184). Washington, DC: U.S. Department of Justice.

Wolf, M. E., Ly, U., Hobart, M. A., & Kernic, M. A. (2003). Barriers to seeking police help for intimate partner violence. *Journal of Family Violence, 18*, 121–129.

Wolfe, D. A., Werkerle, C., Gough, R., Reitzel-Jaffee, D., Grasley, C., Pittman, A. L., . . . Stumpf, J. (1996). *The youth relationship manual: A group approach with adolescents for the prevention of woman abuse and promotion of healthy relationships.* Thousand Oaks, CA: Sage.

Wong, R. R. (1995). Divorce mediation among Asian Americans. *Family and Conciliation Courts Review, 33*, 110–128.

Wood, P. B., Gove, W. R., Wilson, J. A., & Cochran, J. K. (1997). Nonsocial reinforcement and habitual criminal conduct: An extension of learning theory. *Criminology, 35*, 335–366.

Woods, S. J. (1999). Normative beliefs regarding the maintenance of intimate relationships among abused and nonabused women. *Journal of Interpersonal Violence, 14*, 479–491.

Worth, D. M., Matthews, P. A., & Coleman, W. R. (1990). Sex role, group affiliation, family background, and courtship violence in college students. *Journal of College Student Development, 31*, 250–254.

Wuest, J., & Merritt-Gray, M. (1999). Not going back: Sustaining the separation in the process of leaving abusive relationships. *Violence Against Women, 5*, 110–133.

Yang, B., & Clum, G. A. (1994). Life stress, social support, and problem-solving skills predictive of depressive symptoms, hopelessness, and suicide ideation in an Asian student population: A test of a model. *Suicide and Life-Threatening Behavior, 24*, 127–139.

Yegidis, B. L., & Renzy, R. B. (1994). Battered women's experiences with a preferred arrest policy. *Affilia, 9*, 60–70.

Yllö, K. A. (2005). Through a feminist lens: Gender, diversity, and violence. In D. R. Loseke, R. J. Gelles, & M. M. Cavanaugh (Eds.), *Current controversies on family violence* (2nd ed., pp. 19–34). Newbury Park, CA: Sage.

Yoshihama, M. (2002). The definitional process of domestic violence in Japan. *Violence Against Women, 8*, 339–366.

Youngstrom, N. (1992, February). Laws to aid battered women backfire. *APA Monitor, 23*(2), 45.

Yut-Lin, W., & Othman, S. (2008). Early detection and prevention of domestic violence using the Woman Abuse Screening Tool (WAST) in primary health care clinics. *Asian Pacific Journal of Public Health, 20*, 102–116.

Zakar, R., Zakar, M. Z., & Krämer, A. (2012). Voices of strength and struggle: Women's coping strategies against spousal violence in Pakistan. *Journal of Interpersonal Violence, 27*, 3268–3298.

Zeoli, A. M., Norris, A., & Brenner, H. (2011). A summary and analysis of warrantless arrest statutes for domestic violence in the United States. *Journal of Interpersonal Violence, 26*, 2811–2833.

Zink, T., Regan, S., Jacobson, C. J., Jr., & Pabst, S. (2003). Cohort, period, and aging effects: A qualitative study of older women's reasons for remaining in abusive relationships. *Violence Against Women, 9*, 1429–1441.

Zinzow, H. M., Grubaugh, A. L., Frueh, B. C., & Magruder, K. M. (2008). Sexual assault, mental health, and service use among male and female veterans seen in Veterans Affairs primary care clinics: A multi-site study. *Psychiatry Research, 159,* 226–236.

Zlotnick, C. K, Johnson, D. M., & Kohn, R. (2006). Intimate partner violence and long-term psychosocial functioning in a national sample of American women. *Journal of Interpersonal Violence, 21,* 262–275.

Zlotnick, C. K., Kohn, R., Peterson, J., & Pearlstein, T. (1998). Partner physical victimization in a national sample of American families. *Journal of Interpersonal Violence, 13,* 156–166.

Zorza, J. (1991). Woman battering: A major cause of homelessness. *Clearinghouse Review, 61,* 421–429.

Zorza, J. (1994). Woman battering: High costs and the state of the law. *Clearinghouse Review, 28*(Special issue), 383–395.

Zorza, J. (1995). Recognizing and protecting the privacy and confidentiality needs of battered women. *Family Law Quarterly, 29*(2, Special issue on domestic violence), 273–311.

Zorza, J. (1997). Recent cases. *Domestic Violence Report, 2,* 90.

Zorza, J. (1998, December/January). Our clients may affect us: Vicarious traumatization. *Domestic Violence Report, 2*(2), 21–22, 26.

Zorza, J. (1999, December/January). Dual victim treatment helps preschoolers and mothers dramatically. *Domestic Violence Report, 4,* 20, 499.

Zorza, J., & Schoenberg, L. (1995). *Improving the health care response to domestic violence through protocols and policies.* Washington, DC: National Center on Women and Family Law.

Zorza, R., & Klemperer, J. (1999, April/May). The Internet-based domestic court preparation project: Using the Internet to overcome barriers to justice. *Domestic Violence Report, 4,* 49–50, 59–60.

Index

characteristics of, 146–147
childhood abuse and, 148
female survivors of assault and, 147
marital rape and, 147–148
survivors, 149
Poverty, and institutional battering, 50–51
Power, and sexism, 22–23
Powerless responsibility, 79
Prevention, importance of, 169–173
Problem solving, 154–155
Professional women, and
    victimization, 91–92
Protection orders, and IPV cases,
    76–78, 78 (case study)
Psychological abuse, 123–124
PTSD. *See* Posttraumatic stress disorder
Punishment, 125–127,
    126 (case study), 228–233

Quindlen, Anna, 21

Rage, 37
    responses to, 137–138 (case study)
Rape, by an intimate partner among
    U.S. women, 219
Rathmann, Carol, 170
Reasonable man's defense, 164
Reinforcement, 227–228, 231, 232
Relationship commitment, 42–43
Relationships
    ongoing, reducing male violence in,
        179–180
    violent, attributions in, 102–104
Religion, and institutional battering,
    57–60
Repeat victimization, 99, 220
Restraining orders, 67 (case study)
Robinson, Kerry, 59
Rothman, David M., 80
Rural women
    IPV and, 9
    victimization and, 90,
        90–91 (case study)

Same-sex couples, and IPV, 9
Same-sex orientation, false beliefs
    about individuals with, 93 (table)
Same-sex partner abuse, public atti-
    tudes toward, 93–95

Seligman, Martin, 158
Selye, Hans, 233–234
Sexism, 21–22
    power and, 22–23
    therapy and, 26–28
Sexual abuse, 136
Sexual assaults
    battering relationships and, 65–66
    fact sheet, 219
    intimate partners, of, 215
Sheehan, Barbara, 167 (case study)
Sheehan, Raymond, 167 (case study)
Shelters, 174–176
    life in, 52–53 (case study)
Sherman, Larry, 73
Shock, predictable and
    unpredictable, 234
Signaled avoidance, 234
Simpson, Nicole Brown, 6, 26
Simpson, O. J., 6, 26, 190
Sister of Silence (Berry), 91
Skinner, 226
Sleeper effects, 36
Smeal, Eleanor, 50
Snyder, Lynda, 181
Socialization, 19–21
    affiliation and, 19–21
    childhood, 37–39
    sexism, 21–22
    sexism and power, 22–23
Social learning theory, 36–37
Social support, and victimization,
    104–106
Special populations, and victimization,
    88–95
    elder women, 89–90
    immigrant women, 95
    lesbians, 92–95
    professional women, 91–92
    rural women, 90
    teenage girls and college women,
        88–89
Spiraling reactivity, 92
Spontaneous recovery, 226
Spousal abuse
    alcoholism and, 201–202 (case study)
    recovery and, 199–201 (case study),
        201–202 (case study), 202–203
        (case study)

Winner, Karen, 81
Wishful thinking, as a coping
   strategy, 157
Women, victimization of
   college-age, 88–89
   elder, 89–90
   immigrant, 95
   lesbians, 92–95
professional, 91–92
rural, 90, 90–91 (case study)
teenage, 88–89
See also Abuse; Battered women;
   Intimate partner violence (IPV);
   Victimization; Violence

Yamaguchi, Nori, 181

About the Authors

Alyce D. LaViolette has worked with battered women since 1978, first as an advocate at WomenShelter of Long Beach and then in private practice. In 1979, she founded Alternatives to Violence in Long Beach, one of the first programs in the country for spouse abusers. She specializes in anger management, domestic violence counseling for survivors and perpetrators, and gender issues. She also provides couples counseling and counseling for a broad base of individual issues. She has spoken internationally and for the U.S. Department of State. She is an expert witness on criminal and family law cases involving domestic violence and has recently been awarded the Champion of Hope Award by WomenShelter of Long Beach. In addition, she was recently voted onto the Board of Directors for the Alumni Association of California State University at Long Beach and received the Alumni of the Year Award.

Ola W. Barnett is Distinguished Professor Emerita of Psychology at Pepperdine University, Malibu, California. She earned her undergraduate and doctoral degrees in psychology at the University of California, Los Angeles, specializing in learning, personality, and physiological psychology. Her initial research centered on batterers, and she later studied battered women and dating violence. She conducted her doctoral dissertation on a population of imprisoned sex offenders. She has coauthored a best-selling textbook on family violence, now in its third edition, *Family Violence Across the Lifespan*. She remains active in the field by reviewing articles for journals and serving as a guest lecturer for classes and organizations focusing on family violence.

s from the

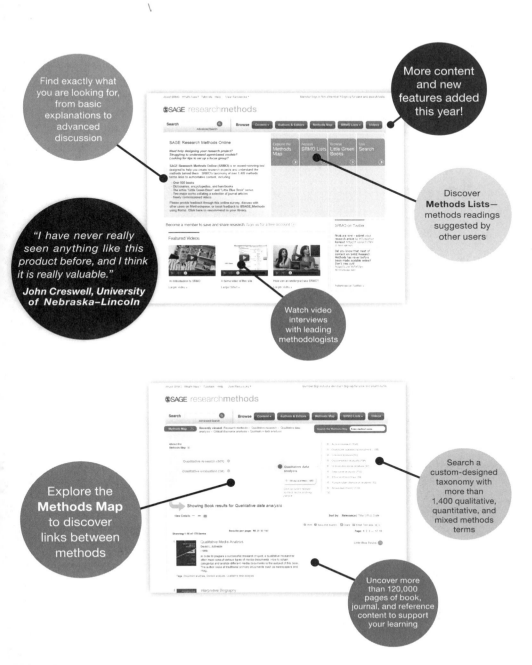

Find exactly what you are looking for, from basic explanations to advanced discussion

More content and new features added this year!

"I have never really seen anything like this product before, and I think it is really valuable."
John Creswell, University of Nebraska–Lincoln

Discover **Methods Lists**—methods readings suggested by other users

Watch video interviews with leading methodologists

Explore the **Methods Map** to discover links between methods

Search a custom-designed taxonomy with more than 1,400 qualitative, quantitative, and mixed methods terms

Uncover more than 120,000 pages of book, journal, and reference content to support your learning

Find out more at
www.sageresearchmethods.com

DATE			
MR 24 '75			